Quite a Good
Time to Be Born

Also by David Lodge

FICTION
The Picturegoers
Ginger, You're Barmy
The British Museum is Falling Down
Out of the Shelter
Changing Places
How Far Can You Go?
Small World
Nice Work
Paradise News
Therapy
Home Truths
Thinks . . .
Author, Author
Deaf Sentence
A Man of Parts

CRITICISM
Language of Fiction
The Novelist at the Crossroads
The Modes of Modern Writing
Working with Structuralism
After Bakhtin

ESSAYS
Write On
The Art of Fiction
The Practice of Writing
Consciousness and the Novel
The Year of Henry James
Lives in Writing

DRAMA
The Writing Game
Home Truths
Secret Thoughts

Quite a Good Time to Be Born

A MEMOIR: 1935–1975

David Lodge

Harvill Secker
London

Published by Harvill Secker 2015

2 4 6 8 10 9 7 5 3 1

First published in Great Britain in 2015 by
HARVILL SECKER
20 Vauxhall Bridge Road
London SW1V 2SA

A Penguin Random House Company

Penguin
Random House
UK

global.penguinrandomhouse.com

A CIP catalogue record for this book is available from the British Library

ISBN 9781846559501 (hardback)
ISBN 9781846559518 (trade paperback)

Penguin Random House supports The Forest Stewardship Council (FSC),
the leading international forest certification organisation. All our titles that are
printed on Greenpeace approved FSC certified paper carry the FSC logo. Our paper
procurement policy can be found at www.randomhouse.co.uk/environment

MIX
Paper from
responsible sources
FSC
www.fsc.org   FSC® C016897

Typeset in Futura and Minion by Palimpsest Book Production Limited,
Falkirk, Stirlingshire

Printed and bound in Great Britain by
Clays Ltd, St Ives PLC

To Mary, with love

FOREWORD

I drew my first breath on the 28th of January 1935, which was quite a good time for a future writer to be born in England, especially one belonging to a lower-middle-class family like mine. It meant that I would have plenty to write about and an education that, though patchy up to secondary level, gave me the skills and motivation to do so. Four and a half years old when the Second World War began, and ten and half when it ended, I retained some personal memories of that epic struggle, the hinge on which twentieth-century history turned. My generation was the first in Britain to benefit from the 1944 Education Act, which established free secondary education for all, and free tuition with means-tested maintenance grants for those who competed successfully for admission to a university. Like many others I was promoted by education into the professional middle class, and lived through an extremely interesting period in English social history, when the stratified classes of pre-war Britain gradually melded to create a more open and fluid society.

I was brought up in the Roman Catholic faith, which had not significantly altered in its beliefs and devotional practice since the Counter-Reformation and had successfully resisted the intellectual and moral challenges of modernity, but which from the 1960s onwards underwent a series of momentous changes and internal conflicts. Catholicism has stimulated my imagination as a novelist both before and since that upheaval. Over the same period there were several technological developments which have transformed social and cultural life, such as ubiquitous access to television, affordable global air travel, the contraceptive pill and the microchip.

This last invention, which enabled the production of the personal computer, the laptop, the internet, email, mobile phones and ebooks, has had a powerful but ambivalent effect on the production of literature. These tools have undoubtedly made the work of writers easier. Information that could only be retrieved in the past by hours or days of research in libraries can now be obtained in seconds with a few keystrokes, and word-processing software has made revision, which is at the very heart of literary composition, physically effortless. On the other hand the same developments now threaten to dissolve the connection between writing as a profession and the book as a mechanically reproducible commodity which has existed since the invention of the printing press, and to render obsolete the interlinked system of publishers, agents, printers, booksellers and copyright law that for more than a century has provided a relatively firm framework within which writers have pursued their vocation and earned income from it. I was fortunate, I think, in having the major part of my career as a writer in that more stable milieu.

This memoir describes how I became a writer, principally of prose fiction and literary criticism, beginning with the early experiences and influences that fed into my work later, and it covers what is, at the time of writing, the first half of my life, up to the age of forty. I hope to write another book about the second half, in added extra time.

D.L., September 2014

1

I was the first and, as it turned out, the only child of my parents.
When I was born, a little over two years after they married, they
were living in a flat in Grove Vale, East Dulwich, then as now the
poorer part of that south London suburb, very near the terraced
house where my father – also an only child – had grown up and
lived with his parents until he married. The birth certificate states,
rather surprisingly, that I was born at 5 Brunswick Square, in
Bloomsbury. I remember being told I was born in a 'nursing home',
but why it was deemed necessary to go into central London for that
facility, I do not know, and now, like so many other questions
that arise from an exercise like this one, it is much too late to find
out. My father's name is given as 'William Frederick Lodge'; he
was known as 'Will' to his family, 'Bill' to his friends, and for a
time he called himself professionally 'Bryan Lodge'. His profession
is described rather grandly on my birth certificate as 'orchestral
musician'. He did play in bands that described themselves as
'orchestras' – Jay Wilbur's, Maurice Winnick's, Arthur Roseberry's

– but they played popular, mainly jazz-derived music generically known then as dance music, and he usually described his profession as 'dance musician'. If he had been born in 1935 instead of 1906 he would probably have become a violinist in a symphony orchestra. He had a natural talent for the violin, and had some private lessons on that instrument as a boy, and on the saxophone and clarinet which he took up later, but he had no formal musical education and was largely self-taught.

His parents were not well off. My grandfather, also called William, but known familiarly as 'Pop', was a shopwalker in the drapery departments of various big London stores. He was said to be an expert on silk fabrics, and he would have been a master of sales patter. For a time he and a colleague had a semi-professional telepathy act which they performed in music halls. I'm not sure how it worked, but it would have required a quick wit and a ready tongue. Unfortunately he had a weakness for drink and a passion for pubs, and was dismissed by several employers on this account. At those times my grandmother, Amelia, or 'Milly', whom I called Nana, and loved dearly, would have been the main source of income for the household, being a skilled furrier who took in work at home, cutting and sewing the pelts which were a staple component of female attire. She was the youngest of thirteen children fathered by John Bush, a bookbinder. After my father died in 1999, I found his birth certificate and the marriage certificate of Nana and Pop among several similar documents in his desk, and was astonished to discover that they were married on 13th July 1906, only six weeks before he was born on 26th August. What story – what drama and distress – was hidden in those bald dates? Why was the marriage delayed till such a late stage in my grandmother's pregnancy? Did she fail to tell Pop of her condition until it could no longer be disguised? Did he have to be persuaded to make an honest woman of her? Or was she perhaps reluctant to marry him, in spite of the stigma that attached to unmarried mothers in those days? The wedding took place in a registry office, not a church, and the bride's age was given on the certificate as twenty-one, though in fact she was only nineteen. My first thought was that this was done to avoid having to get parental consent, but Milly's mother Henrietta was one of the witnesses, so presumably approved, or at least accepted, the marriage, and Nana's father was by then deceased. Another insoluble enigma.

Finding this document prompted me to do some research into my ancestry, helped by a former student who became expert in genealogy. I was particularly keen to verify, if possible, a tradition – so tenuous that one might more properly call it a rumour – that my paternal great-grandfather or great-grandmother was of Jewish extraction. I have always enjoyed Jewish humour and the work of Jewish, especially Jewish-American, writers. I am flattered that my comic writing has sometimes been compared to Woody Allen's, and one of my best-known fictional characters, Morris Zapp, was created out of that empathy. I liked the idea that this strand in my work might have a genetic origin. The Lodge family came from Huddersfield in Yorkshire, and were mostly connected with the wool trade in one way or another, as weavers, cloth dressers and millwrights. In the middle of the nineteenth century a James Lodge moved south to London, found employment as a clerk and married a servant from the West Country. One of their sons, Frederick, also a clerk, married a dressmaker and was my great-grandfather. There was no discoverable Jewish strain in the Lodges of Yorkshire, or the spouses of James and Frederick. My grandmother's line seemed more promising, since her father's name might have been the anglicisation of a European name, but again research drew a blank. The Bushes of the nineteenth century (servants, clerks or craftsmen by occupation) and the spouses they married in Anglican churches were all English, or in one case Irish. The quest for a Jewish ancestor ended disappointingly.

I couldn't help wondering whether Dad ever discovered the circumstances of his birth, and if so, how and when. It was something that must have been known to members of the extensive Lodge and Bush families, but people in the first half of the last century were practised in concealing such secrets. Was it perhaps not until he obtained his mother's marriage certificate after her death in 1981, at the age of ninety-two, that he learned the truth; or did he not examine the document closely and so never discovered that he was nearly born out of wedlock? Certainly no hint or rumour of it ever reached me, but I was conscious that Pop was a marginalised member of our six-person, two-generation family. There wasn't the same affection in Nana's relation to him as she showed towards Dad and me, and my father's attitude to him was always cool and dismissive. He was more of an absence than a presence at our meetings and visits, generally referred to with an ironic grimace or shrug, and when he did join us, usually from the nearest pub (even on Christmas morning he would go looking for one that was open and get back only just in time for the turkey dinner), he adopted a kind of bluff, hearty mask which made intimacy impossible. He was more in his element at the larger Christmas parties of the Lodge clan in Dulwich, seated at an upright piano with a glass of ale to hand, singing a comic song to his own vamped accompaniment. He was a music hall artiste manqué.

Marriage forced on the couple by pregnancy, and the absence of any further children (unusual in that class, at that time), suggest that the union was somewhat lacking in mutual love, and in the course of a long tape-recorded conversation with my father, late in his life, I heard for the first time a story which tended to confirm that supposition, and to explain why Pop was always treated as a quasi-delinquent member of the family, on parole as it were. When the First World War broke out, he and two of his brothers volunteered patriotically to join a local regiment, as so many did. His elder brother Ernie was awarded the Military Cross for Valour, but Pop was invalided out of the Army after a year because of a hernia. It was an unheroic discharge which probably made him an object of envy to fellow soldiers, and certainly of suspicion to civilians. 'Coppers were always knocking on our door asking to see his papers,' Dad recalled. Pop went to work at Woolwich Arsenal, where he met another woman, began a relationship with her and moved out of the family home for a while. Pop and Nana were eventually reconciled, but perhaps he was never really forgiven. 'It was rather a sad time,' was Dad's understated memory of the episode. He also said, regretting his lack of paternal guidance in adolescence, 'I didn't have a proper father. My mother was the sole sustaining force in the household.'

At his elementary school Dad was evidently identified as a pupil with potential. He remembered a teacher explaining to the class the meaning of the phrase *a dark horse* and saying by way of illustration, 'William Lodge is a dark horse.' He was interviewed for a scholarship to a grammar school, but didn't make the cut. The interviewer mocked his pronunciation of 'geography', a subject in which he had professed an interest. 'What's that – jogging the boy next to you?' the man enquired, enjoying his own joke. Dad moved to another, commercially oriented school for the last two years of his education where he learned among other things shorthand and some French. A former pupil called Fred Haydon, who had won a scholarship to the Guildhall School of Music, returned one day to play the violin to the assembled students, and imparted to my father the desire to be a musician. 'I remember thinking, *I'd like to do that.*' He began to take lessons in the violin from 'an enthusiast' who ran a local music shop, probably paid for by his mother until he left school and got a job as an office boy with an insurance company in the City for £1 a week. He could not remember whether he was fourteen or fifteen at the time. A year later he got a job as messenger with a sugar company in Mincing Lane at £2 a week. But he had no ambition to rise to a higher position in the firm, or any firm – he dreamed only of becoming a professional musician. For several years he was a 'semi-pro', working in the City by day and playing in the evenings, beginning as a violinist in the silent-film cinemas of Dulwich and environs. In one of them he encountered Fred Haydon, whose musical career had not perhaps fulfilled its promise. 'I met him in the pit. He wore glasses, glasses like beer bottles. Talk about drink. He worked in a small cinema in Rye Lane – those were silent days of course. They had a six-piece band there and he was first violin – lovely tone. But he must have killed himself with drink.' Dad's anecdotes of his professional life were invariably laced with stories of lives and careers ruined by excessive drinking or womanising, vices of which he himself could not be accused, though he enjoyed a drink in moderation (mainly beer and sweet sherry) and had a keen appreciation of female beauty.

That a small cinema in south London could afford to employ a six-piece band gives some indication of the meagre rate of pay for musicians in the 1920s, but it was more than Dad could earn from his low-level position in the City, and as soon as possible he 'gave up the day-job' (a phrase which I heard at home long before it entered into common parlance). Apart from playing in cinemas, 'gigs' – one-off engagements for dance bands – were the main employment opportunity, and in the Jazz Age instruments such as the saxophone and clarinet were more in demand than strings. When silent films gave way to talkies in the next decade, skilled violinists were often reduced to playing in the street. My father, who responded enthusiastically to the rhythms of jazz like most of his generation, adjusted early to this trend, learning to play a borrowed tenor saxophone when he was still in his teens, and later acquiring an alto sax and clarinet. He took lessons, but in an incomplete, unsystematic way. He never really learned how to read music expertly, and could be embarrassed when faced by a difficult, unfamiliar score. He relied on his natural instinctive ability, a good memory for tunes, and his 'tone'. He was always admired for his tone on all his instruments. With these attributes he got a steady job playing at a nightclub called the 43 Club whose proprietor was eventually sent to prison for selling liquor illegally, and another later run by her daughter called the Silver Slipper, a venue favoured by the Bright Young Things, including Evelyn Waugh. 'But I wasted the opportunity to improve my technique.

I was a bloody fool. I had the tone but not the technique. I did my practice but it was the wrong kind of practice. I should have studied the practical, technical side, not the flamboyant, emotional side of playing, which I was very good at. I could play the violin like a concert platform player, but I couldn't play the music! A lot of it I couldn't read. I never had a musical education of any kind.' Then with a characteristic swerve away from despondency he added, 'But would I have been better off?' He was probably remembering those stories of concert violinists playing in the street. Perhaps because his instrumental ability had its limits, he began also to exploit his talent as a singer, which he inherited from my grandmother, who had a lovely, pure soprano voice with which she would delight those large Christmas gatherings in Dulwich even in her sixties. Dad himself had a high, light tenor voice of the kind one often hears on scratchy recordings of popular music in the thirties, and towards the end of that decade he began a promising career as a singer on the radio, which was cut short when he joined the Royal Air Force in 1940. But long before that, at some point in the 1920s, when he was working as a professional musician and still living at home, Dad met at his local tennis club a young woman who satisfied his exacting standard of good looks. Her name was Rosalie Mary Murphy, and in due course they got engaged. Her family was very different from his: half Irish, half Belgian, and Roman Catholic.

I have no memory of my maternal grandparents, since they died at the beginning and end of the same year, 1936, when I was only one year old. My mother's father was Tom Murphy, the son of an immigrant from Cork. On my mother's birth certificate (she was born on 11th May 1903) his profession is given as 'corn sampler'. Subsequently he became the licensee of a public house in the dockland district of Rotherhithe, and later of the Imperial Hotel in Southwark Street, near London Bridge, one of which establishments was popular with well-known boxers and their entourages. Tom Murphy was by all accounts well fitted to be a pub landlord – charming, witty and much liked by all who knew him; but he was a gambler, and a less reliable tradition suggested that he was for a time involved in smuggling tobacco.

My maternal grandmother was called Adèle Goddaert. Her parents had emigrated from Lille in Belgium in the early 1860s and ran a grocery shop in the Docklands on the south side of the Thames, where Adèle, the younger of their two daughters, was born in 1865. I possess a remarkable group photograph of the wedding of Tom and Adèle which took place around the turn of the century, when both of them would have been in their early thirties. The bridal couple are posed in a garden or yard with trellised walls, surrounded by some twenty relatives and guests whose smart clothes, especially the ladies' elaborately trimmed hats and gowns, suggest they enjoyed a comfortable standard of living above that of the contemporaneous Lodges and Bushes. Tom, in a morning suit, is tallish, slim, good-looking, with a wide, tapered moustache, and stands with his long legs apart, gazing quizzically into the camera. Adèle beside him, in a long white dress and holding a large bouquet, has a smooth oval face, a shapely figure, dark eyes and a slightly anxious expression. The sun is shining on the group but no one is smiling, perhaps a consequence of the long exposure time required for outdoor photography at that time.

On the whole my mother seemed to have happy memories of her childhood, when the family lived over the pubs Tom Murphy was managing, and the children derived some interest and excitement from the social buzz that goes with such a business. Tom prospered sufficiently to send his three children to private day schools – my mother and her sister Eileen to a Sacred Heart Convent school in (I think) Bermondsey, and their brother John to St Joseph's Academy, Blackheath, where I would in due course be a pupil myself. At some point, however, probably in the late 1920s, Tom Murphy lost a great deal of money through gambling and he retired from pub management to live on what was left, with some help from his daughters. Adèle became depressed and, I was told in adult life, attempted suicide once. The general narrative of the family which I imbibed from my mother and aunt over the years was one of prosperity followed by decline into genteel poverty. They were a cut above my father's family on the social scale – the most obvious index of this being their speech: my father could adjust his accent adroitly to the company he was in, but his natural speech had a perceptible cockney flavour, whereas the Murphys had been brought up and educated to 'speak nicely', and my aunt Eileen in particular prided herself on her elocution. I suspect that she and John always felt that their sister had, in the old-fashioned phrase, married beneath her; but Dad was innately more gifted than any of the Murphys, and I owe most of my creative genes to him.

To judge from their parents' wedding photograph, my mother 'took after' her mother, and Eileen and John after their father. Rosalie (whom my father nicknamed 'Pat') had Adèle's womanly figure and soft, symmetrical features, whereas both Eileen and

John had Tom's lean frame and sharply modelled nose and chin. Temperamentally I suspect they followed the same parental patterns. My mother was intelligent but unassertive. She trained to be a shorthand typist and had a secretarial job which made a valuable contribution to the family budget until she married, and did part-time clerical work later, but she was content to be primarily a housewife and mother. Eileen also worked as a secretary, but she was more ambitious than her sister, and had the personality and social poise to become her boss's personal assistant. When my mother left home Eileen became responsible for looking after the parents in their sad old age, and had to suspend her career for a while – a source, understandably, of some discontent on her part. John was no help to her in this situation. He was always described to me by his sisters as being an unruly and unreliable sibling, given to teasing and annoying them in childhood, and a constant worry to his parents when grown up because of his inability to settle into a career or hold a job. He was, however, admitted to be highly entertaining in company, and I found him so when I encountered him in childhood and after-wards. He had a gift for clowning when the mood was on him, and possessed a repertoire of extremely funny walks long before Monty Python invented a Ministry for them – in fact, he looked not unlike John Cleese. When swimming in the sea he would entertain family members sitting on the beach by slipping off his trunks and hoisting them like a flag on the end of one elevated foot. Eventually he joined the Royal Air Force, which seemed to suit him. He flew as navigator and wireless operator in biplanes in India before the Second World War, and trained younger airmen during it. The war changed the direction of his life and Eileen's in unexpected ways that would in due course significantly broaden my own experience.

Dad recalled that he was in no great hurry to get married: 'You know me – "put it off, put it off". I was more interested in getting into a gig network. I remember one day Pat gave me an ultimatum. "When are we going to get married? Mum and Dad want to know." I had to agree on a date then and there.' It was 17th December 1932. According to the marriage certificate, the wedding was 'solemnised' at the Catholic church on Lordship Lane, Dulwich, but it would not have been a nuptial mass because Dad was a 'non-Catholic', as the Roman Catholic Church designated all Christians who had not been baptised into it. It frowned on 'mixed marriages' and actively discouraged them. The Catholic party had to obtain a dispensation to marry a non-Catholic, who was required to attend a series of instructions in the Catholic faith, and to promise formally that any children of the marriage would be brought up as Catholics. These regulations are still in force today, but applied in a more welcoming fashion. My father would have received a basic Christian education from his elementary school and the Sunday School he attended for a time, but Pop and Nana were not churchgoers, and neither was he. In adult life he professed a vague belief in God, and respected the Catholic religion, but showed no inclination to join it. My mother was a dutiful but not devout Catholic. She taught me Catholic prayers, took me to mass every Sunday, and placed me in Catholic schools, but she never got involved in parochial life. In consequence my Catholicism was almost entirely shaped by education. The ambience of home was essentially secular – there were no crucifixes, plaster statues or holy pictures on the walls and shelves. The fact that I was an only child also made me an untypical Catholic.

In the course of his instructions Dad would have been told that the Catholic Church forbade the use of artificial contraception, though moral theologians conceded that the Catholic partner could submit to it if to refuse would endanger the marriage. Catholics, especially Catholic women, who married non-Catholics were often meanly suspected by their co-religionists of seeking such partners deliberately as a way of planning their families without guilt. I have no reason to suppose that was part of Dad's attraction for my mother, but the fact that I was born two years after they married, and that she was not pregnant again until 1939 (she lost the child through a miscarriage), suggests that my father took care of birth control.

In 1936, when I was about one and a half, they bought a small house, with a mortgage of course, which apart from interruptions in wartime would be their home until they died, and mine until I married. It was in Brockley, a few miles east of Dulwich in the Borough of Deptford, where the first range of hills rises from the London plain south of the Thames. Its principal park is called Hilly Fields, and from another park, spread over the top of Telegraph Hill, on a fine day there is a panoramic view of London as far as the landmark buildings on the north bank of the Thames and beyond. Brockley was developed as a residential suburb in the course of the nineteenth century with a wide range of housing, from enormous villas and substantial town houses to humble terraced cottages. After the First World War the larger properties were increasingly divided into smaller units, as their owners migrated to newer, leafier suburbs, and the demographic became predominantly lower-middle and working class, a process that continued after the second war with a growing immigrant element. Although the Southern Railway gave fast direct access from Brockley to London Bridge, its cultural and socio-economic development was hampered, like most of south-east London, by the lack of Tube connections: the only line terminated at New Cross or New Cross Gate, and its trains shuttled back and forth through the Docklands only as far as Whitechapel. When I was growing up there after the Second World War Brockley was a declining, unfashionable suburb, though I did not perceive it as such. After I ceased to live there in 1959, as Goldsmiths College in New Cross grew in size and status it began to attract more sophisticated residents – teachers, artists, actors – and lately it has become almost trendy.

The house my parents moved to was a new one – in fact they bought it 'off plan', while the street to which it belonged was still under construction. Millmark Grove was something of an anomaly in its late Victorian architectural setting: just under a hundred houses with red-tiled roofs, timbered gables, casement windows and pebble-dashed facades, resembling millions of homes built in England between the wars, but terraced, not semi-detached, in order to squeeze as many units as possible on to a sliver of land situated between a deep railway cutting and a main road that ran along the backs of grey, grimy Victorian terraced houses from Brockley Cross to New Cross. The new street bent sharply at one end to join the main road, thus creating gaps for side passages between a few houses, of which ours, number 81, was one. This was a great convenience – it meant that dustbins could be emptied by the garbage collectors, coal and coke delivered, and bicycles stored in the back garden, without having to be carried through the house – but at the cost of having a smaller back garden than those further up the street. The fence at the end of our garden was no more than a dozen paces from the back of the house. But you couldn't see anything over it or be seen, because the houses and gardens were built on raised foundations and landfill some twenty feet deep, and this, helped by the rambling roses my father grew on trellises between us and our neighbours, created a degree of privacy.

The street was named after the developer and his wife, Mark and Milly. The designation 'Grove', weakly justified by the flowering cherry trees planted at intervals in the pavement, was no doubt meant to signify that it was a cut above the drab surrounding streets. But it was successful inasmuch as most of the owner-occupiers took a pride in their houses, and kept them well maintained, regularly repainting the woodwork, often in two colours. Every house had a tiny front garden, usually with a neatly trimmed privet hedge behind the low boundary wall, a patch of grass or crazy paving, and perhaps a flower bed and shrubs. As a child and youth I always felt when I turned into our street that it looked cleaner, brighter and more inviting than its environs. It still has that character, though the cars parked nose to tail at the kerbs on both sides make it seem less of a tranquil backwater. Dad was one of the first residents to own a car, but he chose the site initially because all-night trams ran to Brockley from central London, allowing him to get home from nightclubs and similar venues in the West End in the small hours with his bulky instrument cases. These cases were objects of fascination to me as I grew up: drab and scuffed on the outside, they opened up to reveal moulded recesses lined with richly coloured velvet in which the gold-coloured alto and silver tenor saxophones safely nestled.

One of the things which drew me to write about the life and work of H.G. Wells was his consuming interest in domestic architecture, and his conviction that people's health, happiness and behaviour are crucially affected by good or bad design in their habitat. So I will describe my parental home, and other spaces in which I subsequently lived, in some detail. Internally the houses in Millmark Grove were built to the pattern of most small new homes of the period: a short hallway, giving access to a sitting room at the front of the house, and a dining room and kitchen at the rear; a flight of stairs leading to two bedrooms, front and back, a 'spare room' at the front that could accommodate a cot or small bed, and a bathroom and separate lavatory at the back. Because we had a side alley, there was a window at the angle of the stairs which shed welcome light on the small landing, and the telephone, essential tool of Dad's trade, rested on the window ledge next to his diary and thumb-indexed notebook of musicians' phone numbers. All but one of the rooms were meanly proportioned, and the two most-used rooms were least adequate for their purposes, though I did not really register these facts until long after I had left home and formed higher expectations of domestic comfort and convenience.

The largest and most attractive room was on the ground floor at the front, which we referred to as 'the lounge' or sometimes simply 'the front room'. It was about fourteen feet square, with a shallow bay window, a rather handsome fireplace with deep purple ceramic tiling and a black lacquered mantelpiece, with bookshelves and display cases to each side. It contained a comfortably upholstered three-piece suite which took up much of the floor space, and in my childhood an elegant HMV cabinet gramophone, with a wind-up handle on the side, and a pair of doors on the front. These opened to reveal a kind of wide-mouthed tunnel that tapered and curved as it descended to the inscrutable source of sound, intriguing me much as it did the white fox terrier hearing His Master's Voice in the famous painting adopted by the manufacturer as its trademark. And there was one genuine antique in the room, probably of the French belle époque, which my mother had inherited from hers. A narrow rectangular table made of polished, richly inlaid wood, with legs on wheels splaying out from an elaborately carved central column, it seemed purely ornamental, but its top swivelled and unfolded on hinges to make a card table lined with red felt. It was seldom used for that purpose, and the room itself was seldom used, being reserved for special occasions like Christmas or visits from relatives and friends, and occasionally for listening to records on the gramophone. The dining room, about twelve feet square, was actually our living room, where we not only ate, but also relaxed, sat round a coal or electric fire in the hearth, read, wrote letters at the bureau desk in one corner, listened to the radio, and in due course watched television. It contained an oak sideboard, a small dining table with extendable leaves and upright chairs, and a couple of small easy chairs, so to get from the door to the French windows required something like a ballroom dancer's nimble shuffle. The kitchen was even more crowded and cramped, not more than six feet wide, and accommodated a coke-fired boiler for hot water as well as sink, draining board, electric cooker, larder and wall-mounted storage cupboards. Somehow a small table and chair were squeezed in under one of the cupboards, where we took breakfast individually at different times. It was not surprising that one day in this congested space, when I was about two, the contents of a saucepan of boiling milk on the hob of the electric cooker was accidentally tipped on to my foot, and I bear the scar of the consequent blister under my ankle bone to this day.

Number 81 Millmark Grove no doubt seemed a bright, attractively modern home to the young couple when they took possession in 1936, contrasting favourably with the rented flat, carved out of some older house in East Dulwich, from which they had moved – and as a first step on the property ladder it was not a bad choice. But for reasons of history and personal character they never moved to a more commodious house, nor did they significantly improve or modernise the one they stayed in. This I find very sad to contemplate, especially as it affected the life of my mother.

2

I was four and a half when the war began, so I had little understanding of the anxiety and dread my parents must have been
feeling, like so many others, in the summer and autumn of 1939.
In their case the stress must have been heightened when my mother
lost the baby she was carrying at that time, a daughter, due to a
miscarriage. I don't know what caused it or how advanced the
pregnancy was; indeed I first learned of this lost sister of mine as
an adult – I'm not sure how, perhaps from my aunt Eileen, but
certainly not from my mother, who never mentioned it and with
whom I never raised the subject. The information was a total
surprise, and made me wonder what difference it would have
made to all our lives if this daughter had lived. I had got used to
being an 'only child' long ago, and never consciously regretted it.
There were advantages in being the sole focus of parental love,
care and attention, which were essentially my mother's during the
war years, when my father was mostly absent, serving in the Air
Force. Melvyn Bragg has described vividly, in his autobiographical

novel *The Soldier's Return*, the Oedipal tensions caused when a soldier returns home at the end of the war to his wife and a six-year-old son who was an infant when he left, and to whom he seems a threatening interloper. That was not my situation: I was old enough to have pre-war memories of Dad, and saw him just often enough during the war to keep a filial image of him in my mind and to look forward with longing to his permanent return home. When we were finally reunited as a family I transferred my primary allegiance to him, while still taking my mother's devoted care for granted. Lacking a satisfying career of her own, and having a limited interest in the things that preoccupied Dad and me, like music, literature and sport, she was marginalised and became a kind of servant to both of us: shopping, housekeeping and serving up meals, often individually at hours which suited our separate timetables. It seems to me now that if she had had a daughter, and I a sister, the balance of power in our family might have been more even and her life more fulfilling. How that would have affected my own character is more difficult to imagine, but perhaps I would have been less introspective and self-centred. I presume Mum and Dad avoided conceiving another child during wartime on one of his rare leaves, and by the time the war was over she was forty-two, and it would have seemed too late. Needless to say, the possibility never crossed my own prepubescent mind. I was just happy to have two parents again, all to myself. Later in life I regretted not having siblings with whom I could have shared the responsibility of looking after their welfare in old age.

I know that my mother's miscarriage happened shortly before or after the beginning of the war because of an extraordinary

24

anecdote that was attached to it, which I would hesitate to rely on if my father had not repeated it in the taped conversation I had with him late in life. It seems that they heard of some kind of nursing home in the country south of London which offered a safe refuge for expectant mothers and their young children from the threat of air raids, and my mother had accepted a place there just before she lost her baby. A woman friend urged her to tie a cushion round her tummy and pretend she was still pregnant to get into the nursing home – and, encouraged by my father, she did so and was admitted, taking me with her. I actually have a memory picture of the place: a rather idyllic scene of women and little children strolling and playing on a big green lawn, and a white-painted wooden summerhouse which fascinated me because it could be rotated like a carousel to follow the movement of the sun across the sky. According to my father, Mum didn't have to wear the cushion once she was interviewed and accepted for admission to the place, after which she presumably pretended to be at an earlier stage of pregnancy, but even so the revelation that my rather shy and diffident mother had had the gumption to pull off this somewhat theatrical deception astonished me, and revealed what unexpected resolve people can sometimes show under the pressure of circumstances.

The vivid opening sequence of the 1936 film *Things to Come*, scripted by H.G. Wells from his own novel, had shown a world war beginning in 1940 with a devastating aerial attack on London. It had a chilling effect on the large number of people who saw it, and when Prime Minister Neville Chamberlain announced that Britain was at war with Germany in September 1939 there was widespread panic in the capital and other big cities and an exodus of people to the country, followed by a rather sheepish return home by most of them as the 'Phoney War' set in. I have a memory which must belong to that time, of getting off a train in the warm dark at a country station with a group of grown-ups including my mother, carrying suitcases and walking into a village and knocking at people's houses looking for somewhere to stay. Before long we returned to Brockley.

I am not sure how that memory relates chronologically to the nursing home episode. Indeed the chronology of all our many movements during the war is very vague and now irrecoverable, but I am fairly sure this village was Lingfield in Surrey, where my mother and I lived at times later in the war. We also spent two other periods near St Austell in Cornwall, and returned home to Brockley for at least one long spell when it seemed safe. This itinerant life inevitably disturbed my education – I attended five or six different schools during the war, some of them pretty poor – but I had a much broader and more varied experience as a child than I would have had if there had not been a war, without suffering the loneliness and homesickness of the official 'evacuees', who were packed off to the country by the trainload with gas masks round their necks and labels pinned to their coats, to be billeted on often reluctant strangers. Interesting experience is money in the bank to a novelist, and you can't open an account too early in life.

There was a popular radio comedian called Rob Wilton in the 1940s, who always began his monologues, *The day war broke out . . .*' On the day war broke out all places of entertainment – theatres, nightclubs and dance halls – closed immediately, and my dad was out of work. He was thirty-three, young enough to be conscripted for military service in due course. He got a day job for a while, but as time passed without the anticipated air raids materialising, some nightclubs and similar venues were allowed to reopen and he began to work again as a musician and vocalist, singing with several well-known big bands on BBC radio. A columnist in a magazine called *Bandwagon* reported in March 1940: 'One of Arthur Roseberry's discoveries, a young laddy who seems to be getting a very full share of the broadcasts available to tenor vocalists, is making quite a stir. His name is Bryan Lodge . . . he is easily one of the best vocalists in town.' Dad was well aware, however, that he was bound to be called up sooner or later, and acted on a tip from a fellow musician: that if he volunteered to enlist with the RAF Central Band at Uxbridge he could spend the war playing music for airmen to march to by day and dance to in the evenings, rather than in some boring, uncomfortable and possibly dangerous occupation not of his own choosing. 'Looking after number one as always, I got my application in a bit sharpish,' he told me.

In due course he got a call from a band leader he had worked for, Jack Nathan, who was forming an 'entertainment band' at Uxbridge and was in need of a sax player who could also sing. Dad jumped at the offer and began his basic training forthwith. 'I don't have to tell you about basic training. Those corporals! I don't know how they make them. So ignorant! They're bastards, they are, that's why they give them the job.' But once that was over, he had a fairly cushy time in the Air Force. Musicians were excused menial duties, such as shovelling coal, which might damage their fingers; and when Jack Nathan was made a flight sergeant he was able to get them spared guard duty. The band's first posting was to RAF Cottesmore in Rutlandshire, a base mainly used for training bomber crews. There were frequent crashes, followed by funerals at which Jack Nathan's band played, slow-marching behind the coffins. This regular duty instilled in Dad a keen awareness of the dangers of flying, and he declined all opportunities to experience it himself. In fact he served for five years in the Air Force, travelling to the Shetlands and India, without ever going up in an aeroplane, and maintained this remarkable record in his post-war life.

But Dad was still at Uxbridge, and my mother and I were at home in Brockley, when the long-delayed Blitz on London began, at the beginning of September 1940. I contributed some memories of this time to a feature in the magazine *Areté*, called 'I remember':

> I remember hearing the up-and-down wailing noise of the air-raid siren on being woken by my mother and putting on my siren suit and running up the road to a neighbour's house, where they had an Anderson shelter dug out of the ground in their back garden. The sky was all red with the fires at the docks, and searchlights swept across the sky lighting up the barrage balloons and a big anti-aircraft gun boomed from the railway line behind the houses opposite.
>
> I remember the smells of earth and paraffin oil and cocoa inside the shelter, and feeling very safe and not frightened at all.
>
> I remember my father came home sometimes in his hairy

blue Air Force uniform from a place called Uxbridge. He joked that he was safer where he was stationed than we were.

And so he was. We were only a few miles from the Docks, a prime target for German bombers, whereas he was almost in the country at the western end of the Metropolitan Line.

I drew on those memories at the beginning of my novel *Out of the Shelter* (1970, rev. 1985), changing, combining and embellishing the facts for narrative and thematic reasons. For example, the father of the central character, Timothy, is an ARP (Air Raid Precautions) warden, being too old for military service, while the father of the family in whose shelter Timothy and his mother take refuge is an airman who happens to be at home on leave when a bomb hits the house, an invented episode. I don't know how long we stayed in London once the Blitz began – long enough, anyway, for me to start collecting shrapnel from the street, rough and still warm to the touch in the morning after a raid – but eventually my mother must have decided it was getting too dangerous, and we went back to lodgings in Lingfield.

Lingfield, in Surrey, thirty-odd miles south of London, is best known as the site of a racecourse, for which reason it has its own railway station, reached from the village by a longish walk across fields, pleasant or unpleasant according to the weather. It has a village green with a duck pond, but its only historic and picturesque feature is the part-medieval parish church, flanked by Tudor cottages and containing some exceptionally fine brasses. It evoked no memories when I revisited the place after an interval of some fifty years, and I don't suppose my mother and I ever went inside that church. Catholics in those days were forbidden to attend Protestant services, and the taboo inhibited us from entering non-Catholic churches at other times (not that we would have been tempted to do so by historical or architectural curiosity). We went on Sundays to a building not much better than a large shed, where a visiting priest said mass.

There was, however, just outside Lingfield a convent school run by the Notre Dame order of nuns which took boys as well as girls up to the age of seven, and my mother placed me there as a day pupil; then, after a while, to my dismay, as a boarder. She said she had to return to London to do some kind of 'war work' – presumably of a clerical nature – and that she couldn't look after me there because of the bombing. I doubt if she was impelled by patriotic motives; more likely, now that Dad was on a service-man's pay, she needed to earn some money. This episode figures in *Out of the Shelter*:

His mother kissed him goodbye and told him to be a good boy. She was crying and he couldn't understand why she was leaving him all on his own. He didn't cry but he was frightened and unhappy. The boarding part of the school was cold and dark, with wooden floors and passages that had no carpets and creaked when you trod on them. There was stew for supper with bits of white fat in it and watery gravy that made the potatoes all mushy. He didn't eat any of it, but he was frightened in case Sister Scholastica noticed. After supper they went into the chapel and sang hymns and said long prayers which he didn't know. He opened and closed his mouth soundlessly to pretend that he was singing and praying with the others. Then it was time to go to bed. His bed was in a big room with some other little boys. There was a place to wash, but only cold water. There was only lino on the floor and it was cold under his feet when he took off his shoes and socks, so he got into bed quickly. The Sister in charge asked him if he had said his night prayers and he said his mother let him say them in bed if it was cold and the other boys giggled. The Sister said next time he must kneel down and say them like the other boys. He didn't like being a boarder at the convent. He felt like crying but it wouldn't be any use. When his mother came to see him he would cry a lot and ask her to take him away. He pictured himself crying and saying to his mother, *Take me away, take me away,* and she took him away. It was a nice picture. Thinking of it, he fell asleep.

That was written when I was much closer to the experience than I am now, and I can no longer distinguish confidently between the details that were taken from life, those that were inspired by classic fictional treatments of the subject, like Joyce's *A Portrait of the Artist as a Young Man* and Antonia White's *Frost in May,* and those that I imagined myself. But the passage, and the whole sequence to which it belongs, is certainly true to the sense of abandonment I felt, as a five-year-old used to my mother's devoted and no doubt over-indulgent care, when suddenly thrust into the austere collective life of a boarding school. On parting my mother had promised to visit me soon, bringing my wellington boots from London, and I remember waiting tensely beside the front door of the convent when she was expected, and when I saw her coming down the drive, dashing out of the house and throwing myself into her arms. I don't know whether I said '*Take me away*', but it was something like that, and she did.

I was not a boarder at the convent more than a week or two, but until my mother returned it seemed to me of indefinite duration, like a bad dream from which one wakes with overwhelming relief. I went back to living with Mum in various places, sure that she would never abandon me again; and indeed by the closing stages of the war I was sufficiently self-confident to willingly board with a family in Lingfield for some months while she returned to London to work. But when much later in life I became troubled by anxiety to a neurotic degree I sometimes wondered whether the seed of this tendency was planted by the episode of the convent boarding school – that abrupt, unforeseen, indefinite withdrawal of everything which had made my infant life comfortable and secure.

I continued to attend the convent school as a day pupil, living in lodgings with my mother. For a time we lived with a disagreeable woman called Mrs Green, who complained that I made too much noise, and whose house, like many in Lingfield, had no electricity, only gaslights on the ground floor and nothing on the first floor, so that you had to go to bed with a candle, and no bathroom, so that I had my weekly bath in our living room in a tin tub filled with hot water from jugs. I believe it was not very long afterwards, probably in the spring or summer of 1941, that we left Lingfield to live in Porthpean, a seaside hamlet near St Austell on the south coast of Cornwall. Mum had an older cousin on her mother's side, Victor Wood, whom she and Eileen had known and liked when they were girls. Victor grew up to be a successful businessman who moved to Cornwall and owned two chemist's shops there, one in St Austell and the other in Newquay on the north coast. Having discovered the rather miserable circumstances in which my mother was looking after me in Lingfield, he generously invited us to go and live with him in his spacious house in Porthpean, and so we did.

We travelled by coach, I suppose for economy's sake – an interminable journey in those pre-motorway days, involving a change in Exeter. But I imagine that I soon cheered up once we arrived at our destination. Porthpean was a more appealing place to a child than damp, muddy Lingfield, and Victor Wood's house infinitely more comfortable than the lodgings we had occupied there. The area around St Austell is not one of the most picturesque parts of Cornwall. It is the centre of the china clay industry, and conical hills of the whitish-grey waste this produces rear up from the fields like spectral slag heaps. The town itself lacks charm, but scenic Fowey and quaint Mevagissey are not far away, and there are several small bays in the area with attractive beaches, like Porthpean. My uncle Vic's house, called The Retreat, was only a short steep walk from that beach, and although it was disfigured by a long barricade of obstacles constructed of concrete and rusting iron, designed to repel a German invasion, they did not prevent us from getting to the sea. It was a perfect beach for a child, with plenty of sand at low tide, and a stretch of rocks at one end that were easy to clamber over, their hollows and fissures becoming seaweed-lined pools when the waves withdrew, home to mussels, limpets, crabs, shrimps, sea anemones and tiny fish. When I revisited the place in 2002 the rock pools were still there, but with little sign of life in them. Being 'evacuated' here felt, at least for a while, like being on an extended holiday rather than being in exile from home. To my joy Dad was able to join us for a reasonably long leave, and I have a snapshot of him and me smiling side by side in an identical pose, legs apart, with our thumbs hooked into the waistbands of our shorts. Dad is shirtless, so it must have been taken in the summer of 1941. I dare say I was very sad when he had to put on his uniform and return to base, but I was proud of him too, and somewhat idealised his contribution to the war effort. I took intense interest in a little book on aircraft recognition which he gave me, and learned to distinguish between the silhouettes of Spitfires and Hurricanes, and Dornier and Heinkel bombers.

Just east of Porthpean was Duporth House, home of the Rankin family, who before the war had converted the estate into an upmarket holiday camp, building chalets on the land that sloped down to their private beach. At the commencement of war the site was requisitioned for the accommodation of troops, but Mr and Mrs Rankin continued to live in the manor house with their son Alan, who was about my age. My uncle Victor knew the family and as a result I was invited to Duporth House on several occasions to play with Alan, a rather mischievous boy with a mop of golden curls. He led me through the rooms of the (as it seemed to me) vast house, and we explored the big echoing buildings that had once served the holidaymakers – a dining room, a ballroom with a sprung floor – and the boardwalks and paths outside. We peered through trees at the Indian troops who were at that time occupying the chalets, swarthy men in turbans who cooked their food over fires in the open air. It seemed to me a magical place, and the *pièce de résistance* was a magnificent model railway

Mr Rankin had constructed in an attic room, as big as the one I had seen in Hamleys of Regent Street before the war, which he enjoyed demonstrating to us.

Alan's parents were always chiding their son for his behaviour and, I believe, hoped I would be a good influence on him. I certainly had a much greater respect for authority, as an incident I recall from that period illustrates. I was playing, or rather hanging out (the American phrase is more expressive of the aimless congregation of unsupervised children), with a few kids on the corner of the road in Porthpean where my uncle's house was situated. A small car came up the hill from the beach, and on a naughty impulse, to impress my playmates I threw a stick I was holding at the vehicle as it passed. I doubt if I meant it to hit the car, but it did, on a side window. To my horror the car stopped and the driver got out, revealing himself as an army officer in uniform. The cliché 'frozen to the spot' is the only possible description of my state of mind and body as he walked back towards us. I don't think I feared anything specific, like being summarily arrested and hauled off to a police station. I was just aware of having committed some terrible transgression which would be punished. Of course all the man did was to speak sternly to us about the danger of throwing things at cars – I'm not even sure that he identified me as the culprit. But for years afterwards, in moments of reverie, especially when trying to go to sleep, I would mentally relive those traumatic moments, and struggle vainly to escape the memory of my guilt and fear of retribution.

An occasional visitor to us in Porthpean was my aunt Eileen, my mother's younger sister, who had moved from London to the south-west in search of war-related employment in a safer environment than the capital. She worked as a Land Girl for a time, then later as a secretary to the CO of the American troops who replaced the Indians at Duporth House. I was always glad to see her, as were most people. She was attractive, vivacious, always elegantly turned out and groomed, very good company, a great talker, slightly 'actressy' in her speech and body language, and full of amusing anecdotes about her experiences which would keep the adults around her in fits of laughter. There was a sadder side to her character, as I would discover later in life, but to me as a child she was a fascinating figure who banished boredom whenever she appeared, and she in turn was very fond of me. I looked forward eagerly to her visits, and on one occasion, when I was about six, I proposed to her a secret compact between us, namely that I would confess to her when I had been naughty and she would have to punish me, beating me on the bottom with a stick I supplied from the garden, and make a record of it. She giggled in a rather embarrassed way, as well she might, when I explained this plan to her, and found ways to avoid implementing it, apart from a token 'practice' stroke, as light as a fairy's wand, which I insisted on. What would a psychoanalyst make of the scheme I concocted? Obviously I didn't really want to be physically hurt, and relied on my aunt's tenderness towards me to ensure that. Was it then an expression of infantile sexuality, for I was in a way in love with my aunt and this may have been the most intimate connection between us that I could conceive of at that age? Or was it an unconscious effort of the child to rid himself of the uncomfortable emotions associated with the episode of the officer in the car (a stick figures in both episodes), to purge the memory of that traumatic moment of transgression and fear by a ritual performance of punishment? I shall have more to say about my aunt Eileen later. She was a very important figure in my life, and her own partly inspired two of my novels.

My uncle Vic was a thoroughly nice man. Slight of build, he wore glasses, had grey, thinning hair, and his face broke frequently into a broad, toothy smile. He had retained his Yorkshire accent, which was a novelty to me, but seemed eloquent of his homely warmth and generosity. He was in his early fifties, too old for military service, though he was in Civil Defence. He had a small car and, because of his business, a petrol ration, from which we benefited. Once he drove Mum and me across the Cornish peninsula to Newquay, which was then a quiet and modestly sized resort very different from the crowded and somewhat tawdry place it is now. Even at that early age I was struck by the contrast between the rugged windblown north Cornwall coast and the gentler, more sheltered south, and awed by the great rollers that surged in from the Atlantic to break on the vast Newquay beaches.

I have made this time we spent in Cornwall sound idyllic and in many ways it was. But there were tensions in the ménage at Porthpean created by Vic's wife Isabel, who resented the presence of Vic's relatives in her house. This feeling was perhaps under-standable, but her way of expressing it was often bizarre. Looking back, it seems obvious that she was psychologically disturbed, but she was an alarming figure to me then, liable to sudden changes of mood, given to fits of anger and hysterics which we would hear through closed doors. She was a Protestant and seemed particularly aggravated by the fact that we, like her husband, were Catholics; on Sundays she would sit at the piano in the drawing room singing

'Onward, Christian Soldiers' and other Protestant hymns at the top of her voice to demonstrate her religious allegiance. She and Vic had two teenage children, Ralph and Mary. Ralph, who was the elder, seemed to side with his mother, to judge by his reserved manner towards us, while Mary was much more friendly. The saintly Vic did his best to keep everyone happy, but I presume my mother decided at some point that we had better not stay with the family any longer. We went back, rather surprisingly it seems to me in retrospect, to London, to Brockley, to Millmark Grove.

3

I presume there was a lull in the bombing of London in 1942, when Hitler was preoccupied with his campaigns in Russia and North Africa, which made my mother think it was safe to return there. Or perhaps it was the installation of a Morrison shelter in our front room that was the crucial factor. This was a large black box made of girders and thick steel plate, about the height of a table and occupying the floor space of a very large double bed. The sides were heavy-duty wire mesh, one of which lifted up to give access to the mattresses and bedding within. You crawled in when the siren sounded an alarm, or slept there routinely every night, protected from all but a direct hit by a bomb. I was very fond of the Morrison shelter, which was in many ways like the 'dens' that children love to build for themselves. It felt cosy and safe when you were inside, and I used the top to lay out an airfield for my motley collection of model planes.

I know we were back in London in 1942, because I was seven that year, and made my First Communion at the Brockley parish church of St Mary Magdalen at that age, as was customary, on the assumption that seven was 'the age of discretion' at which a child could understand the nature of the sacrament and the concept of sin. In fact there were two sacraments to be understood, because you had to cleanse your soul of sin in the sacrament of Penance (usually referred to as Confession) before receiving the Eucharist. Children were prepared for this rite of passage at the parochial elementary school. Like, I believe, most of those who experienced it, I found confession more daunting than communion, even though I had invented a profane version of it with my auntie Eileen as confessor. Occupying a pew in a row of apprehensive and fidgety classmates, 'examining your conscience', moving along to take your turn in the confessional, a wooden structure like a large wardrobe at the back of the church, pulling aside the curtain, kneeling down in the semi-darkness, and reciting a prepared list of sins to the vague priestly presence behind a grille that resembled the door of a meat safe, wondering afterwards if, out of embarrassment, you had omitted something which would invalidate the whole process (that distant occasion, for instance, when a playmate's sister lowered her knickers and lifted her skirt to show you the dimpled cleft between her legs, though you unchivalrously declined to reciprocate by displaying your own weeing apparatus) – this was an anxious business, although the priest was kindly and the 'penance' (silent recitation of a few 'Hail Marys') was light. In communion you received Jesus into yourself in some mysterious way in the form of a consecrated wafer placed on your tongue by the priest, which was a kind of magic that a child could accept readily enough. The main challenge was to swallow the host without chewing it, which would be disrespectful, and possibly sacrilegious, but not so easy to manage when your mouth was dry because you'd had to fast from food and drink since going to bed the previous evening. We practised with unconsecrated hosts in the communion class. The real thing, we were told, would be the happiest day of our lives. I didn't feel that it was, though some ladies of the parish did their best to make it memorable, laying on a special breakfast with jellies and cakes for us first communicants in the school afterwards. I thought the happiest day of my life would be when the war was over and my dad came home for good.

The school was a utilitarian two-storey brick building adjacent to the church, with classrooms on the ground floor divided by partitions which folded back to make a parish hall outside school hours, and a high-walled asphalt playground, with toilets for boys and girls on opposite sides. I have a mental image of that drab playground crowded with children running and skipping, kicking and catching balls, like the stick-figures in a Lowry painting. The boys' urinal consisted of a gutter and a wall against which older pupils would vie with each other to pee the highest. It was open to the sky, and sometimes they would be seen by the headmaster, looking down from an upper-floor window, and get caned. As in all Catholic schools of the period, there was a good deal of corporal punishment. I was in the class of Mrs Clark, a pale-faced, ginger-haired, short-tempered lady who administered it freely, not just for misbehaviour but for what she regarded as culpable ignorance or incompetence. Her method was to roll up the sleeve of the offender and slap the soft flesh on the underside of the forearm with her hand. The careful, deliberate way she rolled up the sleeve was more frightening to me than the sound of the slap. I feared her wrath, but was clever enough to elude it.

The church was a more ornate redbrick building constructed at the end of the nineteenth century in basilica style. There was a Lady Chapel next to the high altar which was hit by a bomb and left in its ruined state, partitioned off from the main body of the church for the duration of the war, an open wound in the side of the holy building and a constant reminder of evil German aggression as you passed it in the street. The priests who served the parish were Augustinians of the Assumption, a French order founded in the nineteenth century whose mission was to oppose the godlessness of modern society. The parish priest, Father Louis, was French and preached sermons of passionate exhortation with a strong accent. He was advanced in years, with a full, grizzled beard, and looked like a biblical prophet in an old painting.

On Monday mornings he or one of the other priests from the presbytery would often appear in school at the first session when the register was taken, and order any children who had not been to mass the previous day to stand up. These unfortunates (believing, I suppose, that their absence had been noted and that to pretend otherwise would only make a bad situation worse) would then have to offer their explanations and excuses, which would be received with varying degrees of scepticism and disapproval. We would be reminded that to miss mass on Sunday, deliberately and with no good reason, was a mortal sin. According to the Penny Catechism (then the standard guide to Catholic doctrine, and still in print), mortal sin is so called because 'it is so serious that it kills the soul and deserves hell'. So if you happened to die after culpably missing Sunday mass, without having obtained absolution in confession or managing to make a 'perfect act of contrition' on your own (a difficult feat, because your sorrow for sin had to be motivated purely by the love of God, and not by the fear of punishment), you would go to Hell for all eternity. This was so patently absurd – the punishment so grotesquely disproportionate to the putative offence to God – that it is hard in retrospect to credit that anyone really believed it, but such was the power of clerical authority that no one challenged it. The concept of mortal sin (as distinct from venial or minor sins) was a crucial element of traditional Catholic moral theology by which the Church defined how salvation might be forfeited, and it acquired special force in the first half of the twentieth century, as John Cornwell has convincingly demonstrated.[1] Before then, only very devout Catholics received communion frequently, and the majority did so only at Christmas and Easter and on other special occasions. Pope Pius X (1903–14) began a campaign urging the faithful to receive communion at every opportunity, and in due course the majority of attenders at Sunday mass did so. At the same time the 'age of discretion' at which a child should be introduced to confession, which had been flexibly assessed in the past, was defined as seven. Frequent communion required frequent confession to ensure that one was in 'a state of grace'. In this way the clergy was able to police the moral lives of the laity continuously from childhood till death, and ensure that they were obedient to the dictates of the Church. After the Second Vatican Council of the early 1960s, which shook up the whole system of Catholic belief and practice, the distinction between mortal and venial sin largely disappeared from the language of religious instruction, as did the habit of frequent confession among practising Catholics.

---

1 John Cornwell, *The Dark Box: a secret history of Confession* (2014)

I walked to school and back – a distance of about a mile – initially in the care of an older girl recruited for this task by my mother. Later I became more independent, but usually came home with a group of pupils who lived in the same direction. One afternoon we were a few hundred yards from the railway bridge that traversed Brockley Road just before Brockley Cross when a German aeroplane flew low over our heads firing its machine guns, perhaps at a train on the line, though its main target was said later to be an anti-aircraft battery on Telegraph Hill. These rare hit-and-run raids, as they were called, by fast fighter-bombers that flew under the British radar, were not heralded by the warning ululation of an air-raid siren. Some of the bullets hit the white-tiled walls under the bridge and left pockmarks which were still discernible the last time I looked, about fifty years later. We children had a narrow escape, which may have been the reason why Mum and I left London again in 1943.

We returned to Cornwall. This time we lodged with a very hospitable family called Smith who lived in the village of Mount St Charles, a mile or so from Porthpean, to whom we had been introduced by my uncle Vic. Mr Smith was an industrious man: a butcher with his own shop and slaughterhouse, he also had a smallholding and a milk round in the locality. Needless to say, we ate extremely well while we lived in the house behind the butcher's shop. I particularly remember the lavish provision of clotted Cornish cream at teatime to accompany home-made scones and jam, and the rare experience of spooning honey from the comb on to one's bread and butter. The Smiths had two daughters: one, Dorothy, was a teenager, and the other, Jenefer, was much younger

44

– indeed too young to be a playmate for me, though adults liked fondly to imagine that we might be sweethearts when we grew up. A snapshot guaranteed to draw a murmured '*Ah, aren't they sweet?*' survives from this period, of Jenefer and me in front of the butcher's shop, she in a white summer frock, with plump dimpled cheeks under a dense mass of dark hair in ringlets, and I in short flannel trousers and rolled-up shirtsleeves beside her. Our suntanned arms are linked, and with our free hands we are stroking the Smiths' collie sitting patiently between us. My most vivid memory of Jenefer is less romantic: watching with a mixture of fascination and pity as Mrs Smith combed her tightly curled natural ringlets with a steel comb to remove the nits she had acquired at school, crushing them on a sheet of newspaper and treating her scalp afterwards with gentian violet, while her daughter wriggled and whimpered.

In the summer of 2008 I talked about my book *Deaf Sentence* at a literary festival in Fowey, and afterwards a smiling, grey-haired lady came up to the table where I was signing copies and introduced herself as Jenefer. There was no opportunity to talk much, for she had another appointment, but we exchanged addresses and in due course letters. She told me that some time ago she had deduced from reviews of my books and a profile of my life that I must be 'the little boy who came to stay with us during the war'. She remembered well the nit-picking ordeals, and told me that the photo of us together with the dog was taken in the summer of 1943, when she was six and a half and I was eight and a half. It is one of the very few precise chronological markers that I have for this phase of my life. She wrote: 'I always remember your mother and Aunt Eileen as such beautiful women', and recalled that her elder sister Dorothy used to go horse-riding with Eileen.

Mr Smith was a kind, friendly man who did his best to compensate for my fatherless state. If I was willing to get up very early on holidays or weekends he would take me in his van to collect the churns of milk which the local farmers left at the gates of their properties, and once I helped, rather ineffectually, to bring in the hay from a field that belonged to him. I had a sneezing fit as dust and pollen swirled about in the air, and when I became susceptible to hay fever in adolescence I wondered if my allergy originated on that day. I never really took to the rural and agricultural way of life, in spite of Mr Smith's kind efforts to initiate me into it. For me, 81 Millmark Grove in its grimy urban setting was still 'home' and I yearned to return there. There was a song made enormously popular in the war by Vera Lynn's rendering of it, beginning, 'There'll be bluebirds over the white cliffs of Dover, tomorrow, just you wait and see . . .' which projected a sentimental vision of the peace to come:

> *There'll be love and laughter*
> *And peace ever after*
> *Tomorrow, when the world is free*
> *The shepherd will tend his sheep*
> *The valley will bloom again*
> *And Jimmy will go to sleep*
> *In his own little room again.*

I always identified with Jimmy when I heard the song.

I don't know how long we lived with the Smiths, or why we left Cornwall and went back to live in Lingfield. Possibly my mother was concerned about my education because the standard of the village school at Mount St Charles was poor. The Notre Dame convent school in Lingfield, which normally took boys only up to the age of seven, was prepared to make exceptions in wartime, and I and another boy who lived locally were admitted into a class of girls of our own age, some of whom were boarders. Neither of us had the slightest sexual interest in them. In their brown gym tunics and thick stockings they seemed like an alien race, who were often mean to each other and cried easily. At breaks we played with the younger boys, and rather enjoyed the power we had over them due to our seniority. It was for me an agreeable change from the rather rough and intimidating Cornish school.

Mum and I had lodgings in a street of what were probably council houses, with the mother of a little girl called Pauline, whose husband was away in the forces somewhere. We had the front sitting room and a bedroom to ourselves, and Mum shared the kitchen. How she managed financially at this time, how much she suffered from boredom, loneliness and the frustrations of house-sharing (though we got on well enough with our landlady), I have no idea. Lingfield was more congenial than it might otherwise have been, especially to me, because my grandmother had also left London at the time of the Blitz, and settled there for the duration, as living-in housekeeper to an elderly single gentleman called Mr Sandal, while Pop stayed in London, working at Barkers department store in Kensington and fire-watching from its roof at nights, coming down to the country by train at weekends. Nana was the person I most loved in the world after my parents, and she remained very dear to me in adult life. I knew she loved me too, because whenever we met her face would light up with pleasure in a way that cannot be faked. She was small in stature, with a matronly figure, strong well-fleshed features and fine black hair. She was quick-witted though not formally well-educated, gentle, kind and transparently sincere, and she had the rare ability to relate directly to a child, talking to him without any trace of condescension or adult self-consciousness. Mr Sandal's house was a redbrick villa at the end of a short cul-de-sac that led to the village recreation ground. I loved to spend time with Nana in the kitchen-parlour, playing cribbage, helping her shell peas from the garden, drinking tea and asking her to read our futures in the pattern of the tea-leaves left at the bottom of the cups, and watching her light the gas as dusk fell outside, holding the spill up to the pale mantle until it ignited with a faint 'pop' and glowed red and then white. Some of her favourite expressions – like 'a nice game played slow', applied ironically to tedious and futile tasks – have stayed with me ever since.

At some point Mr Sandal died and Nana became housekeeper to a GP, a bachelor or widower whom she always referred to as 'the Doctor', so I have forgotten what his name was. In fact I don't recall ever meeting him, though I suppose I must have done, since I visited Nana frequently in her living quarters at the back of his fine house. It had a splendid garden well stocked with vegetables and fruit – raspberries, loganberries, redcurrants and blackcurrants, apples, pears, damsons and quince. Nana was a good plain cook, especially of pastries, puddings and conserves, and made excellent use of the garden's produce. She was very happy there, and stayed on for a year or two after the war was over. I missed her then, and used to visit her occasionally, travelling on my own from London on a Greenline bus that passed through Lingfield on its way to East Grinstead.

East Grinstead is the nearest sizable town to Lingfield, and during the war Mum and I went there occasionally for shopping. It was the site of the famous Queen Victoria Hospital where the pioneering plastic surgeon Sir Archibald McIndoe and his team treated Allied airmen who had been badly burned, and occasionally one saw these brave men in the streets in bright blue hospital suits with white bandages wrapped round their faces. Their presence was only one of many continual reminders that 'there's a war on', along with the vapour trails of planes in the sky on their way to bomb Germany, and the convoys of military vehicles on the roads moving towards the coast in preparation for the invasion of occupied France. In 1944 I was nine, old enough to begin to take an intelligent interest in the progress of the war, with a comforting sense that we seemed to be winning. The prospect of an early return home to London, however, was extinguished by the bombardment of the capital by V1 flying bombs which began in June, shortly after D-Day. At the beginning of August one of these missiles landed smack in the middle of Millmark Grove, demolishing sixteen houses and damaging many others. Remarkably, only two people were killed. Our house, being near the end of the street, suffered light damage, mainly to windows, as Dad reported after being given leave to inspect it. A family whose house had been destroyed asked if they could move into ours temporarily, and it is pleasing to record that he agreed, and that many years later I received a letter via my publisher from a member of that family expressing gratitude for the loan of our house. Before long the V1s were followed by V2 rockets, and in November one of these hit a crowded Woolworth's store in New Cross, killing 168 people, the worst disaster of the V-weapon campaign. The closest I came to personal experience of these dangers was when I was walking across a field near Lingfield with my grandmother one day and a black V1 suddenly appeared overhead pursued by a Spitfire, low enough for us to see the camouflage markings on the fighter and the orange flame coming out of the flying bomb's jet engine before they disappeared out of sight. I presume the fighter was looking for a safe place to shoot down the V1, or else to tip its wing and make it crash.

Dad spent a long period of the war very far from any action, and from us, stationed with Jack Nathan's band at a base near Lerwick in the Shetlands, relieving the monotony by fishing and playing golf in his off-duty hours, and sending me amusing strip cartoons of himself engaged in these activities, stared at by sheep. But the band must have been back in England in 1944, because Mum and I joined him for Christmas together in Millmark Grove (rather surprisingly, because the odd V1 or V2 continued to fall on London into the New Year). I remember him meeting us at Victoria station and saying to my mother, 'I see we're losing the war again', a hyperbolical reference to the Battle of the Bulge in the Ardennes, then in progress, which worried me. But by the early spring of 1945 it was obvious that the war in Europe was approaching its end, and my father and his mates were looking forward to demobilisation, when to their dismay Jack Nathan's band was ordered to go to India to entertain the troops there. They travelled by sea, and I possess Dad's dog-eared copy of an American paperback in a 'Fighting Forces Series', called *What To Do Aboard the Transport*, which must have been distributed to the troops on embarkation since it has no price on it. It included guides to star-gazing and bird-watching with which Dad passed the time more profitably than most of his fellow passengers, who played endless games of cards. Always good at adjusting to unalterable circumstances, he quite enjoyed the voyage, but he disliked what he saw of India, its heat and insects and squalor, and the experience probably put him off foreign travel for the rest of his life, because he never left the shores of England after his return, except once to join me and my family on holiday in Guernsey.

At about the time Dad went to India Mum returned to London from Lingfield to work at Deptford Town Hall in the department concerned with ration books. She probably wanted to earn some money and get the house straight before Dad came home, and she gauged correctly that I no longer needed her constant protective presence. I boarded with the family of the boy of my own age who was my classmate at the convent. I have forgotten his name, but I liked him, and his mother, and her cooking, and I was quite happy to accept the arrangement. That Nana was living nearby, where I could visit her frequently, was reassuring. Nevertheless I looked forward eagerly to moving back to 81 Millmark Grove, the only source of anxiety being the prospect of another change of school in the autumn. Mum arranged for me to sit an entrance examination at my uncle

John's old school, St Joseph's Academy, Blackheath, which was in the process of becoming a state-aided Catholic grammar school. I passed the exam successfully (I wrote a 'composition' plagiarised from the novel *Black Beauty*, but perhaps the examiners found this enterprising rather than culpable) and was given a place for the new school year beginning in September as a fee-paying pupil, with the understanding that if I passed the newly established 11-plus exam after my next birthday there would be no more fees to pay. The fees would in any case have been modest, for the school had an honourable policy of adjusting them for eligible pupils from low-income families. I had been introduced to algebra and French in my last months at the convent without making much progress in either, and I remember asking my mother anxiously if I would be expected to have a grasp of these subjects when I started at St Joseph's. She thought not.

I have no distinct memory of the end of the war in Europe in May, but I was back home in Millmark Grove for the surrender of Japan in July and the celebrations of VJ Night, described in *Out of the Shelter*:

> They had a bonfire in the street, on the bomb-site. Everybody came out of their houses and stood around the bonfire laughing and talking and drinking beer and lemonade out of bottles. Like all the children, Timothy had a red, white and blue ribbon pinned on his coat in the shape of a V. There were bonfires that night on lots of bomb-sites all over London. They lit up the sky in a red glow like the Blitz.

That bomb site would soon become a kind of adventure playground for me and my friends in the street, and until the gap was filled in with new houses it gave us illegal access to an immense railway embankment with trees and bushes and hollows ideal for playing a game called the Lost Commandos we developed from a comic. Servicemen began to come back from the war, welcomed by home-made banners and posters on the walls and in the windows of their houses. I made my own 'Welcome Home Dad' posters and waited impatiently to display them, which took some time as he cautiously declined the offer of a lift in an RAF transport plane and travelled by sea. But eventually we were happily reunited and a new chapter of our lives opened. I had to start secondary education; Dad had to rebuild his professional career; and Mum . . . well, Mum had to cook and keep house for us in the era of post-war 'Austerity' when rationing and shortages made that occupation an unrewarding struggle.

Dad tried to resume his career as a singer with bands broadcasting on radio, but had no luck. His 'tenor sweet style', as it used to be described in music magazines, had been superseded by the 'crooning' style made popular by American singers. I remember that he was excited about getting an audition with the Ted Heath band, probably the best of its kind at the time, and very disappointed when he was unsuccessful. (The singer who got the job was Jimmy Young, later to become a celebrity broadcaster.) Nevertheless, Dad's ability to sing as well as play several instruments meant he was usually fully employed with gigs and occasionally longer engagements in clubs. He returned home from work in the small hours of the morning to sleep late, with a pillow over his face to keep out the light. After an hour or so of music practice, the rest of his day was devoted to one of the many interests and hobbies which he took up, dropped and sometimes returned to, such as painting, calligraphy, golf, sea-angling off the pier at Brighton, collecting antique pottery and playing the stock market. My mother participated in none of these activities. In the evening he had a meal we called 'tea', which was a kind of early supper, and sat down afterwards in his reclining armchair for a short rest, covering his face with a newspaper. Then he would suddenly cast the newspaper aside, glance at the clock, swear and rush out of the room and up the stairs to change into his dinner suit, and down again to collect his instruments from the front room, and up again to get something he had forgotten, while Mum and I did our best to keep out of his way until the front door slammed behind him. Dad rarely left himself enough time to leave the house in a leisurely way, and I recognise the same tendency in myself.

The work he went off to do was providing entertainment for other people, in a branch of the music business that was essentially social. On the stand the musicians in a dance hall or club were always exchanging jokes and quips between sets, laughing among themselves to convey a feeling of bonhomie and enjoyment to the customers, and when Dad became leader of his own resident quartet at a nightclub in the late forties he would circulate and chat to the regular patrons. Having exercised his social skills at work he had no inclination to do the same in his leisure hours, which in any case were not those of most other people. He and my mother therefore had virtually no social life together – no friendships with other couples, no entertaining or being entertained at home, no outings to theatres or cinemas or restaurants together. My mother's social life consisted almost entirely of informal contact with women friends and relatives. From old snapshots in photograph albums it is clear that in their courting days and the early years of marriage Dad and Mum had a fuller social life together, and in that period of economic depression they were probably better off than most of their neighbours; but after the war Dad established a domestic routine that served his own needs and priorities while neglecting Mum's, and she was not sufficiently assertive to do anything about it. Both my father and I were the only children of doting mothers, who lived at home until early adulthood, 'waited on hand and foot' in the proverbial phrase, and we assumed that it was the natural order of things.

Mum's siblings, meanwhile, had been living, and continued to live, much more exciting lives. Eileen got a job as a civilian secretary at the American Army HQ in Cheltenham prior to the Normandy invasion, and volunteered afterwards, with a number of other adventurous women similarly employed, to serve in France. They didn't know their destination until their military plane broke through the clouds and they saw Paris spread out beneath them and a cheer went up in the cabin. She worked in the Chaplain's Department, which as a good Catholic she found congenial, wore a smart quasi-military uniform, and sent us a snapshot of herself wearing it jauntily in a snow-covered Parisian street, smiling and obviously exhilarated by the atmosphere of the liberated capital. At the end of the war the secretaries followed the military into Germany, and Eileen was sent first to Frankfurt and then to Heidelberg, where the US Army of Occupation set up its headquarters because, unlike Frankfurt and most other German cities, it was almost entirely undamaged by the war.

In this picturesque setting she enjoyed all the privileges and comforts that the American Army could supply to its personnel on a scale unattainable by other nationalities. In the middle and late forties American society, having rapidly recovered from the Great Depression of the pre-war era, embodied the whole world's desires for the materialistic Good Life, mediated through its movies and magazines in the imagery of huge cars, huge refrigerators, huge steaks, ice cream, candy and Coca-Cola *ad libitum*, consumed by human beings who looked happier, healthier and about a foot taller than their equivalents in war-weary Europe. Having access to the PX store which provided American goodies to the military community in Germany, Eileen was able to pass on some of them to us in England when she made her occasional visits – nylon stockings for Mum, candy bars for me with strange names like 'Baby Ruth' and 'Oh Henry!' and cartons of Lucky Strike for Dad. As time went on, and the tourist resorts of Europe began to open for business again, she used her dollars to visit some of them during her leaves and sent back postcards and letters with lyrical descriptions to us in England, where the annual foreign currency allowance of £25 per person severely restricted Continental travel, even if we had desired it.

Meanwhile my uncle John was also starting a new life in Europe. After doing duty as an instructor for most of the war, he was posted to Brussels at the time of the liberation of Belgium and there he met a young woman called Lucienne at a party. They fell in love and married. It was a civil wedding, because she was a divorcée with a son of about my age, and John, unlike his sisters, had long ceased to be a practising Catholic. He brought his bride to London soon after the end of the war to meet us and other friends and relatives. He was tall and handsome in his RAF officer's uniform, with crisp wavy hair and a dashing moustache, and Lu obviously adored him. She herself was not a beauty, but she was a vivacious and charming person whom I liked immediately and remained attached to for the rest of her long life. She was of Flemish and Jewish stock but belonged to the well-off Brussels bourgeoisie who spoke mainly French. Her father owned a whole-sale textile business in which he promised to find John a job. Thus John returned to the homeland of his mother, Adèle.

The occasional visitations of Uncle John and Aunty Eileen in the immediate post-war years were like sudden splashes of colour and explosions of noise in our quiet monochrome existence. We rarely entertained at home, and never more than a few people at a time, but when Eileen was visiting us there would be gatherings of her and Mum's women friends in our lounge, powdered and perfumed and dressed to the nines, sipping sherry and gin-and-orange, exchanging anecdotes and shrieking with laughter, parties on the fringes of which I lurked, fascinated and uncomprehending. Eileen and John were both emotionally volatile individuals, quick-tempered, prone to sudden changes of mood, and whenever the siblings came together sooner or later the initial euphoria and hilarity would be followed by arguments, reproaches and, on Eileen's part, tears. Dad, who disliked immoderate displays of emotion, found these visits a strain and used his work commitments as an excuse to get out of the associated socialising. He also resented Eileen's comments on the shortcomings of our domestic arrangements and suggestions for improving Mum's lot. His reaction was understand-able, but so, in retrospect, were the comments and suggestions.

4

I was now halfway into what Freudian psychoanalysis designates the latency phase of personal development, 'a period of emotional quiescence between the dramas and turmoils of childhood and adolescence'.[1] I think it is a good name. Looking back on myself between the ages of ten and fourteen, I cannot perceive many signs of the person, especially the writer and academic, I was to become – unless it was that when asked 'What do you want to be when you grow up?' my standard reply for some time was: 'Sports reporter.' My main interest in life and the chief focus of emotion during those years was sport; sport of various kinds but especially football and cricket, whose seasons divided the year between them.

Dad took me to watch Charlton Athletic one Saturday not long after his return home, and I was immediately hooked. At some point in the 1970s I went with a friend to watch a professional football match for the first time in at least twenty years, at the

---

1 Charles Rycroft, *A Critical Dictionary of Psychoanalysis* (1972)

Birmingham City ground, and revived the experience of entering the unappealing back parts of a football stadium, squeezing through its stiff turnstiles, mounting a dark, dank concrete staircase, and the thrill of emerging at last into an arena packed with humming, expectant humanity, looking down on a vividly green rectangle of grass on which a contest would shortly be enacted by twenty-two brightly clad athletes; and I understood then more clearly than I had as a boy the magnetic attraction of this colourful spectacle for the inhabitants of drab urban environments. It was especially appealing to men who had been deprived of it for several years by the war, and attendances in those days were high. Charlton's ground, known as the Valley, was a vast bowl carved out of a former quarry which attracted crowds of up to 70,000 spectators, mostly standing on uncovered terraces, a mass of bodies that swayed and surged like the sea at moments of excitement. (It has since, I believe, greatly shrunk in scale and improved its amenities.) Charlton was not, strictly speaking, our local league club – Millwall was nearer. But Millwall was in the lowly Third Division and its ground, appropriately called the Den, had (and still has) the reputation of attracting a rough crowd, whereas Charlton was one of the elite teams of the First Division, the equivalent of today's Premier League.

In 1946 they got to the FA Cup Final at Wembley, only to lose 3–1 to Derby County in extra time. I listened to the BBC radio commentary and was inconsolable at the end. But Jimmy Seed, Charlton's brilliant manager, who had steered them from Third to First Division in two seasons before the war, vowed they would be back at Wembley next year – and by golly they were, just like a story in one of the boys' magazines, *Hotspur, Wizard* and

59

Champion, on which I spent my weekly pocket money – and this time they won! The FA Cup, now overshadowed by European competitions, was then the Holy Grail of English professional football, and I felt privileged to be a supporter of so successful a club. After that peak a slow decline in Charlton's fortunes began, but I remained loyal. I no longer needed to be escorted to matches by Dad, but travelled to the Valley by tram with a couple of friends in Millmark Grove. My heroes in the team were the goalkeeper Sam Bartram and the centre forward Charlie Vaughan. Bartram was a virile and genial figure, with a grin like Burt Lancaster's and dense auburn hair set off by the green woollen jerseys goalkeepers invariably wore in those days. Jimmy Seed defined a good goal-keeper concisely as 'a gymnast with ball skills', and Sam Bartram was certainly that, but he also showed, in the style of his flying saves, an instinct for what transforms a game into a spectacle. Charlie Vaughan had been a star of the amateur club Sutton United before he joined Charlton, and something of the gentlemanly amateur lingered in his deportment at the Valley. I don't remember him ever committing a violent foul or protesting against a referee's decision, and when caught offside in possession of the ball, he would place it for the opposition's free kick before retreating. His posture was straight-backed, with arms usually held close to his sides as if to emphasise that football was played with the feet, and he would have been appalled by the holding and shirt-grabbing that is now tolerated in professional football. He was a good role model for a football-mad boy.

One of the great disappointments of St Joseph's Academy for me was that, in common with most grammar schools, its winter sport was rugby. I never liked the game. I was always the youngest member of my class, small and slight in stature, and shrank from the violent collisions with larger bodies that were inevitable in rugby. It seemed to me a vastly inferior game to football, favouring brute strength over skill, and I have not changed my mind since. Rugby consists essentially of physical struggle, and the rules devised to make it a game have the effect of spoiling it as a spectacle – witness the number of international matches that are settled by penalty kicks which interrupt the play and are awarded for reasons often invisible and sometimes incomprehensible to spectators. Admittedly, a flowing passing movement that results in a try can be thrilling to watch, but such moments are rare. And there must be something fundamentally wrong with a field game in which a basic tactic is to kick the ball out of play.

The majority of pupils at St Joseph's were, like me, primarily interested in football, and at breaks in the school day the playground was a pitch on which half a dozen games were played simultaneously with rubber balls of various sizes, up and down and from side to side, 'crossed' like a Victorian letter for the Penny Post, so that considerable skill was needed to avoid not only tackles from opponents, but collisions with players in other games. I was very good at playground football – good at dribbling and trapping the ball and shooting with either foot. These skills I honed in the road outside our house in Millmark Grove, kicking a small rubber ball against the low wall that bounded our front garden, and in games with friends that were only very occasionally interrupted by the passage of a car. I was obliged to play rugby at St Joseph's in games periods, but I got out of it whenever possible and ensured by my apathy that I was never considered for matches with other schools at weekends. This freed me to play football in parks with a full-size leather ball and proper boots, eventually for the team of St Mary Magdalen's parish youth club. We played in a league of South London Catholic parish teams, experience I drew on for a section of my novel *Therapy*. (It was reviewed in *The Observer* under a heading which was a quote from the text: 'Immaculate Conception 2, Precious Blood nil.')

I stopped going to see Charlton play at the Valley when I was about fifteen, and other interests and demands on my time began to take priority, but I continued to follow their fortunes in the newspapers, and I still glance occasionally at their position in whichever league they are in (they have been relegated and promoted several times over the years). Watching the highlights of top-class football on television is one of the very few activities that I could describe as relaxation unadulterated by any connection with work. My relationship with cricket in boyhood was much the same as with football. I was deeply interested in the game as a spectator, spent days watching Surrey at the Oval, learned all the rules and technical terms, listened to Test Match commentaries, and was familiar with the achievements of the great players of the day like Hutton and Washbrook, Compton and Edrich, Laker and Lock. I was good at cricket in the street or playground, played with a worn tennis ball and a wicket chalked on a wall or constructed from a cardboard box, and like Timothy in *Out of the Shelter* I suspended a solid rubber ball on a string from the clothes-line in our tiny back garden on which I practised stroke play with a cheap cricket bat. But never the real thing, with pads, gloves, a full-size bat and that hard, intimidating leather ball. At some time in the 1980s I was pressured into participating in an English Department Staff–Student match at Birmingham

University, and was embarrassed to find the bat so heavy that I was unable to achieve any backlift before the ball reached it, which restricted me to the leg glance and the dead bat by way of strokes. I scored one run in quite a long innings before being bowled out.

I have tried several other sports and forms of physical recreation at different times in my life – cycling, tennis, table tennis, squash, badminton, golf, swimming, dinghy sailing – sometimes briefly, sometimes intermittently, and none of them with distinction. The one I pursued for the longest time and greatly enjoyed was tennis, but I never had any coaching until I was well into my sixties, when it was too late to get rid of bad habits, and I never had a decent backhand.

I read a lot in the latency years, but somewhat indiscriminately. I read some classics – *Ivanhoe*, for instance, which I enjoyed; but I was also addicted to cheap story magazines for boys, as previously mentioned. From the excellent Deptford public library, which was only a mile from home, I borrowed all the Just William books by Richmal Crompton I could find, and all the Biggles books by Captain Johns. Some children's classics like *Winnie the Pooh* and *The Wind in the Willows* had passed me by, perhaps because of the disturbances of wartime, but I did read *Alice's Adventures in Wonderland*, on Dad's recommendation.

He enjoyed reading and, considering his abbreviated education, had excellent though selective literary taste in fiction. He possessed a complete edition of the works of Dickens, obtained in the 1930s through loyal readership of the *Daily Express*, and tried to pass on his genuine enthusiasm for this writer to me. I enjoyed *Pickwick Papers* for its comedy, and for many years as Christmas approached

I would re-read the chapters about the Christmas festivities at Dingley Dell as a kind of secular liturgy to get myself into the seasonal mood. I read *Oliver Twist* and I tried some of the longer novels but did not, as I remember, finish any of those. It was not just the number of their densely printed pages that put me off – so did Dickens's highly rhetorical language and the dark, grotesque illustrations by Phiz and Cruikshank. I was not ready for Dickens, and in fact it was not until many years later, when I began to teach and write about him, that I read most of the novels for the first time. Other writers to whom Dad introduced me, and whom I found more accessible, included the short story writers W.W. Jacobs and Damon Runyon, and Dad himself wrote short stories in later life influenced by these authors and by Dickens. I was surprised to find after he died how many typed manuscripts of these stories there were among his papers. They all display a feeling for the expressive power of language, but were too old-fashioned in tone and subject matter to get published, except for some amusing sketches of the musician's life he contributed to the Musicians' Union journal, for example 'Overheard in Archer Street' (a short, drab street near Piccadilly Circus, where musicians gathered every Monday afternoon to look for work, arrange gigs, and gossip):

'Put down Sunday same time as Saturday. I'll give you the time for Friday when I see you Thursday, better still, phone me Wednesday – I'm out of town Tuesday, and by the way, they've scrubbed Monday.'

'So we packed up at twelve and they said well don't leave a full crate behind, so we stopped and finished that, then I dropped Joe home and he said have one for the road, so we all had a few at Joe's then I dropped Sid off and Sid said come in, so I had a few with Sid, so I got in about five, I think, being very careful not to wake the wife as I picked up the television which sprang at me, then I remember waking up in bed just as she came home from work, and would you believe it, she hasn't spoken to me since! There's no doubt about it – women don't understand this business.'

Dad loved Jerome K. Jerome's *Three Men in a Boat,* but I owe my introduction to that classic to my aunt Eileen, who gave me a copy, which I still possess, as a Christmas present in 1944. I loved all the comic set pieces, and often used them as comfort reading all through my adolescence. Many years later a Bulgarian post-graduate who was writing a thesis about comedy in my novels enquired if I had been influenced by Jerome K. Jerome. It had never occurred to me before, but I realised at once that she was right.

In that pre-television era BBC Radio was the main source of home entertainment, and I listened with Mum and Dad to popular comedy programmes whose characters and catchphrases became part of folk culture. The archetype was *ITMA* ('It's That Man Again'), which lifted the nation's spirits during the war and continued afterwards till 1949. Its presiding comedian, Tommy Handley, interacted with a gallery of cartoon-like characters such as Colonel Chinstrap, who converted every remark addressed to him into an invitation to drink ('I don't mind if I do'), the char Mrs Mopp ('Can I do yer now, sir?') and the Middle Eastern street vendor, Ali Oop ('I go – I come back'). *Much-Binding-in-the-Marsh,* set on a shambolic RAF station, performed and written by Kenneth Horne and Richard Murdoch, was another, subtler favourite, and at least one of its catchphrases, 'Read any good books lately?' is still used by people much too young to know where it originated. It was a great age of radio comedians, some of whom came to the medium from music hall, others who started their careers on the radio: Arthur Askey, Rob Wilton, Vic Oliver, Max Miller, Max Wall, Frankie Howerd, Tony Hancock . . . On Sunday evenings, when Dad was not usually working, we would sit round the hearth and listen to *Variety Bandbox*, a long-running programme on which many of these comedians featured. If I have some ability in comic writing it may be in part due to that early saturation in radio comedy.

I went to the cinema in these years with increasing frequency, sometimes to children's matinées on Saturday mornings, and sometimes with my mother in the afternoon or evening. It was rarely with my father, presumably because of his work, though he was never a keen cinemagoer. There were two cinemas we mainly patronised: a big Gaumont in New Cross which showed new releases, situated at a busy road junction known as the Marquis after its contiguous pub, the Marquis of Granby; and the Ritz, a smaller cheaper cinema just round the corner from Brockley Cross, which showed older films. My attitude to the cinema at this stage of my life was conditioned by experiences much earlier in childhood. When I was only six or seven I had been taken to see some excellent films like *The Wizard of Oz*, Disney's *Snow White and the Seven Dwarfs* and *Bambi*, which were deemed suitable for children but had elements that frightened and upset me. The graphically depicted malevolence of the Evil Queen in *Snow White*, and of the Wicked Witch in *The*

Wizard of Oz, images like the Scarecrow's straw arm bursting into flame in the latter film, or the tears rolling down Bambi's nose at the death of his mother, were distressingly unforgettable. The brilliance of *The Wizard of Oz* is that it resembles a dream in structure and imagery, so that watching it is like being trapped in a dream from which, like Dorothy, you awake at the end, but it continued to disturb me for some time with new dreams.

During the war I seldom went to 'the pictures' (as we called cinema) by choice, and my opportunities in any case were limited. When I acquired the habit back in London, I favoured comic films – the short animated cartoons of Disney's family of anthropo-morphic animals, or Tom and Jerry, or slapstick comedy like the Three Stooges and Laurel and Hardy, or formulaic westerns like the Hopalong Cassidy and Gene Autry movies, with plenty of action and not much to pluck at the heartstrings. That was the sort of thing you could see for sixpence at the Gaumont on a Saturday morning in an auditorium full of shouting, cheering and occasionally misbehaving children. If I went to the cinema with my mother I would steer her towards comedies or musical comedies – Danny Kaye was a great favourite – and away from love stories and melodramas. Then one day, when I was probably thirteen or fourteen, I went to the Ritz on my own to see the Powell and Pressburger film *A Matter of Life and Death,* now an established classic, and was transfixed and transported by it. In the brilliant opening sequence a British pilot, Peter, is piloting a burning Lancaster bomber back to England after a bombing raid on Germany, having told his crew to bale out, but is unable to do so himself because his parachute has been destroyed. He com-municates his plight in nonchalant British understatement by radio to an American girl called June serving in the WAAF, and within minutes they have fallen in love. Peter jumps out of the plane over the English coast and should have died, but the 'Conductor' delegated to escort him to the afterlife (the spirit of a French aristocrat guillotined at the Revolution) loses him in the fog over the English Channel and he finds himself alive on a beach, not far from June's base, and meets her. The rest of the film chronicles a struggle for Peter between the agents of the afterlife and his friends on earth, conducted in parallel on two levels – naturalistically and supernaturally. Powell and Pressburger conjured up a witty and pleasing visualisation of the threshold to the afterlife, which is connected to earth by an enormously long escalator that deposits recently deceased airmen, still wearing their flying suits, in a calm all-white reception area like a hotel. (In America the film was retitled *Stairway to Heaven*.) At the climax a celestial tribunal debates whether Peter should be allowed to escape the death that was his allotted fate, while down below he is undergoing a critical brain operation. There were so many things in this film which appealed to me: the vivid evocation of the war in the air, the imaginative and strangely comforting transformation of orthodox notions of the afterlife, the comedy of the embarrassed Conductor, and the touching relationship between the RAF hero (dashingly played by David Niven) and his comely American sweetheart (Kim Hunter), which perhaps for the first time seriously engaged my emotions in the 'love interest' of a film. Seeing it contributed significantly to my passage from childhood to adolescence, stirring in me a more mature sense of the complexity of life and how it might be represented in art. Its themes and images stayed with me, and when some friends kindly purchased for me as a sixtieth birthday present the right to command a showing of a film at the National Film Theatre, I chose *A Matter of Life and Death*.

One afternoon at about the same period, I went to see another film on my own – I have quite forgotten what it was – at the New Cross Gaumont, and a man sat down beside me while it was in progress. This in itself did not surprise me, since in those days of double features customers often entered in the middle of a film and watched the whole programme until they reached the point where they came in. ('This is where we came in' was a popular idiom, now almost obsolete.) What did puzzle and somewhat annoy me was that the man had chosen the seat next to mine when the cinema was more than half empty. Then after a few minutes I felt his hand on my thigh. I froze. Why had he done that? What should I do? Had he mistaken my leg for the seat-arm, or was he a pickpocket? After a few moments of anxious hesitation, I got up and moved to another part of the cinema, reluctant to leave it immediately and miss the rest of my film. The man did not follow me, but the episode spoiled my enjoyment of it. When I returned home, Dad was alone in the house, doing something in the kitchen, making a cup of tea perhaps, and I told him about the man in the cinema and my theory that he was a pickpocket. Dad was concerned but, to his credit, remained calm, carrying on with whatever he was doing as he explained to me that some men were 'perverts' who were attracted to young boys, and this led to a brief and fairly rudimentary 'facts of life' talk. I had already learned the basic mechanics of the sexual act from a conversation with a boy at school (needless to say, there was no sex education at all at St Joseph's Academy), and I didn't learn much that was new to me, except how to pronounce the word 'penis', which I had only seen in print and pronounced silently to myself as if the first syllable was 'pen'. I remember too that I got some welcome reassurance on the subject of nocturnal emissions, which I was beginning to experience. I was too shy to ask any questions that might have extended my scanty knowledge of sexuality and, probably like most children in the same situation, gave the impression that I knew much more than I did, to cut the conversation short. Nevertheless it was a bonding conversation. It may surprise today's parents that I was allowed to go to the cinema unaccompanied in early adolescence, and not forbidden to do so after this episode, but children then were given more freedom, and expected to be more self-reliant, than nowadays.

One thing I did *not* do in the latency phase, and later regretted, was learn to play a musical instrument. I joined the Brockley parish Scout troop when I was about eleven or twelve, which offered an opportunity to play the cornet, and I was loaned an instrument for that purpose which I bore proudly home. Dad had once commented that I had 'trumpeter's lips' (i.e. thin ones) so I thought he would be pleased and helpful. However, I proved incapable of blowing into the cornet with sufficient power and continuity to produce more than a few discordant notes, and I quickly lost heart. Dad did not encourage me to persist, probably judging correctly that I would never get on with the cornet and that my efforts to learn would be painful to listen to. It was certainly not an instrument suited to a small semi-detached house. He himself practised daily for an hour or two on the saxophone and clarinet – all scales and brief disconnected phrases designed to keep his fingering in good nick, never a tune, and rather irritating to other ears – so probably Mum was also relieved when I returned the cornet (and not long afterwards dropped out of the Scouts). I can remember only one occasion when I heard Dad play a tune from beginning to end, probably when I was thirteen or fourteen. We were staying at a Butlins-style holiday camp where Dad joined Mum and me at the end of a summer job in the vicinity, bringing his instruments with him, and one evening there was a concert at which the 'campers' were invited to 'do a turn'. Dad went up on the stage with his alto sax and played a sweet, lyrical ballad without accompaniment, receiving warm applause which made me feel very proud. Perhaps if I had seen and heard him play in a band I would have been more motivated to learn an instrument myself, but the nature of his work precluded that. And I sometimes think that if we had had a piano in the house, a more domesticated instrument than the cornet or the saxophone, I might have learned to play it, but we didn't because Dad had no use for one. As long as I lived at home he was always ready to share the experience of music with me on records and the radio, to inform me and educate my taste in the several kinds of music that interested him – popular, jazz and classical. In the 1950s he was very excited by the emergence of modern jazz in America in the form known as 'bebop', and communicated some of his enthusiasm for Charlie Parker, Dizzy Gillespie and Lee Konitz to me; later I shared his taste for the cooler jazz of the Modern Jazz Quartet, Chico Hamilton, Miles Davis, and the exquisite solos of the Dave Brubeck Quartet's saxophonist, Paul Desmond, and began to collect their records myself. In due course he persuaded me to listen sympathetically to symphonic music of the kind he liked – mostly late Romantic and early modern, like Rachmaninov, Ravel, Elgar and Delius. Long after I had left home and was living with my family in Birmingham, he regularly recorded music from the radio or from LPs he had bought or borrowed from the Deptford library, and sent the cassettes to me with enthusiastic recommendations. But he never gave me any encouragement to learn an instrument when I was young, which surprises other people when I tell them. I think he may have been apprehensive, consciously or unconsciously, that if I should become addicted to making music as he was himself in his youth I might be drawn into what he regarded as an insecure profession. If my school had offered tuition in music I might have learned to play an instrument there, but in that respect, and several others, the education it offered was lacking.

5

St Joseph's Academy was situated on the crest of a hill that rose
from the centre of plebeian Lewisham, on a road that led after
half a mile or so to bourgeois Blackheath Village. A dignified
square building housed the offices and living quarters of the
brothers. Behind it there were two blocks of classrooms, built at
right angles to each other and enclosing a lawn, and beyond these
were the playground and playing fields. It had a two-form entry,
with fifty to sixty boys in each year. Its uniform (blazer and cap)
was a very bright green, trimmed with gold, and its badge a five-
pointed star with the motto *Signum Fidei* (Sign of Faith). The De
La Salle brothers who owned and largely staffed the school wore
black cassocks and collars, with two slightly splayed white linen
panels at the neck. They belonged to an order founded in the
mid-seventeenth century by St John Baptist De La Salle, a French
aristocrat who had a laudable mission to provide education for
the people. The full name of the order is the Institute of the
Brothers of the Christian Schools, and they are sometimes

understandably confused with the Christian Brothers, a similar order but founded much later, in Ireland. The De La Salle order also had a presence in Ireland, and several of the brothers at St Joseph's were Irish. Both sets of men took religious vows of poverty, chastity and obedience, but were not ordained priests, and were not of the same intellectual calibre as teacher-priests in orders like the Benedictines and Jesuits. I had a sense, however, that the De La Salle order considered itself a cut above the Christian Brothers, perhaps because of its longer history.

St Joseph's was not an academically distinguished school when I joined it, though it improved somewhat while I was there, thanks mainly to the addition of several lay teachers to the staff. Immediately after the war both human and material resources for education were limited, but even allowing for that I believe I received an education inferior to that of my peers at other London grammar schools, Catholic and non-Catholic, especially in the junior forms. Grammar itself was reasonably well taught in an old-fashioned way, and for that I am grateful; but the teaching of literature was uninspired and uninspiring. We studied the same texts in successive years, perhaps because there was a shortage of books, and 'did' *Julius Caesar* so many times that I finally knew it almost off by heart. A class typically consisted of each boy reading aloud a section of the text in turn and then the teacher commenting and asking questions about it. We had an elderly teacher called Brother Palladius, known as 'Polly', whose regular homework was to require us to read a few pages of a set text, for example *Treasure Island*, and be prepared to take a spelling test on words in it at the beginning of the next day's lesson. He would call out five words, and if you got any wrong you would get the strap, one whack (not very hard) on the hand for each mistake. In its pedagogically incorrect way it was quite effective as a method of improving pupils' spelling. English was always my best subject, and I vividly remember my mortification when for once I misspelled a word (it was 'cofee') and had to go up to the front of the class to receive chastisement. The strap was made of several layers of leather sewn together, and short enough to be concealed in the pocket of a cassock. The teacher who introduced us to physics in the third form (one of the less successful lay additions to the staff) also used a strap to punish faulty homework, which did not help me to find his lessons any more comprehensible. I dropped the subject with great relief, along with chemistry, when we were split into arts and science streams at the end of the academic year. Biology was not taught at the school at that time, so I left it lamentably ignorant of the natural sciences. There was no music either, apart from occasional lessons called Singing; so though appreciative of music and possessed of a good ear, I never acquired even an elementary understanding of its structural principles.

Surprisingly, religious instruction was probably the worst-taught subject of all, though the ethos of the school was intensely Catholic. Its War Memorial featured a statue of St Joseph cradling the infant Jesus in the crook of his arm and apparently teaching him to read. There was a crucifix on the wall of every classroom. There were prayers at morning assemblies, and every subsequent lesson of the day began with the recitation of the 'Hail Mary'. On feast days we were marched down to the Catholic church in Blackheath for mass. But there were no specialist teachers of religious instruction. It was the responsibility of form teachers, occupying the first period of the day after the register was taken, and in the lower forms it consisted mostly of indoctrination in the Catholic faith by working through the Penny Catechism, the answers to whose questions we were required to memorise and repeat on demand. '**Where is God?** God is everywhere. **Does God know and see all things?** God knows and sees all things, even our most secret thoughts. **What is the Catholic Church?** The Catholic Church is the union of all the faithful under one Head. **Who is the head of the Catholic Church?**' That was a trick question, the correct answer being not the Pope, but 'Jesus Christ our Lord'. The Pope was defined in succeeding questions and answers as 'the visible head of the Church and Vicar of Christ'. He was of course infallible. '**What do you mean when you say that the Pope is infallible?** When I say that the Pope is infallible, I mean that the Pope cannot err when, as Shepherd and Teacher of all Christians, he defines a doctrine concerning faith or morals, to be held by the whole church.' The Penny Catechism was not a document sensitive to the views of non-Catholic Christians.

Towards the end of this little book there was a section on Virtues and Vices with lists that were more of a challenge to memorisation, like '**Which are the seven gifts of the Holy Spirit?**' (Answer: 'Wisdom, Understanding, Counsel, Fortitude, Knowledge, Piety and Fear of the Lord'), easily confused with the answer to '**Which are the twelve fruits of the Holy Spirit?** (Charity, Joy, Peace, Patience, Benignity, Goodness, Longanimity, Mildness, Faith, Modesty, Continency, Chastity)'. Longanimity, in case you are wondering, for it is an archaic word my spellchecker refuses to recognise, means forbearance, patience under suffering. One wonders who drew up these lists, and named them, and what was supposed to be their usefulness in the effort to lead a good life. Some had footnotes with abbreviated references to verses of Scripture, but we never studied the Bible as a text, nor later in our schooling were we entered for public examinations in religious instruction which would have entailed such study. Our teachers sometimes seemed as bored by RI as we were. In the fourth year we had as our form teacher Brother Peter, an Irishman whose close-cropped grey-haired head and craggy features made him look a bit like a convict. He was also our maths teacher and insisted on using the first period of the day to give us additional maths, which he claimed we badly needed. When some bold spirits in the class protested that the lesson should be religious instruction he pulled a long rosary from the pocket of his cassock and shook it in the air, declaring with a triumphant, gap-toothed grin, 'Say your rosary! Say your rosary! That's all the religious instruction you need!' The Rosary is the most mind-numbing of all Catholic devotions, consisting in the recitation of multiple 'decades' of prayers, namely the 'Hail Mary' repeated ten times, preceded by one 'Our Father' and concluded by one 'Glory be to the Father, and to the Son, and to the Holy Ghost, Amen'. While reciting these prayers, silently or aloud with others, using your beads to keep track, you were supposed to meditate on one of the 'Mysteries' of the Faith to which each decade was dedicated, and these Mysteries were themselves divided into three sets of five; for example, the first Joyful Mystery was the Annunciation, the first Sorrowful Mystery was the Agony in the Garden, and the first Glorious Mystery was the Resurrection. But the repetitious droning of the prayers, and the disconnection between their words and the theme of each decade, made focused thought impossible.

Brother Peter's suggestion that saying the Rosary could be a substitute for religious instruction was preposterous.

I couldn't help wondering in retrospect what motivated these men to choose their way of life. To take religious vows of poverty, chastity and obedience without acquiring the status and sacred privileges of the priesthood, in order to pursue a vocation that was also open to laymen, would seem to betoken exceptional dedication and self-sacrifice in the cause of education. I did encounter brothers at the school of whom one could believe this was true, but not many. In most cases there were probably other motives. I raised this subject recently with a friend of about the same age, who had been a postulant with the Christian Brothers in youth. As a boy, he attended one of their grammar schools in Bristol, where he was happy and looked up to his teachers as role models. To him, coming from a Catholic working-class family in a council house, the brothers' communal lifestyle seemed enviable, combining camaraderie with social status in this life and more or less guaranteed salvation in the next. The prospect of being trained as a teacher by the order, and possibly sent to university, was attractive, and when at the age of about twelve the boys were asked if they felt they had a vocation to join the order, he put himself forward. He was then transferred to a junior seminary, a boarding school which prepared boys to become postulants. This was traditional practice in the Roman Catholic Church: to place likely candidates for the religious life as priests or brothers in a sequestered, all-male environment before puberty to prepare them for a life of dedicated chastity and keep them from temptation. For some time my friend continued to be happy in this milieu, but when the sexual urges of adolescence kicked in the moral theology with which he was indoctrinated produced extreme spiritual anxiety, leading eventually to a kind of nervous breakdown at the age of nineteen. The order sensibly discharged him, and he went to Bristol University, where he met his future wife, and subsequently had a successful career as a lay teacher and headmaster of progressive Catholic views.

In recent times both the Christian Brothers and the De La Salle order have been implicated in shocking revelations of sexual and physical abuse of children by Catholic priests, brothers and nuns in many countries going back to the 1950s, revelations which have rocked the Church internally, badly damaged its reputation and exposed dioceses to ruinously expensive compensation claims from the victims. The record of the Christian Brothers in Ireland, Australia and Canada is particularly shameful. It is impossible not to connect this evil with the vow of celibacy required of Roman Catholic priests and brothers, to which many committed themselves without sufficient experience of life to make such a decision, and which must have become more difficult to keep as society at large became increasingly open and permissive in sexual matters. There is also evidence that many candidates for the priesthood in this period were homosexually oriented men for whom heterosexual celibacy was no sacrifice and who consciously or unconsciously sought to sublimate their desires through a religious vocation, only to find that it provided plentiful temptations and opportunities for pederasty.

I asked my friend if he was ever conscious of such behaviour in his time at the junior seminary, and he answered emphatically in the negative. He claimed proudly (and I have no reason to disbelieve him) that the Christian Brothers in England, unlike their brethren in other countries, have never been found guilty of sexual abuse. The English De La Salle order has, however, been implicated in at least one serious case of this kind: 170 people filed compensation claims for abuse suffered from 1958 onwards at St William's care home and school in Yorkshire, owned and staffed by the order. The headmaster, Brother James Carragher, was tried twice, and sentenced for seven years and fourteen years, for a series of offences including buggery, indecent assault and taking indecent photographs of young boys, and was expelled from the order. Other brothers at the school narrowly escaped prosecution. Such stories continue to emerge in various countries, disgusting and disillusioning Catholic laity and undermining the vocations of honest, decent priests and brothers. In January 2014, at the beginning of the Northern Ireland Historical Institutional Abuse Inquiry, the De La Salle order admitted with deep regret that abuse took place at their boys' home in Kircubbin. This was on the second day of an inquiry that was expected to last six months, taking evidence from 400 people.

Never at any time when I was at St Joseph's did I observe, or hear of, or feel personally threatened by, any untoward behaviour of a sexual nature from any of the brothers. Indeed I was completely unaware of any case of sexual abuse of minors by priests, brothers or nuns in the Catholic Church anywhere until reports began to appear in the press in the 1990s. That is why it is not mentioned in *How Far Can You Go?* (1980), generally considered to be an accurate portrayal of English Catholic life in the post-war period up to the mid-seventies. If I had known about it I might have made it an element in the novel. Clerical abuse in England was possibly less common in my boyhood than later, and it was always most likely to happen in boarding schools, junior seminaries, orphanages and similar institutions, where the young were defenceless against adults in authority. A school like St Joseph's, where pupils returned home at the end of every day, was an incomparably safer environment.

There was a good deal of corporal punishment at the school, which caused me some anxiety in my early years there, since it was easily incurred; but it was not sadistic and was part of educational culture in that time, though it seems barbarous from today's vantage point. It was gradually phased out in the UK, but probably lingered longer in Catholic schools than others. I remember in the late 1970s going to pick up my wife after school hours at the Catholic comprehensive where she was a school counsellor, and seeing a few cowed-looking youths lurking outside an office who, she told me, were waiting to be caned by the deputy head. She went off to complete some task and soon the burly teacher came briskly down the corridor to usher the boys into his office with a curt command. I moved off before I might see or hear any more of this atavistic ritual, feeling sickened, and surprised by the strength of my own reaction.

Most writers owe a debt to a particular English teacher in their schooldays, and I am no exception. When I was in the fourth form, and approaching the age of fourteen, a new teacher joined the school and took over the teaching of English to my class. He was an Irish layman called Malachy Carroll (though it was some time before we discovered that unusual and potentially mockable first name). He was probably then in his late thirties, with a big ruddy-cheeked face under thinning black hair, and often wore an amused smile as if enjoying a secret joke, though he also made overt jokes for our benefit. He was like no other teacher we had encountered

– relaxed, unthreatening and unorthodox. The first thing he did was to announce that he would set us no English homework for four weeks. Instead we were to write a long essay on 'The Techniques of Poetry'. The teaching of poetry we had received up till then had consisted mostly of learning poems 'off by heart', with very little analysis of their verbal form, and this assignment spread alarm and despondency in the class, especially as the new teacher gave us no guidance on how to research the topic – it was left to our own initiative.

Fortunately for me, the Deptford public library had excellent holdings in literature and literary criticism, and on its shelves I found exactly what I needed. It was a short book, whose title and author's name I have forgotten, on the elements of poetry – metre, rhyme schemes, verse forms and the figures of speech. These latter – metaphor, simile, alliteration, assonance, onomatopoeia and the rest – particularly fascinated me, and in retrospect I traced my later specialisation as an academic critic in formal and linguistic analysis of literary texts back to that seminal exercise on 'The Techniques of Poetry'. Mr Carroll commended my essay and must have identified me as a pupil with literary promise, for over the next few years he became my mentor as I began to develop an interest in both critical and creative writing. In 1950, when I was fifteen, he encouraged me to polish a homework essay on the poetry of Wilfred Owen for the annual school magazine, *Signum Fidei,* which was my first published work. It seems a sadly stilted piece to me now, but a humorous sketch on 'The Child in Church' and a short story called 'Major County Award', also selected by Malachy Carroll for publication in the magazines for 1951 and 1952, respectively, were more promising.

Malachy was himself a published author of a rather specialised kind: he supplemented his teacher's salary by writing commissioned histories of religious orders or biographies of their saintly founders, such as *The Charred Wood: the story of Blessed Julie Billiart, foundress of the Congregation of Sisters of Notre Dame of Namur.* He also wrote a novel called *The Stranger,* published in Dublin in 1951. It carried an acknowledgement to a Gaelic novel 'for the bones of the plot' which he told me, when he gave me a copy, he had been pressured to insert by the publisher, although his debt was slight. The plot is in fact its weakest element, as I have just reminded myself, skimming through it for the first time in sixty-odd years: a stranger with a mysterious past arrives in a small rural Irish community, makes himself respected and loved, but is denounced by the villain of the piece as an ex-convict who served a prison sentence for theft. It is eventually revealed that the stranger is a defrocked priest who was innocent of the crime but unable to exculpate himself without breaking the seal of confession, and at the end he is vindicated and restored to his vocation. It's a rather contrived and melodramatic story, but there is some fine descriptive writing and excellent vernacular Irish dialogue. You can tell from the first page that this author has a gift for metaphor and simile (e.g. 'the breeze passing over the wheat, like fingers caressing plush against the pile') and in his teaching Malachy imparted an appreciation of figurative language which influenced my own early attempts at writing – perhaps to excess, but it was a good fault. One of our set texts for A level in the sixth form, which he had selected from the list offered by the exam board, was a selection of Browning's dramatic monologues, and he taught us to relish the combination of human interest and lyrical intensity in those poems. I found them immensely exciting, not least for Browning's vivid portrayal of Catholic clergy whose faith was worm-eaten with worldliness, envy and lust, in poems like 'The Bishop Orders His Tomb' and 'Soliloquy of the Spanish Cloister'.

There were two other lay teachers who arrived at St Joseph's during my time there of whom I have positive memories. One was Mr Dalton, who taught Latin. He was short-tempered and had an alarming habit of hurling bits of chalk at pupils who were inattentive, but was dedicated to his subject and taught it well. He told us when he arrived that he was going to teach us a newly approved method of pronouncing classical Latin, but I discovered when I left school that most educated English people used a different pronunciation, which has sometimes caused confusion or puzzlement when I utter a Latin word or phrase. That apart, I am very grateful for Mr Dalton's teaching. Latin is the only foreign language in which I achieved any real competence and, although it is a dead one, knowledge of it is invaluable for anyone professionally concerned with the English language and its literature.

The third memorable teacher was the art master, Archie Brew, a very unlikely member of staff in a Catholic grammar school of the 1950s. Whether he was Catholic himself I never discovered. He arrived to replace an elderly teacher who set us to draw boring objects like brooms and teapots and seldom permitted the messy business of painting. Archie Brew encouraged colour and creativity. He was tall: very tall and thin, like an Aubrey Beardsley drawing, with a big Roman nose and hair that was long for the times, and he had a manner that I would later identify as 'camp'. He called pupils by fanciful nicknames, pulled them by their ears or hair if they misbehaved, and threw tantrums of anger which might rapidly elide into peals of laughter. I knew nothing about homosexuality as a schoolboy, but retrospectively I was sure he must have been gay, as were other former pupils of St Joseph's. However, I discovered recently, after his death, that he was happily married with two daughters. I was fairly good at art (another gene I inherited from my father, who was quite a skilful self-taught painter in oils and whose pictures still give pleasure, hanging on the walls of our house) and I always looked forward to a double period in the art room on Friday afternoons when I was in the fifth form – a perfect way to end the school week, it seemed to me. I obtained a GCE O level in Art – but not at the end of that academic year, 1949–50, for reasons that had a significant effect on other aspects of my education.

At that time the school-leaving examinations had just been revised and renamed as the General Certificate of Education, Ordinary Level and Advanced Level, and the Department of Education, or whatever its equivalent was called in those days, made a rule that candidates for the O-level examinations must be at least fifteen by the beginning of the year when they sat them. I would be fifteen on the 28th of January 1950, and so was disqualified from sitting them with the rest of my class in June. As far as I can remember, no reason was ever given for this diktat. Perhaps it was decided on egalitarian grounds that precocious pupils should not be encouraged to demonstrate their ability by taking examinations earlier than normal, a practice more common in private schools than state schools; or perhaps it was a bureaucratic mania for uniformity. Whatever the cause, the effect of the new rule on me was wholly negative. My teachers were confident, as I was myself, that I could pass the exams with good marks in all my subjects. It would be unprofitable and almost punitive to hold me back in the fifth form for another year and make me do the same syllabus all over again. To the credit of the school, and especially the headmaster, Brother Fabian, they protested vigorously, but to no avail. In the spring term I sat the school's Mock O-level exams (designed as practice for the real thing) with the rest of the fifth form, and my papers were marked, typed and sent to the relevant authority as evidence of my ability, hoping this would prompt a change of heart.

Looking through a box of papers and documents relating to this period of my life recently, I found a typescript of my answers to five questions on the English Literature paper, with Malachy Carroll's handwritten endorsement: 'This is an exact copy of the answers given. Spelling mistakes – most of them being "speed slips" are included.' He awarded marks ranging from 20/20 to 16/20, with an aggregate of 92/100 – a 'DISTINCTION +'. But it was a lost cause: the authorities were unmoved. The school therefore proposed that, rather spend another year pointlessly in the fifth form, I should proceed to the sixth form and begin the two-year A-level curriculum, taking the O-level exams at the end of my first year.

This was a formidable undertaking, because I had to revise for the O levels, especially in subjects I was no longer studying, like maths, in parallel with new A-level work in English, History, Latin and French. I had never been very good at French, and I found the A-level set books, Balzac's *Père Goriot* and a play by Molière, heavy going. I would need only three A levels for university entrance, so in the spring term I decided, against the advice of the brother who taught the subject, to drop French in order to reduce my workload, using the time saved to revise for O levels. It was a decision I deeply regret, since in consequence I have never been able to read French without constant recourse to the dictionary and am quite unable to conduct a conversation in the language. This has been particularly galling to me in the later years of my career as a writer, from 1989 onwards, when my novels began to have a remarkable success in France and I visited the country frequently to promote my books. Even if I had had the will and time to improve my spoken French, it was by then too late because of increasing deafness. I blame myself for the decision to drop French when I was sixteen, but I also blame the politicians, educationalists and civil servants who pressured me into it by the arbitrary rule which prevented me from taking my O levels in 1950, when I was ready for them.

In July of that same year there was a general election in which the Labour government, elected in 1945 by a landslide, experienced a huge swing against it that was driven partly by the electorate's impatience with just such unnecessary interference with individual freedom. Its reduced majority of 5 was unviable, and in the following year it was replaced by a Conservative government under Winston Churchill. Labour was out of office for the next thirteen years. I did not take much interest in party politics in early adolescence, and the subject was rarely discussed at home by my parents. I have no recollection of how they voted in the 1950 and '51 elections, but it was almost certainly Conservative, because they shared the general public mood of discontent with the post-war economic regime of 'Austerity' and grumbled about the rationing, shortages and taxes it entailed. Dad had probably voted Labour in 1945, like the vast majority of servicemen in the forces, but as a freelance musician he would have found the levelling and controlling tendency of its policies unsympathetic. He was a loyal member of the Musicians'

Union, which was immensely powerful at that period, but had mixed feelings about its restrictive practices. There was, for instance, something called 'needletime', by which the Union strictly rationed the amount of recorded music the BBC was allowed to broadcast, in order to compel them to employ musicians performing live. Incredible as it may seem to younger people today, there were only two or three weekly radio programmes on the BBC (which had a monopoly on broadcasting) in the late 1940s and early '50s that consisted of a presenter playing records of popular music. The term 'disc jockey' did not become current in Britain until the mid-fifties. The agreement created employment for British musicians in a lot of indifferent radio band shows, but Dad complained that this lucrative 'session work' was difficult to break into unless you had the right contacts. And like other people he hankered after more American popular music, including jazz, on radio. This state of affairs continued until the 1960s, when pirate radio undermined the compact between the Musicians' Union and the BBC and it eventually crumbled.

The newspaper we took at home was the *Daily Express,* then at the height of its circulation, a populist right-wing paper with similar views to those of the modern *Daily Mail,* so I imbibed a regular diet of anti-socialist opinion, illustrated by caricatures of leading Labour ministers, like Bevan, Bevin, Shinwell and Cripps. This reinforced a prejudice against Labour, and perhaps a distrust of the political process itself, that I had formed in 1945, when – inexplicably to a ten-year-old boy – the country voted to replace Winston Churchill, the heroic winner of the war, as Prime Minister with the far-from-heroic-looking Clement Attlee. In my late teens I began to appreciate the merits of the Beveridge-designed welfare state that Attlee's government put in place, especially the National Health Service and the free secondary and tertiary education from which I benefited. Apart from a period in the 1980s when I supported the SDP, in its brief existence as a moderately left-of-centre breakaway party from Labour, I have been a rather luke-warm Labour supporter since attaining the age of twenty-one, voting on principle rather than from enthusiastic commitment, and always opposed to the dictatorial, ideology-driven tendencies of the party's left wing. This antipathy I am inclined to trace back to that frustrating encounter with the edict of faceless educational bureaucrats when I was a schoolboy.

6

In spite of the pressure of taking O levels and A levels in successive years, I really enjoyed school for the first time as a sixth-former.
One was treated with more respect by staff and younger pupils,
and given more independence. Teaching was more casual and
intimate, in smaller groups than in the lower forms, and we had
'free periods' which could be spent in the library – where, in spite
of its limitations, I first discovered the essays of George Orwell.
Even religious instruction became interesting as we discussed
issues in moral theology, and learned how to defend the Catholic
faith against Protestant and atheistic attack with the aid of a
textbook called *The Question Box* written early in the century by
an American Paulist priest, the Rev. Bertrand L. Conway, but
substantially revised in 1929 and issued in an abridged form in
1950. This consisted of objections to Catholicism (many of which
had never occurred to me before) in question form, followed by
vigorous and dogmatic refutations. I began to define my Catholic
faith in more intellectual terms than previously.

As the only child in a mixed marriage, growing up in a home where religion was rarely discussed, and experiencing little of the social interaction with parish clergy and laity that is characteristic of a typical Catholic family, I always felt myself to be a somewhat marginal Catholic, especially in the latency phase. I did not, for instance, learn to serve at mass, as did most boys of my age in the parish who were deemed capable. It was suggested to my mother by one of the priests at St Mary Magdalen's when I was about twelve, and I had a couple of trial sessions at the presbytery, learning to recite the responses in the Latin liturgy, but I didn't feel comfortable in that ambience – nor, I fancy, did I relish the prospect of cycling to church before breakfast to serve at early-morning masses – so I did not take it further. I did, however, perform a devotion known as the Nine Fridays, which for a period entailed just such early rising once a month.

The Catechism-centred religious instruction I received at school laid a heavy emphasis on sin, how easily sins could be committed and how one would eventually be punished for them in Purgatory, even though they had been forgiven through the sacrament of confession. I was therefore much interested in the concept of indulgences, especially the Plenary Indulgence. For the benefit of non-Catholic readers I will quote the sardonic authorial explanation of this practice in *How Far Can You Go?*

An indulgence was a kind of spiritual voucher, obtained by performing some devotional exercise, promising the bearer so much off the punishment due to his sins, *e.g.* forty days' remission for saying a certain prayer, or two hundred and forty days for making a certain pilgrimage. 'Days' did not refer to time spent in Purgatory (a misconception common in Protestant polemic) for earthly time did not, of course, apply there, but to the canonical penances of the mediaeval Church, when confessed sinners were required to do public penance such as sitting in sackcloth and ashes at the porch of the parish church for a certain period, instead of the nominal penances (recitation of prayers) prescribed in modern times. The remission of temporal punishment by indulgences was measured on the ancient scale. There was also such a thing as a plenary indulgence, which was a kind of jackpot, because it wiped out *all* the punishment accruing to your sins up to the time of obtaining the indulgence. You could get one of these by, for instance, going to mass and Communion on the first Friday of nine successive months.

I managed to perform that feat once, much to my mother's surprise and admiration, but was never quite sure whether I had fulfilled all the requisite conditions, including a 'right disposition'.

It took me a long time to grow out of the self-interested and superstitious element in Catholic faith – the belief that you could not only ensure your eternal salvation but also get God on your side in the quotidian trials and challenges of earthly life by petitionary prayers and performing devotions beyond those minimally required for membership of the Church. But in the sixth form my faith became a bit more sophisticated, informed not only by *The Question Box*, but also by literature, especially Catholic writers like James Joyce, Graham Greene and Evelyn Waugh. Malachy Carroll included Joyce's autobiographical novel *A Portrait of the Artist as a Young Man* in a list of books and authors he suggested

I should read 'outside the syllabus' – quite a bold recommendation in a Catholic school of that period – and I found it riveting, in spite of the challenging nature of its form, shifting from one prose style to another as it charted the hero's development from infancy to young adulthood.

The ethos of English Catholicism at the parochial level in the late 1940s and early 1950s was not very different from Irish Catholicism at the beginning of the century. Doctrine and devotional habits had not changed much in the interval, and the majority of priests, nuns, teaching brothers and Catholic laity in England were Irish or descendants of Irish immigrants, so I experienced the 'thrill of recognition' frequently as I read. The experience of Stephen Dedalus was much more dramatic than mine, but I could identify with it at several points. The vulnerability of the sensitive child sent away to a Jesuit boarding school in the early chapters, for instance, evoked memories of my brief stay in the Lingfield convent. As an adolescent I had not sinned as spectacularly as Stephen (far from it) and I never heard hellfire sermons as pornographically vivid as the ones he hears at his school retreat, but I understood the eschatological fear they instilled and Stephen's recoil into a phase of extreme piety, accumulating indulgences which he selflessly dedicates to the souls in Purgatory. (*That* was definitely a 'right disposition'.)

Stephen, like his creator, eventually rebels against Church and faith, refusing to make his Easter Duty (i.e. the obligation to receive Holy Communion at least once a year between Easter and Trinity Sunday or be automatically excommunicated) in spite of his mother's pleas on her deathbed, and at the end of the novel he is a defiant apostate. The effect of the book on me, however, was not to disturb my own faith, but to make me marvel at how rich a work of art Joyce's saturation in that faith had provoked, to make me grateful that I had enough understanding of his experience to appreciate the achievement, and to feel the first stirrings of a desire to attempt creative writing myself. The novels of Graham Greene had a similar effect on me, though as an English upper-middle-class convert he had a very different take on the Catholic faith from Joyce's, and my own. Greene did not deal with ordinary English Catholic life (of which he had little personal experience) but with Catholic characters like the teenage gangster Pinkie Brown in *Brighton Rock* or the nameless Mexican whisky priest in *The Power and the Glory,* deeply flawed human beings who are distinguished from the secular societies in which they move, and thus made more interesting, by their awareness of a supernatural dimension to existence.

In the early novels of Evelyn Waugh, this dimension was indicated negatively by its signal absence in the lives of nearly all the characters, though it was some time before I perceived that. My father, whose interest went back to his time at the Silver Slipper nightclub which Waugh patronised in the twenties, enjoyed these books primarily for their comedy and gave me a tattered Penguin edition of *Decline and Fall* (which I still possess) when I was fifteen. I was soon searching the Deptford library for its successors and requested hardback copies of the titles not available from the library, *Vile Bodies* and *Put Out More Flags,* as Christmas presents in 1950. Nothing could have been further from my own experience than the world of these novels, and much of the implied depravity of the characters' behaviour went over my head, but I found them fascinating – as well as hilariously funny – precisely because they opened my eyes to the existence of a social milieu utterly different from my own: adult, glamorous, hedonistic and quintessentially 'pre-war'. In due course I discovered *Brideshead Revisited,* Waugh's first explicitly Catholic novel in which he showed the operation of divine grace in a fallen world. For a Catholic teenager with aspirations to be a writer, it was encouraging and inspiring that these two men, probably the most famous living English literary novelists in the 1940s and early '50s, were both Catholics and wrote on Catholic themes.

I am touching here on a process that began in the sixth form at school but developed more consciously at university, to explain why I became more rather than less committed to the Catholic faith at a time of life when many people begin to doubt the truth of the religion in which they have been brought up and throw off its constraints on their behaviour. Joyce, growing up in the repressive culture of Irish Catholicism, had to rebel against it and go into exile if he was to fulfil his artistic vocation, but for me, as a member of the Catholic minority in a nominally Christian but in fact largely secular England, it was a positive act of self-definition to remain a practising Catholic, and a source of ideas, symbols and moral dilemmas which writing, especially prose fiction, could draw on. The Catholicism I encountered in the parish church and for the most part at school was often philistine, but writers like Greene and Waugh gave the faith a compensatory literary prestige, while the most highly esteemed poet in England, T.S Eliot, expressed in his poetry an Anglo-Catholic faith that was theologically nearly identical to Roman Catholicism. Evelyn Waugh took the title of his novel *A Handful of Dust* from *The Waste Land* ('I will show you fear in a handful of dust') and in due course, I would find in Eliot's essay on Baudelaire a quotation which seemed a key to Graham Greene's obsession with the idea that the sinner was at the heart of Christianity:

> So far as we are human, what we do must be either evil or good; so far as we do evil or good, we are human, and it is better in a paradoxical way, to do evil than to do nothing: at least we exist. It is true to say that the glory of man is his capacity for salvation; it is also true to say that his glory is his capacity for damnation. The worst that can be said for most of our malefactors, from statesmen to thieves, is that they are not men enough to be damned.

That seems to me now pernicious nonsense, or at best self-indulgent hyperbole – it is obviously better to do nothing than to do evil – but there was a time when it seemed a thrilling insight.

That time had not yet come, however, when I was a sixth-former at St Joseph's, between the ages of fifteen and a half and seventeen and a half. It seems to me in retrospect that I matured rapidly in those two years, though in many respects I remained extraordin-arily innocent by comparison with today's teenagers, especially in regard to sex, as were most of my peers. There was no sex education in any of the schools I had attended, and books on the subject were not easily obtainable. The representation of sexuality in literature and the other arts was subject by law to strict control and censorship, nudity and any suggestion of simulated sexual intercourse in films or stage plays being forbidden, as was explicit description of sexual acts in fiction. There was a social consensus to clamp down on the licence that the conditions of war had allowed or concealed. Monogamous marriage was reaffirmed as the foundation of society, and divorce frowned on. Premarital and extramarital sex was considered scandalous, and single parenthood a stigma on both mother and child. Homosexuality was a criminal offence. In bohemian and artistic circles, and in high society, sexual freedom was still practised with discretion, but middle- and working-class life was at this period dominated by a code of moral respectability, and breaching it could have unpleasant consequences.

In the Catholic 'ghetto', as parochial communities like St Mary Magdelen's have been described, and in Catholic schools, this ethos was reinforced by the theological doctrine of sin and salvation and the institution of regular confession. The Penny Catechism was particularly severe on any propensity to sexual sin. The structure of this book required that all sins had somehow to be classified under one of the Ten Commandments of the Old Testament. The two relevant ones were the sixth (seventh in the Protestant Bible), 'Thou shalt not commit adultery', and the ninth, 'Thou shalt not covet thy neighbour's wife', neither of which were common temptations for adolescent boys. The Catechism, however, asserted that 'The Sixth Commandment forbids whatever is contrary to holy purity in looks, words, or actions', and broadened the remit of the ninth to forbid 'all wilful consent to impure thoughts and desires, and all wilful pleasure in the irregular motions of the flesh'.

I presume this last phrase included masturbation (though it was never spelled out in school and indeed teachers tended to hurry through these parts of the Catechism), an activity which caused Catholic adolescents, especially males, a good deal of guilt and anxiety at this period, as I discovered later in life from books and private conversations. It didn't trouble me because I didn't masturbate. I knew neither the word nor the deed. I handled my penis in bed as a comforting accompaniment to reveries of various kinds, sometimes sexual in content, but it did not occur to me that by more vigorous manipulation I could provoke an ejaculation such as occasionally woke me from sleep with a pleasurable sensation, followed by the discovery of an uncomfortable sticky dampness inside my pyjamas and a stain on the sheets the next morning. I think that my peer group at St Joseph's must have been an exceptionally pure-minded set of boys, because I don't recall any of them referring to masturbation in more vernacular terms, or indeed much smutty talk at all in my schooldays.

Some of my fellow sixth-formers were positively prudish. I remember when I praised Graham Greene in a casual group conversation, one boy condemned him for the episode in *Stamboul Train,* the first of the thrillers the writer called 'entertainments', published in 1932, in which the Jewish businessman Myatt has sex with the chorus girl Coral Musker. When she faints in the corridor of the train, Myatt chivalrously vacates his first-class compartment so she can sleep in it, and later treats her to a meal in the dining car. Coral, already falling gratefully in love with him, comes to his compartment that night, nervous because she is a virgin.

He kissed her and found her mouth cool, soft, uncertainly responsive. She sat down on the seat which had become converted into a berth and asked him, 'Did you wonder whether I'd come?'

'You promised,' he reminded her.

'I might have changed my mind.'

'But why?' Myatt was becoming impatient. He did not want to sit about and talk. Her legs, swinging freely and touching the floor, excited him. 'We'll have a nice time.' He took off her shoes and ran his hand up her stockings. 'You know a lot, don't you?' she said. He flushed. 'Do you mind that?'

'Oh, I'm glad,' she said, 'so glad. I couldn't bear it if you hadn't known a lot.' Her eyes large and scared, her face pale under the dim blue globe, first amused him, then attracted him. He wanted to shake her out of aloofness into passion. He kissed her again and tried to slip her frock over her shoulder. Her body trembled and moved under her dress like a cat tied in a bag; suddenly she put her lips up to him and kissed his chin. 'I do love you,' she said, 'I do.' . . . The sense of strangeness survived even the customary gestures; lying in the berth she proved awkward in a mysterious innocent fashion which astonished him . . . She said suddenly and urgently, 'Be patient, I don't know much,' and then she cried out with pain. He could not have been more startled if a ghost had passed through the compartment dressed in antique wear which antedated steam. He would have left her if she had not held him to her with her hands, while she said in a voice of which snatches only escaped the sound of the engine, 'Don't go. I'm sorry. I didn't mean . . .' Then the sudden stopping of the train lurched them apart.

In comparison with post-1960 novels, the description of the sexual act in this scene is very restrained, with no specification of its 'customary gestures'. To my censorious classmate, however, it would have fallen under the proscription of the sixth or ninth commandment, or perhaps both, because it invites the reader's vicarious, imaginative participation in the action. As an adolescent reader I was probably aroused by it, but I also found it a very convincing and moving scene (and still find it so, except for the intrusively literary simile of the antique ghost). It was all the more appealing to me because, like Coral, I didn't know very much when I first read it. I learned that it might be painful for a girl when she had intercourse for the first time, and it was almost unbearably poignant to me that the plot denied the lovers the more satisfying lovemaking they promised themselves later.

Passages like this in novels gave me glimpses into the adult world of sexuality, and in a culture where representations of sexual behaviour were so strictly censored and controlled they could have an extraordinarily powerful effect. Compare and contrast the situation today when nudity and simulated sexual intercourse are commonplace in network TV drama and films with a 15 and sometimes a 12A certificate, hardcore pornography is accessible on the internet with a few clicks of a mouse, graphic sex instruction manuals, videos and DVDs are freely available, and the literary treatment of sexual behaviour can be as explicit as the author wishes. Naturally teenagers are interested in this stuff and it is impossible to prevent them viewing or reading it. Inevitably this has had an effect on their behaviour. In 1991 the first National Survey of Sexual Attitudes and Lifestyles in Britain revealed that a sixth of girls and a quarter of boys under sixteen were sexually experienced. This would have been unimaginable forty years earlier. The second NATSAL in 2001 revealed a continuing trend: a quarter of girls and nearly a third of boys were sexually experienced before the age of sixteen. Every newspaper reader is aware of the social consequences: teenage promiscuity, schoolgirl mothers, fatherless families, the spread of sexually transmitted diseases, and psychological damage from addiction to pornography. The repressive sexual ethos of the 1940s and '50s had its drawbacks, but we seem to have exchanged them for a different and more extensive set of problems.

I had no ambitions to have sexual intercourse as a teenager – it was simply not imaginable, given the social and religious constraints of my upbringing – but I did want to meet girls, and my main opportunity for doing that was the parish youth club, which I joined as a result of being recruited to play in its football team. We played our matches against other parish teams on Sunday afternoons, and in the evening, having washed the mud off my knees in the bath at home, I would put on my best sports jacket and flannel trousers, and a white nylon shirt – an enviable rarity in those days, a gift from my aunt Eileen, purchased from the Heidelberg PX – and go along to the youth club.

The youth club met twice a week in the Infants' School attached to the church: on Wednesdays for games, mainly ping-pong, and on Sundays for a 'social'. This consisted of dancing to gramophone records and partaking of sandwiches and orange squash or tea prepared by teams of girls working to a roster. The boys were required to stack the infants' desks at the sides of the room at the beginning of the evening and replace them in rows at the end. We had the use of two classrooms normally divided by a folding partition wall. The floor was made of worn, unpolished wood blocks, the walls were covered with infantile paintings and educational charts, and the lighting was bleakly utilitarian. The gramophone was a single-speaker portable, and the records a collection of scratchy 78s. But to me, just emerging from the chrysalis of boyhood, the youth club was a site of exciting and sophisticated pleasures.

Thus Tubby Passmore, the narrator of my novel *Therapy*, recalling the Catholic youth club he joined, despite lacking any belief or interest in religion himself, because at the time he was smitten with a young Catholic girl who was a member. His description is closely based on my own memories of the St Mary Magdalen parish youth club (though it was rather confusingly called the St Ignatius Youth Club – perhaps the fathers thought a reformed sinner was not an appropriate patron saint for the purpose). I learned to dance, though I could not remember how, or who taught me, and had to invent a character with that function for Tubby in the novel. It was of course ballroom dancing – quickstep, foxtrot and waltz, with an occasional old-time dance for variety, and no jiving allowed. So one got to know girls, and to touch them, and to feel reasonably at ease with them, but there was none to whom I felt strongly attracted. The most beautiful was a girl called Aurora, the daughter of Italian parents, who had a magnificent bosom and lustrous black wavy hair. I would often see her on weekday mornings when waiting for a tram on my way to

St Joseph's, coming down the hill towards Brockley Cross on her way to the technical school where she was doing a commercial course, and we would smile and exchange a brief greeting. There was an opportunity here to develop a more intimate relationship than the publicity of the youth club allowed, but having danced with her and struggled to maintain a conversation I could not discover a single interest or taste that we had in common. There was no basis for genuine friendship between us, and Aurora had an elder brother who was also a member of the youth club and kept a watchful eye on his sister.

Then I met Peggy, my first girlfriend. But exactly when in 1951, my sixteenth year, did I meet her? It must have been not long after my holiday in Heidelberg that summer as the guest of my aunt Eileen, an experience from which I gained a huge increase in self-confidence.

7

That holiday in Heidelberg in 1951 was not my first experience of Continental Europe. In the summer of 1947, when I was twelve, Uncle John and Aunt Lu invited my mother and me to visit them in Brussels. (Dad was unable to accompany us because of his work, but he wouldn't have wanted to go anyway.) John and Lu enjoyed a standard of living considerably above ours. They occupied a very comfortable apartment in an exclusive residential area of the capital, and owned two cars: John had one for his job as travelling salesman for his father-in-law's business, and Lu had a new Morris Minor, a coveted vehicle in England for which there were long waiting lists, which she drove con brio, swerving in and out of the Brussels traffic, a cigarette smouldering between her fingers on the steering wheel. She also had a Flemish-speaking maid who came in daily to clean the apartment and help her prepare meals. The rationing which was still in force in Britain, and was sometimes more severe than during the war, did not apply in Belgium and the Brussels shops displayed food that astonished Mum and me with its quantity, quality and variety. Lu was an excellent cook, but I was too young and unsophisticated to appreciate much of what she served to us, or indeed to appreciate the whole experience of 'abroad', a privilege which at this time was available to very few British people. I enjoyed some of the more familiar food, and I enjoyed being driven at exhilarating speed by Lu in the Morris Minor, its tyres pattering on the cobbled roads. (Dad's first post-war car was an old Ford Anglia which frequently had to be started with a handle.) An excursion to the site of the battle of Waterloo genuinely interested me, but for the most part I felt ill at ease in the foreign environment.

Lu's son Philippe was several inches taller than me, but a year younger. I did not speak enough French and he did not speak enough English to allow us to communicate very well. We were both shy and there was no spark of instinctive liking between us, so we did not become playmates. The domestic atmosphere of the Brussels ménage was volatile and this added to the strain of being a guest, for Mum as well as for me. In retrospect it is obvious that John was already finding his fairly humdrum job – travelling round the country selling English tweed and worsted to Belgian tailors – irksome and somewhat infra dig, and that he resented Philippe's claims on Lu's attention as much as Philippe resented his alien presence. Both John and Lu were emotional and quick-tempered people who relieved their feelings in outspoken and often angry terms. Their rows never lasted for long, and they soon recovered their good humour – John usually cracking the jokes and Lu providing the laughter; but to Mum and me, used to a much quieter tenor of domestic life, their vocal disagreements were alarming. I think we were both relieved to get back home.

*   *   *

Nevertheless that visit was an educative experience, and meant that when my aunt Eileen proposed, early in 1951, that I should have a holiday with her in Heidelberg that summer, the challenge of travelling there on my own was not quite so daunting as it might otherwise have seemed: I had some idea of what was involved in crossing the Channel and what to expect on the other side. Eileen wrote an enticing description of the attractions of the historic city, of which I already had some idea from the postcards she had sent us, showing its situation on the river Neckar, over-looked by a castle halfway up a tree-covered mountain. She prom-ised that she would spend as much time as possible with me, and obtain a PX card which would allow me to use all the facilities reserved for American personnel – restaurants, snack bars, local transport, the riverside swimming pool and the PX store – while she was at work. It certainly sounded a lot more interesting than the holidays I had shared in the last couple of years with Mum and Dad. When he was a jobbing musician Dad was always reluc-tant to arrange holidays in case he missed some lucrative gigs, but in the late forties he obtained a steady job as leader of his own trio (piano, drums and saxophone/clarinet) at the Studio Club in Knightsbridge, where his boss for a short time was Clement Freud before he became famous. It closed briefly in the summer and so Dad had no excuse not to take Mum and me on a proper holiday. We went in successive years to a boarding house in Shoreham near Worthing. Timothy in *Out of the Shelter* went on such holi-days. 'He was lonely and bored – bored with his parents' company and bored with Worthing; bored with the promenade and the pier and the putting green and Mrs Watkins' Spam salads' – and so was I. I decided to accept Eileen's invitation.

Dad and Mum gave me the money for the journey, but no other assistance in making the necessary arrangements. I had to obtain my rail and boat tickets from Victoria station, a passport from the Petty France Passport Office, and a visa from the West German Embassy. All required separate journeys into central London and much tedious waiting in line. There were moments, especially as I stood in a queue for hours at the West German Embassy, when I regretted what I had let myself in for. But it wasn't just the tedium of the bureaucratic formalities that drained my enthusiasm for the trip: the ugly German eagle stamped on my passport by a rather surly clerk at the embassy triggered some apprehension about venturing into the land of the hereditary enemy, whose evil deeds in wartime had overshadowed my childhood. It was now safely disarmed, but the defeated population would surely be hostile to a young British visitor who they might think had come to their country to gloat. I comforted myself with the thought that I would be under the protection of my aunt and her American friends, and resolved to go through with the adventure. It turned out to be one of the formative experiences of my life.

The journey had five stages: London to Dover, Dover to Ostend, Ostend to Brussels, Brussels to Mannheim, and a short final leg from Mannheim to Heidelberg. I set off in the morning, and was met in Brussels by John and Lu, who gave me a meal, transferred me to a different terminus and put me on the overnight train to Mannheim. I had not thought of reserving a seat and I was unable to find a vacant one. The train was incredibly crowded, its corridors packed with passengers and their luggage. I had to stand for the whole journey, though I spent the latter part of it sitting or reclining on the floor, propped up against my bag, a large RAF officer's holdall that had belonged to Uncle John and for some forgotten reason had been left in our loft, collecting dust, for years. Timothy Young, the sixteen-year-old central character of *Out of the Shelter*, makes this same journey and in the course of it has an intuition that perhaps owes something to *Stamboul Train*: 'a sense that, in Europe, life had always been like this, like an endless train journey through the night, across frontiers, loudspeakers blaring harshly over bleak platforms, uniformed men waking you up to examine your papers, no more immediate end in view than to make a little space for yourself and snatch a little sleep'. Like Timothy, I derived a gratifying increment of self-esteem from completing this gruelling journey, successfully changing at Mannheim on to an antiquated little local train which trundled out of the city past bomb sites rendered grimly spectral by early-morning mist and delivered me half an hour later into the embrace of my aunt Eileen on the platform of Heidelberg station.

My first day unfolded almost exactly as described in *Out of the Shelter*. Eileen checked my unwieldy bag at the station and took me to a nearby guesthouse where she had found a room, warning me that it was not great but the best she had been able to find, as accommodation was 'like gold dust' in Heidelberg. It turned out to be a bleak, barely furnished garret at the top of a tall, gloomy house, owned by a large middle-aged German woman who spoke little English. I spoke no German, a language which was not taught at St Joseph's, except for a few words picked up from comic-book stories about the war, like '*Achtung*' and '*Dummkopf*', which were not much use to me in the circumstances. Eileen, who had acquired some basic German, and quickly sensed that I didn't relish making this place my home for the next two weeks, told the landlady that we would make a decision after I had had some breakfast, as I was extremely hungry, which was true enough. She took me to a cafeteria reserved for US personnel in the middle of a green square near the station called the Stadtgarten, where I had my first introduction to the plentiful food the occupying forces enjoyed – *two* fried eggs were served with rashers of bacon and sausages – and learned two new idioms when a white-coated cook asked me if I wanted my eggs 'sunny side up' or 'over easy'. While I tucked into this meal she apologised for the uninviting guesthouse room and said she would try to find something better in the coming days, but meanwhile I would have to make do with it. Then a *dea ex machina* rescued me from this fate. An American friend of Eileen's greeted her, sat down at our table, and was introduced to me. Informed of my plight, she said that she was just leaving for a three-week vacation, and offered me the use of her room in a hostel for civilian employees of the US Army while she was away. Just like that. This was another revelation – of a quality of friendliness and generosity in large sections of American society, bred of affluence and uninhibited manners, utterly different from the cautious, calculating, protective attitude to personal possessions that most English people display to anyone who is not 'family'. I would frequently experience it again when I lived for two longish periods in America. This woman – I think she was called Ruth – was not an especially close friend of Eileen's, but she was willing to let a sixteen-year-old English schoolboy whom she had never previously met occupy her room for the duration of his holiday. There was only one snag: the room was in a *women's* hostel. Ruth saw no problem, as men were allowed in the building till midnight. Eileen could take me to the room and leave me there at night and

I would just need to lie low until the girls had gone to work in the morning. Eileen responded enthusiastically to this idea. In retrospect I decided this was not just because it offered me much more comfortable accommodation than the guesthouse garret, but also because it would save her quite a few Deutschmarks, and because she was tickled by the element of intrigue and role-playing in the proposal. I was much more doubtful, precisely for that last reason. 'Well, think it over,' Ruth said. 'I must be on my way. Here's the key to my room.' She took it out of her handbag and gave it to Eileen.

That holiday was the primary inspiration for *Out of the Shelter*, and in writing it I drew extensively on my memories of those two weeks, adding material garnered on two later visits to Heidelberg. It is probably the most autobiographical of my novels, though it contains too many fictional elements added to, or displacing, the reality of my experience to be classified generically as an 'auto-biographical novel'. The wartime and post-war childhood of Timothy closely resembles mine, but his experience of the Blitz is more traumatic. It is not his aunt but an older sister, called Kate (perhaps an unconscious incarnation of the daughter my mother lost, though the conscious reason was to avoid portraying Eileen), who works for the American Army in Heidelberg and invites him to visit her there. All the sexual episodes are invented, including Timothy's initiation into heavy petting with the American teenager Gloria. I returned to England as innocent in that respect as I had left; but I did feel enormously more grown-up.

One reason was that I had to pretend to be older than I was much of the time in Heidelberg, beginning with my first evening when I agreed to try out the room in the hostel. The plan was to give the impression that I was a male friend of Eileen's escorting her home and being invited up for a cup of coffee: she would let us into the room and then leave after a discreet interval. All went well that first evening – and subsequently. Even though Eileen looked at least ten years younger than her true age of about forty-five, we would have seemed an odd couple to anyone who scrutinised us closely, but no one did. It helped that the hostel was a larger, more impersonal establishment than the one in which Eileen had her own bedsit, where I sometimes spent time during the day with the co-operation of the friendly German caretaker. There was no visible caretaker in the larger hostel, and the residents scarcely gave us a second glance as Eileen and I made our way to Ruth's comfortable room in the evenings. It had a washbasin but no en-suite bathroom. I peed in the sink at night and waited till the women had all gone to work in the mornings before using the nearest lavatory along the corridor. Sometimes the German women cleaners mopping the floor of the entrance hall would look at me curiously when I appeared at about nine o'clock on my way to take breakfast at the Stadtgarten canteen, but they never said anything except *'Guten Tag'*. The expression 'toy boy' didn't exist then, but perhaps that was what they thought I was. It still astonishes me that, as an unsophisticated and temperamentally cautious English schoolboy, I had the chutzpah to live clandestinely for two weeks in a women's hostel in a foreign city, always conscious that at any moment someone might challenge me to explain what I was doing there. I can only suppose that my fear of exposure was weaker than my reluctance to spend a lot of time alone in the forbidding ambience of the German *Gasthaus*.

The longer I evaded detection, the more confident I became in the nightly charade of escorting Eileen to Ruth's room. I was acquiring a more grown-up appearance and manners from other sources at the same time. Eileen bought me some new clothes at the PX, more suitable for the hot and humid August weather than the thick Utility garments I had brought with me: cotton shirts and trousers, and a lightweight jacket of fine wool in a pale oatmeal shade, with fashionable draped shoulders, to wear in the evenings. Eileen and her mainly American circle of friends, all civilians working for the US Army, lived a very full social life and dined out frequently. A favourite place was the Officers' Club, to which civilian staff like Eileen belonged, a large requisitioned restaurant high up on the mountain overlooking the town, which offered an American-style menu that suited my taste perfectly. I don't remember eating out with my parents in England except occasionally on holiday, and then it was a purely functional matter of filling one's stomach as expeditiously and economically as possible. Now I began to learn that a meal might be made to last for several hours very pleasantly, from aperitifs to coffee, with entertaining conversation. I was introduced to gin in a delicious long drink called a Tom Collins on my first evening, to wine later in the holiday (we never drank table wine at home), and was encouraged to smoke the occasional cigarette – the health risks were not understood at that date, and it helped to make my presence in adult company seem more natural.

I led a largely solitary existence in Heidelberg during weekdays when Eileen was at work. Often I took a book to the open-air swimming pool beside the river, which had been commandeered by the Americans to the understandable resentment of the local

Germans. There I observed teenagers of my own age swigging Cokes and engaging in flirtation and horseplay, but I lacked the nerve to speak to any of them. Sometimes I took a sketch pad and watercolour box to the other side of the Neckar and painted views of the Castle and the Old Bridge with its graceful arches and two cylindrical towers, capped with domes shaped like German helmets, at the entrance to the Old Town. Occasionally I took a yellow-painted American bus to the PX, to browse the displays of consumer goods unobtainable in England and had a hamburger and milkshake at the soda fountain. In the evenings and weekends I became an honorary adult, with access to the world of leisure and pleasure which my aunt and her friends pursued in their off-duty hours. Over a memorable weekend I accompanied a group of them on a trip to the resort of Garmisch-Partenkirchen in the Bavarian Alps, where the Americans had established a Rest and Recreation facility for their personnel. We travelled overnight by train in sleepers and stayed in a vast timbered hotel beside a lake surrounded by mountains, where swimming, waterskiing, boat trips and excursions were available to visitors. One day I took a bus tour of the region on my own and visited the site of the Oberammergau Passion Play and a fairy-tale castle built by mad King Ludwig of Bavaria. I had become a tourist, and had travelled a long way, psychologically as well as geographically, from Brockley Cross.

Eileen was an enthusiastic participant in this round of pleasure and recreation. She was a popular member of her circle, regarded as a good sport and good company, always with a new joke or amusing anecdote to tell, often against herself, admired for her elegant clothes and manners, and for her beautiful English accent, softened by acquired American intonations and varied by the occasional Irish idiom. She played up her half-Irish descent, finding it went down well with her friends, who called her 'Ei*leen*', with the stress on the second syllable, which sounded much more euphonious and glamorous to my ear than the downbeat British '*Eileen*'. She had an engaging spirit of mischief and daring, as the following story illustrates. On a weekend break away from Heidelberg she and her companions were in a very posh restaurant at Baden Baden, where the Duke and Duchess of Windsor were dining with some friends. Eileen bribed a waiter to ask if he could take a photograph of the royal party to record the occasion for the restaurant and they agreed. At the crucial moment Eileen walked past their table, and paused just long enough behind the unsuspecting Duke and Duchess to smile at the camera and give the impression that she was a member of the party. The resulting photograph was circulated to all her friends and relatives, and provoked much merriment and admiration for her cheek.

I suppose I must have wondered, or overheard adults at home wondering, why such an attractive and popular lady had not married, and showed no intention of doing so. At that time she seemed happy to be single and independent, free to enjoy the company of male friends without strings. It is hard for me to recall the stages by which I gradually acquired a deeper knowledge of her character and experience. She may have confided in me at some moment in my holiday that when she was working in Paris she had met a charming American officer and started going out with him, but discovered that he had a wife in the States, and broke off the relationship. It was at a much later date that she told me how deeply she was in love with him, and how close she came to becoming his lover, and that she felt this disillusioning experience had prevented her from forming a close relationship with any other man subsequently. She also admitted to having an inhibition about the idea of physical intimacy which she connected to an episode of sexual abuse by an older cousin when she was a child – I don't know at what age, but she was old enough to feel fear and disgust and guilt, compounded by her Catholic upbringing. It was a sadly familiar story, though it never seems so to the victim. At some point in the late 1950s, perceiving that the military occupation of Germany was approaching its end, and unable to face returning to England, Eileen emigrated to the United States, but she remained single and celibate till her death.

In the summer of 1951, however, she seemed to be having the time of her life in a Europe that was an uncrowded playground for those with the dollars to enjoy it. On my holiday, thanks to the generosity of Eileen, who paid for most of my expenses, and her American friends who treated both of us on several occasions, I had a foretaste of the consumerist good life which the peoples of Western Europe, still recovering from the aftermath of war, would soon aspire to and to a large extent achieve. Eileen and her friends did not live within the bubble of 'America Town' – they dwelt in the older part of Heidelberg, and she at least made an effort to relate to members of the German community with whom she came into contact. With her encouragement I spent a day with the friendly caretaker of her hostel, and made an excursion with him on a borrowed bike to meet his equally friendly parents in a dusty dilapidated village in the country outside Heidelberg. These contacts began to displace the stereotypes of Germans derived from the British mass media in my consciousness.

And one day I accompanied Eileen to visit an American friend of hers in Frankfurt, which revealed to me how utterly untypical of post-war Germany Heidelberg was, a picture-postcard historic town almost untouched by the war. Large tracts of Frankfurt were still bomb sites – cleared and tidied, in the meticulous German way, but still awe-inspiring evidence of the destruction wrought by Allied carpet-bombing, beside which the scattered holes made in the fabric of London seemed comparatively slight. Not that I felt any guilt by association on this account. It was not until I read David Irving's book *The Destruction of Dresden* (1963) that I became interested in the ethical and strategic issues of the Allied bombing campaign, and then I was as much shocked by the scale of Allied air crews' casualties as by the sufferings of German civilians. At the age of sixteen I shared the general British opinion (which is still valid, though not the whole story) that Germany had brought the devastation on itself, but after my sight of Frankfurt I held it with more compassion and understanding.

Flattened Frankfurt was more representative of the state of Germany in 1951 than Heidelberg, but the latter gave me an attractive image of the country's history, topography and architecture to take back to England. Soon after I returned home I painted a mural in my bedroom, between the picture rail and the ceiling, of the Old Bridge, with a stretch of the river and a boat in the foreground and the tree-covered mountain rising over the roofs of the riverside houses in the background. I had had plenty of practice with that view, and it was a successful picture. The poster paints I used on the whitewashed wall kept their colours surprisingly well in the years that followed. After I left home Dad redecorated the room, probably more than once, but he did not paint over the mural. It was still there, only slightly faded, when he died in 1999 and I had the melancholy task of clearing the house and arranging for it to be sold. I took a photo of the painting before I left 81 Millmark Grove for the last time.

8

In the autumn of 1951, the beginning of my second year in the sixth form at St Joseph's, I was standing outside St Mary Magdalen's church one Sunday morning in the throng that had just emerged from mass, chatting to a couple of friends, when a tall, smartly dressed youth came up and invited them to a birthday party he was having that evening at his home. I scarcely knew this boy, who was a year or two older than me, and whose parents were reputed to be well-off. He had once been a member of the youth club, but had evidently outgrown its simple pleasures. He emphasised that he was hosting the party himself without parental interference and promised it would be fun. I got the impression that he had decided to have a party at the last moment and was urgently rounding up guests for it. He looked at me, and said: 'Would you like to come?' I said I would. I'm not sure that before my holiday in Heidelberg I would have accepted the invitation so readily – or perhaps at all.

I remember nothing of the house except the room where the

party took place: a large room with a wooden floor from which the carpets had been rolled up for dancing to a gramophone, and a number of chairs, some easy, some upright, pushed back against the wall. There was a table with sandwiches and cakes, and drinks, including a fruit punch which had alcohol of some kind in it. The host organised games designed to create a party mood, including musical chairs in which the boys sat on the chairs and the girls paraded round and sat on the boys' knees when the music stopped. The last couple left had to kiss. The game was played several times. Afterwards I continued talking to a girl who had perched on my knee in a friendly, unembarrassed and unembarrassing way. She belonged to the parish, but was not a member of the youth club, and I had never met her before. Her name was Peggy, and I found her very easy to talk to. She had fair hair, a pretty elfin face, a nice smile, expressive eyes and a very pleasant voice, which was not 'posh' but had no trace of the south London vowels and glottal stops that accented the speech of me and most of my friends to some degree. When amused, she gave an unusual and attractive low-pitched chuckle. Above all she seemed as keen to make a favourable impression as I was. As the evening went on it became evident that boys and girls were pairing off, curled up together in armchairs or sitting on upright chairs with the girls on the boys' knees, and kissing, or in the current idiom, 'necking'. I suggested to Peggy that we should sit down while there was still a spare chair, and she sat on my knee. Affecting a nonchalance I was far from feeling, I said something like, 'Perhaps we should do what everybody else seems to be doing,' and she smiled and replied in the same tone of light-hearted dalliance, 'Perhaps we should.' And so I kissed a girl, properly, for the first time. It was a delicious sensation. How could one have guessed how incredibly soft a girl's lips were? I saw Peggy home after the party, arranged to meet again, gave her a last kiss in the porch of her terraced house and walked back to my own, blissfully rejoicing in my good fortune. It seemed that she had no other steady boyfriend. I had found a girlfriend at last, superior to anyone I had met at the youth club.

Peggy was a year older than me, had left school, and worked as a telephone switchboard operator for a big company that manufactured lifts. I would phone her there to arrange dates (not that we used that transatlantic term) because she didn't have a phone at home, and if one of the other operators answered I'd ask them to transfer me to Peggy. Her family background was always something of a mystery to me. During the year that we went out together I often entertained her at home in Millmark Grove, but I never got beyond her own front door. Sometimes this would be opened by her mother, who would give me an unsmiling, slightly sardonic greeting before summoning her daughter. There seemed to be no father in residence, but I never discovered anything about her family life and personal history, nor did she volunteer any information. If I touched on the subject she replied evasively, and I did not feel I had the right to press her for details. I felt very lucky to have met her at this juncture in my life. She was too short and stocky to be called beautiful, but she was attractive, dressed with good taste, and, unlike the girls I met at the youth club, she had some high-cultural interests and enthusiasms, through which I sensed that she was trying to make up for having left school at sixteen because of her family circumstances. Perhaps she thought I would help her in this project, but initially she was my tutor. She took me to my first classical concert, at the Albert Hall, to hear her favourite piece, Tchaikovsky's Piano Concerto No. 1, and she introduced me to the gallery of the Old Vic, only half an hour's journey from Brockley, where, sitting on a bench seat, you could see great productions of Shakespeare for a shilling. She joined the youth club, and we went on their organised rambles and other excursions together, and she came to Sunday afternoon football matches and cheered me from the touchline. The house she lived in, probably with shared occupancy, was a terraced town house with steps down to a basement area and another flight up from the pavement, at the top of which was a recessed porch where we necked for a while when I saw her home at the end of an evening. We never did anything more than kiss and cuddle. If the hall light was illuminating the porch through the frosted glass in the front door, Peggy would quietly slip inside and switch it off before returning to my embrace, but the situation was still too public to attempt anything more intimate. In any case, I was inhibited by moral scruples and a temperamental cautiousness. I sometimes meditated feeling her breasts through her clothing but resisted the temptation, reasoning that if she took offence I would be mortified and if she didn't it would be an invitation to go further – and where would that lead? To mortal sin, certainly, and all kinds of other possible complications. Perhaps the temptation was lessened by the fact that her breasts were not very prominent. So I contented myself with necking in the porch, leaving me with an erection like a small crowbar in my trouser pocket which gradually subsided as I walked home. I was only sixteen and a half when we met, and did not pretend to her or myself that I was in love with Peggy. I liked her a lot and enjoyed being with her and I was proud to have her as a girlfriend. When I had occasion to introduce her to my classmates, they were impressed. But I had other things on my mind besides sex, like experimenting with writing and getting to university.

There were about fifteen of us in the second-year sixth form, divided roughly equally between Arts and Sciences. Although there had been a few pupils at St Joseph's in the past who had gone on to Oxford, we beneficiaries of the 1944 Education Act were the first sixth-formers in the school's history nearly all of who applied for university entrance. Dad had needed some persuading that this was a good idea for me. I still nourished vague ambitions to be a journalist (though not specialising in sport) and he had questioned someone he knew who worked in newspapers about the best way to enter that profession. The answer had been: leave school, get a job as a cub reporter on a local paper, and work your way up the ladder. This was perfectly sensible advice in those days, before newspapers started recruiting graduates as a matter of course, and Dad, who knew nothing about universities, thought I should take it. But Mum was uncertain, and went to see the head-master, Brother Fabian, who convinced her that I had the potential to go to university and should be encouraged to do so.

We had little help at St Joseph's in applying. I don't recall anyone telling me there were universities in England other than Oxford, Cambridge and London, and I didn't presume to apply to Oxbridge, which I associated chiefly with the annual Boat Race and thought of as far too posh for the likes of me. Probably, in spite of the confidence-building experience of going to Germany on my own, I was also reluctant to leave the protection and comforts of home. So I applied to two colleges of the University of London, University College and Queen Mary College. I don't remember why I applied to only two – perhaps it was a London University rule at the time. I made Queen Mary my second choice rather than the more prestigious King's College because I thought Queen Mary was more likely to accept me if I failed to get into UCL, but I was rejected by Queen Mary without being interviewed. Everything therefore depended on the interview to which I was summoned at UCL. Their application form had contained a blank page on which you were asked to write a brief essay explaining why you wanted to do a degree course in English Language and Literature, and I suspect my offering must have impressed or intrigued them because I was closely questioned about it by my two interviewers, Professors A.H. Smith and James Sutherland. They were the only full professors in the Department at the time, and Smith was head of it. I must have given a good account of myself because to my great joy I was offered a place. All I had to do now was pass in my three A-level subjects, English, Latin and History. No specific grades were required, for another curious feature of the new examination system, as well as the minimum age for taking O levels, and also perhaps prompted by egalitarian ideology in the Department of Education, was that the pass/credit/distinction categories of the old School Certificate had been abolished. No marks for O and A levels were published, and they were supposed to be confidential, though schools were informed of them and would often pass them on to pupils unofficially. This took a lot of the anxiety out of getting to university if you were lucky enough to be offered a place. Tuition was free, and maintenance grants were available, means-tested against parental income. There were two kinds of grant: a State Scholarship, awarded to a limited number of candidates who excelled in a special S-level examination in their chosen subject, with no set syllabus; and a less valuable Major County Award, given by the candidate's local education authority. I was entered for the S-level exam in English and was advised to apply for a Major County Award as well. Accordingly I went one day to London's imposing County Hall on the south bank of the Thames to be interviewed once more, this time by a committee of four people. (If it seems surprising that so much bureaucratic time was expended on this exercise, remember that in the early 1950s university entrance was not the mass operation it has since become: places were available for only about five per cent of the relevant age group in the population.) This interview gave me the idea for my first published short story.

Around this time my life was made more interesting not just by Peggy, but by the reappearance in London of an old friend, Daniel Moynihan, whom I knew as 'Dan' and would later learn to call 'Danny'. He and his younger brother Michael were the sons of one of my mother's convent school friends, and I used to play with them in their tall, rather shabby town house beside the tramlines at New Cross Gate until the family moved to Hastings when I was about twelve, and as a teenager I visited them occasionally at weekends or during school holidays. Dan was a year or two older than me, and nearly a foot taller, but we always enjoyed each other's company, going for long walks along the Hastings seafront, sometimes in darkness and rain, talking of our hopes and anxieties and aspirations. Dan had not had an academic education, had left school at sixteen and was an apprentice cabinetmaker, but he was restive in this occupation and dreamed of becoming an actor, an ambition inspired mainly by cinema-going. It seemed to me pure fantasy when he talked of it on those walks in Hastings, but one day when I thought he was doing his National Service in the RAF Dan turned up at our house in Millmark Grove and announced that he had been given a medical discharge, and had come to London in a make-or-break effort to become an actor. He was lodging with his gran, who lived just ten minutes away from us, and he had taken an office job in London to support himself, while attending evening classes in drama at Morley College in Southwark, that splendid institution of adult education which has helped and inspired so many generations of students. I thought this was an exciting and impressive move, though his parents were not pleased, and my own were sceptical of his chances of success. Dan was good-looking in a lean, athletic way (he had been a competitive hurdler at county level as a teenager), carried himself well, and had a good speaking voice – all valuable attributes for an actor. Most importantly he had the vital spark of desire to act. But he was culturally under-nourished and diffident about preparing for some of the exercises in his course which involved finding a monologue from a play to perform, or writing one yourself. I was very willing to help him with such tasks, especially the latter, and with rehearsing his performances. These were my earliest experiments in dramatic writing. Before long Dan won a scholarship to the Webber Douglas Academy of Dramatic Art, and I used to go to the end-of-term shows in which the students performed extracts from classic plays, enhancing my knowledge of the history of drama in the process.

I admired Dan's determination to fulfil his ambition, and combined it with my experience of being interviewed at County Hall to write a short story about a young man who applies for a grant to go to drama school. At the interview he pretends to be the Devil, and succeeds so well in frightening the committee that when he reveals the impersonation they award him the grant. 'Major County Award' was published in *Signum Fidei* in my last term at St Joseph's, over the name 'D.S. Lodge'. (My second name is John, but I didn't see proofs.) A former pupil who had a senior position in the London County Council came to give out prizes at the end of the school year and made a speech in the course of which he said that the headmaster had privately remarked to him that there were no geniuses at St Joseph's, but he had been given a copy of the latest school magazine in which there was a story which suggested to him that Brother Fabian might be wrong (or words to that effect). Perhaps the visitor had been tickled to come across a story set in his own workplace. Needless to say, I was immensely chuffed by this very public compliment.

By now I definitely harboured ambitions to be a writer. For a combined Christmas and birthday present I requested and received a portable typewriter, an expensive gift, to which I think my aunt Eileen contributed. It was an Oliver, a British make perhaps hoping to be associated or confused with the more famous firm of Olivetti. It served me well for many years. What pocket money I had, I spent mostly on books. My best friend at school was not in my class, but in the Lower Sixth. He was called John Hodgson, a good-looking youth with a head of blond hair worn rather long, who shared my enthusiasm for literature and scorn for the 'school spirit' St Joseph's aimed to instil. In our lunch break we regularly sauntered down to Blackheath Village – arm in arm, I recall, something that would no doubt attract homophobic catcalls from schoolboys today – to browse in a bookshop that sold second-hand Penguins. There I acquired some bargains which I still possess – Aldous Huxley's *Antic Hay*, for instance, old numbers of John Lehmann's book-format magazine *New Writing*, and several volumes of plays by Shaw, with his prefaces. The moment in Huxley's novel when a boy comes into a classroom and asks the teacher for 'the Key to the Absolute', and the man hands over an ordinary Yale key, has lodged in my mind ever since (it is the key to a cupboard in the chemistry lab where absolute alcohol is kept); so has the moment when Shearwater calls on Coleman and from the doorway glimpses the pink and naked Rosie on a rumpled bed. When I re-read the novel decades later I was surprised to discover some much more erotic passages, but that one made the deepest impression, perhaps because it encapsulated my own sense of exclusion from such experience. This was the era when Penguin dominated quality paperback publishing, and I sometimes lashed out on new copies of books like E.V. Rieu's translation of *The Odyssey* in the Penguin Classics series, and the *Penguin Book of Contemporary Verse*, edited by Kenneth Allott. It was an indication of how much I valued these two books that I converted them into hardbacks with the aid of a special kit you could buy from Penguin, including a little wafer of gold leaf with which to stencil the titles on the spines. I still have them: the covers have not prevented the pages from turning yellow, and the binding on the spines is coming away from the boards where the gum has dried. I'm glad I didn't persist with this practice. What, after all, could compete with the elegant sans serif lettering and bold colour-coding (orange for literary fiction, green for crime and detection, purple for classics) of the Penguin covers of that era?

I left St Joseph's that summer without any regrets or subsequent fits of nostalgia. I had never felt really comfortable in its hearty Catholic ethos, and if Malachy Carroll hadn't come to the school at just the right moment I don't think I would have learned much that was inspiring for my future development. The school improved considerably in the decade following my departure, sending increasing numbers of boys to university; and it acquired a reputation for rugby and other athletic prowess under the aegis of an ex-military PE teacher known as 'Chiefie', a short, assertive, energetic man who arrived in my last years as a pupil, and whom many found charismatic, though not I. His speciality was something called 'log-work', which entailed teams of boys in singlets and shorts hurling a long, stripped and varnished tree trunk up in the air and catching it while performing marching manoeuvres. Perhaps my relationship with the school might have been different and more positive if it had been a soccer school instead of a rugby school. It inspired a loyalty and affection in some old boys that I never felt, but I understood their dismay at its later history.

When grammar schools were abolished in London in the 1970s St Joseph's, which had drawn pupils from all over south-east London and parts of Kent, became a boys' comprehensive with a local catchment area consisting mainly of Lewisham, one of the most socially deprived and troubled London boroughs. As the proportion of disadvantaged and delinquent boys entering St Joseph's increased, the level of academic achievement went down and the school developed a bad reputation locally. The bright green blazers became the livery of unacceptable behaviour on the streets and public transport, and *Signum Fidei* on their breast pockets a badge of dishonour. Middle-class parents ceased to send their children to the school and withdrew those who were there. The school came under 'special measures', but in spite of strenuous efforts these failed to make it viable. Early in the present century it was decided to close and demolish the existing school and to build a new co-educational Catholic comprehensive called St Matthew Academy; an academy in the new sense of a school independent of local authority control and supported partly by private enterprise, offering specialised teaching in selected subject areas. Apparently St Matthew was chosen as the patron saint of the new school because he was a tax gatherer before he became an apostle, and the special emphasis of the new Academy's curriculum was to be 'Business and Enterprise'. The absence of an apostrophe 's' after his name was never explained to me. The new school is reported to be working well, but the demise of the old one is a sadly familiar story of unintended consequences in the implementation of an educational policy that claimed to be progressive.

In July 1952 I was informed by mail that I had passed in all three A-level subjects, but naturally I wanted to know how well I had performed, so went back to the school to find out. The headmaster, having cautioned me that he was not supposed to divulge the marks, wrote down some words and figures on a piece of paper and passed it to me, holding out his hand for its return when I had perused it. The marks ranged from 62 to 66. I was slightly disappointed as I had expected to do better, especially in English, which was the 66. I had not been awarded a State Scholarship, but I had done well enough in the exam to be put on a waiting list in case scholarships offered to other candidates were not taken up, and not long afterwards I received a letter to say that I had obtained one in this way, replacing the less prestigious Major County Award which I had been given provisionally. The news greatly cheered me and I hastened to share it with Peggy, who congratulated me warmly. With this encouragement I was ready and eager to start my BA course at University College, but the beginning of the academic year was still a couple of months away. I looked in the small ads of the *Evening Standard* for a job with which to earn some pocket money in the interval. The first one I found, which seemed like good pay for easy work, was advertised by a photographer in Brixton requiring teenage boys as models, but Dad quickly vetoed that. Eventually I took a job with the W.H. Smith bookstall on Waterloo station. It was poorly paid, even by the meagre standards of those days – £3 10s. for a six-day week. I joined a team of two permanent employees, slightly younger than me, whose job it was to push specially designed wooden barrows around the station from platform to platform, selling magazines and newspapers to passengers who had not supplied themselves from the main bookstall. Many years later I wrote a short story called 'My First Job', narrated by a sociologist recalling a similar experience when he was between grammar school and university:

I did not dislike the work. Railway stations are places of considerable sociological interest. The subtle gradations of the English class-system are displayed there with unparalleled richness and range of illustration. You see every human type, and may eavesdrop on some of the most deeply emotional moments in people's lives.

I reacted similarly to the work at first, but after a while it grew monotonous and I tried to inject interest into it by competing with my two colleagues to achieve the highest takings at the end of the week. They were two scruffy cockneys who had left school at fifteen, with whom I had nothing in common, and there was an edginess to our relationship, especially after the senior one tricked me into asking the pleasant young woman who issued us with our stock for some copies of the *Wanker's Times*. (I was not familiar with the word 'wank', less common then than it is today, or with its colloquial application to the naturist magazine *Health and Efficiency*.) There was no financial incentive for us to increase our takings – no commission on sales or bonuses for effort. It was competition for its own sake, but the other two boys were drawn into it, and the results naturally delighted the bookstall manager. In the story, a somewhat heightened version of these events, the narrator, now a successful academic of leftist views, recalls how he was victorious, breaking all previous records for sales from a barrow before he went off to university, but he is guiltily haunted by the faces of his two co-workers

as I last saw them, with the realisation slowly sinking in that they were committed to maintaining that punishing tempo of work, that extraordinary volume of sales, indefinitely, and to no personal advantage, or else be subjected to constant complaint and abuse.

9

University College London is situated in Bloomsbury, so unknowingly I began my life as an undergraduate only a few streets and
squares distant from where I had been born. UCL is the oldest,
largest and most prestigious of the London colleges, and now a
university in its own right. It was founded in 1826 to provide
higher education for those who were not members of the Church
of England, then obligatory for students and their teachers at
Oxford and Cambridge, and was open to freethinkers as well as
members of other sects and faiths, earning itself the soubriquet
of 'the Godless University'. The mummified body of Jeremy
Bentham, the Utilitarian philosopher regarded as 'the spiritual
founder' of the college, is famously preserved, and occasionally
displayed, in a wooden cabinet in its main building. This is an
imposing domed edifice designed by the architect of the National
Gallery, fronted by flights of steps, on which students perch with
their books in summer, and by a massive columned portico reminiscent of the Parthenon. It was always a visual thrill to come into

sight of this building, set well back from the road behind a turfed quadrangle and screened by the dull facades of Gower Street, when one reached the entrance to the Quad and the Porter's Lodge, guarded by a Dickensian-looking porter in antique livery.

But as a student I seldom entered the college by the main entrance. The English Department was reached by a less impressive side entrance known as Foster Court and accommodated in a former warehouse. It was built of dirty brick, several storeys high, and faced another building of the same grim aspect. The lift was off-limits to students, and you had to climb several flights of stairs to reach the English Department's administrative office, teaching rooms and the rooms, separated by partition walls, occupied by individual members of staff. The ceilings were low, the corridors narrow and the floors covered with durable lino. One fine, sunny morning in late September 1952, in the largest of the teaching rooms, I joined my fellow 'freshers' for the first of several days of initiation into aspects of the college, the Department, and the courses we would follow. After some speeches of welcome and briefings by members of staff, there was an interval when coffee was served and we milled about, excited and nervous, trying to take the measure of the group of strangers to whom we now belonged. Some seemed to know each other already, and chatted with enviable ease. I approached a girl who had caught my eye: she had flawless features, blonde hair drawn back into a ponytail, and a shapely figure. She responded with a spontaneous friendly smile when I spoke to her. Her name was Mary – Mary Jacob. I can't remember what we talked about – banal things, no doubt, such as where we came from, and what aspects of the course before us seemed most interesting or most forbidding. She seemed very nice. Later on that day I was lingering outside the Foster Court building before the afternoon session of our programme, and wondering where she had gone in the lunch break, when I saw her with two or three other girls walking abreast towards me, the autumn sun bathing them in light. I was struck more powerfully than before by her beauty, though she seemed quite unselfconscious about it. She looked strong and confident, glowing with health and a simple happiness at being where she was. As I moved towards her she flashed a pleased smile of recognition. The group stopped as I came up to them. 'Where have you been?' I asked Mary, and she said, 'We've been to join the Catholic Society, or Cath Soc, as they call it.' 'Are you a Catholic?' I said excitedly, hardly able to believe my luck. 'I am too.'

I suppose I fell in love at that meeting, at second rather than first sight, though I didn't define my feelings in those romantic terms. But I remember thinking, if not at that precise moment, then not long afterwards, that Mary had a kind of beauty that would last – a rather extraordinary reflection for a seventeen-year-old, as if I were already sizing her up as a possible wife. Perhaps I was, unconsciously. Consciously I was only aware that she was an exceptional girl, and that I wanted urgently to attach myself to her before someone else did, having sensed the vibrations in the air emanating from clever young people on the threshold of adult life and away from home for the first time, eager to make relationships with the opposite sex. I kept close to her in the days that followed, sat next to her at lectures and accompanied her to the bazaar-like events at which various student societies solicited membership. I signed up for the Catholic Society, of course. We explored together the various facilities of the college, including the Students' Union, a large smoky basement with a bar, its walls festooned with hand-painted posters, furnished with battered armchairs and sofas where young men argued noisily and uninhibited couples necked. I asked Mary if she would like to go to a gallery one evening. She looked puzzled until I explained that I meant the gallery of a theatre, not an art gallery, and then she agreed readily. Mary was obviously very intelligent – she had won a State Scholarship, without going on to a waiting list – but she was unsophisticated, and her experience of theatre-going was limited to being taken with her older sister by a friend of the family to see variety shows and Christmas pantomimes. She had been brought up in Hoddesdon, Hertfordshire, a small town about twenty miles north of central London, and had attended a convent secondary school in Enfield, where she had been head girl and captain of games. I gathered that both her parents were Irish, and that she had six brothers and sisters. She had hardly any knowledge of London, which gave me a great advantage in securing her friendship, since I was able to be her guide to aspects of metropolitan life, such as how to reserve gallery seats. You went along in the morning before the performance and paid sixpence to have a numbered ticket stuck on one of the small folding stools which were arranged outside the theatre in the form of a queue, and came back in the evening to claim your place before the doors were opened, being entertained in the meantime by buskers who sang, tap-danced and played musical instruments. The seats in West End theatres were dearer than the Old Vic's – two shillings, I think – but also slightly more comfortable, with backs to the benches. Galleries, colloquially known as 'the gods', were certainly a godsend to impecunious students, but they disappeared long ago from London theatres as their owners ripped out the benches, replaced them with more expensive upholstered seats and renamed the space 'Upper Circle' or 'Balcony'.

I was of course conscious of a disloyalty to Peggy, to whom I owed my own introduction to that economical source of cultured entertainment, as soon as I began to seek Mary's company at college. Very soon – about a week after I first spoke to Mary – I went round to Peggy's house to tell her that I had met another girl and was going out with her. I don't remember details of our conversation, which as usual took place in the porch of her house, and was brief. She looked at her feet as I spoke, with an expression both sad and wry, and said little. I had a feeling that she had feared this would happen, but perhaps not quite so quickly. I felt pity for her and some remorse, but there was no honourable alternative. I was quite sure that Mary was the girlfriend I wanted, and although I had no reason to suppose she was as strongly attracted to me, I had known from the moment she gave that smile of recognition in Foster Court that she liked me. She was nine months older, but even more innocent as regards sex – of knowledge about it, never mind experience. She had lived as a boarder in her last eighteen months at the convent school, since her home was so crowded that she couldn't study properly there. At the school, I would learn in due course, she had been the unwilling object of schoolgirl crushes and the embarrassing embraces of an intense young nun, but had little contact with boys as a teenager. She had learned to dance and went to parish socials on occasion, but I quickly established that she had had no boyfriend before she met me, which for so attractive a girl in her eighteenth year was remarkable. That summer she had spent a month as an au pair with a wealthy family in south-west France, which was her first experience of Abroad, and something like a rite of passage for her, as my holiday in Heidelberg had been for me. Apart from that, family, school and parish had defined the limits of her world. Now she was free, at least in term-time, of her ties and duties to all of them, an independent adult in a big city, and – you could see it in her clear blue-green eyes – expectantly open to new experiences and new friendships. My desire to be the most important of the latter was of course greatly helped by the fact that I was a Catholic and therefore shared the same moral code. She had come up to London early to settle into her digs, and gone to a Union dance at the very beginning of Freshers' Week which I had skipped, and been affronted by the behaviour of a boy who had danced with her, holding her too tight and trying to lure her outside for a snog. Mary was happy to accept me as her first boyfriend.

There were several Catholics in our year in the English Department, and we discovered fairly soon that it was an advantage to have had a Catholic education, even one as narrow and shallow as mine, in pursuing the BA Honours English course at the University of London. The curriculum was heavily loaded towards early literature, from the Anglo-Saxon period to the seventeenth century, much of which was saturated in Christian and often specifically Catholic doctrine, practice and allusions. Knowledge of these was especially useful for the study of medieval literature, and I recall that in our second year we Catholics tormented the young lecturer who was taking us through the *Ancrene Riwle* by pointing out his misreadings of religious references in this text (a devotional manual written by the chaplain to a group of nuns, generally thought to be the finest extant example of Early Middle English prose). Catholicism wasn't much help, however, in coping with the epic poem *Beowulf*, partly because it had its roots in the pagan period of Anglo-Saxon culture, but mainly because it was written in Old English, which to us was a foreign language that had to be learned. There was an Old English Finals paper waiting for us at the end of our three years, with compulsory questions requiring the translation of passages of *Beowulf* into modern English. Students who were good at languages, like Mary, took to the task willingly; others like me found it a wearisome chore. One of our particular friends in the year was Derek Todd, who was older than all of us because his commencement of the course had been delayed by National Service in the Navy, followed by serious illness. He gave up the attempt to learn Old English as a decodable language, and prepared for the final examination by memorising the visual appearance of the text of *Beowulf* and the prose translation of it available in an Everyman anthology, so exactly that he would be able to recognise the passages of the former selected for the exam and match them with the modern English translation. This stratagem evidently worked because he obtained a First-class degree.

The disproportionate prominence of Old English in the degree course at London and most other British universities at this time had a historical origin. UCL had been offering courses on English literature from its foundation, but degrees in the humanities at the more prestigious ancient universities continued to be based chiefly on the study of classical texts in Greek and Latin, until a School of English was established at Oxford in 1893, against some opposition. To meet the objection that studying literature in the mother tongue was too easy to be worth a university degree, the curriculum was made as 'hard' as possible, mainly by requiring students to study Old English and its roots in other Germanic languages revealed by historical philology. Cambridge refused to offer a BA degree in English at all until 1917, when it introduced one with a different syllabus from Oxford's, beginning the study of English literature with Chaucer, and incorporating courses such as 'Tragedy' and 'Practical Criticism' designed to provide cultural breadth and intellectual rigour. This syllabus also had an influence on the development of English studies elsewhere, but Oxford had been first in the field and its model was more widely adopted by other British universities, including London.

I had come to UCL expecting my course to be an extension in more depth and detail of my A-level studies, which began with Chaucer's General Prologue to the *Canterbury Tales,* and went up to the late nineteenth century, supplemented by reading in more modern literature for S level. Instead I was disconcerted to find myself in the first term having lectures on nothing later than seventeenth-century prose, and discovering that 'English' as a university subject incorporated not only Anglo-Saxon literature, but specialised courses in subjects like palaeography, the historical study of handwriting, especially of the 'secretary hand' in which most Elizabethan and Jacobean manuscripts were written, and bibliography, the historical study of books as physical objects, including their printing and binding. We did have something called 'Essay Writing', a course taught in seminar groups of about ten students, which included some practical criticism and even a few creative writing exercises, but the teacher I had was unsympathetic to my efforts, and my personal tutor was also critical of the essays I wrote for him on seventeenth-century prose writers. The truth is that they didn't appeal to me, and I lacked the cultural and historical knowledge to appreciate them, which was not surprising, given my age and patchy education. It took me some time to find my feet as a student.

Among the other Catholics in our year was Anthony Petti, who had no such difficulty. He was the son of Italian parents, and in appearance bore a slightly caricatured likeness to portraits of Renaissance aristocrats, prelates and soldiers of fortune. He was very tall, with long arms and legs protruding from his jacket cuffs and trouser turn-ups, a shock of stiff black hair like the head of a broom, high cheekbones, dark, close-set eyes and an impressively large Roman nose. He lived at home in north London, where he had been very well educated at a Jesuit school. His manner was slightly theatrical, though not in the least camp: when he had something serious to say his body language sema-phored its gravity and his expression underlined its import with frowns and the lowered pitch of his voice; when he was amused or being amusing he snorted and giggled, capered and clowned, and he could switch from one mode to the other in an instant. He had a passion for music, especially classical opera and Renaissance church music, on which in due course he became an expert as both musicologist and choirmaster. Indeed I often wondered why he hadn't chosen to study music instead of English. But as a first-year undergraduate Tony was impressively familiar with the canon of English literature. He was one of the few men in our year who had already done his National Service, so was older than most of us, which helped to make him a leader in departmental student activities, and one of the first things he did was to organise our year's contribution to the entertainment at the departmental Christmas party. We had a meeting of those interested, and decided to present a burlesque poetic drama about a freshman's life loosely modelled on Milton's *Samson Agonistes*, a neoclassical verse drama that I and several others had studied for A level. I still have a creased, yellowing copy of the cyclostyled script, which was composed by various hands, but mostly Tony's. It was called *Simpson Agonistes* (a title used decades later by Robert Metcalfe for a book about the trial of O.J. Simpson). I was cast as Simpson, and contributed his opening speech, in which Milton's lines, '*O dark, dark, dark, amid the blaze of noon, / Irrecoverably dark, total eclipse / Without all hope of day*', were replaced by:

> O work, work, work amid the days of gloom.
> Unmitigated work, unutterable work
> Without all hope of play.

Tony directed the piece, which was a tissue of literary quotations and allusions, some familiar, others less so. Dramatically it pillaged Shakespeare and morality plays as well as Milton's neoclassical tragedy, but it ended appropriately with Simpson's death offstage under the collapsing pillars of the college portico, described by the Porter in the ancient Greek manner. Mary was in the female chorus that chanted the play's closing lines:

> Simpson is dead, in sleep of peace he lies.
> More geese than swans now live
> More fools than wise.

Not until sixty years later, when I googled these lines, did I discover that the first echoes Psalm 4, and the last two were lifted from Orlando Gibbons's madrigal 'The Silver Swan' (1612). Tony Petti had a very well stocked mind.

Our performance was warmly received by the assembled staff and students, and several of the former said that it was the best of its kind that had ever been presented at the annual party. Later the text was printed on the Department's own hand press as an exercise for Bibliography students. Most of the credit for its success was due to Tony, but in fact we were, without knowing it, an exceptionally bright year, as our Finals results would eventually demonstrate, so we educated and stimulated each other as bright students always do. We were also fortunate, again without knowing it, to be in what was at the time probably the best English Department in the country after Cambridge and Oxford. The staff included several men at the rank of lecturer whose careers had been interrupted by the war, and who, shortly after we graduated, moved on to professorial chairs at other universities: George Kane, world authority on *Piers Plowman,* Harold Jenkins, editor of the Arden *Hamlet,* and T.J.B. Spencer, a versatile scholar who lectured on everything from classical background to W.B. Yeats. In our second year the youngish Randolph Quirk returned from leave of absence in America to introduce us to modern linguistics in dazzling style, and the recruitment of Charles Peake strengthened the teaching of modern literature. The two full professors in the Department were less inspiring. A.H. Smith was a philologist whose speciality was the etymology of English place names. He lectured to us on the history of the English language from well-worn notes, and on one occasion read out a lecture he had delivered the previous week; it did not improve on second hearing, but nobody dared to interrupt his discourse to tell him. James Sutherland was a traditional literary historian best remembered for his edition of *The Oxford Book of Literary Anecdotes*, which had a long life before it was superseded by John Gross's. His lectures on eighteenth- and nineteenth-century literature also tended towards the ramblingly anecdotal. Attendance at lectures was obligatory; a register was passed round the benches to be signed, and although it was not checked very rigorously, frequent absences would provoke a reproof.

The member of staff most revered by us students was Winifred Nowottny – Mrs Nowottny, we called her, since she did not have a doctorate, which was not unusual in those days. She was married to a Czech, but she herself was English, and her quiet voice had a perceptible northern accent. She was probably in her late thirties at this time. She was completely lacking in feminine allure: slight, pale-faced, with a long chin and lank mousy hair, she looked always on the edge of exhaustion, as if she had given blood in exchange for knowledge. Her reputation as a charismatic teacher filtered down to us from the senior students in the Department, and was confirmed when she lectured to us on Shakespeare in our second year. She somehow conveyed that she was giving us the benefit of her own latest thoughts and research on the play under discussion, and it was from her that I first apprehended the intellectual excitement and satisfaction that analytical literary criticism could yield. She had a legendary reputation as a personal tutor, and was greatly oversubscribed by final-year students, who were allowed to register a preference for a tutor. She took her pick, and in due course I was one of the lucky ones.

The tutorial system in UC's English Department was (and I believe still is) its most distinctive and valued feature. Every student received a one-to-one tutorial for half an hour (though some tutors would be more generous with time) every fortnight, for which they wrote an essay on a topic related to their current courses that was read to and discussed with the tutor, who subsequently marked it. At this time one-to-one tutorials were rare in British universities outside Oxford and Cambridge, especially in popular subjects like English, and students were usually tutored in pairs, or more commonly threes and fours, normally for an hour each week. That was the system at Birmingham University until the 1980s, when it collapsed under the pressure of student numbers and was replaced by larger groups taking modular courses. It was a very expensive system in terms of staff teaching hours and, I came to think, a wasteful use of them. What students want and need most from a tutor is dedicated advice and feedback on their written work. When more than one student is involved the tutorial becomes a partly social event, and the role of the tutor is to encourage discussion between the participants, to put the shy and tongue-tied at ease, to prevent the bright and articulate from dominating the conversation, and to guard against doing the same himself. If you have a group that is clever and evenly matched it can be a stimulating experience for all concerned, but more often than not the social dynamics of the event hamper its educational effectiveness.

When Winifred Nowottny was my tutor, I was building up a body of knowledge in preparation for Finals by my fortnightly essays, so she allowed me to nominate the topics, and she would honestly tell me in a few cases – Joyce's *Ulysses* was one of them – that she knew little about my choice. But such was the incisiveness of her intelligence that I would always learn something useful from her comments, and draw encouragement from her approval. About three years later, when I was a postgraduate student, she gave a series of intercollegiate lectures on the language of poetry at Senate House, the headquarters of the University of London, by which I was deeply impressed. It formed the basis for her first book of criticism, *The Language Poets Use*, published in 1962, by which time I was a university teacher myself, and I reviewed it favourably in *The Tablet*, the Catholic weekly. It consists mostly of close analysis of poems or parts of poems, which is designed to show how poetry 'works' – for example, on Milton's lines '*in the lowest deep a lower deep / Still threatening to devour me opens wide*' she comments: 'the device is to run language back on its tracks by making "lower" worse than "lowest"; infinity is given a linguistic index by unfixing the fixities of grammar.' The book belonged to the Anglo-American critical movement of 'close reading' generally known as the New Criticism, but it drew also on systematic stylistics and linguistics to give the analysis more-than-usual precision. It was a direction in which my own critical practice was moving in relation to the novel, leading to my first book of criticism, *Language of Fiction*, published in 1966. I toyed with the idea of calling it *The Language Novelists Use*, but decided that would be too ostentatious an *hommage*.

I kept in touch with Winifred in the 1960s, and once I visited her at home near Banbury in Oxfordshire when a lecture engagement took me in that direction. She seemed subdued and rather melancholy and she was alone except for her cats – I recall stepping over bowls of half-consumed cat food spread across the floors. She told me that she was working on the new Arden edition of Shakespeare's sonnets, and I said truthfully that I could not think of anyone so well qualified to undertake it. After that I had no contact with her, and I was shocked to learn after many years had passed the sad story of her later life. She never completed the Arden edition of the Sonnets, but hung on to the commission for many years until the publishers cancelled her contract and gave the task to someone else. Perhaps like other scholars who have tackled the Sonnets she became obsessed by the insoluble enigmas they contain. Meanwhile her husband had died and she had become alienated from her only son. She became increasingly paranoid, and when she retired, refused to vacate the university flat in Bloomsbury which she then occupied. Rather than evict her, the University allowed her to stay but had no communication with her. She became a recluse, and one day was found dead in a flat that was filthy and full of scattered pages of notes about Shakespeare's sonnets. It is one of the saddest stories I ever heard. But I was glad to discover recently from several links on the internet that *The Language Poets Use* is still a book that is sought and read, and that other scholars have recorded their debt to Winifred's teaching.

Simpson Agonistes was not the only dramatic production in which I was involved in the weeks preceding Christmas 1952. The parish youth club was now known as the St Ignatius *Social* Club, with a more mature membership, and I did not sever my links with it on becoming a university student. One Sunday after mass at St Mary Magdalen's I was approached by a young woman of the parish, who took an interest in the club and must have known about my literary aspirations, with a surprising but irresistible request. It appeared that the Nativity play normally performed by children in the parish junior school had been cancelled for some reason. Would I consider writing a Christmas play to be performed by members of the youth club instead? I would. I did. I not only wrote it, I directed it, acted in it, designed it, chose the music for it – did just about everything connected with it except sew the costumes. I used this experience many years later in a short story called 'Pastoral', one of a series commissioned by the BBC to be broadcast in the intervals of Prom concerts with some thematic connection to the music. My hook was Beethoven's Pastoral Symphony, which had provided the background music to the Crib Scene of my play. The story begins:

'Dah *dah* dah, dah *dah* dah, dad*a* dad*a* dad*a* . . .' I never hear the opening strains of the 'Shepherds' Song' from Beethoven's Pastoral Symphony without remembering my scheme to embrace the Virgin Mary. That is to say, Dympna Cassidy, who was impersonating the Virgin Mary at the time.

A few years later I used the same material, with numerous variations and additions, in an episode of my novel *Therapy,* whose hero recalls acting the part of Herod in a Catholic youth club Nativity play to keep a proprietorial eye on his girlfriend, playing Mary. These fictional versions of the Brockley youth club production had the curious effect of displacing the original in my memory, so that when I tried to recall it for the purpose of this book the images in my head were all of the familiar Bible story, performed in appropriate costumes, but with more colloquial dialogue and contemporary 'relevance' than usual. In fact the play was much more ambitious than that. Looking through a box of old papers I came across a copy of the script, entitled *A Dream of Christmas*, and found that it was a three-act play in which the traditional story was presented in the second act as the dream of a group of travellers marooned in an inn on Christmas Eve, whose characters correspond to the biblical ones. All of them have problems in their lives (e.g. there is a husband who suspects that his pregnant wife has been unfaithful, and another woman who is barren like Mary's cousin Elizabeth) which the dream of Christmas, interpreted by a priest called Father Brown ('No relation to Chesterton's,' he quips), who is also stranded at the inn, helps them to understand and accept. The dramaturgy is incredibly schematic and the dialogue often stilted and sententious, especially in the third act, when all the characters' difficulties are effortlessly resolved. Perhaps conscious of these improbabilities, and in an effort to wrong-foot the audience, I resorted to a sensational denouement in which Father Brown is revealed to be a lunatic, escaped from the local asylum, who is under the delusion that he is a Catholic priest – God working in mysterious ways. I know the play was performed as written because it was reviewed in the youth club's stencilled news-sheet by an anonymous critic who complained of the frame story's simplistic structure and baffling conclusion, and yet I still can conjure up no memory of its first and third acts. It was not suppressed by embarrassment or shame, because the play, performed on a makeshift stage in the school hall, was well received by a full house that included my admiring mum. A note in the news-sheet records that it raised £9 for the Bishop's School Fund.

I found the whole experience very exciting and satisfying, and the more enjoyable because Mary was part of it, albeit somewhat reluctantly. I persuaded her to play the part of the Virgin Mary in the second act, and buxom Aurora to play the invented character of a simple young friend of hers, who is impressed by, but cannot emulate, Mary's unworldliness. I played the part of Joseph myself, and made more of his shock at, and eventual acceptance of, Mary's pregnancy than the New Testament does. A psychoanalytic critic could no doubt make something of the unconscious motivation behind both the dramaturgy and the casting.

Mary was not a natural actress and had no pretensions to be, but she participated gamely for my sake. She had to stay overnight in our house for the final rehearsals and performance, sleeping in my bed in the back bedroom, while I had a made-up bed on the floor of the lounge. She had already met Mum and Dad several times, but not on such intimate terms. Dad liked her and appreciated her good looks, and Mum – well, I think Mum would have preferred that I didn't have a girlfriend at all, but if it was inevitable then she couldn't fault my new choice. There was some tension between them because Mary was used to helping at home with domestic tasks, but Mum was always reluctant to let any guest into her kitchen and at first resisted all Mary's offers of assistance. For her part, Mary was somewhat scandalised by the way my mother cosseted me and my nonchalant acceptance of this treatment.

I think it was earlier, during the autumn term, that I accompanied Mary by Green Line bus to her home in Hoddesdon, and encountered a family life that was very different from mine. They lived in Lord Street, a turning off the High Street that eventually became a winding country lane, in a semi-detached house that was almost identical in size and design to 81 Millmark Grove, but had to accommodate nine people instead of three. Not all nine of them had been continuously in residence together, because some of the children had lived with friends or boarded at school for periods when the pressure on space was acute, and of late the older ones had begun to live away from home, but it was always an over-crowded house, as its worn carpets and furniture showed. Mary and I made our visit on a weekday, and both parents were out at work when we arrived. Our lunch was prepared by their oldest child, Brian, who was in his early twenties, and living at home temporarily while he looked for a job, having been recently sacked from a chemical company, Mary told me, for causing an explosion. He had graduated from King's College London with a poor science degree, and Mary thought he had wasted his time there. She had applied to King's College herself, and had taken exception to the way he had paraded her for the admiration and badinage of his hearty beer-drinking cronies when she went there for interview. (She was offered a place, but opted for UCL.) She had no more affectionate memories of him earlier in her life, claiming that he borrowed her meagre pocket money and failed to repay it, and cheated at Monopoly. But on first acquaintance Brian seemed friendly and hospitable, and I was impressed by his ability to cook a meal. His speech struck me as very different from Mary's correct but neutral register – much more clipped and assertive, in an upper-class style which seemed out of place in this humble dwelling. I learned that he had done his National Service in the Army before going to university, and been commissioned as a second lieutenant, which would partly explain the accent.

In the course of the afternoon and evening the other members of the family returned home from their various schools and work-places, except for Mary's older sister Eileen, who was doing a diploma course at a Catholic teacher training college in Roehampton, and fourteen-year-old Alice, for reasons I don't recall. All the young children seemed to me very charming, and all gave me the same spontaneous friendly smile on being intro-duced that Mary had given me at our first meeting. She was the third-eldest child, followed by Alice, John (twelve), Kathleen (ten) and Margaret (nine). Mrs Jacob, who was a teacher at a local school, came in at about teatime, and greeted me cheerfully in a strong Irish accent. I always had some difficulty in following what she was saying, not so much because of the accent as because her train of thought kept branching off into abrupt digressions and uncontextualised memories, interspersed with proverbs, quota-tions, jests and pious ejaculations; but her fundamental goodwill was always evident. She was a stout, vigorous woman of fifty, with a fresh complexion and a head of dark, thick, naturally curly hair. She belonged to the large family of a farmer called O'Reilly in County Clare in the west of Ireland, who had offered her the choice of extended education or a dowry. She opted for the former and emigrated in 1922 to London, where she was trained as an elementary school teacher and worked in the East End. She had digs in Hampstead where she met Frank Jacob, a very different kind of Irish immigrant. He was a Dubliner, descended from English Quakers who had emigrated to Ireland in the seventeenth century, and he possessed a family tree to prove it. They founded the famous Jacob's biscuit-manufacturing business, but unfortu-nately Frank belonged to a less prosperous branch of the family.

He had served briefly as a private soldier in an Irish regiment of the British Army at the end of the 1914–18 war, probably without leaving Ireland. Despite his Protestant background he was an Irish patriot, and told a tale of being persuaded at that time by a member of the IRA to convey a parcel containing a gun to somebody, which would have had serious consequences if discovered. He came to England to find work and met Mary O'Reilly in a London branch of the Gaelic League, an organisation dedicated to the promotion of the Irish language, which Mary, who was bilingual in Gaelic and English, helped him to learn.

Through courting her, Frank became converted to Roman Catholicism. This was not simply an expedient to marry her, for he was a totally convinced, indeed fundamentalist Catholic for the rest of his life, and suffered great distress at the thought that his unbaptised Quaker family must be eternally damned, until his elder daughters explained to him the most liberal interpretation of the doctrine of Baptism of Desire, which promises that those who live righteously according to their lights will be saved. The young couple came under the spell of Father Vincent McNabb, a remarkable Dominican friar of Irish origin, based in the Hampstead Dominican Priory. He was a regular and much-admired speaker at Hyde Park Corner, taught Thomist philosophy, pursued the cause of ecumenism when it was not as fashionable as it is today, published numerous books on religious topics and was a friend of G.K. Chesterton and Hilaire Belloc. Like them, he was a strong believer in distributism (the distribution of property, especially in the form of smallholdings, to a large proportion of the population) as being more conducive to social justice than either capitalism or socialism. Under his influence the newly married Frank and Mary Jacob bought a bungalow just outside Hoddesdon, in an acre of ground on which Mary grew vegetables and raised chickens and a goat, while Frank commuted to London where he had a clerical job with the Crown Agents. The young couple suffered a personal tragedy in the death of their second child in infancy from convulsions, and the smallholding did not prosper, so they decided to cut their losses and moved into Hoddesdon, renting one of the newly built houses in Lord Street. They and their three children, of whom Mary was the youngest, fitted reasonably well into the three-bedroomed semi. But they went on to have four more children, three of them quite close together, for reasons obviously connected with Catholic teaching on birth control, about which I shall have more to say later in this book. All were born in the master bedroom, and slept there for the first year or so of their lives, and the front reception room had to be used as a bedroom most of the time.

Frank Jacob was too old to be called up in the second war and served in the Home Guard, continuing to commute to his job in the City. His salary was modest, and his wife was fully occupied with her babies and infants for many years. The family was hard up in the late 1930s and early '40s. Only the introduction of Family Allowances by the Labour government elected in 1945 made life tolerable, and even so the children had to make do with clothes and shoes that were handed down or donated by sympathetic friends in the parish. For want of a toothbrush in childhood, Mary would suffer from gum disease later in life. The house was an inferior example of its type: the hot water system never worked properly and the bathwater had to be heated in the kitchen washtub and carried upstairs in a bucket. The only thing to be said in favour of this house as a place to bring up children was that there was common land beyond the fence at the end of the back garden, with a brook that made an inviting play area, and further off there were fields and woods to be explored.

The Jacob family were poor by economic criteria but middle class by birth, education and aspiration, striving to maintain respectability in a very Irish way. Thus the parents spoke with an Irish accent but the children were brought up to use received English pronunciation and punished if they ever lapsed into the local Hertfordshire dialect; and during the war they were forbidden to use public shelters when the air-raid sirens sounded, because of the low class of people who frequented them. They mixed with the children of more affluent families, some of whom generously treated them to holidays and excursions, and as they grew up they became more and more conscious of what was lacking in their own domestic habitat, but they did not apologise for it or shrink from inviting their friends to visit. When I met them I was over-whelmed by their friendliness, vitality and sheer numbers, and although I registered the absence of comfort in their domestic arrangements, it did not bother me. They had the fascination of otherness: it was a family antithetical to my own in almost every respect, except that I shared with them a common faith – and their lifestyle was much more typically Catholic than mine. At home they said grace before meals, and the walls and shelves of the house were crowded with holy pictures, plaques and statues. Most of the children had been educated at the parish junior school by an order of German nuns who were refugees from Nazism, and there was a strong bond between the sisters and the family which endured. The angelic-looking younger son, John, rose early to serve at mass for a different community of enclosed nuns in the town before going off to school – the same Jesuit college that Tony Petti had attended. It was thought that he might have a vocation to the priesthood.

The last member to arrive home was the paterfamilias. Frank Jacob was delighted to see his daughter Mary for the first time in weeks, kissed her, and shook hands with me. He sank down in the armchair reserved for him in a corner near the fireplace of the crowded living room, where one of his young daughters sat on his knee and another brought him a cup of tea. He was a person very different in character and temperament from his wife and the rest of the family: quietly spoken, with a flat Dublin accent, and not quick to speak in the first place. His expression gave little away about what he was thinking. Photos of him early in the marriage, especially one with a hunting rifle tucked under one arm, portray a good-looking, virile young man, with a head of fair, wavy hair, but the passing of the years had thinned the hair, and thickened his waist. He moved slowly and with deliberation, as if conserving his energy. He had been commuting to his job in the City for a quarter of a century, a journey by bus, train and on foot that must have taken him at least ninety minutes each way, year in and year out, in peace and war, rain and shine, six days a week (a half-day on Saturday). It was an exhausting routine, but it also largely relieved him of practical involvement in bringing up a large family in an unsuitable house and on an inadequate income, a task which devolved upon his wife, who was hardly equal to it, as my Mary was keenly aware. I created a somewhat idealised fictional version of this family in my first published novel, *The Picturegoers*. There were tensions and conflicts in its history of which I then had no knowledge, and psychological traits in some of its members that would create serious problems in the future. Much of this unhappiness was connected, directly or indirectly, with their Catholic faith, but for most of them only the faith made it bearable.

10

My life as an undergraduate was more like that of a student in a Continental European city, where it is still common practice to study at your local university and live with your family, than that of most post-war British students, for whom living away from home for part of the year, on the historic Oxbridge pattern, has been an essential part of their tertiary education. When the system began to expand rapidly in the 1960s and '70s, new universities were constructed on the American campus model with integral student accommodation, and civic redbrick universities provided their swelling intakes with what were called 'halls of residence' – a somewhat archaic phrase which covertly invoked the Oxbridge heritage. I lived at home, and commuted daily to college by train and Tube along with office workers and shop assistants. I have sometimes wondered if missing the experience of a residential university was a deprivation, but there are enough accounts by people who were made miserable by it to make me think that at seventeen and a half I might have been one of them. At home I was looked after by my mother, who cooked my meals and did my laundry and performed other mundane tasks for me more solicitously than any Oxbridge 'bedder' or 'scout'. I had a nice room to myself, with an electric fire, and in very cold weather a coal fire, to keep me warm, and a desk at the window to work at. I had nothing to do but pursue my studies and extracurricular interests.

For Mary, going to university was more of an adventure and a challenge, though her daily journey was very similar to mine. She obtained university-approved 'digs' in Stockwell, a drab older suburb in south London between the boroughs of Lambeth and Brixton, served by the Northern Line of the Tube. She shared a bedsitter with another first-year student in the English Department, a tall, buxom girl with a rather affected posh manner and accent, and an obsessive interest in 'boys', with whom Mary found she had little in common, so she was grateful that my companionship and frequent invitations to Millmark Grove reduced the time she had to spend with her room-mate. Their landlady observed the rules prescribed by the University Lodgings Office scrupulously, and I was never allowed to cross her threshold until the very end of our first year. I splashed out on tickets for the college summer ball, held on the South Bank Festival site, and when I called at the house for Mary I was permitted to step inside and wait in the hall for her till she descended the staircase, looking stunning in the full-length blue taffeta dress she had made herself. Even so, after escorting her home at the end of the evening I had to kiss her goodnight on the porch, as usual. This was a repetition of my routine with Peggy, except that I had a much longer journey afterwards, and often I had to run to Stockwell station to catch a Tube that would connect with the last train to Brockley or New Cross. Occasionally, if it was very late, I would travel to Knightsbridge and wait in the vestibule of the Studio Club for a lift home with Dad.

That summer ball was one of the few occasions when our lives resembled those led by students at Oxford and Cambridge. Another was the annual Rag Week, when we rode down to the Strand on the backs of lorries in fancy dress and taunted our rivals at King's College with the chant *'All King's Students Are Illegitimate'*, repeated four times, and concluding *'Buggering About the Strand'*, Mary singing with gusto a word which had never previously passed her lips, or perhaps even impinged on her ears, and the literal meaning of which was known to neither of us. A more useful taste of traditional university education which we enjoyed occasionally was a condensed version of the undergraduate Reading Party, held at Cumberland Lodge, a fine seventeenth-century house in Windsor Great Park donated to the nation by King George VI as a conference centre. Initially it was specifically designed for use by institutions like UCL which did not have a residential communal life. Twice a year a group of up to thirty students from different years in the English Department and perhaps half a dozen staff would go down to Windsor by coach for a weekend of reading and discussions around a theme. We paid a subsidised rate for the privilege – and a privilege it was to chat and eat with our teachers in such surroundings. The food I remember was fairly dire, but the table settings were elegant and the furnishings and décor quite luxurious, with deep upholstered armchairs and sofas in the vast drawing room. The grounds, and the park itself, invited conversational strolls in good weather. I have warm memories of those weekends at Cumberland Lodge, which were a bonding as much as an educational experience. It moved intellectually upmarket in later years, and I think ceased to host undergraduate groups.

Mary and I were soon recognised as a couple by others in our year and none of the boys tried to displace me, but I was always watchful of potential rivals for the attention of this obviously attractive girl. I was somewhat apprehensive when a postgraduate in the Law Department called Marcus Lefebure made contact with Mary. His sister had been at the Enfield convent school with her, and they were slightly acquainted through that connection. He was a few years older than us, of French extraction, handsome in a refined, ascetic way, cultured, articulate and Catholic. It seemed to me that he and Mary got on well with each other, and that if he made a pitch for her affections he would be a formidable rival. He asked her out to a meal once, and I was relieved when he went off to do postgraduate research in Cambridge, but in fact I had no reason to be jealous. He invited us to visit him in Trinity College, and took us to lunch at a little Indian restaurant where I had a curry for the first time in my life and found it delicious. He told us that he had decided to try his vocation as a priest in the Dominican order, and in due course he was ordained. Marcus was chaplain to the Catholic students of Edinburgh University for many years, until he had a serious psychological breakdown and left the order and the priesthood, but not the Church, to become a lay counsellor. We kept in touch with him until his death at the age of seventy-eight from a particularly distressing, slowly crippling disease which he bore with saintly fortitude. It is a story which, like many others of a similar kind, I find difficult to reconcile with the idea of a loving personal God.

On a lighter note, I recall that Mary had another admirer at the University whose attempt to impress her ended unfortunately for him, though I did not discover the full farcical facts of the matter at the time. John Paddy Carstairs, then in his early forties, was a prolific British director of popular films, including comedies starring Norman Wisdom and a series based on the 'Saint' novels of Leslie Charteris. The films were of little artistic merit, but he nourished an interest in English literature and desired to improve his knowledge of it. He accordingly signed on as an 'auditor' in the UC English Department, meaning that he paid a fee to attend lectures of his choice, but received no tuition. He was a friendly, boyish-looking fellow who evidently enjoyed mixing with young people, and he took a fancy to Mary, whose looks inspired him to call her 'Peaches and Cream', subsequently shortened to 'Peaches'. Eventually he invited her to have lunch with him and she accepted. Suspicious as I was, I couldn't think of any good reason to dissuade her that wouldn't seem silly and possibly insulting. She just thought he was being friendly, and probably that was the case; if he hoped to lay the foundations for a seduction he was certainly disappointed. Off she went to the date in her best dress and a new pair of high-heeled shoes. When I next saw her and asked her what the lunch had been like she said it had been very nice, but was vague and evasive about details, and it was only many years afterwards that she revealed to me what a disaster it had been. The high-heeled shoes were a mistake to begin with, for John Paddy Carstairs was extremely short in stature, and she towered over him as he escorted her into the smart restaurant he had chosen. She was quite unfamiliar with the protocol and routines of such a place, made imprudent choices from the menu, and had a prolonged coughing fit when something stuck in her throat, which alarmed the whole dining room. She told Carstairs that she did not drink wine (in fact she had never drunk anything alcoholic) but he ordered a bottle anyway, vainly hoping to persuade her to try it, and was obliged to consume all of it himself or see it wasted. Perhaps it acted as a welcome anaesthetic. He did not ask her out again.

It is very difficult to recall accurately how one felt and behaved sixty years after the event, so any written trace of such experience is illuminating, and sometimes surprising. When we were separated during vacations Mary and I exchanged letters, and a few handwritten pages from the middle of one I wrote to her in our first year, probably in the Easter vacation, have survived to give me some idea of how I courted her (that now distinctly archaic verb seems appropriate):

I have read your letter through several times & I find it delightfully typical. However I linger on the rare affectionate passages & skip through the rest, which has something of the conversation of a shy young girl at her first 'tête à tête' with her sweetheart. I am sure you have something more to say underneath, and if you could only break down your barrier of shyness it would make me so happy. Remember that you did so once when you first told me you loved me, – a gesture so miraculous on your part that I shall never cease to marvel at it, and a moment so thrilling that I shall never forget it. Let me refresh your memory & do a little homework for Mr Palmer as well . . .

That epistolary style now strikes me as highly artificial, like something lifted from a period novel, affecting a maturity I certainly didn't possess, and the letter gets even more literary as it goes on. Kenneth Palmer was the lecturer who taught the Essay Writing class we both attended, and I recalled the 'thrilling moment' in the form of a creative writing exercise. It begins with an atmospheric evocation of rain falling on a London street at night, reflections of streetlamps, the gurgle of water in the gutters, etc., and a young couple sheltering under an umbrella.

The boy has his arm round her waist, and her cheeks are wet as dewy peaches are wet as she nestles against him, and they stand in a silence vibrating with unsaid thoughts. But his mind fidgets and he has to say something:

'Penny for your thoughts.' Then, remembering a former conversation as she does not reply, 'Oh, I forgot: you don't like saying what you're thinking.'

She answers, rather hastily, 'O yes I do – sometimes.'

A long, long pause, while he ponders & the never-ceasing accompaniment of the rain goes on. Then, delivered in calm, level tones, but coming in their supreme import like a new & dazzling meteor hurled into the heavens from another cosmos – seven simple words: 'I was thinking that I love you.'

And still the rain fell. But the world had changed.

Cue violins and the close-up of a prolonged kiss. This must have described a real event, rhetorically heightened in the hope of drawing from Mary some equivalently ardent declaration which she had so far evidently withheld, because she was more reticent or perhaps just less certain about her feelings. But what interests me most about this fragment is that I was trying out different literary styles in a love letter, in the effort to define my own feelings. The letter continues in its original primly formal manner – 'It is with reminiscing on such incidents that I console myself during your absence' – but then suddenly takes a less ingratiating, even aggressive turn:

> Incidentally I should love to read out the above extract in an Essay class and watch your reactions. I think perhaps if I was a little more brutal in that way I might make you more callous towards your own emotions. But then I'm not sure I should like you any different from what you are.

And I'm not sure now what I meant by 'callous', but this passage seems a more authentic expression of feeling than the overblown rapture of the rain-drenched tryst.

At the beginning of our first long summer vacation Mary and her elder sister arranged to work for a month as cooks on a student farm camp near Wisbech in Cambridgeshire. Eileen had a boyfriend, a student at Oxford, whom she had met at a camp the year before, and he would be joining her. I didn't like the idea of Mary spending several weeks out of my sight in such a community, so I decided to accompany her for the first two of them, little as I relished the prospect of agricultural labour, and reluctant as I was to put aside the novel I had started writing. The camp was situated in the flat featureless Fens, next to a farmhouse where Eileen and Mary slept and worked in the kitchen. The student labourers, male and female, lived in tents. I shared one with a genial Norwegian who was older and certainly more experienced than I. One afternoon during working hours I went to our tent to look for something and found him lying on his camp bed under a blanket with one of the girl students. He grinned up at me without embarrassment as I mumbled an apology and hurriedly withdrew. He told me later that he came on these farm camps chiefly to have sex with girls, and urged me to let him know if I wanted to have the tent to myself and Mary one day. I did not bother to explain the chaste nature of our relationship, but I was glad that by coming on the camp I had warned off such potential predators from being a nuisance to her. There was a group of bearded Persian students who could not disguise their lust for the bare-headed English girls in their revealing shorts and skimpy tops, and exchanged no doubt obscene remarks with each other on the subject in their own language, laughing and rolling their eyes, but Eileen and Mary managed to control their behaviour by treating them like naughty children.

The work itself consisted mainly of picking strawberries, planted in long rows that seemed to stretch to infinity, in a stooping or squatting posture, putting them in a large punnet and taking it, when filled, to be weighed and credited to your individual account. Before long, muscles I never knew I possessed were aching painfully and my delicate townee's fingers were chafed and sore. At the end of each day I was exhausted. The rate of pay was low and I was not adept at the task, so I did not earn a great deal. But

I saw Mary every day and spent some time with her in the evening when she and Eileen had finished clearing up the kitchen after dinner, and I returned home a fitter and healthier-looking young man. I settled down to finish my novel, while Mary, after returning from Wisbech, went off to visit her many relatives in Ireland for the first time.

The novel was entitled *The Devil, the World and the Flesh,* and had as its epigraph Question 348 in the Penny Catechism: '**Which are the enemies we must fight against all the days of our life?** The enemies which we must fight against all the days of our life are the devil, the world, and the flesh.' I don't know if anyone has remarked that this triad is ordered differently in traditional theology as 'the world, the flesh, and the devil', '*mundus, caro, et diabolus*', or explained why the Catechism put the devil first. I suspect it was to emphasise the connection between sin and damnation, for the answer to the next question, '**What do you mean by the devil?**' is: 'By the devil I mean Satan and all his wicked angels, who are ever seeking to draw us into sin, so that we may be damned with them.' It wouldn't have been a bad title for somebody's novel, but was ludicrously portentous for mine. I preserved the typescript and read it, or rather skimmed through it, when writing this book, frequently cringing with embarrassment at the naïvety of my eighteen-year-old self.

The hero is Paul Fletcher, sixteen years old at the beginning of the story, a pupil in the fifth form of a Catholic grammar school with an entirely lay staff. (I must have invented this institution to avoid identification with St Joseph's.) He is an orphan, brought up by an aunt and uncle, a practising Catholic but alienated from the conventional piety of his parish community, something of a loner at school, bookish, self-obsessed, nourishing literary ambitions, desiring sexual experience but restrained by his religious beliefs – in other words a self-portrait modelled on the adolescent Stephen Dedalus. Early on in the narrative he goes to a party very like the one at which I met Peggy and meets a girl of voluptuous good looks who introduces him to necking. She is Ruth Seed, the daughter of Paul's history teacher, and has a sister called Teresa who has just returned home after unsuccessfully trying her vocation as a nun. The family belongs to the same Catholic parish as Paul. He begins a relationship with Ruth which leads to their having sex. The story takes a soap-operatic turn when Ruth finds she is pregnant, and this becomes known in the parish and at the school, provoking great scandal, the stigmatisation of Ruth and harassment of Paul. A comic subplot about the organised humiliation of the martinet headmaster of Paul's school delays the denouement, which I can hardly bring myself to summarise even at this distance in time from its composition. Shortly before Christmas, Ruth is rushed to hospital seriously ill. When Paul visits her she confesses that she has a history of sexual delinquency, and set out to seduce him. She tells him not to blame himself if she dies and, it is revealed after her demise, refuses the abortion that might have saved her life, in accordance with Catholic teaching. The medical and gynaecological details are left vague, since I did not know what they might plausibly be.

The flaws in the novel become more and more evident as it goes on and the novelist gets more and more out of his depth in the subject matter. But it must have been written at considerable speed, mostly in that long vacation, and to have finished it at all, a novel of about 60,000 words, was a kind of achievement. Stylistically it was often lively and imaginative, teeming with metaphors and similes. 'The moon suddenly appeared from behind a cloud, like a silver disc slipped through a button-hole in the sky' is one I could still find a use for. I showed the novel to Malachy Carroll, with whom I remained in touch and occasionally visited at his home in Greenwich. I don't remember now what he said, but he thought it was promising enough – presumably on grounds of style rather than substance – to send it to someone he knew at Michael Joseph, then an independent publishing house, for an opinion. I received a letter on their headed notepaper to say that they would like to meet me and suggesting an appointment. Highly excited, I presented myself at the Michael Joseph premises and met two men who I presume were editors. Any dream I might have nourished of having my novel published as it stood were quickly but kindly dispelled. But they kept the MS, and one of them, a Mr P.H. Hebdon, wrote to me when returning it to say that it had 'an extremely difficult theme which you will be able to tackle very much better when you have had a little more experience', and that they would be interested in seeing any further work.

I knew I would have no time to write another novel until I had finished my degree course, but I was encouraged by their interest. It would also, I hoped, impress Mary, and make her take a more favourable view of *The Devil, the World and the Flesh*. She had been the first person to read it, and had not liked it at all. She had read very little contemporary literary fiction – I doubt if she had read even Greene and Waugh by that time – and she was somewhat shocked by the novel's preoccupation with sexual desire, complicated by Catholic morality and guilt, as experienced by a character in whom she could of course recognise aspects of me. She was certainly anxious to erase any traces of herself in the novel. Ruth calls Paul 'fish' in affectionate mockery on occasion. 'You can't write that,' Mary said firmly. 'It's something *I* say' – as indeed it was, when she wanted to tease me.

She would not have been reassured by Paul's mental response to a seductive whistle he hears from the shadows of a bomb site early in the story:

> He quivered with a breathless surge of emotion and excite-ment. After all, the experience. And he wanted to be a writer, didn't he? Graham Greene, Evelyn Waugh – how did they get their experience, and they were Catholics, weren't they? A mortal sin. But was it? Some fragment: 'A young man and a young woman in a green arbour on a May morning – if God would not forgive it, I would.' Besides, there was always confession . . .

Indeed there was always confession, which was the means by which those eminent Catholic novelists managed to reconcile the practice of their religion with illicit sexual activity. Greene, who became a Catholic while courting the devoutly Catholic Vivien Dayrell-Browning, was resorting to prostitutes within a year of marrying her. Much later he tried to persuade the great love of his life, Catherine Walston, who was married and had become a Catholic as a consequence of reading his books, to live with him with this enticement:

Whenever we settled for any length of time, we would have two rooms *available,* so that at any time without ceasing to live together & love each other you could go to communion (we would break down again & again, but that's neither here nor there).

The parenthesis betrays a rather superficial understanding of the 'firm purpose of amendment' which is required of a penitent to make the sacrament of Penance valid, but Greene was a man who liked to live on what Browning called 'the dangerous edge of things', and seemed to derive a kind of spiritual exaltation from transgression. 'I'm a much better Catholic in mortal sin! Or at least I'm more aware of it,' he wrote to Catherine on another occasion.[1] This was a paradoxical stance that a boy from the Catholic suburban ghetto could not emulate. I was saddled with an unresolvable conflict between a biological urge to have sex and a mental conviction that to do so outside marriage (a prospect so distant as to be not worth thinking about) would endanger my immortal soul. The urge is of course a normal condition of youth, but in my case it was reinforced by a belief that sexual experience was necessary to become a writer of fiction. My sense of being in a double bind was comically expressed in an undated and unpublished story called 'The Wages of Sin', which I had completely forgotten until I came across it in a file of typescripts belonging to the 1950s. It begins:

---

1 Letters quoted by Norman Sherry, *The Life of Graham Greene, Volume Two: 1939–1955* (1994), pp. 227 and 324.

The envelope fell on to the mat with a dull thud, but I didn't hurry to pick it up, being a young writer, still a student and struggling to get work published, and thus used to such a sound. However it wasn't one of my rejected manuscripts, but a large official envelope that wore its embossed crests and other decorations as self-importantly as a general with three rows of medals. The letter inside was from the Apostolic Delegate, and it was short and to the point. 'Dear Joe,' it ran (my name's Joe). 'I am pleased to tell you that the Pope has granted your request for an unlimited right to commit sin for one day in order to get material for your new book. Yours truly, etc.'

The story, which describes the serial frustration of Joe's efforts to make the most of this dispensation, is too tame to live up to its promising beginning, but there was a lesson in it which it took me a long time to recognise: that the best way to treat Catholic hang-ups about sex was through comedy.

11

I showed my novel to Mary shortly after she returned from her holiday in Ireland. When I met her at Euston off the Holyhead train, she had put on half a stone in weight and was bursting out of the tailored jacket and skirt she had left London in. Her farmer relatives in the west of Ireland had fattened her up like a Christmas goose on gammon, cabbage and potatoes with an occasional chicken, serving up huge portions and watching her as she struggled to clear her plate, conscious that they would be hurt if she didn't. She had visited three of her aunts, one of whom insisted on her niece being measured and fitted with a corset, because all respectable women, young and old, fat or thin, wore corsets, apparently for reasons of modesty, and it was simpler to submit than resist. There had been enjoyable occasions during her tour, ceilidh dances and sing-songs and excursions to the coast, but the culture shock had been challenging, especially the sanitary arrangements, or rather lack of them (on one of the farms 'you went in the cowshed – there was nowhere else'), and she was glad to get back to England. Her figure soon resumed its normal shape.

Just before the beginning of our second academic year, she went into University College Hospital for an operation on her leg. She had torn a muscle in her thigh in some heroic athletic effort at school, and made it worse by playing hockey at college before it was properly healed, so surgery was required to repair it. The operation was rather clumsily executed, or so it seemed to us when the plaster cast was removed and revealed a long serpentine scar, cross-hatched where the stiches had been like a railway line on a map. Mary accepted this blemish, which would be clearly visible when she wore a swimming costume for many years afterwards, with what seemed to me remarkable resignation, pleased that the operation had been a success and that she could run again without pain. As it happened, I was an inpatient at the same hospital myself in the Christmas vacation for surgical treatment of a comparatively trivial problem – an ingrown big toenail. But the first attempt was unsuccessful, and became infected, and I had to go in again. This time the surgeon sliced away the side of the nail down to the root, and required me to spend a week in the ward confined to bed, giving the toe a chance to heal. I was taken in a wheelchair to the WC to move my bowels, so spared the indignity of a bedpan, but I had to use a bottle to urinate. This regime entitled me to a daily bed bath. A comely, well-built young nurse, who had an interest in literature and had taken rather a fancy to me, would draw the curtains round my bed, spread a waterproof sheet on the mattress, and sponge down the upper half of my body as we discussed classic novels she had read. She handed me the sponge and towel to attend to my private parts, tactfully averting her gaze, and then, when I turned over, rubbed surgical spirit into my buttocks to prevent bed sores. I used to look forward to these sessions (especially the finale), which were physically more intimate than anything I had experienced with Mary. I did not mention them to her.

That year we regularly attended a weekday early-morning mass at a Catholic church off Goodge Street, whose priest acted as a chaplain to the UC Catholic Society. The church of St Charles Borromeo was very convenient for a weekday mass, being a short walk from Goodge Street Tube station, which was also the closest to UC's Foster Court entrance. It is a Victorian building in early English Gothic style, quite handsomely proportioned and (as I have discovered from the internet) now elegantly decorated, and enhanced by the addition of a spectacular sunken baptistery in the middle of the nave. But in the early 1950s it was a gloomy and chilly place, especially in winter, and in need of refurbishment.

Either the priest at St Charles Borromeo's at that time offered, or some pious students requested, the celebration of a mass once a week for members of the Catholic Society at an appropriate hour before our first lectures of the day. Many years later I created a fictional version of this ritual and its participants as a starting point for my novel *How Far Can You Go?* The authorial narrator describes a dozen college students assembling for a low mass (a mass without music, singing, incense, etc.) at eight o'clock on a bleak February morning in 1952:

They do so at considerable cost in personal discomfort. Rising an hour earlier than usual, in cold bed-sitters far out in the suburbs, they travel fasting on crowded busses and trains, dry-mouthed, weak with hunger, and nauseated by cigarette smoke, to be present at this unexciting ritual in a cold, gloomy church in the grey indifferent heart of London.

Why?

It is not out of a sense of duty, for Catholics are obliged to hear mass only on Sundays and holydays of obligation . . . So why? Is it hunger and thirst after righteousness? Is it devotion to the Real Presence of Christ in the Blessed Sacrament? Is it habit or superstition, or the desire for comradeship? Or all these things, or none of them? Why have they come here and what do they expect to get out of it?

To begin with the simplest case: Dennis, the burly youth in the dufflecoat, its hood thrown back to expose a neck pitted with boil scars, is here because Angela, the fair beauty in the mantilla, is here. And Angela is here because she is a good Catholic girl, the pride of the Merseyside convent where she was Head Girl and the first pupil ever to win a State Studentship to University.

My own motivation was in part like Dennis's, though in other respects he is quite unlike me. Not to join Mary at the mass would have weakened the bond between us, and possibly exposed her to the attentions of rival Catholic youths. But there was also an element of genuine religious faith in my attendance: I believed it was good for my soul to make this regular pilgrimage to hear a weekday mass in addition to the obligatory Sunday one, and that the quasi-penitential effort it entailed was a guarantee of its efficacy. And I believed that conduct like this would earn me God's help in my earthly life as well as contributing to my salvation – indeed my hopes were far more sharply focused on the former than on the latter. Although this seems to me in retrospect a naïve and superstitious attitude, there is perhaps something to be said for self-denial, whatever the motive. A feeling of virtuousness can enhance the enjoyment of life, and there was an agreeable solidarity in sharing it with a group of like-minded young people, kneeling together in the cold, dimly lit, almost empty church, reciting the Latin responses of the dialogue mass (a recent innovation, designed to increase lay participation in the liturgy), knowing that to most of the men and women hurrying to work on the pavements and in the streets outside what we were doing would be incomprehensible. Not that we felt smugly superior to them, but we were aware of our difference, and valued it. Our breakfast after mass at the ABC cafeteria in Tottenham Court Road was a high-spirited gathering, and the food was relished all the more because of our fast.

The cast of characters introduced in the first chapter of *How Far Can You Go?* was meant to show a cross-section of young practising Catholics at the time, whose fortunes would be followed over the next twenty-five years; and in the interest of representativeness I invented a troubled character called Michael, who belongs to the group but feels spiritually compromised by a habit of masturbation which he cannot kick and cannot bring himself to confess, so that he is obliged to find various excuses to avoid going to communion, finally pretending to have doubts about the doctrine of transubstantiation, 'though in fact he believes the whole bag of tricks more simply and comprehensively perhaps than anyone else present at the mass, and is more honest in examining his conscience than some'. When the novel was published in 1980 it was reviewed on BBC Radio 4 by the Oxford don Valentine Cunningham, who, when describing the cast of characters, stated that 'Lodge himself is presumably the guilt-ridden masturbator, Michael.' It was disconcerting to hear this assertion broadcast to the nation, but I did not issue a denial. There were other traits in Michael's character which invited an identification with me – he is reading English at the University, writes a postgraduate thesis on Graham Greene, later becomes a college lecturer and published critic; and in any case by 1980 there was no shame attached to masturbation – *au contraire*, it was accepted, indeed recommended, as a natural stage in sexual development, and it would have been more embarrassing to admit to never having passed through it.

In our second year at UC Mary left her Stockwell digs and rented a small flat – a bed-sitting room, kitchenette and a shared bathroom – with her sister Eileen, who had started work as a teacher of art at a comprehensive school in London. The flat was in Highbury, near enough to the Arsenal football ground to hear the roars of the crowd on Saturday afternoons. It was not subject to the rules of university-approved lodgings and I was able to spend time with Mary there, studying or relaxing and sharing meals with her and sometimes Eileen, with whom I got on well. Our relationship continued on its affectionate and companionable path, almost like a *mariage blanc*, as it would for many years. We saw each other constantly during term, less frequently in vacations, kissed discreetly on meeting and parting and cuddled when we had the opportunity, but those were the limits of our intimacy.

Of course I desired her, and fantasised about making love with her, seeking clues in literature to what it would be like, but in reality that would entail marriage, a possibility so distant that even getting engaged would have been premature. We both had to complete our education, and then I would have to do two years' National Service before starting some kind of career, as yet undefined; while Mary told me she had resolved to give a significant proportion of her earnings to her parents for some years after she started work, thus making clear that marriage was not at present on her agenda. She had seen what a hard life her mother had had, and was not eager to re-enact it. Nowadays two students in the same kind of relationship, even Catholic ones, would most likely have been sexual partners by this time. Obviously the social mores of the early 1950s, and of Catholic subculture in particular, made our restraint more normal, and therefore less stressful, than it would be today, but I recognise in retrospect that there was something in my character that contributed. I was always inclined to postpone an anticipated pleasure rather than risk diluting it by too hasty an indulgence, just as I would habitually reserve the choicest titbit on my dinner plate for the final mouthful. Perhaps I inherited this trait ('delayed gratification', in psychological jargon) from my father who, having chosen his mate and won her assent, never wavered in his commitment but was in no hurry to consummate their union.

Taking advantage of having close relatives on the Continent, I planned a holiday for Mary and myself in our long vacation that would be more hedonistic than her Irish excursion. I wanted to impress her by showing her a good time, as Americans say, such as I had enjoyed in Germany three years before. My aunt Eileen, who had met Mary on a visit to Brockley and thought she was 'a lovely girl', agreed readily when I wrote asking if I could bring her to Heidelberg for a week or so, and John and Lu needed the gentlest of hints to invite us to stay with them in Brussels on our way there. They had not met Mary but I was confident that they would like her, and they did. She got on particularly well with Lu, to whom perhaps she seemed like the daughter Lu would have liked to have herself; that at any rate was the impression I received when watching her teach Mary how to cook a soufflé. That Mary spoke French well was another point in her favour, and made up for my own deficiencies in that respect. John was glad to have a pretty girl around the place and a new audience for his funny walks and amusing anecdotes. He was still chafing somewhat at having to conform to the manners of the Belgian bourgeoisie – for instance, it was the custom at large family gatherings for each individual to shake hands with all the others on his or her first appearance in the morning, which struck John as tiresome and excessively formal. One day on such an occasion he sat down at the breakfast table concealing a prosthetic hand, which he then produced and gave to his neighbour, bidding him to 'pass it round'. Like most practical jokes it had an element of aggression in it, and not everyone present, we gathered, was amused. But Lu indulged his pranks as she tolerated his quick temper, because she loved him. Mary and I did the usual tourist things in Brussels, like the Grand Place, the Musée des Beaux-Arts, the Manneken Pis, staying with John and Lu for five days or so before they put us on the train to Heidelberg. It was a successful and enjoyable visit and a precedent for several more in the future, mostly to Knokke-le-Zoute, the upmarket end of a seaside resort east of

Ostend, where they had an apartment to which they eventually retired.

The West German *Wirtschaftswunder* ('economic miracle') was by now a recognised phenomenon, but its effects were less obvious in Heidelberg than elsewhere because it had never been a commercial or industrial centre and the fabric of the city had not been damaged by the war. The German people on the street looked a little more prosperous and less sullen than when I was last there, but the Americans still provoked local resentment by their monopoly of the swimming pool and other facilities. Tourism was beginning to be encouraged in the Old Town and on the river, where pleasure boats plied up and down, but British visitors were rare. Eileen provided Mary and me with passes to all the American eating places, and scrip (the US Army's special currency) with which to pay for our meals, but we thought we should try a German restaurant at least once. We had a limited amount of Deutschmarks and chose what looked like a cheap one at which to have lunch. I regretted the decision as soon as we sat down. The other diners stared at us in an unfriendly manner on hearing our English voices, and the waiter gave us no help in interpreting the menu. Neither Mary nor I knew any German and he didn't appear to know, or pretended not to know, any English. In desperation I jabbed my finger at random at something unpronounceable, which proved to be a swollen haggis-like thing sitting in a puddle of gravy, which burst open when punctured with knife and fork to spill its unappetising contents over the plate. We ate very little, departed as soon as we could, and did not repeat the experiment, though we did go with Eileen and an American friend one evening to a *Bierkeller* in the Old Town which was more welcoming.

Eileen had found lodgings for Mary, and I was given a bed in a large house overlooking the river that Bill and Jim, two friends of Eileen's – 'the boys', as she called them – shared with some other single men. We met up after breakfast and amused ourselves doing the sort of things I had done alone on my first visit – exploring the Castle, swimming in the riverside pool, drawing and painting the Old Bridge from the other side of the Neckar, and walking on the Philosopher's Walk above it. Our only excursion of any distance was to Baden-Baden. Since my previous visit Eileen and several of her friends had taken up golf and developed a taste for gambling, and the famous spa town in the foothills of the Black Forest, which offered both diversions, had become their favourite destination for short breaks. Eileen had arranged for Mary and me to accompany them there one weekend during our stay. It was a memorable experience, which I later incorporated in Timothy's holiday in *Out of the Shelter*, perhaps at the cost of some anachronism, for I doubt if Baden-Baden was quite as lively in 1951 as it was in 1954.

We were in a party of eight or ten people who set off early in the morning to drive south into the French Occupation Zone, where Baden-Baden was situated. The smart French soldiers patrolling the streets, with flashes of scarlet on their tight-fitting uniforms, looked as if they were understandably pleased with their posting. Like Heidelberg, the town had survived the war unscathed, and was an oasis of pre-war pleasures, with its famous baths, neoclassical casino, historic golf course, riverside promenades and elegant hotels where the baths had three taps, for hot, cold and spa water. As soon as we had checked into our rooms, we went off to the golf course to have lunch on the terraced restaurant overlooking the fairways and well-groomed greens. Afterwards the party split up into two groups of golfers, the competent and those like Eileen and Bill who were still learning. I offered to haul Eileen's clubs. Mary elected to watch from the shade of the clubhouse terrace.

Golf was one of Dad's more consistent enthusiasms, from the 1940s to the 1960s. It was an ideal sport for a musician, for he was free to play on municipal courses on weekday afternoons when they were uncrowded. Sometimes in my school holidays I accompanied him, pulling his bag of clubs along on its two-wheeled trolley and helping to look for balls that had gone into the rough, which happened quite often. Ever the autodidact, he studied golf manuals and magazines intently to improve his technique, but never managed to get his handicap lower than eleven. Occasionally he would meet a friend by arrangement, or pick up another solitary golfer to play against for a modest wager, and these games would occasion a good deal of swearing under his breath and cigarette smoking – he would usually get through a packet of ten Woodbines, a small, cheap brand, in the course of a full round. Gradually I picked up the rudiments of the game, and when he joined an unpretentious club with a nine-hole course next to a cemetery at Honor Oak Park, just a couple of miles from Brockley Cross, he encouraged me to learn, and paid for junior membership and a few lessons. I was never good enough to play with him very often, but I used to knock a ball around the Honor Oak course on my own occasionally as a break from studying, and on the strength of this experience I borrowed clubs from Eileen's bag as she went round the Baden course, and tried some shots of my own.

I was not outclassed. Seldom, I believe, had a group of such incompetent golfers been let loose on such an exclusive course, which had been a venue for championships before the war and was the third-oldest in all of Germany. They swung and missed, sent tee shots that should have soared into the air hopping along the ground or sliced them into adjoining fairways, hacked divots out of the turf, sent fountains of sand into the air in vain attempts to play out of bunkers, and putted their balls back and forth several times across the greens before sinking them. It was a very hot afternoon and our energy flagged well before we had completed the eighteen holes. The bright blue rectangle of a swimming pool belonging to a hotel on the boundary of the course caught our eye and we gazed at it longingly. Surprisingly, it seemed to be unoccupied. Bill led us over to investigate and with the aid of some dollars persuaded the man in charge not only to let us swim but to find us some swimming costumes – old and faded, but laundered. Mary had got bored in the clubhouse and joined us by this time, so she enjoyed this unexpected treat. It was an episode which encapsulated for me the uninhibited hedonism and casual sense of entitlement that characterised the expatriate social set to which Eileen belonged. A visit to the glamorous casino that evening confirmed this impression, though Mary and I were not allowed to gamble, for reasons of age, and had to remain observers at some distance from the gaming tables. This was no great depriv-ation, as neither of us had any interest in gambling. Eileen was intensely interested, and could not conceal her excitement as we made our way to the casino, but she prudently set herself a limit for the evening and kept to it.

I can't remember whether she won or lost that night, but I hope it was the former, because she must have paid for our hotel accommodation, as she paid for much of our holiday. Her friends probably picked up the tab for some of our meals and drinks on that and other occasions, and it embarrassed me later to recall how readily we had accepted their largesse, as if it was a personal extension of wartime Lend-Lease. I hope we expressed our gratitude adequately, and that they got some entertainment from our company. Of course we thanked Eileen profusely and sincerely at the end of our holiday for making it possible. Always an emotional person, who wept easily, she smiled through tears when she saw us off at Heidelberg station. And so, refreshed and stimulated by our travels, we returned home, to prepare for the final year of our degree course.

12

During my second year at college I had begun to develop a more mature critical approach to literature, shedding the expressive, highly metaphorical style which Malachy Carroll had tended to encourage, and giving my essays a tighter argumentative structure. My marks improved, and so did my confidence. At the end of that year I had to submit a long essay related to the course on the History of Literary Criticism, which I had chosen in preference to the History of the English Language. T.J.B. Spencer gave us back our essays in the last class of the session. I had never had any personal contact with him. He began by pronouncing my name interrogatively as he looked round the room, and when I identified myself he handed me my essay with some congratulatory words. The mark was a straight A, and evidently the best of the set. This was a pleasant surprise, and made me think that I was capable of getting a very good degree, perhaps a First, though like most students with the same ambition I kept the thought to myself, except for telling Mary. She herself had been told by her tutor of that year, George Kane, that her sessional exam results had been 'borderline First', and she was awarded a prize for her performance in Old English.

In the early 1950s, and for some time after, British higher education in the humanities was still what might be called a 'First-degree' culture. A young man's or woman's intellectual calibre was judged primarily by their performance in the final under-graduate examinations. A First-class Bachelor's degree was the gateway to coveted careers in the civil service, the professions and academia, and some older university teachers had never bothered to obtain a postgraduate degree, though by now it was expected of new entrants to the profession. (The Oxbridge MA was, and still is, a mere title obtainable on payment of a nominal fee some time after the award of the Bachelor's degree; and the Scottish MA is a degree equivalent to the English BA.) Among the first things one learned as a fresher were the five classes of the bachelor's degree: First, Upper Second, Lower Second, Third and Pass (which was not an Honours degree). And there was, of course, Fail – a rare occurrence, given the competition for university places at the time. Such a finely calibrated degree classification is, I believe, unique to Britain and countries where higher education was shaped by British influence. Historically, it reflected our national obsession, which has somewhat abated during my life-time, with fine distinctions of social status, and the terms 'Upper' and 'Lower', which derive from the terminology of class, have been largely displaced by the more neutral '2.1' and '2.2'. Happily there was never a fixed equivalence between the two scales, and clever young people of low degree socially could overcome this disadvantage by getting a very good university degree, given the opportunity. The five tiers of a Bachelor's degree remain in place today, but the same drama does not attach to the means by which they are earned and awarded. Continuous assessment has taken much of the risk out of the process, and grade inflation, driven by a buyer's market in higher education, has made First-class degrees and Upper Seconds commonplace. Postgraduate qualifications have correspondingly become more important.

In aspiring to get a First I was not motivated by desire for an academic career. In our third year some of us received a form letter asking if we wished to be considered for a postgraduate scholarship, should our Finals results warrant it. For me it would have been a way of postponing National Service for another two or three years, but I wanted to get that over with. In fact I could have avoided it altogether, by training as a schoolteacher after graduation and undertaking to work in that capacity for at least five (I think it was) years, under a scheme devised by the government to make up for a shortage of teachers. But I didn't want to be a schoolteacher, and I had a feeling that to be a writer I needed a broader experience of life than academia could provide. Military service, though I did not look forward to it, would be a start in that direction. So I returned the form with a negative answer, and worked hard to get a First just to prove that I could.

In those days Finals were a test of character and stamina as well as knowledge, three years' work being assessed in a series of three-hour written examinations (eight, in our case) taken in a period little longer than a week, sometimes two on the same day. Three years of learning were judged on the evidence of twenty-four hours of writing. It was the antithesis of the legendary examination system for entry to the Imperial Chinese Civil Service, when

187

candidates were locked in a hut and told to write down everything they knew. At UC we had plenty of practice in the art of writing examination answers, having mid-sessional and sessional exams in our first and second years, and were required to write long essays (as well as our regular tutorial essays) in connection with certain courses. But none of this written work counted towards the final degree result. So you could study industriously for three years, receiving good marks, and still get a disappointing degree if at the time of your final examinations you were physically unwell (but not too ill to sit them), or suffering from acute nervous stress, or bereavement, or other possible misfortunes. The system was particularly hard on women (who were of course excluded from higher education when it evolved) because they might be menstruating or suffering from PMT at the crucial time.

Today very few British universities, if any, award degrees exclusively on the basis of three-hour written examinations taken at the end of three years. There is normally a considerable element of continuous assessment and perhaps a short dissertation or project. To succeed in the classic version of Finals it was essential to be able to write fluently under pressure, and with that facility it was theoretically possible to do well by preparing just a few topics in the run-up to the exams; but if you were unlucky with the questions you could be scuppered. To be confident you had to store much more knowledge in your memory than you could possibly demonstrate. An extreme example was the Shakespeare paper which all candidates for English Honours at London colleges had to take. Five plays were set for special study, and the final paper had a compulsory section on those five which required the candidate to paraphrase a long speech from one of them and comment on a number of shorter passages from others, putting these in context and elucidating problematical expressions and textual cruxes (disputed readings of specific words and phrases, which sometimes varied between the early Quarto and Folio editions). 'Paraphrase' meant rendering Shakespeare's densely metaphorical, idiosyncratic, allusive and often archaic language into modern English prose which made clear that you understood every nuance. It is a very demanding exercise. To be ready to perform it under exam conditions on any passage taken from any one of five plays, and to answer the commentary questions, you had to read those texts very closely and ensure that you understood every line. Nowadays there are numerous annotated editions cheaply available which would assist students in this task if anything like it were required of them, but in the early 1950s there were very few in print, and none in paperback. The Penguin Shakespeare and similar series did not yet exist. Only two of our set plays, *Love's Labour's Lost* and *Richard III*, had recently been published, in expensive New Arden and New Cambridge editions respectively. For the others we had to make do with plain texts which we annotated ourselves from the old Arden editions and other sources in libraries, sometimes buying a plain text edition, removing the binding, and putting the pages in a ring binder interleaved with pages of handwritten notes. All that preparation for just one exam question! Not that I resented or regretted it in the case of Shakespeare – I found preparation for the paraphrase question fascinating and highly educative – but the dissociation of our broadly spread coursework from the drastically condensed assessment of Finals examinations was a constant source of anxiety and complaint.

Another grouse was that the main literature syllabus ended at 1880, roughly when modern English literature began. We were, however, allowed to choose a special subject in our third year from a range of options, and, having discovered that the University of London syllabus offered an optional course in Modern English Literature which was taught at several other colleges, we petitioned the UC Department to offer it, and they agreed to do so. Two authors were set for special study, and questions on them, of which at least one had to be answered, occupied the first half of the Finals paper; the second half consisted of questions on a range of other writers and topics in the period from 1880 to the present. The two set authors for our year were Henry James and W.B. Yeats. Of Yeats I'd known nothing until I started reading his poetry then, but I have been grateful ever since for the incentive to do so. His interest in the occult, and the elaborate system he developed out of bits of Neoplatonism, theosophy and his wife's automatic writing, to explain life, the universe and everything, was alien to my orthodox Catholic mindset, but he made great poetry out of it. Lines of his I learned then have stayed with me ever since: '*And what rough beast, its hour come round at last, / Slouches towards Bethlehem to be born? . . . That is no country for old men. The young / In one another's arms, birds in the trees / – Those dying generations – at their song . . . O body swayed to music, O brightening glance, / How can we know the dancer from the dance? . . . I must lie down where all the ladders start / In the foul rag and bone shop of the heart . . .*' I was impressed by the remarkable extent of change and development in Yeats's work over his lifetime, from the wistful romanticism of his early poetry ('*Tread softly, for you tread on my dreams . . .*)' to the frank sensuality of the late poems ('*Belly, shoulder, bum, / Flash fishlike; nymphs and satyrs / Copulate in the foam*'). It was also reassuring to learn that this author of great poetry about sexual love did not lose his virginity until he was well into his thirties.

But as an undergraduate I didn't get on at all well with Henry James. Since I have written extensively about him in later life – not only literary criticism but also a long biographical novel, *Author, Author,* very sympathetic to its subject – this may seem a surprising confession, but there were several reasons. My first acquaintance with his work was unfortunate. His name was on the list of modern authors Malachy Carroll advised me to read in the sixth form. Knowing nothing about his work, not even a title, I went to the Deptford public library and from the books by James on the shelves I plucked *The Sacred Fount*, because it seemed to be the shortest. This novel, first published in 1901, just before two of his late masterpieces, *The Wings of the Dove* and *The Ambassadors*, is the most obscure and eccentric piece of fiction Henry James ever produced. A deeply unreliable narrator observes a number of people at a country house party. Noticing a striking disparity in physical vitality between the partners of a married couple, he develops a bizarre theory that one is draining a 'sacred fount' of energy from the other, and then begins to detect the same phenomenon linking male and female guests who are not married to each other, suggesting illicit relationships. It is impossible to believe in or make sense of the story, and even the most devoted Jamesians regard *The Sacred Fount* as a misbegotten work. Needless to say, I was totally baffled by it at the age of sixteen, and read no more James until I discovered he was a set author for my final exam in Modern Literature. I read several of his novels in the long vacation before the start of the course, but I chose badly. When people who have had unhappy experiences with James, or been put off by his intimidating reputation, ask my advice on what to read by him I always direct them first to *Daisy Miller*, and to other short and accessible works such as *Washington Square*, *The Aspern Papers* and *The Turn of the Screw*. But I started with James's first attempt to make his mark as a novelist, *Roderick Hudson*, which I found uninvolving, and moved on to *The Portrait of a Lady*, *The Princess Casamassima* and *The Tragic Muse*. The first of these was obviously a great improvement on *Roderick Hudson*, but it seemed to me to move painfully slowly, and the other two enormously long books even more so. Frankly, James bored me, as he bores many young readers: he is a writer for mature minds. But my basic mistake was trying to read him quickly, in order to acquire an overall sense of his *oeuvre* for examination purposes. Henry James did not write page-turners. You have to match your reading speed to the leisurely tempo and complex syntax of his narrative style, relishing every nuance, waiting patiently for each periodic sentence to deliver up its meaning. I learned that lesson some six years later, when in my first year as an assistant lecturer at Birmingham University I was required to give a lecture to first-year students on *The Ambassadors*. I had never read it before; I did so then, very carefully, and was overwhelmed with admiration for the subtlety of its rendering of consciousness and the beauty of its prose, and my serious engagement with James's work began then. In the autumn of 1954 I decided I was not going to 'do' James for Finals because I was not enjoying his work. Instead I would prepare to answer a question on James Joyce (I took a calculated risk that there would be one, or one that could be answered with reference to him, in the second part of the paper). It was a project which entailed reading *Ulysses,* and that was a seminal experience.

All I had read of *Ulysses* up till this time was the chapter about Leopold Bloom's attendance at Paddy Dignam's funeral, in a short selection of Joyce's work, *Introducing James Joyce,* edited by T.S. Eliot. In his very brief Introduction, Eliot mentioned that every chapter of the novel is connected in some way with Homer's *Odyssey,* but gave no other help to the reader. The title of the book is the only textual clue to that fact, but when it was serialised in *The Little Review* prior to completion each section was named after an episode in Homer's epic poem, and that is how they are referred to in criticism. Although I was unable fully to appreciate 'Hades', as the funeral chapter is known, out of its context, it was fascinating enough to leave me with a desire to read the entire book one day. Now the moment had come; but obtaining a copy was not straightforward. The ban imposed for many years in Britain and America after the novel's publication in Paris in 1922, on grounds of obscenity, was lifted in the USA by a legal judgment in 1933. It was published in Britain by John Lane, The Bodley Head in 1937, and had a limited circulation henceforth. By 1954 it was available in some libraries, but only on request and at the discretion of librarians. Respectable bookshops did not display it and most did not stock it. I bought my copy from one of the slightly louche bookshops in Charing Cross Road that had in their windows illustrated books on the Nude and treatises on exotic sexual customs. It cost £1 sterling – equivalent to just over £23 in 2013, based on the retail price index, and nearly £60 in purchasing power, based on average wages, so a formidable investment for a student; indeed for anybody who wasn't well off. The high price was a form of voluntary censorship by the publisher. I'm fairly sure that if Bodley Head had issued a cheap edition there would have been a legal challenge, and possibly an anticipation of the *Lady Chatterley* trial of 1960, although anyone seeking to use *Ulysses* as pornography would have to search through a great deal of densely allusive experimental prose to find what they were looking for, and would probably give up in bafflement long before they got to the most sexually explicit episode, Molly Bloom's monologue, at the very end.

The copy I bought, and laid reverently on my desk at home, was the sixth reprint of the Bodley Head edition. It had a distinctive squarish shape, the width of a normal octavo but shorter, with 740 closely printed pages that gave it a chunky feel in the hands. It had a green paper dust jacket which carried a generous tribute from – rather surprisingly, for he was generally regarded as a popular middlebrow writer – J.B. Priestley: 'As a literary feat, and example of virtuosity in narration and language, it is an outstanding creation. Nobody who knows anything about writing can read the book and deny its author, not merely talent, but sheer genius.' No doubt the publishers thought Priestley's approval would carry more weight with the great British public than, say, T.S. Eliot's, but the former's words were well chosen. The cover bore the image of an ancient Greek longbow, which was also impressed on the green board beneath, this being the favoured weapon of Ulysses, the Latin name of Odysseus. Like all decent hardback books in those days, its pages were gathered and stitched, not glued together, so that when opened it stayed open, without the need for any digital pressure on the pages as I began reading:

> Stately, plump Buck Mulligan came from the stairhead, bearing a bowl of lather on which a mirror and a razor lay crossed. A yellow dressing-gown, ungirdled, was sustained gently behind him by the mild morning air. He held the bowl aloft and intoned:
>   – *Introibo ad altare Dei.*

These words ('I will go in unto the altar of God') were spoken by the celebrant at the beginning of the Latin mass, which Buck Mulligan travesties, substituting his shaving bowl for a chalice, and a few lines later mocking the Eucharistic doctrine of transubstantiation by comparing it blasphemously to a conjuring trick:

> He added in a preacher's tone:
>   – For this, O dearly beloved, is the genuine Christine: body and soul and blood and ouns. Slow music, please. Shut your eyes, gents. One moment. A little trouble about those white corpuscles. Silence, all.

Immediately I was hooked. This prose, combining humour, religious allusion, archaisms (*ungirdled, ouns* [wounds]), colloquialisms (*Shut your eyes, gents*), scientific terminology (*corpuscles*) and mimetic syntax (that long predicate concluding the second sentence imitates the way the skirt of the dressing gown is lifted by the morning breeze) endowed the familiar with the shock of the new. It was like nothing I had encountered before – except to some extent in 'Hades'. But Leopold Bloom, whose narrative point of view Joyce adopts there, is *l'homme moyen sensuel,* the average man of average sensuality (though of course, like every human being, he has a unique personal identity), and his perception of the world is quite different from that of Stephen Dedalus, Joyce's portrait of himself as a young man, through whose consciousness the opening chapter of *Ulysses* (known as 'Telemachus', the name of Odysseus' son) is narrated. Its style is complex, allusive, intellectual, literary. 'Hades' is in a quite different register, homely and colloquial in diction, using repetition and redundancy which would be a fault in conventional prose to imitate actions and attitude:

> Mr Bloom entered and sat in the vacant place. He pulled the door to after him and slammed it twice till it shut tight. He passed an arm through the armstrap and looked seriously from the open carriage window at the lowered blinds of the avenue. One dragged aside: an old woman peeping. Nose whiteflattened against the pane.

One of Joyce's great achievements in this novel was to create distinctive styles for his two main characters, Stephen and Bloom, not just in the way they speak, but in the way they perceive and think, and then to find a third, quite different and equally expressive one for Molly Bloom. But as well as evoking the physical and mental life of these personages with unprecedented fine-grained realism, he shows them to us in the course of the book through the distorting lens of various specialised and artificial kinds of discourse – newspaper journalism, literary parody, surrealism, catechism, cheap romantic fiction for women, and several others – so that the novel is as much about its own medium, language, as about the world. That is why, when literary novelists are asked to name the work of fiction they most admire, *Ulysses* so often comes top of the poll; and why readers simply in search of entertainment seldom get very far in it.

With *Ulysses*, as with medieval literature, I found my Catholic background immensely helpful in picking up its religious references, but for details of the Homeric parallels, and other kinds of allusion and patterning (each episode, for instance, has its own special colour, art and symbol), I needed the assistance of Stuart Gilbert's guide and commentary, *James Joyce's Ulysses*, a book written with Joyce's blessing and co-operation. I also read Herbert Gorman's biography, the best available at the time, and was impressed by the determination with which Joyce pursued his vocation in his early adult life, in the teeth of all kinds of discouragement, condemnation and bad luck. From that time onwards he was my literary hero.

Joyce's direct influence on my own writing is not observable until my third novel, *The British Museum is Falling Down* (1965), with its parodies of various modern writers and *hommage* to Molly Bloom's monologue in the last chapter. The style of the first section of *Out of the Shelter* (1970) owed a good deal to the corresponding section of *A Portrait of the Artist as a Young Man*, in acknowledgement of which, when I issued a revised edition of that novel in 1986, I used an introductory dash at the beginning of direct speech, which Joyce preferred to what he scornfully called 'perverted commas'. And in *Small World* (1984) and *Nice Work* (1988), like other authors before me I took a tip from Joyce and used precursor texts as structural scaffolding for stories of modern life: the Grail

Legend and chivalric romance in the former, and Victorian industrial novels in the latter. But I would like to think that the most important lesson about writing I learned from reading and teaching Joyce over the years, and have tried to implement at my own level of literary endeavour, was to take pains to make the work as good as one is capable of making it. Joyce, meeting his friend Frank Budgen in the street one day, told him that he had spent all day working on a single sentence in *Ulysses*. When Budgen asked if he had been searching for the right words, Joyce replied: 'No, I have the words already. What I am seeking is the perfect order of words in the sentences I have.' That anecdote has become for me the literary equivalent of a Zen parable. From my first reading of *Ulysses* I also learned a lot of interesting and surprising things about sex; certainly more than I would have derived from further reading of novels by Henry James. (I have revised and rearranged the words of that sentence thirteen times.)

In the Easter vacation of 1955, a couple of months before Finals, I took part in an event called Student Cross. This pilgrimage (which is still performed annually on a larger scale, along several different routes) consisted of a group of Catholic students from various colleges walking in Holy Week from St Etheldreda's church in London to the Marian shrine of Walsingham in Norfolk, a distance of about 120 miles, carrying a large wooden cross. It was described as a penitential act of reparation for the sins of students everywhere – a tall order, one might say – and a demonstration of Christian faith. We set out on the Saturday before Palm Sunday, and to get to Walsingham by Good Friday, where the last mile was customarily walked barefoot, we would have to average about twenty miles a day. There were a couple of dozen of us, all male, and a Dominican friar who was chaplain. I sent the principal character of my first novel, *The Picturegoers* (1960), on this pilgrimage, and the diary Mark Underwood keeps is probably a more accurate account of it than anything I could summon up from my ageing memory now. These are some extracts from his record of the first day:

First there was Mass in the crypt, with the Cross standing before the altar. A plain wooden cross, about twelve feet tall, and six feet from arm to arm. It weighs, I believe, about 120 pounds. It is grubby from the sweat and dirt of several pilgrimages. We walk in a column, in lines of three. The Cross leads, carried horizontally on the shoulders of three students, one to each arm, and the other at the foot. You carry it for the duration of the Rosary (about ten minutes) recited by the trio immediately behind. Then they move up to take the Cross, and you drop back to the end of the file. The body of the column sing hymns now and again, led by the Dominican chaplain Fr Courtney. Otherwise we talk quite freely . . . On the whole I enjoyed the day. It has certainly been a curious experience to flaunt one's religion in the face of London . . . The reaction of spectators was less marked than I had expected. Plenty of curious stares of course, but quite as many people would look hastily away, more embarrassed than we were.

Soon, however, Mark is sorely afflicted with suppurating blisters on his feet, which make walking agonisingly painful and do not respond to treatment. On the third day he gives up and returns ignominiously home by train from Cambridge. Exactly the same thing happened to me, and not surprisingly. I was slight of stature and, having given up playing football, not particularly fit. My walking experience consisted of a few easy rambles with the youth club. I had never done a hike of twenty miles in my life, let alone a series of them, carrying a rucksack with clothing, etc. on my back, plus an additional 40 pounds of wood at regular intervals. But I might have struggled on if it hadn't been for my soft and vulnerable feet, unprotected by proper walking boots and socks.

Why did I do it? There was a mixture of motives. I did not want to spend the entire Easter vacation at home revising for Finals, with a risk of becoming stale and jaded. On the other hand, I would not have felt easy about taking a purely recreational break, and Mary would not have been willing to join me. It so happened that the first overnight stop of Student Cross was in her home town, Hoddesdon, and that was how I first heard of it. The pilgrims slept in the parish hall there, and she told me how in past years she and her sisters provided an evening meal for them. I rather fancied the idea of impressing her and the rest of the Jacob family by appearing there as a pilgrim. This pilgrimage was an ostentatious example of what theologians call supererogation, the performance of religious acts in excess of what is required for salvation, and I nourished a secret hope, barely acknowledged even to myself, that if I did it the God of Roman Catholics would look kindly on me when I took my final examinations. It seemed to offer an ideal combination of healthy exercise, relief from studying, enhanced esteem, and supernatural grace. I just miscalculated the physical stamina it would require.

But I did not feel too bad about my failure: after all, God would know that I had tried.

In late May or early June we took our final examinations in a huge hall in South Kensington, on which candidates from all the constituent colleges of the University of London converged. It was not a convenient venue for someone living in south-east London, but as the appointed day for the first exam drew near, the problem of getting there in time for a morning session starting at 9.30 suddenly became critical, when service on the Southern Railway was halted by a strike. The railway was my only fast and reliable means of transport to central London – travelling by bus from Brockley in the rush hour could take for ever. What to do? Fortunately Mary's sister Eileen had a friend and colleague at the school where she taught, Bill Carlos, who had a flat in Highbury with a spare couch where he kindly offered to put me up for the duration of the exams. I gratefully accepted, travelling to and from South Kensington by Tube, which was running normally. So far from disturbing me, this sudden change of routine had a positive effect: my confidence was boosted by circumventing the effects of the strike, and the company of Mary, Eileen and Bill in the evenings removed the temptation to solitary brooding at home on my performance in the day's exams. Mary and I agreed to avoid inquests on the papers we had taken, and exchanged the minimum of information with fellow students as we poured out of the examination hall at the end of the three-hour sessions.

There was widespread dismay about the passage set for paraphrase in the compulsory section of the Shakespeare paper. It was taken from *Cymbeline,* one of Shakespeare's late plays sometimes called tragicomedies, a tortuously complicated story about the eponymous

Ancient British king, which so outraged Dr Johnson that he refused 'to waste criticism upon unresisting imbecility, upon faults too evident for detection, and too gross for aggravation'. The play is not quite as bad as that – it is very rewarding if you are prepared to go with the flow of its romance structure – but its language is often challenging. The passage sadistically chosen by the examiners was the long speech of the disguised Posthumus in Act V describing the battle in which Bellarius and his two sons (actually Cymbeline's lost offspring) rallied the fleeing Britons and defeated the Roman invaders. It is one of the knottiest pieces of bravura rhetoric in the whole of Shakespeare. Of our five set plays, this one had been given least attention in lectures, and some students had skimped their revision of it, so were unprepared to cope with lines like:

> Our Britain's harts die flying, not her men.
> To darkness fleet souls that fly backwards. Stand,
> Or we are Romans, and will give you that
> Like beasts which you shun beastly, and may save
> But to look back in frown.

At this distance in time I need the help of an annotated edition and the *OED* Online to construe the speech,[1] but as an examinee in 1955 I was fairly confident I had got it right.

---

1 The lines quoted mean something like: 'British deer die when running away, not British men. Souls that fly backwards vanish into darkness. Make a stand against the enemy, or we will act as the Romans have done, and like wild beasts give you the treatment you shrink from like cattle, a fate which you could avoid if you would only look back at the enemy with grim resolution.'

There is nothing quite comparable to the relief that follows the last Finals exam, like the lifting of a weight that one has been carrying for a very long time. Did we celebrate? I suppose we must have, but not in the usual bibulous fashion. Mary let her hair down literally not metaphorically: she released her ponytail from its fastening, had her hair cut and shaped, and bought herself a new summer dress. She never wore the ponytail again. I borrowed Kingsley Amis's *Lucky Jim* from Deptford library (the first paperback edition did not appear until 1959, and the hardback would have been an unthinkable extravagance) and read it thirstily, a treat I had been saving up for more than a year since it was published. I knew from reviews and word of mouth that I would love it, and I did. It articulated perfectly, and hilariously, the suppressed rebellious feelings of many first-generation university students in the post-war period towards the social and cultural norms of what would soon become known as 'the Establishment'. (The term was put into currency in September 1955 by Henry Fairlie in an article in *The Spectator*.) In its way, *Lucky Jim* was to be as important an influence on my own writing as *Ulysses*, though antithetical in artistic aims and literary form, a paradox I would recognise and wrestle with later.

We had a couple of months to wait for our results. Not long after that I would be called up into the Army – I had passed my medical – and Mary would begin earning her living. Like me, she'd had enough of studying for the time being, and had not considered doing a postgraduate course. She applied for a job as a teacher at a convent school and for a place on a graduate management training scheme with Marks & Spencer. She was offered both, and chose Marks & Spencer as more challenging. While we waited for these significant new chapters of our lives to begin, we felt we owed ourselves a holiday, preferably abroad. I noticed a small ad in the *Evening Standard* which ran something like: 'A group of students driving to the Costa Brava in a Bedford van in late July/ early August are looking for two more passengers to contribute to the cost of petrol.' I phoned the number that was given and Mary and I met the organiser of the trip, Ron, and his big, blonde girlfriend who I think was called Lynn. They seemed much older than Mary and me, more like mature students, and I never did quite grasp what or where they were studying. But they seemed pleasant enough and maturity was a desirable attribute to lead such an expedition, so we decided to join it. The Bedford van was a model later converted to make a camper or mobile home called a Dormobile, but ours was more like what is now called a people carrier, with windows on each side and bench seats on which the passengers sat facing each other. The party that finally assembled for departure numbered nine or ten, mostly female. There was another vehicle, a saloon car driven by a fat man who also looked like a mature student, if indeed he was a student at all. Perhaps he was a medical student, because the passengers in his car were two nurses.

I had never been to France before and still remember the shock of the hole-in-the-floor lavatory at the café where we first stopped for refreshment after crossing the Channel. Our route took us down through France to Perpignan and then into Spain at the foot of the Pyrenees. There were no autoroutes, progress was slow, the weather was warm and the Bedford became increasingly uncomfortable the further south we travelled. Leaving the sliding door open was our form of air conditioning, dangerous for Lynn in the front seat because the vehicle had no seat belts. But the tedium and the discomfort all seemed worthwhile when we reached the Costa Brava. The first place we stopped at was Cadaqués and I remember strolling along the seafront there, past brightly illuminated food stalls and cafés and bodegas and barber shops, relishing the wonderful velvety warmth of a Mediterranean evening for the first time, that warmth which continues after the sun has set and darkness falls, unlike the damp chill that nearly always overtakes summer evenings in Britain.

We drove along the beautiful coastline in easy stages, stopping at different places for two or three days. The Costa Brava was completely unspoiled by commercial development in 1955, and picturesque little seaside resorts like Tossa de Mar and Lloret de Mar, soon to be swamped by package tourists from Britain and disfigured by high-rise hotels, were frequented mainly by Spanish families and retained their pristine charm. The beaches were inviting, the sea was blue, the food and drink and simple accom- modation were astonishingly cheap and the sun shone unfailingly day after day. There were tensions within our party that made the holiday less than totally euphoric, partly due to the gender imbal- ance. Ray and Lynn were obviously sexual partners, though I can't remember whether they shared the same room. Mary and I were the only other couple, and of course did not. The fat driver of the saloon car tried to get off with each of his passengers in turn and was rebuffed by both nurses, who said he was horrible. There was another young man travelling with us in the Bedford who was pleasant enough, but he didn't seem to be interested in girls, and the female members of the party had little opportunity to find other male company as we were constantly on the move.

Our last destination was Barcelona. Spain was ruled by Franco at this time, and the atmosphere of the city was repressed and gloomy, very different from the vibrant, elegant, hedonistic place it is today. Apart from the Ramblas with its colourful flower market, the streets seemed drab and dusty, the expressions of people on the pavements serious or sullen, and I was struck by the number of women who wore all-enveloping black clothes in the summer heat. Armed soldiers patrolled the streets and squares, watched warily by beggars and vendors of American cigarettes. But the cheerful young woman who ran the cheap *pension* where we stayed spoke some English and was friendly and helpful. Her first name was Montserrat, a metonym for Mary, being the name of a mountain about thirty miles from Barcelona where there is a Benedictine abbey that houses the Black Virgin, a statue of great antiquity venerated throughout Catalonia. Mary and I took a bus to the spectacular site of this shrine, perched on a bare mountain top, and paid our respects to the Black Virgin in the abbey church. Montserrat has long been a popular place of pilgrimage, and the abbey has accommodation for visitors. According to a brochure I picked up in the church, many Catalonian newly-weds spent their honeymoons there. I remember thinking it would be an inhibiting venue for what I imagined honeymoons were about.

When we set off on the return trip Mary and I were well aware that our Finals results would have been published by now, and letters conveying them to us would be waiting at our respective homes; but we did not think of phoning our parents to enquire. Aside from the difficulty and cost of making international calls in those days, we preferred to remain in suspense rather than risk getting disappointing news on the road. In fact the road nearly prevented us from getting news of any kind. On our way through the foothills of the Pyrenees, Ron, who was our only driver, pulled into a lay-by for a break. After we had stretched our legs and admired the panorama for a while, we boarded the van and set off again. Ron pulled out into the road and proceeded up the gradient – on the left-hand side. It is easily done when you emerge from an exit that has no central dividing line, and none of us immediately noticed. A minute later a car came round the sharp bend ahead of us, travelling fast on the same side of the road. Ron wrenched at the wheel of the Bedford just in time to avoid collision and the Spanish car passed us with an outraged blast of the horn. We had narrowly escaped a very serious accident, and all felt very shaky for the rest of the day.

I don't have any memory of the rest of the return journey through France, which I imagine was even more tedious than the one out, but once we got off the ferry at Dover, the idea of home and the letter waiting for me there began to exert a kind of magnetic attraction. Millmark Grove is less than a mile from the old Dover road, so Ron was happy to drop off Mary and me at number 81. I phoned ahead from a callbox to tell Mum we were on our way, and to ask if I could invite the others in for some refreshments. It was getting dark by the time we arrived. The group squeezed into our lounge, and Mum served up tea and sandwiches, which were much appreciated. (Dad, as usual in the evening, was at work.) I slipped into the dining room, found the envelope I expected propped up on the mantelpiece, opened it and read it. I had got a First. I went back into the lounge, told the others, and received their congratulations; but it was only after they had all gone, apart from Mary, that I began to realise how pleased I was.

Mary phoned home to tell her parents that she was back in the country, safe and sound, but did not want them opening her mail. The next morning we went to the college, where she read on a noticeboard that she had got an Upper Second. She would have been bitterly disappointed by anything less, but in those days an Upper Second was a real distinction, as the university-wide list comprehensively demonstrated. It also revealed an astonishing dominance by the forty candidates from University College. A hundred and forty-two internal students at various colleges in the University of London had sat their final examinations for the BA Honours degree in English that year. Only six First-class degrees were awarded (just over four per cent of the total) and five of them were to students at UC. We also accounted for fifteen of the thirty-three Upper Seconds (which were just over twenty-three per cent of the total). These figures were impressive evidence of our collective ability, and are also an index of the grade inflation that has occurred since then. As previously noted, our friend Derek Todd had got a First, but Tony Petti, who had worked himself almost into a nervous breakdown in the run-up to Finals, had to be content with a 2.1, which was, however, good enough to earn him a postgraduate scholarship. Mary's 2.1 would certainly have been a very good one too, but we received no details, officially or unofficially, about how we had performed in our final examinations. In due course I was informed that I had won the Morley Prize, which gave me a clue. Founded in honour of Henry Morley, Professor of English Literature at UCL from 1865 to 1869, it was awarded to the 'best third year student of English Literature' and took the form of a handsome bronze medal with the bearded professor in relief, and £5 in cash 'to be spent on books'. I invested it all in the *Shorter Oxford English Dictionary*, a condensed version of the multi-volume *OED* in a single enormous book of 2,500 pages that cost five guineas. I made up the five-shilling balance and this magnificent reference book served me well for many years.

Students who obtained First-class degrees were automatically offered postgraduate scholarships by the University, so I was given a second chance to consider this option. I decided to accept but to postpone the scholarship for two years while I did my National Service, reasoning that I had nothing to lose by doing so, and might change my mind about not pursuing an academic career. It was a very wise decision. A few weeks of Basic Training was enough to convince me of the desirability of an occupation in which one was paid for reading and thinking and talking about books, while writing some of one's own.

13

My career as a soldier is easily summarised. On receiving my conscription papers I had expressed a preference (as one was invited to do) for the Education Corps, but I was assigned to the Royal Armoured Corps, which is composed of mechanised cavalry regiments of various historic origins and numbered battalions of the Royal Tank Regiment formed in the First World War. I received my Basic Training with the 7th Royal Tank Regiment at Catterick Camp, a huge garrison spread over the moors near Richmond in Yorkshire. Because of my education I was classified as a 'Potential Officer', but I withdrew from this category before the end of basic training. After trade training as a clerk I was assigned to the Royal Tank Regiment and posted to Bovington Camp in Dorset. This was (and still is) the Royal Armoured Corps centre for training in driving and maintenance of armoured vehicles, staffed by a motley collection of soldiers belonging to various regiments in the RAC and the Royal Electrical and Mechanical Engineers. I worked in Bovington as a clerk, rising eventually to the rank of corporal, until I was released in August 1957.

A more detailed account of what my military service was like can be gathered from my novel *Ginger, You're Barmy,* published in 1962. The story that links the narrator, Jonathan Browne, his rebellious fellow conscript, the ginger-haired Mike Brady, and Pauline, the young woman with whom they are both involved, is entirely fictional; but Jonathan's service in the Army follows the pattern of mine closely, and almost every detail of setting and daily life in the novel, many small illustrative incidents, and numerous lines of dialogue, were recalled from memory, beginning with Jonathan's account of waiting to have a medical examination on his very first day:

We sat round the walls of a warm, stuffy room which smelled of perspiration, wearing only jackets and trousers, waiting to be called in to the Medical Officer. Three soldiers in denims were making some adjustments to the lights. We sat, quiet and depressed, hoping perhaps that the medical might result in a last-minute reprieve, while the three soldiers conducted at the tops of their voices, as if oblivious of our presence, the most obscene conversation I had ever heard in my life. It might almost have been laid on as an introduction course in Army language. It was obscene not only in its liberal and ingenious use of the standard expletive that lingers like a persistent echo throughout any conversation in the Army, but also in its use of words whose obscenity, at that stage, I could only guess at, and in its content: sexual encounters experienced at the last weekend, or anticipated at the next . . .

It may be hard for younger readers to believe now, when various forms and applications of the word 'fuck' occur frequently in the casual speech of all classes and are commonplace in dialogue on the stage, in films and in television drama, but up to that time, in my not especially sheltered life, I had very rarely heard, or overheard, the word spoken, so I was as shocked by its frequency in this conversation as by the sexual references. Needless to say, I had never uttered the word myself, and during my service I did not acquire the habit of doing so – one of several ways in which I resisted assimilation to the military subculture.

Basic training, which occupies a substantial portion of the novel, is a stereotyped rite of passage which does not vary much between different military services and countries. Its object is to turn a random collection of raw recruits into an obedient body of soldiers by conditioning: cutting their hair brutally short, clothing them in coarse, ill-fitting uniforms or fatigues, shouting at them, sneering at them, swearing at them, drilling them, marching them, depriving them of sleep by setting absurd but exhausting tasks that last long into the night, like scrubbing khaki webbing clean until it is white and then coating it in khaki blanco again, ironing and pressing clothing into precisely measured squares and rectangles for kit layouts, and polishing the toecaps of boots made of leather never intended to shine into a gleaming glassy carapace (activities collectively referred to in army slang as 'bull', a contraction of 'bullshit').

All this is faithfully described in *Ginger, You're Barmy*, but there was one episode in my experience which does not figure in the novel because it was untypical, indeed possibly unique. The effectiveness of basic training partly depends upon the recruit being deprived of liberty for the duration of the course. We were not allowed to leave Catterick camp until after our 'passing out' parade, when there would be a 72-hour leave which we looked forward to with inexpressible longing, and the threat of being denied it by some major failure or misdemeanour and being 'backsquadded' (made to do basic training again from the beginning) was the Army's most powerful sanction for instilling obedience. But due to an ironic coincidence, I was given the unusual privilege of a weekend leave during the course.

In our first year at UCL Mary and I became acquainted with a plump, vivacious young woman a few years older than us called Avril Doyle-Davidson, who had returned to the college after a year's absence for health reasons to complete a general arts degree. One of her subjects was English, and her father, she informed us, was a senior lecturer in Medieval English Literature at Leeds University. She was a Catholic and a member of the Catholic Society. Mary's brother Brian, who was still looking for a job, turned up at a Cath Soc hop one evening and spent most of it dancing and flirting with Avril. Whatever sequel there was to that meeting did not last long because he had decided to rejoin the Royal Signals as a regular officer, and in due course he was sent abroad. A couple of years later he returned to England, renewed contact with Avril, wooed her and won her. A wedding was arranged to take place in Leeds on a Saturday morning in September 1955, in the middle of my basic training. Mary was to be a bridesmaid, and had put my name on the guest list. Having nothing to lose, I submitted my impressively printed invitation with an application for leave to attend the wedding and, to my surprise, it was granted – only because it was a military wedding, I'm sure, and because Brian was at that time serving with the Royal Signals in Catterick. But that he knew or approved of my being invited, I doubt.

I was given leave from Friday evening to Sunday morning. It felt great to escape the prison-like atmosphere of basic training, but the weekend was a bitter-sweet taste of freedom, and physically exhausting. Although Leeds and Richmond are both in Yorkshire, travelling between them through the night by train entailed two changes, at Darlington and York, with long hours spent on hard benches in station waiting rooms. I arrived in Leeds at about six in the morning, tired and dishevelled, and was delighted to find that the station had a facility where you could have a bath for the price of a shilling. I was its first customer, and luxuriated in a deep hot tub before getting myself some breakfast and going in search of Mary. She had had a similarly gruelling overnight journey from London, being driven in a van by her cousin Brendan, which in those pre-motorway days took eight hours or more. This arrangement was made partly for the sake of economy, and partly because she had been at work on Friday at a branch of Marks & Spencer in north London, where she was learning about the retail trade by serving behind the counter. I found her with her sister Eileen at the hotel where the Jacob family were staying, trying on their full-length bridesmaids' dresses, made of a brick-red taffeta about which they had not been consulted and which did not become either of them. I was wearing the starkly plain khaki battledress of a new recruit not yet assigned to a regiment, with no cap badge or other insignia except for a small white felt triangle on the upper arm, reminiscent, it seemed to me, of the pink and yellow triangles homosexuals and Jews were compelled to wear by the Nazis. Nothing could have been less appropriate as a wedding garment. It was a full military wedding, attended by many of Brian's fellow officers, resplendent in their dark blue dress uniforms, who formed a guard of honour for the bridal couple as they emerged from the Catholic cathedral under a glittering arch of drawn swords. I spent most of the occasion hiding behind pillars and skulking in corners to avoid eye contact with these men, not being sure if I was supposed to salute them, and I had the impression that they thought my presence was in bad taste and were doing their best to pretend that I didn't exist. When the reception, held at the University, was over Mary and I had some hours alone together, and walked aimlessly about the centre of Leeds. There was nowhere to go where we could sit down except a cinema, in which we spent a few hours watching an unmemorable film before it was time for me to go sadly back to camp, and her to London. The ultimate effect of my brief escape from Catterick was to reinforce my depression at being trapped in the Army.

The fact that I was two or three years older and better educated than the average conscript helped me deal mentally with the shock treatment of basic training, but it also made me all the more dismayed by the prospect of the two years stretching ahead, in which I could see little hope of enjoying and developing the intellectual and cultural interests I had acquired at university – certainly not in the Royal Armoured Corps. At the interview with the personnel officer we all had in our first week I asked if I could apply for a transfer to the Education Corps where I thought my qualifications might be of some use, but he brusquely informed me that it was impossible because of a rule that a soldier could not transfer from a corps that was 'senior in the line' to one beneath it. I learned that, as a potential officer, I would take part after basic training in a series of trials and courses, of increasing duration and rigour – 'Uzbee' (Unit Selection Board), 'Wozbee' (War Office Selection Board) and the Mons Officer Training School – to determine whether I possessed the attributes required of an officer. If I was successful, I would obtain a commission, though probably not in the RAC, since the senior-in-the-line rule did not apparently apply to officers. As an officer I would enjoy a more comfortable lifestyle and escape the coarse society of the barrack room. But the more I learned about the selection process, which sounded like an inordinately long and more exacting version of basic training, though much worse in being competitive and infused with a public-school OTC ethos completely alien to me, the more convinced I became that I would fall, probably at the first hurdle and certainly at the second, for lack of both aptitude and enthusiasm. I was used to doing well in examinations. Rather than allow the military hier-archy to reject me, I decided to resign the status of potential officer.

I was fortunate in finding a kindred spirit in my intake, called Clive Rees, who had just come down from Cambridge with a BA in English, and shared my disaffection with the Army as well as an interest in literature and the arts. I showed him some of my stories and he talked about his ambition to work in films. Clive was my best friend during basic training, though we didn't have much else in common. He was older, had led a more dissipated life as a student than I, and had an exotic family background which, he told me, included an American great-grandmother who had been raped by a Native Indian. In conse-quence he had some indigenous American blood in him, a claim that was supported by his complexion and features. When I told him I had decided to withdraw from being a potential officer he said he would do the same. Then to my surprise I discovered that a contem-porary of mine in the English Department at UCL had joined the 7th RTR, in the intake behind ours. Chris Woods-McConville had been an amiable but notoriously idle student who spent a great deal of time in the Union bar and failed to get an honours degree. This did not prevent him being classified as a potential officer, but after conversations with Clive and me he decided to withdraw from the cadre too. When we conveyed our wishes to the callow second lieutenant nominally in charge of our squad he took no action, hoping perhaps that we would change our minds. In due course we were paraded to appear before the 2IC (second in command) of the Regiment along with the other POs for a routine interview designed to wish us good luck with the Unit Selection Board, and had to explain to him, one by one, that we didn't want to become officers. I was quite glad that I went first since apparently he became increasingly annoyed by this display of disrespect for the honour of a commission. After the interviews we were escorted by the grim-visaged personnel officer to another building where he typed out what was called a 'Non-desirous' statement, which we had to sign. Evidently it was not a common enough event to merit a printed form.

Though I felt quietly proud of inspiring this little rebellion, the alternative careers open to us in the RAC were limited. The 'trades' of 'Other Ranks' in the Royal Tank Regiment were signaller/gunner, gunner/driver, driver and clerk. Our squad had been allowed to get inside a tank one afternoon to discover what it was like, namely claustrophobic and uncomfortable, and I had no desire to repeat the experience even once. I opted for clerk, as did Clive. Chris I think chose driver. The one component of the clerk's training that might have been useful to me was learning to touch-type properly, but there was so little time devoted to it (the whole course was only four weeks long) that we struggled to reach the very modest word-per-minute rate required, and rather than risk failing the final test I reverted to my own two-finger method, and continued to use it for the rest of my army service, and indeed my life. The rest of the course consisted of copying from a blackboard a few simple facts about army procedure which a bright schoolboy could have mastered in a morning, while the instructors, a couple of cynical and depraved-looking corporals, questioned us about our sexual experience or lack of it, and punished insolent responses by standing the culprit against a door and hurling tennis balls at him.

When the course was concluded we had a 48-hour leave, though a good many of those hours were spent on trains and the euphoria of escape from camp was soon clouded by the imminence of returning to it. We were then assigned to 'general duties', which meant menial tasks like shovelling coal, peeling potatoes in the cookhouse and doing the occasional guard, while we waited to be assigned and posted to a regiment in the RAC. Guard was the most irksome of these duties: first the parade and inspection, for which your kit had to be in immaculate order on penalty of a charge if it wasn't; then the boredom and debilitating rhythm of the guard itself, recalled by the middle-aged hero of a later novel of mine, *Therapy*:

Two hours on, four hours off, all through the night, and all through the day too, if it was a weekend . . . snatching sleep lying on a bunk fully dressed in ankle-bruising boots and neck-chafing battledress under the glare of a naked electric light bulb, and then being roughly woken to gulp down sweetened lukewarm tea, and maybe some cold congealed eggs and baked beans, before stumbling out yawning and shivering into the night, to loiter for two hours by the barrack gates, or circle the silent shuttered huts and stores, listening to your own footsteps, watching your own shadow lengthen and shorten under the arc-lamps.

*

The few letters I wrote to Mary in this period that have survived seem to me now embarrassingly sententious. For instance:

> So many people have sad frustrated lives because of failure or difficulty on the plane of personal relationships, that we should be very, very grateful for the key to happiness that has been thrust into our hands. Let us clutch it together, my darling and never let go. The years stretch ahead, clouded with uncertainty, doubt and arduous challenge; but only one certainty – the certainty of our love, makes the way clear and straight, even if just as difficult.

Evidently I was feeling deeply apprehensive about the likelihood of long separations from Mary over the next two years if, as was likely, I was posted abroad, probably to Germany, and I was seeking to bind us together in mutual fidelity by this high-minded rhetoric. Paradoxically, when given an opportunity to express a preference to the officer in charge of postings, I asked for the Far East, which would mean no home leave at all as long as one's regiment was based there. My motive was to try and wring something positive out of military service by broadening my experience, seeing something of the big wide world at the Army's expense. But what about Mary? I suppose I reasoned that if we couldn't be together all the time perhaps it would be better not to be together at all, relying on the special nature of our relationship to endure, rather than live from one infrequent leave to another on an emotional see-saw of meeting and parting. After all, it would make no difference to the postponement of our physical union, and might even make it easier to bear. The tales of opportunities for dissipation in the fleshpots of the Orient that circulated in the camp, brought back by soldiers who had served out there, may have influenced this decision. Perhaps at the very back of my mind, scarcely acknowledged, was a Graham Greeneish fantasy that I might lose my virginity in a Hong Kong brothel, and be quickly shriven by a regimental chaplain, without real disloyalty to Mary. I decided not to tell her about my request unless and until it was granted. I was uncertain how she would react, and was relieved rather than disappointed when I was told that there were no vacancies for a clerk in the Far East.

Fate dealt me a very different posting. The sergeant in charge of the clerks' training course had been impressed by my performance in the final examinations, and took a benevolent interest in me during the tedious weeks that followed. He had me attached to the regimental orderly room doing clerical work, which was infinitely preferable to the fatigues I had been doing. (I took the opportunity to sneak a look at my own file and read the personnel officer's report on my first interview: 'Educated up to university level. Thinks too much of himself.') One day the Sergeant called me into his office and told me that an old friend who was chief clerk at the RAC Driving and Maintenance School at Bovington needed a new clerk and had asked my sergeant to send him a good one. He proposed to nominate me. I asked him where Bovington was, and he said it was in Dorset, about a hundred miles from London. A hundred miles was a comfortable distance for 48-hour leaves, and feasible for a 36. I accepted the offer gratefully. I was assigned to the Royal Tank Regiment and henceforward wore its black webbing, its cap badge with the rhomboid image of a First World War tank, and brown, red and green shoulder flashes, an iconic allusion to the regimental motto: '*Through mud and blood to green fields beyond*', which Jonathan Browne in *Ginger* mentally rewrites for the National Serviceman as: '*Through boredom and discontent to blessed civvy street beyond.*' At Bovington, however, I found ways to mitigate the boredom and discontent.

Bovington Camp is situated on the heathland between Wareham and Dorchester, in the heart of Thomas Hardy's Wessex. The depiction of Egdon Heath in *The Return of the Native* and *The Mayor of Casterbridge* was partly inspired by Bovington Heath. I was not then as familiar with Hardy's fiction as I became later, when I published several essays about his novels, so I did not immediately register the connection, and the irony that Hardy's wild and almost primeval landscape was now scarred by tank tracks, and its silence broken daily by the roar of 1,000-horsepower diesel engines. The place had another literary association which at the time meant even less to me. T.E. Lawrence had occupied an isolated cottage called Clouds Hill a mile or so from Bovington Camp, and died in an accident when speeding along the road to it on his Brough Superior motorcycle in 1935. Clouds Hill was donated to the National Trust after Lawrence's death, but I had not read *The Seven Pillars of Wisdom* and the little I knew about Lawrence of Arabia did not draw me to visit this shrine to him until quite late in my service at Bovington, when I found it closed and could only walk round the outside. An NCO had aroused my curiosity by telling me that Lawrence had been billeted in Bovington as a soldier. I thought this must be an apocryphal version of his service in the RAF after the First World War, which I vaguely knew about, and it was not until long afterwards that I discovered the story was quite true.

Lawrence joined the Air Force under the alias of Aircraftman Ross in 1922, allegedly (there is much dispute about his motivation) to write and save his soul, undistracted by the celebrity he had acquired from his exploits in Arabia. He was compelled to leave in the following year when his cover was blown by the press, and enlisted in what was then called the Tank Corps, as Trooper Shaw, at Bovington Camp. According to his letters to various friends at this time, he was miserable there. In one of them he wrote, 'The Army is unspeakable; more solidly animal than I believed Englishmen could be. I hate them, and the life here.' He added: 'and am sure it is good medicine for me', but there was a limit to how much of it he could take. As a refuge from barrack-room life he rented the Clouds Hill cottage where, in his spare time, he read books, listened to music and worked on the second draft of *The Seven Pillars of Wisdom*. Although in due course he obtained what he described as a 'cushy' job assisting the quartermaster, Lawrence was still so unhappy after two years at Bovington that in letters to some influential friends he dropped hints of suicidal intentions, which eventually reached the Prime Minister himself, Bonar Law, securing his release from the Tanks and permission to rejoin the RAF. He purchased Clouds Hill and continued to use it as his main residence until he died. It is a fascinating story, and in one or two respects I unknowingly re-enacted it at Bovington.

Coming from the austerities of the Catterick camp, where we occupied stone-floored Nissen huts heated by a single stove, I was delighted with the superior amenities of Bovington, and wrote jubilantly to Mary shortly after my arrival:

After Catterick it is Paradise. The billets, though not affording as much privacy as I hoped for, are comfortable and centrally heated. The washroom is in the same building and there is always hot water. The canteen, NAAFI and library are within a stone's throw of the billet. The cinema and church are 10 mins walk away. The food is good . . . I have got a good job in a very pleasant office . . . I should be able to work down here pretty well. There is a Quiet Room in the NAAFI, and I have made friends with the 'Librarian' and I think he will let me work there after hours. So you see, my darling I am really very lucky in my posting. The fare home is a bit more than I expected – 16 or 18 shillings. However I shall make renewed efforts to get published. I hope to be home on a 36 next weekend . . .

And there, essentially, in that letter to Mary, I mapped out my future as a conscripted soldier.

The Army had, in effect, made me an embryonic Angry Young Man, though the phrase did not come into general currency until the following year, 1956, when the press agent of the Royal Court Theatre applied it to the author of a new play called *Look Back in Anger,* and the media found it a convenient label for a whole new generation of English writers who in their different ways took a critical and satirical view of the state of post-war British society. John Osborne, Kingsley Amis, John Wain, John Braine, Arnold Wesker, Alan Sillitoe and Colin Wilson were some of the key figures. There was no common ideology uniting them. Although some were sympathetic to socialism, they were rebels rather than revolutionaries, and several of them moved to the right as they grew older. They expressed the frustration and resentment of the lower-middle- and working-class younger generation that the levelling effects of the war and the landslide victory of the Labour Party in 1945 had not fundamentally altered the distribution of power and influence in English society. There was still a self-serving Establishment which controlled opportunities and rewards, as the grammar school beneficiaries of the 1944 Education Act discovered when they left university with their good degrees in their pockets. Of all public institutions, the peacetime Army, with its rigid hierarchy of officers, NCOs and men, and its fetishistic devotion to precedence, insignia and traditions, epitomised this resistance to change very clearly. Jonathan Browne's view of his situation was very much my own: 'I dimly perceived that I had been wrenched out of a meritocracy, for success in which I was well qualified, and thrust into a small archaic world of privilege, for success in which I was singularly ill-endowed.' A year later, on one of my weekend leaves, Mary and I saw the famous first production of *Look Back in Anger* at the Royal Court Theatre, and I doubt if any member of the enthusiastic audience delighted as intensely as I in Jimmy Porter's withering denunciations of the English Establishment – especially as represented by his wife's ex-officer brother, Nigel.

'Have you ever seen her brother? Brother Nigel? The straight-backed, chinless wonder from Sandhurst? . . . Well, you've never heard so many well-bred commonplaces come from beneath the same bowler hat. The Platitude from Outer Space – that's brother Nigel. He'll end up in the Cabinet one day – make no mistake. But somewhere at the back of that mind is the vague knowledge that he and his pals have been plundering and fooling everybody for generations.'

National Service had requisitioned two years of my life – two of the most interesting and exploratory years of any man's life – and turned it into what at Catterick felt like a prison sentence for a crime I hadn't committed, filled in prospect with repetitious, unfulfilling duties in mostly uncongenial company, the only thing to look forward to being its eventual termination. But in the relaxed atmosphere of Bovington Camp, which had no regimental identity to maintain, and in its relative proximity to London, I sensed at once the possibility of turning my situation to positive account. I would spend all my spare time from Mondays to Fridays reading and writing, try to make some money from the latter, and spend as many weekends as possible with Mary in London. If I could manage that, I thought, National Service would not be a wholly futile and tedious interruption of the life I desired.

The job I mentioned in that first letter to Mary was that of release clerk. Men from RAC units stationed all over the world who were approaching their release date were often temporarily billeted at Bovington Camp, and my work involved briefing the soldiers and issuing them with the relevant documents. There was some irony in my being given this job when my own release was so distant; but the soldiers I dealt with were very pleased to see me, and I found the work congenial. Soon, however, I was given a new position, that of PRI clerk, assisting the officer designated as President of the Regimental Institutes (i.e. responsible for the welfare and recreational facilities of the camp). He was an amiable but barely competent middle-aged officer, always carrying a riding crop and accompanied by a pair of hunting dogs, who might have stepped from the pages of Evelyn Waugh's *Sword of Honour* trilogy, and had evidently been eased out of the cavalry regiment to which he belonged and put in a post where he could do least harm until he could be pensioned off. Captain Pirie (as I called him in *Ginger*) was also in charge of 'Admn Squadron', the administrative unit of the camp, so my new job entailed a move from the central orderly room to another building where I shared an office with a civilian clerk, a polite and friendly middle-aged man, and was subject to much less scrutiny than before. My work consisted mainly of keeping the PRI accounts (I learned double-entry bookkeeping from my civilian colleague), ordering various commodities from condoms to football boots for whose acquisition the PRI was responsible, and putting letters and cheques in front of Captain Pirie for him to sign. The workload was light and I was able to use the upright typewriter on my trestle-table desk for my own purposes.

Behind my back as I sat at the desk was a partitioned-off space, about six feet by twelve, known as a 'bunk'. There was one in every barrack room, where usually a lance corporal slept, acquiring a little privacy in acknowledgement of his rank, but not much peace, since until 'lights out' and for some time afterwards, the air would vibrate with noises: slamming doors, booted footsteps, shouts, groans, oaths, expletives, laughter, insults, smut. The air itself was usually pretty fetid too. I had mentioned to Mary in my first letter from Bovington that the lack of privacy was the only disappointing feature of my situation. In the empty bunk behind my desk I saw a possible solution, one which would greatly facilitate my projected programme of reading and writing. After some months, and when I had established myself as honest and reliable with the officers and NCOs who mattered, I asked if I could move my bed and kit into the bunk and sleep there, thus enhancing the security of the Admn Squadron building, which contained stores as well as offices. This was a specious argument because I had no intention of sleeping there at weekends, but amazingly my request was granted. There was a toilet with wash-basins just down the corridor from my office. I thus enjoyed the unusual privilege, as a trooper, of having self-contained accommodation all to myself, where I could read and write undisturbed every evening. The bunk was my Clouds Hill.

During my time at Bovington I produced two long prize-winning essays, a 20,000-word pamphlet about Catholic writers, a number of short stories, and more than half of the first draft of a novel. Both essay prizes were awarded by University College London, and named after nineteenth-century alumni: the John Oliver Hobbes Scholarship and the Quain essay prize. Both still exist, though their regulations and monetary value have changed. In my day they were open to recent graduates, and were on specified topics, which in 1955–56 happened to coincide with my own literary interests. The John Oliver Hobbes, which I won with an essay on 'The Satirical Novel', was worth £30 and the Quain, for which I submitted an essay on 'The Eccentric Character in English Fiction', was worth £50. There was not much publicity for these prizes and I gathered afterwards that I was the only candidate for the former and had only one competitor for the latter. For that I produced a substantial piece of work some 25,000 words long, spanning the history of the English novel from Fielding, Sterne and Smollett to Aldous Huxley, Ronald Firbank and Evelyn Waugh, not neglecting the influence of Cervantes.

The pamphlet *About Catholic Authors* was my first monograph, published by St Paul Publications, the same religious press that produced *The Question Box*, my sixth-form textbook, in a series called *Tell Me Father*, aimed at young adult Catholics. The concept was to convey information to such readers in the words of a priest responding to questions from them about a particular topic. I owed the commission to Malachy Carroll, with whom I was still in touch, and who had been asked by the Paulist fathers to suggest someone who would write on Catholic literature in this format for a flat fee of £45. The pamphlet was not published till 1958, but was written in the second year of my army service, and bears the 'Nihil Obstat' and 'Imprimatur' of the Catholic hierarchy, dated October 1957, guaranteeing freedom from heresy and incitement to immorality – the only one of my publications to be thus approved. It was a new venture and only two other titles were commissioned along with mine: *Tell Me Father About Living* and *Tell Me Father About Confession,* neither of which was available to me as a model, so I invented my own fictional frame: a bored National Serviceman asks the priest who had taught him at school to suggest some books by Catholic writers he should read, and the rest of the pamphlet consists of the priest's letters in response. I covered a huge amount of ground in its 64 pages: fiction, poetry, history, biography, even theology, from St Augustine and Chaucer to Graham Greene and Evelyn Waugh, and cited scores of books, some of which I had read about rather than read. I took the opportunity to plug Malachy Carroll's work, and had a diplomatic kind word for *The Question Box*. By this time I had informed the University of London, of my intention to take up its postgraduate scholarship in the academic year beginning September 1957, and the subject I wanted to study was the development of a distinctively Catholic contribution to English literature in the nineteenth and twentieth centuries, so researching and writing this pamphlet was useful preparation for that project. I have no memory of how I managed to get hold of the books I needed for all this writing; presumably I brought them back to camp from home and the Deptford public library on my frequent leaves.

The novel I started writing at Bovington was not about the Army, though it had a National Serviceman among its minor characters, and was not published until 1960, so I will discuss it later. Of the short stories I wrote in this period, the only ones I got published were of a rather pietistic type that found a home in Catholic family magazines published by religious orders who paid me a few pounds for them. But they helped towards the cost of travelling to and from London, where I spent nearly every weekend. I was entitled to a monthly 48-hour pass and on other weekends I was free to absent myself from midday Saturday to early Monday morning unless I was down to do guard duty. I travelled by coach since it was cheaper than the train and my pay at the beginning of my service was only £1 a week. Later I applied to take trade tests for two higher grades of clerk, studying the *Manual of Military Law* and other set texts on my own, passing with ease, and consequently adding first one stripe and then two to my uniform, and several pounds to my weekly pay.

*

There was a regular private coach service from the camp to London on Fridays and Saturdays which I used until I met a trooper with a wealthy father who had given him an Austin saloon in which he ferried three or four passengers back and forth to London for a reasonable fee. Either way, it meant arriving back at the camp in the early hours of Monday morning and making do with a few hours' sleep, but it was worth it. If it was a 36 weekend, I would go straight to the Marks & Spencer in Turnpike Lane where Mary and the other counter staff would be checking their stock to make sure it tallied with the week's sales, and wait outside the closed doors until she was released.

She was obliged to work on Saturdays, the busiest day of the week for shops, and when I had a 48-hour leave it was frustrating to have to spend most of that day on my own. So I was pleased for that reason, among others, when Mary decided after nearly a year in the M&S graduate training scheme that the retail business was not for her. Though she was being trained for personnel management, and M&S had a name for looking after its employees' health and welfare, it became evident to Mary that this was only in order to make them more efficient and thus generate more profit for the firm. She had no natural instinct or enthusiasm for business and decided to take up teaching instead, the profession of her mother and sister Eileen (and in due course of every other sibling, including Brian when he retired from the Army). In those days an honours degree was an accepted qualification for teaching in state schools, and Mary had no difficulty in finding a job in a comprehensive school, though she prudently enrolled in a part-time course leading to a Postgraduate Certificate of Education while she was in post.

Teaching was her true métier, but the year with Marks & Spencer was by no means wasted. It gave her invaluable knowledge of the world of work that most of her pupils would eventually enter, and also some eye-opening knowledge of the lives and preoccupations of working-class women.

In that respect it was a parallel experience to my army service, which showed me aspects of English society that I might not otherwise have been exposed to, and I was aware that this was useful to an aspiring novelist. My grudge was that it went on for so long, much longer than was necessary for what one learned from it – from a military point of view, as well as my own. A minority of National Servicemen had an interesting and fulfilling time. Some had a genuine enthusiasm for soldiering and exercised it in exotic places, while others found opportunities to employ their abilities usefully or acquire new ones. There was, for instance, a privileged cadre including several famous literary names, like Alan Bennett and Michael Frayn, who were selected to learn Russian in the Intelligence Corps, and spent most of their two years at Cambridge in agreeable anticipation or continuation of their undergraduate lives. But for the vast majority it was predominantly two years of servitude and boredom. The periods of training we received were ridiculously brief in duration: my basic training was only five weeks long, and a couple of sessions on the shooting range were the only occasions when I fired a gun throughout my service. The process of making us into soldiers could have been accomplished much more efficiently in six months of intensive training, and the only reason for keeping us in uniform for two years was to have a cheap standing army. The rhythm of life encouraged idleness and apathy, what was called 'skiving', and this had a demoralising effect on regular soldiers as well as the conscripts. From what I observe of the fully professional British Army today, mainly from television reporting and documentaries, it is a much more efficient and effective force than it was then – and less class-conscious.

There were two, almost simultaneous, political events in the autumn of 1956 which put my situation temporarily in a new perspective: the popular revolt against the Soviet-backed Communist regime in Hungary, which began on 23rd October and was crushed by Russian tanks by 7th November; and the Suez crisis, which lasted from late October to late November, when Britain joined with France, in secret collusion with Israel, to try to wrest back control of the Suez Canal after the Egyptian President Nasser had nationalised it. A joint Anglo-French military operation was mounted, involving bombing, paratroops and a seaborne invasion of Egypt. Suddenly, being a soldier in the British Army seemed a real and serious matter, even in the sleepy backwater of Bovington, as men on training courses and some members of the permanent staff were recalled to their regiments. Since I did not belong to any particular battalion of the RTR I was in little danger of being caught up in the action, and in any case it was all over very quickly, as Britain and France withdrew from Egypt under pressure from the United Nations. This misconceived and mismanaged adventure was a political disaster, the true scale of which would take some time to become apparent, but it dismayed many British people while it was happening, for reasons eloquently expressed by the Liberal politician Lady Violet Bonham Carter in a letter to *The Times*:

I am one of the millions who watching the martyrdom of Hungary and listening yesterday to the transmission of her agonizing appeals for help (immediately followed by our 'successful bombings' of Egyptian 'targets') have felt a humiliation, shame and anger which are beyond expression . . . We cannot order Soviet Russia to obey the edict of the United Nations which we ourselves have defied, nor to withdraw her tanks and guns from Hungary while we are bombing and invading Egypt.

British Catholics identified strongly with this point of view. We had been brought up to regard Soviet Communism as the enemy of our faith and the Church. Every Sunday throughout the cold war there were prayers at the end of mass for 'the conversion of Russia' (whether to Roman Catholicism or to the Orthodox faith which most Russians historically practised was never made clear). We felt a special identification with the Hungarian people because of the heroic figure of their leading Catholic prelate, Cardinal Mindszenty, who had been imprisoned twice for protesting against the oppression of his country, first by Nazism and then by Soviet Communism, and was briefly freed in the Revolution of 1956.

One weekend in the midst of these momentous events, dressed as always when on leave in civilian clothes, I accompanied Mary to a big demonstration in Hyde Park in support of the embattled Hungarians organised by students of the University of London. A speaker appealed for volunteers to join a party which intended to join the struggle. 'All you need is to know how to handle a gun,' he said. It occurred to me that even if I were a free agent and reckless enough to volunteer, my two dimly remembered sessions on the Catterick shooting range would not be of much use. Later I read in a newspaper that about twenty students had made their way to Hungary but were turned back at the border. Cardinal Mindszenty was soon forced to take refuge in the US Embassy in Budapest and spent the next fifteen years there, a prisoner once again, and something of an embarrassment to his Western protectors. Years after doing National Service I met Chris Woods-McConville by chance, and learned that he had been part of the task force that invaded Egypt from Cyprus, as the driver of some kind of support vehicle. He said he was terrified throughout the operation, and deeply relieved when it was called off. I believed him. No soldier's death would have been more futile.

The year turned, and the end of my National Service became imaginable in sharper focus. Counting the months turned into counting the weeks, and then days. Clive Rees, who was due for release at the same time, turned up at Bovington for that purpose. He did not seem to have changed much: still quietly spoken, laconic, still nursing an ambition to be a filmmaker.[1] He had spent

---

1 He should not be confused (as he is on some internet websites) with the younger Clive Rees who directed When the Whales Came and other movies. At some point in the 1960s I ran into my Clive on a Soho pavement and we chatted briefly. He was working in the film industry, but directed only one film, called The Blockhouse (1973), based on a true story of the Second World War about a group of foreign slave workers in German-occupied France, who were trapped at the end of the war in a concrete bunker and remained there undiscovered for several years, dying one by one. Surprisingly, it starred Peter Sellers. It was shown at some film festivals to appreciative audiences, but panned by critics and never widely released. Sadly, this failure apparently prevented Clive from getting another opportunity to direct.

an uneventful two years with a tank regiment in northern Germany – at least I can't remember anything specific he said about it, except that one night when he was doing a guard it was so cold that he cried, and he dropped some hints of a louche off-duty lifestyle. He suggested that we should celebrate our imminent release by going into Poole one evening, getting drunk and picking up a couple of girls – he had already ascertained that they were easily found in the harbour-front pubs. I declined, regretting anew that we could never be real friends because of our incompatibility in this respect. I had a different kind of celebration planned, a holiday in Spain with Mary and a couple of college friends, as soon as I was free.

14

One of our particular friends doing English at UCL was a girl of striking looks, with jet black hair and olive skin, called Jeswyn Buckwell. Her Italian (and as she would discover late in life, half-Jewish) father had adopted an English-sounding name after immigrating. In her third year she became seriously attached to Martin Jones, a student of chemistry who had come to UCL after doing his National Service in the Air Force. He was very interested in cinema and became President of the college Film Society, a position which, amazingly, was considered important and onerous enough in those days to merit an extra sabbatical year at college with no required academic work. Not long after Jeswyn had graduated with an Upper Second, Martin spotted an advertisement for someone competent in modern languages to join a company that subtitled foreign films, for which Jeswyn, who was well qualified in Italian and French, applied successfully.

The four of us got together occasionally when I was on leave during my army service. I was impressed when I discovered that

Jeswyn subtitled well-known films like *And God Created Woman*, starring Brigitte Bardot, and envied her opportunity, much less interesting though it would have been to her, to see the shots of Bardot in the nude that she told me had been cut by the British censor. I liked and was impressed by Martin, who seemed exceptionally well informed, for a chemist, not only about film but also modern American literature. He subscribed to the *New Yorker*, and was the first person to tell me about a writer called Vladimir Nabokov before the *Lolita* controversy made him famous. When Jeswyn and Martin suggested a joint holiday in Ibiza following my release from the Army we agreed readily, although like most Brits in 1957 we knew nothing about the island. There was a difficulty about dates, because Mary and Jeswyn had to return to work only a week after I was released. It was decided that I would join the others after they had been in Ibiza for a week, to spend the second week with them, and then the girls would return to England while Martin and I toured southern Spain for another couple of weeks. He had recently been recruited by the huge oil company BP, but would not be taking up his job immediately.

It is interesting that 'release', rather than 'discharge' or some other synonym, was the official military term for the conclusion of a conscript's service, the word that is applied to prisoners who have done their time. The day after I was freed, I flew from Heathrow to Barcelona on a student charter flight, in a Dakota so old and infirm that it did not attempt to fly over the Pyrenees, but shuddered and groaned its way down to the south coast of France at about 10,000 feet and then turned right. There was no airport on Ibiza then. I took an overnight boat from Barcelona, sitting up on deck since the accommodation below was so crowded and filthy. I did not mind: the night was warm and star-speckled, and in the early morning I had the thrilling sight of the island of Ibiza and its port slowly rising, as it seemed, out of the blue-green sea, the steeply stacked houses, tenements and churches behind the harbour catching the light of the risen sun. And there on the quayside were Mary, Jeswyn and Martin, waving and smiling. Everything had gone according to plan. Mary, who was getting tired of playing gooseberry to the other pair, was very glad to see me and we embraced warmly. We all sat down outside a harbour-front café, and as I sipped delicious coffee and heard about their first week, with the unaccustomed heat of the sun warming my back through my shirt, I felt happy. Released.

There is a special charm about an island as a holiday venue, as long as it has no airport. The effort of getting there by sea gives one a sense of achievement, and the practical limitation on the number of visitors enhances one's enjoyment of its attractions. Becoming temporarily an islander encourages relaxation and imparts a feeling of peace and well-being. I have not been back to Ibiza since 1957, but I am well aware of how much it has changed under the impact of mass tourism. Martin had booked our accommodation for that week in San Antonio, on the opposite side of the island from the port, a small, quiet, unpretentious resort, still recognisable as a fishing village, which was described recently by London's *Time Out* magazine as 'arguably the clubbing capital of the universe'. We stayed in a cheap but clean little hotel on *demi-pension* terms. It was near the beach, but we preferred to walk each morning about a mile to a small, tree-shaded cove that we usually had to ourselves, where we read and swam. After a late Spanish lunch and a long siesta we would take the air and stroll along the seafront, have a light supper, and end up sampling liqueurs in a bodega. A shot of Cointreau, Benedictine or Green Chartreuse cost about sixpence. For the same price you could have yourself shaved by a barber with a cut-throat razor, and I indulged myself in this luxury several times, urging Mary to test the baby's-bottom smoothness of my cheeks by nuzzling them. There were, needless to say, no discotheques – the word and its referent had not yet been invented. There were one or two open-air cafés which had live music and a concrete dance floor on which we gamely attempted the Ibizan equivalent of ballroom dancing. That was our very agreeable holiday. Years later I wrote a short story called 'Where the Climate's Sultry' about two going-steady English couples, just graduated from university in the late 1950s, who take a similar holiday and stay in a similar hotel, the boys sharing one room and the girls another, but pair off differently for their siestas, with consequences that should not be taken as biographical.

At the end of the week we separated: Mary and Jeswyn went back to England and work, envying Martin and me as we took a different boat from Ibiza to Alicante. Our plan was to see something of Andalusia by bus, visiting Murcia, Granada, Seville and Cadiz, then to return home by train via Madrid. Our budget was limited. We stayed in the cheapest hotels, in rooms without air conditioning and sometimes without windows, in often stifling temperatures, ate in cheap restaurants, suffered diarrhoea, and managed with very little Spanish between us. In Madrid one day we were followed for some time by two juvenile beggars who had accosted us and been refused, pleading or jeering unintelligibly at our heels, until I remembered that cowboys in westerns used to tell unwelcome Mexican characters to '*vamoos*'. I turned on the couple and yelled the word fiercely in their faces, upon which they fled. It was a small, and for me rare, triumph in a foreign language. The Spanish word is actually *vamos* – I have just looked it up – but I think I'm right about the cowboy pronunciation: there is an American insect repellent called Vamoos. It was quite a challenging trip for both of us, and the last lap, a long train journey by night from Madrid to Paris in a third-class compartment, was gruelling. Unable to stretch out on the bench seat to sleep, I climbed into the netted luggage rack and used it as a hammock until ordered by a conductor to get down. These are the memories that survive from such journeys in youth, rather than the castles and cathedrals and museums one visited. We arrived home from this one weary but pleased with ourselves for having accomplished it. Martin went off to Aberdeen to join BP and I went to Bloomsbury to get myself a card admitting me to the British Museum's round Reading Room, where I would spend much of the next eighteen months.

The Museum then housed the British Library, the first and greatest of the nation's Copyright Libraries, to which one copy of every published work must be submitted by law. The collection is now housed in a new building on the Euston Road with modern technology and amenities, but less charisma. The round Reading Room cast a spell on me as soon as I entered it: the floor a perfect circle nearly fifty yards in diameter, from which rose a wall of bookshelves and a gallery, surmounted by a vast dome; exactly in the middle of the floor was a hub where books were issued and returned, surrounded by concentric circles of shelving in which the catalogue was stored, composed of millions of printed slips which had been pasted into huge leather-bound volumes. From this core the rows of desks splayed out: spacious, leather-covered desks, separated from those on the adjoining aisle by a high partition, equipped with retractable shelves, bookrests and reading lamps, and provided with comfortable chairs of upholstered leather, whose wheeled legs moved soundlessly on the floor. There are photographs of this exquisitely symmetrical floor design, taken from the apex of the dome, in which it looks like a gigantic roulette wheel, but viewed from any angle it was deeply impressive. And the place was hallowed by all the famous persons who had read and written there – you were always conscious that you might be sitting at a desk once used by Thackeray or Karl Marx or Oscar Wilde or Virginia Woolf, or any one of a hundred other famous writers. One day I would write a novel set in and around this wonderful building. Meanwhile it was the ideal place to do my postgraduate research, conveniently situated only half a mile from University College.

I was registered for the London University MA, which in those days was a two-year research degree awarded for a substantial thesis, supplemented by a single examination paper on the literary period to which one's subject belonged. The title I eventually settled on for my thesis was: 'Catholic Fiction since the Oxford Movement: its Literary Form and Religious Content'. I was surprised, in retrospect, that the Board of Postgraduate Studies approved it, for it was much too big a subject for a Master's thesis. Perhaps they thought there couldn't be a lot of English Catholic fiction in the past hundred-odd years. But there was – much, much more than I had supposed myself.

The first English Catholic writer of note after the Catholic Emancipation Act of 1829 was John Henry Newman, who converted to Roman Catholicism in 1845, having for some years been the leading light of the Oxford Movement. This was a group of academic divines who sought, by publishing a series of 'Tracts for the Times', to shift the Church of England, historically founded upon a combination of predominantly Protestant Articles of Faith and an essentially Catholic liturgy, and therefore always prone to split into parties and factions, towards the Catholic end of the religious spectrum, in order to combat the worldliness which they saw infecting the Established Church and to raise the level of spirituality in its members. It owed a good deal of its inspiration to the Romantic Movement's nostalgic celebration of medieval culture, and its three-dimensional manifestation was the neo-Gothic architecture of Pugin. Newman's own thinking moved so far in this direction that he finally 'went over' to Rome, taking many disciples and admirers with him, and provoking a spate of 'No Popery' outrage in the population at large. He was re-ordained as a Catholic priest, joined the Oratorian order, and founded an Oratory in Birmingham where he spent most of the rest of his life, writing theological, philosophical and polemical works in the Catholic cause, for which he was eventually honoured with a Cardinal's hat. Interestingly, one of the first things he wrote after his conversion was a novel, published anonymously, called *Loss and Gain* (1848). It describes the gradual conversion to Catholicism of a young undergraduate at Oxford, but not at all in a solemn or pietistic way. It gives a vivid picture of university life and ecclesiastical politics at the time, in a sparkling, often satirical style, with several brilliant dialogic set pieces showing that differences of opinion about doctrine and liturgy were argued about as fiercely and sometimes as foolishly in the Church of England then as issues of gender and sexual behaviour are today. (A striking index of this contrast and continuity is that the word 'pervert' as noun or verb had the same meaning in the nineteenth century as 'convert' does in modern English.)

I discovered early in my research that a large number of novels engaging polemically in the religious debate from the High, Low and Broad Church points of view were published at this time, and that *Loss and Gain* was actually a riposte to one of them: *From Oxford to Rome, and How it Fared with Some Who Made the Journey*, by Elizabeth Furlong Shipton Harris, a sensational and tendentious account of a group of Anglicans who convert to Rome under the influence of the Tractarian movement and are painfully disillusioned by the experience. It acquired extra notoriety when it became known that the authoress had herself made the journey, and regretted it. The novel began with a conversation between the hero Eustace and his Oxford tutor who, the *Quarterly Review* thought, was 'plainly intended for Mr Newman'. Newman himself, who later described the novel's contents as 'wantonly and preposterously fanciful', rightly thought the best response would be another, much better and more truthful novel on the same theme.

Putting his achievement in its context entailed reading many greatly inferior religious novels, and so did tracking the subsequent development of Catholic fiction in England in the nineteenth century. The surge of conversions in the upper and professional classes triggered by Newman's, and the growing confidence of the English Catholic community, which had kept a low profile until Catholic Emancipation, created a literary market that many writers, especially female ones, were eager to supply. I found the best way to identify novels with Catholic content was to read reviews of fiction in journals like the *Athenaeum* and the Catholic *Dublin Review*. It was the age of the circulating library, and the novels were usually in the three-volume form that suited that institution. I filled in large numbers of request slips, and the library's assistants brought the books from the stacks and piled them up on my desk. I could tell that I was the first person to read many of them because their pages were uncut, and I was provided with a paper-knife with which I hacked my way through this literary undergrowth to the understandable annoyance of readers at neighbouring desks. I reckoned to get through two three-deckers a day and lived in hope of finding a novel as good as *Loss and Gain*, without being rewarded. I did, however, detect a general trend. The religious novels of the 1840s reflected controversies and competition between different Christian churches and factions within them. In the latter half of the nineteenth century all versions of Christian belief were challenged by various forms of doubt and disbelief, driven by the advances of science, especially the Darwinian theory of evolution, and by demythologising biblical scholarship. One of the upmarket bestsellers of the late nineteenth century was Mrs Humphry Ward's *Robert Elsmere* (1888), about an Anglican clergyman's loss of faith. Catholic novelists in this period seldom engaged with this theme. Instead they took the truth of the Catholic faith for granted and contrived sentimental and often melodramatic stories, narrated in cliché-ridden prose, which exhibited the piety, sacrifice and moral heroism it demanded in personal life.

As the century drew towards its end, this emphasis on the moral and emotional rather than the cognitive aspects of religious faith continued, but with an improvement in literary quality. I found some Catholic writers who, though minor, had genuine ability – among them the John Oliver Hobbes whose scholarship I had won. That name, I discovered, was the nom de plume of Mrs Pearl Craigie, an American expatriate and Catholic convert who had been a mature student at UCL before she turned to writing novels that dealt thoughtfully with personal relationships in a Catholic ethical perspective that was usually implied rather than explicit. They were admired by Henry James and Thomas Hardy, among others. I already knew something about a very different Catholic convert, Frederick Rolfe, self-styled 'Baron Corvo', a homosexual spoiled priest who compensated for his life's disappointments in the extraordinary fantasy *Hadrian VII* (1904), in which a humble English priest acting as a candidate's chaplain at a Papal conclave is himself elected Pope and turns the Church upside down. I enjoyed exploring Rolfe's other equally idiosyncratic writings.

Catholicism became fashionable in literary circles at this time, and the poet Ernest Dowson spoke for many when he declared, 'I'm for the old faith. I've become a Catholic as every artist must.' Oscar Wilde did not do so until he was dying, but this action was foreshadowed in the eponymous hero of *The Picture of Dorian Gray*, of whom 'it was rumoured . . . that he was about to join the Roman Catholic communion; and certainly the Roman ritual had always a great attraction for him.' For Dorian and his creator, and other converts of the Decadence like Aubrey Beardsley, the attraction of Catholicism was partly aesthetic and partly existential. The work of the French writer J.K. Huysmans, which reflected his spiritual journey through sin and satanism to redemptive faith, was a potent influence, especially *À rebours* (1884), translated into English as *Against the Grain,* which was described by Arthur

Symons as 'the breviary of the Decadence', and which Dorian Gray reads with devout fascination. For these writers, exploring the reality of sin in personal experience, riskily deferring the redemption offered by the Catholic Church, was a sign of authenticity and a way of resisting the materialism and philistinism of the modern world. Huysmans wrote to a friend, 'it was through a glimpse of the supernatural of evil that I first obtained insight into the supernatural of good . . . With his hooked paw the devil drew me towards God.' I perceived a link here with the work of Graham Greene, which was to be studied in the last chapter of my thesis, preceded by one on Evelyn Waugh, but I kept on discovering earlier Catholic writers of some interest who had to be explored and discussed first, and the horizon of my project seemed to move further and further away.

I was living at home again and travelling every weekday to the BM on a second-hand Vespa scooter. In those days there was free parking of two-wheeled vehicles in the British Museum forecourt for visitors, and I commuted from home with my bag of books, files and index cards strapped to the luggage rack behind the saddle. My daily companion was Derek Todd. Like me he had been offered a university postgraduate scholarship on getting his First, and having already done his National Service in the Navy he was free to accept it, but by a cruel twist of fate he discovered at the same time that he had contracted TB and must be admitted immediately to a sanatorium for treatment. His doctor had in fact diagnosed the condition earlier and delayed telling him until he had sat his Finals. Derek spent most of the academic year 1955–56 in a sanatorium on the Isle of Wight, where Mary and I visited him during one of my leaves, so he was just a year ahead of me when I began my MA. His thesis topic, 'Attacks on Scholars and Scholarship in the Late Seventeenth and Early Eighteenth Centuries', had been suggested by his supervisor, James Sutherland. Swift and Pope were the major authors it concerned but there was also a swarm of minor satirists, poets and essayists whose work had to be tracked down and considered. In due course Derek accepted Sutherland's advice to convert his MA thesis into a PhD, which normally took three years, and was covered by the university scholarship. My own project was also of a scale more appropriate to a PhD, but I had no wish to extend its duration, since I was determined to get married as soon as I had submitted it.

I saw Derek almost every day at the British Museum. The first of us to arrive would save a seat for the other by putting some books on a desk, taking care not to pick one favoured by any of the Reading Room's resident eccentrics, a little band of regular readers, mad-looking, weirdly attired and unkempt, who had been coming there every day for as long as anyone could remember and seemed to think they had territorial rights. We would take smoke breaks together in the colonnade that extended on two sides from the building's massive portico, and exchange news, anecdotes and observations on life in general. Derek had a mind more like a philosopher's than a literary critic's, and liked to speculate about whatever subject presented itself in an analytical manner which his friends found amusingly provocative. He appreciated other people's humorous remarks and rewarded them with a series of high-pitched laughs, his head thrown back and each laugh punctuated by a pause for breath. Sometimes at lunchtime we would meet John Jolliffe, a friend of Derek's and a graduate of UCL, who was on the staff of the British Library and rising rapidly up the career ladder. (John was a pioneer in the application of computers to cataloguing and would eventually become Head Librarian of the Bodleian at Oxford until an aneurism of the brain cut his life brutally short.) One day he took Derek and me on a tour of the labyrinthine book-stacks behind the graceful walls of the Reading Room – out of bounds for readers, and an experience that I drew on when writing *The British Museum is Falling Down.*

In an earlier chapter I described the teaching of the humanities in British universities at this time as a 'First-degree culture'. One consequence of this was the haphazard management of postgraduate studies. At UCL, and I believe at most British universities, postgraduate research was an almost entirely unstructured activity. You submitted a subject for your thesis, and, if it was approved, got on with it largely on your own. You would have a supervisor with whom you could discuss your project and get occasional feedback on work in progress, but there was no timetable for these consultations, and some supervisors were less scrupulous than others about arranging them. If the postgraduate chose his or her own thesis topic, rather than taking up the suggestion of a member of staff, one might have a supervisor who knew little or nothing about it, especially if it was an unusual one; and fully stretched as most of them were by their undergraduate teaching, which had priority, they could not reasonably be expected to keep up with the candidate's growing body of knowledge about his subject. This was my situation. The supervisor assigned to me was MacDonald Emslie, who had joined the Department shortly before I obtained my BA. He was a youngish

Scotsman who always seemed rather harassed and depressed – perhaps he was homesick for Scotland, for he moved back there later in his academic career, where I have been told he became a notorious alcoholic. I could never ascertain what his academic specialism was; the little I have been able to discover about his publications recently suggests a wide range of interests from the sixteenth to the nineteenth centuries, but the history of the Catholic novel was not one of them. He told me frankly that he could not help me with the content of my thesis, but he would read whatever I cared to submit to him and give me his non-specialist opinion for what it was worth. I don't think I saw him more than once or twice a term. I was quite happy with this arrangement because I knew what I wanted to do and how I intended to do it, but I felt the absence of any corporate life in postgraduate study. Apart from a few lectures on research methods at the beginning of the academic year, there were no seminars or group activities of any kind for postgraduate students in the English Department. So I decided to organise something myself, by forming a group of postgrads working on English literature who would meet regularly to discuss some topic or text of common interest. As it would be an unofficial and informal gathering it would be appropriate to meet in the evenings and outside college. But where? Chance provided an ideal venue at just the right moment.

In January 1956 Jeswyn and Martin got married – sooner than they had planned, but Martin was doing well in BP. He was moved down to Rochester in Kent, and they rented a small, brand-new house there. In consequence Jeswyn had to move out of her flat in Endsleigh Street, a few minutes' walk from UC, which she was renting from a friend who was working abroad. Jeswyn offered to sub-sublet it to Mary, who was looking for new accommodation since her sister Eileen had decided to make her career as a teacher in Canada. It was a top-floor flat with a large living room that provided an ideal space for the discussion group.

I recruited friends like Derek and Tony Petti directly, and sent invitations through the internal mail to other likely participants. Most of them responded positively. Sadly, I can recall little about our meetings – how often they occurred and what we discussed – but we did not talk about our own research. The idea was to have a break from our daily scholarly labour and be made to think more broadly about literature and criticism. After a while we invited one or two sympathetic members of the departmental staff to join us, and they were glad to do so. The venture came to an end with Mary's tenancy of the flat, which lasted for six months or so, but it was generally enjoyed by those who took part. The most vivid memory I have of it was quite trivial, and is of the very first meeting. As people assembled and arranged the chairs in the living room, in an excited and expectant mood, Tony Petti plucked a book from a bookshelf, opened it, and began to recite a *faux naïf* comment on a famous line of Wordsworth's:

> 'The child is father to the man.'
> How can he be? The words are wild.
> Suck any sense from that who can:
> 'The child is father to the man.'
> No; what the poet did write ran,
> 'The man is father to the child.'
> 'The child is father to the man!'
> How <u>can</u> he be? The words are wild.

The wedding of my maternal grandparents, Tom Murphy and Adèle Goddaert, probably in Rotherhithe *circa* 1900. No documentary record of the marriage has survived.

Dad with alto saxophone, early 1920s.

My mother (left) and her sister Eileen (right) with friend (centre), perhaps dressed for an amateur performance, *circa* 1920.

Dad, on tenor sax (right) wrote 'Piccadilly Hotel' at the bottom, with a date that looks like '1920'. But he was only fourteen in that year, so the last digit must be an imperfect 6 or 8. The imprint of 'The Bungalow, Brockley Rise' is another enigma.

Mum and Dad, perhaps early in their marriage.

Mum with me, aged about six months, at the seaside in 1935.

On holiday with Mum and Dad, a year or two later.

Snap of Mum and Dad, probably taken by a seaside photographer, early 1930s.

Group photograph of my first classmates at St Joseph's Academy, Blackheath, probably taken in 1946. I am in the middle of the front row.

The Station Band of RAF Cottesmore, supplemented by volunteers, marches through the village on Battle of Britain Day 1941 or 1942.

81 Millmark Grove. DL aged 13/14 in proprietorial pose.

'*Aaah . . . aren't they sweet?*' Jenefer Smith and I outside her father's shop in Mount St Charles, Cornwall, summer 1943.

In the back garden of 81 Millmark Grove. If there had been a ball it would have gone straight through the kitchen window.

Mary looking down on Heidelberg and the river Neckar from the parapet of the Castle, summer 1954.

Mary and I with my Aunt Lu at the Brussels Expo, 1958.

Looking into the future, on a walk in the country near Hoddesdon, 1958/59.

Members of Adm Squadron, RAC Centre, Bovington Camp, Dorset, in 1956 or 1957. Lance-Corporal Lodge is on the left of the second row.

The Bovington Camp PRI clerk at work, probably in 1956.

Our Whitsun wedding in Hoddesdon, May 1959.

A reunion with my Aunt Eileen at Palm Springs, California, April 1965.

Mary and the somewhat alarmed Julia and Stephen beside a geyser at Yellowstone National Park, Wyoming, July 1965.

Christopher learns to walk in our garden in El Cerrito, California, 1969.

Leonard ('Lenny') Michaels and I at Stinson Beach, June 1969.

Malcolm Bradbury as a young man in the late 1950s or early 1960s.

Mary and Park Honan, in Providence, Rhode Island, February 1965, at a farewell meal before we set off on our trek westwards.

The Honan family: Park, Jeannette and their children Corinna and twins 'Thieu and 'Tasha, at St Brévin-les-Pins, 1961 or '62.

Richard Hoggart, photographed in his office at Birmingham University by Clayton Evans, *circa* 1963.

Portrait of DL by Paul Morby, with Birmingham University Library in the background, 1974.

We all thought this was hilariously funny, and demanded to know the author. Tony held up the book, open at the title page: *Collected Poems* of Gerard Manley Hopkins. I admired Hopkins's poetry but had never suspected that he had a sense of humour.

Among the postgraduates whom I approached by mail was an American called Park Honan. We had not met, but I was aware of his existence as a contributor of stories and poems to the college literary magazine, *New Phineas*,[1] of which I had become assistant editor, and I had seen a play he had written and performed in under the auspices of the Dramatic Society, of which I have now only the haziest memory. According to Park's own account, in an essay he published many years later, the subject of the first session he attended in Endsleigh Street was the short story as a literary form, and I had prescribed for preparatory reading a story of his own in *New Phineas* (which was distributed free within the college), in addition to some classics of the genre by writers like Hemingway and Katherine Mansfield. In the essay he claimed to have been crushed by the critical comparisons this invidious juxtaposition elicited from the group. That was certainly not my intention, and Park cannot have been really offended because soon after that meeting he invited Mary and me to dinner in the flat he and his French wife Jeannette occupied in Catford, only a few miles from Brockley. It was the first of many delicious meals Jeannette cooked

---

1 The wooden figure of Phineas Maclino, a kilted Jacobite, stolen by students from outside a tobacconist's shop in Tottenham Court Road, was a UCL mascot earlier in the century. The magazine, originally called *Phineas*, became defunct, probably because of the war, and was revived in the mid-fifties with the addition of the epithet 'new' to its title.

for us over the years to come. She spoke fluent English studded with American idioms in an enchanting French accent, and Mary and I immediately warmed to her. It was a cold winter evening, and in the cosy glow of the open fire in the basement kitchen–dining room a lifelong friendship between the four of us began.

Park was then about twenty-seven, Jeannette a few years younger. They had a little girl, Corinna, aged three or four, and Jeannette was heavily pregnant with twins. Their story was unusual and romantic. Park had grown up in New York City and just outside it in Bronxville. His father, a surgeon who commanded a hospital behind the Western Front in the First World War, was much older than his mother and died when Park was aged seven. The boy was named Leonard Hobart Park Honan – 'Leonard' after his maternal grandfather, and 'Hobart Park' after his father's best friend, whose surname Park adopted as his first name, perhaps unique for a Caucasian. It is a common surname in Korea, and those who know him only through the printed word sometimes think he is part Korean. To save his mother the cost of higher education fees he obtained a scholarship at Deep Springs, an unconventional college in the Californian desert, which prepared a small select group of male youths for life with a combination of high-level academic courses and practical manual work for at least four hours a day, such as cooking, irrigation, planting, and looking after the college's own cattle herd. From there he won a scholarship to Chicago University, where he studied English and History and graduated with an MA. He then moved back to New York, and scraped a living from odd jobs on the fringes of publishing while trying to get his own writing into print, and waiting apprehensively to be claimed by the draft, from which he intended to seek exemption as a conscientious objector. At that juncture he met Jeannette, through his younger brother Bill who was a student at Oberlin College, where she was a Fulbright Scholar, and a mutual attraction was sparked. Jeannette had grown up in Paris under the German occupation, and as a schoolgirl was caught tearing down a Nazi poster by the French police, who told her father, a headmaster who was counterfeiting documents for the Resistance at the time, that they would report her to the Germans if she repeated the offence. She was never able to recall those years of oppression and fear without a shadow passing over her normally smiling features and subduing her effervescent personality.

Defying the uncertainty of their circumstances and future prospects, she and Park married and soon found themselves in difficulties. His claim to be a conscientious objector was rejected because it was based on secular, not religious, moral principles, and at one stage he was arrested and jailed for a few hours. Protracted appeals and negotiations with the authorities followed, during which time Jeannette returned to France, where she gave birth to Corinna, and there was some doubt as to whether she would get a visa to return to America. In the end Park accepted the inevitable for the sake of his wife and child, and was drafted, but with an official undertaking that he would not be given combat duties. It all worked out very well because after doing his basic training and serving for a while in Maryland (where he collaborated with a fellow conscript and Harvard graduate in writing a 1,000-line poem in heroic couplets satirising the US Ordnance Corps, printed for circulation on an army mimeograph) he was posted, either by extraordinary luck or some unwonted exercise of compassion by the authorities, to an American military unit in south-west France, where he was allowed to live off-base with Jeannette and young Corinna. Furthermore, on his release from the Army he was entitled under the GI Bill to a government grant towards three years of higher education, which he decided to spend in England rather than the USA, partly so that Jeannette could remain within easy reach of her family, and partly because the lax British system of postgraduate studies, contrasting sharply with American PhD programmes (a closely monitored combination of courses and dissertation), suited his individualistic temperament perfectly. He elected to work on the poetry of Browning and was being supervised by Paul Turner, a versatile scholar familiar with Greek and Latin as well as English literature, with whom he got on very well, though progress with his thesis was hampered by all the poetry, plays and prose fiction he was writing.

I did not hear the whole of this story on that first evening in Catford, but I got the gist of it and the more I heard subsequently, the more it fascinated me. It was in many ways a more dramatic and adventurous version of my own life to date: the aspirations to be a creative writer, the early attachment to a female partner, the resistance to the ethos of military service, the decision to pursue an academic career, were all parallels between us. But Park had taken more risks, and he created a kind of mythical aura around himself, his family and friends which gave him energy and confidence to face an uncertain future with a wife and child and two more on the way – just the sort of plight I had imagined and prudently avoided by opting for a long, celibate courtship. It had made a difference, of course, that Park was five years older than me, and unburdened with a Catholic conscience. But he seemed to me in every respect a little larger than life, especially educated middle-class English life, with its fondness for understatement and light irony. His manners were boisterous, his speech commanding, his laughter was hearty, his handshake firm. He tended to hyperbole in expressing both likes and dislikes, whether of persons or books, and he habitually nicknamed people as they became characters in his myth. His daughter Corinna acquired several names, including 'Poupi' and 'Bear' because of her devotion to *Winnie-the-Pooh* in infancy. Jeannette was 'Froggy'. His younger brother Bill was 'Driz'. In due course I was 'Davido', and after Mary and I were married, she was always '*Marielodge*', pronounced as a single word, with a French accent. I had never met anyone quite like Park, and I never would again. Through our friendship I extended my education in American culture, speech and manners which had begun in Heidelberg, and acting as his guide and interpreter of their English equivalents I perceived my own country in a new, and sometimes comical, light. His energetic commitment to writing in various forms, including a novel in progress called *Eat Rocks, Tame Tigers* (a title lifted from Shakespeare's *Troilus and Cressida*), made him a stimulating friend and confidant as I pursued my own literary goals. Chief among these was the completion of the novel I had started at Bovington, called *The Picturegoers*.

Set in a London surburb called 'Brickley' which closely resembles Brockley and New Cross, the novel depicts the lives of seventeen people of varying ages and social backgrounds who live there and go to the same local cinema, called the Palladium, on Saturday evenings. (There was a popular film magazine published at the time called *The Picturegoer*.) The several Catholics among them also go to Sunday mass at their local parish church, and the story suggests a kind of analogy between the rituals of religion and immersion in the dream world of film, each providing compensation for, or escape from, the frustrations and disappointments of ordinary life. 'Saturday Night and Sunday Morning' would have been a good alternative title when the novel was eventually published, if Alan Sillitoe hadn't already used it. At the centre of the narrative is the Mallory family, middle-aged Catholic parents of seven children, three of whom are still living at home. Clare, the eldest, has just returned after being rejected by the convent where she was a postulant (a theme carried over from *The Devil, the World and the Flesh*). Into this household comes a lodger, Mark, a student at a London college with aspirations to be a writer, who was baptised a Catholic but has never practised because his parents 'lapsed' in his infancy. The novel traces the relationship that develops between Mark and Clare, and the intersecting fortunes of all the other characters, by describing the events of three weekends separated by several months. While Clare, initially disturbed by Mark's cynicism and frank references to sex, gradually falls in love with him, he becomes more and more attracted to the family's Catholic faith and feels he may have a religious vocation. (It wasn't until I got into structuralism as a literary critic in the 1980s that I realised how pervasive such binary oppositions and reversals are in my fiction.) The minor characters include Mr Berkeley, the manager of the Palladium who has despondently overseen its decline from a popular music hall to a struggling independent cinema, and the Mallorys' parish priest, who keeps an anxious eye on falling attendances at mass and Benediction. One of the first notes I made about this novel was for a scene in which Father Kipling goes to the cinema for the first time in his life to see *The Song of Bernadette*, a biopic about the saintly visionary of Lourdes, but gets the date wrong and is scandalised by a Hollywood comedy very like the Marilyn Monroe movie *The Seven Year Itch*, after which he preaches against immorality in the cinema, with unhappy results. Two other films are featured in the novel under their real names: Vittorio De Sica's classic *Bicycle Thieves*, which Mr Berkeley shows in an effort to raise the cultural tone of his cinema but which merely depresses most of his customers, and *Rock Around the Clock*, which is a huge success with a mainly youthful audience who dance in the aisles (a much-publicised phenomenon when the film was released in 1956), leading rather improbably to the redemption of a delinquent Teddy boy character. First novels do not usually contain as many subplots and points of view as *The Picturegoers*, and in retrospect I recognise the influence of two favourite sources: the 'Wandering Rocks' episode of *Ulysses*, which represents the actions and thoughts of a large number of characters, major and minor, moving about Dublin at the same hour of the day, and Dylan Thomas's radio play, *Under Milk Wood*, which does something similar with the inhabitants of a fictional Welsh fishing village, and which I listened to with delight and read many times after it was broadcast by the BBC in 1954. (I still tease my wife with the henpecked Mr Ogmore's line, '*I must put my pyjamas in the drawer marked pyjamas,*' when reproached for untidiness.)

There was another book which exerted a different kind of influence. Shortly after I was released from the Army in the summer of 1957, with more than half of the novel written, I accepted an invitation from the University of London to attend an interdisciplinary seminar at Cumberland Lodge for students beginning postgraduate degree courses, on a subject called something like 'The Arts in Society'. I have no memory of the seminar, but the invitation came with a reading list that included *The Uses of Literacy* by Richard Hoggart, which had been published earlier that year to enthusiastic reviews, and I do remember borrowing a copy from the Deptford public library and reading it with rapt attention, for it seemed to have much in common with the 'Saturday night' side of my novel. Hoggart argued that the commercially driven products of 'mass culture', such as Hollywood movies, were displacing the simple entertainment and reading matter which had traditionally served English working-class communities and reinforced their values. At first sight this seemed to reiterate a familiar complaint of F.R. Leavis and his disciples, but whereas they dismissed all twentieth-century popular culture with generalised contempt, Hoggart studied it with discrimination and without patronising those who consumed it, understanding how even meretricious and formulaic art can help people to negotiate and interpret their lives. This was very much my aim in describing the collective, habitual experience of 'going to the pictures', in the era before television largely took over its social and cultural function. Richard Hoggart studied the popular fiction and entertainment of a slightly earlier era, but in the remarkable first section of *The Uses of Literacy* he described the working-class society that consumed them with the kind of evocative specificity that novelists strive to achieve. Reading Hoggart's book strengthened my faith in my novel-in-progress, and helped me develop its themes in the second half. A decade later I was able to tell Richard this when he became a colleague and friend at Birmingham University, where he founded the Centre for Contemporary Cultural Studies and instigated the development of a whole new subject in the humanities.

In spite of all the other claims on my time I managed to finish *The Picturegoers* by the late spring of 1958 and set about finding a publisher. I began by sending the novel to Michael Joseph, who had responded encouragingly to my first attempt, and I was disappointed when they turned down its successor – kindly ('it is well above the average first novel') but without much explanation. Next I tried Gollancz, which was the trendy publisher of the day, having issued both Kingsley Amis's *Lucky Jim* and Colin Wilson's *The Outsider* in its trademark bright yellow jackets. I wrote to them first, describing the novel, and received a personal letter from Hilary Rubinstein, a director of the firm, saying they would be 'delighted to consider it'. It is hard to imagine an unknown, unpublished and unrepresented novelist getting such a response today. Quite soon I received a letter from another director, John Bush, to say that they did not see the novel as publishable, but their readers' reports had praised several features of it and they would be glad to consider anything else I might submit. Then I happened to see in the *Evening Standard* a report about a small, relatively obscure publishing house called MacGibbon & Kee, which was expanding and actively looking for new authors, so I decided to try my luck with them, delivering my manuscript by hand as usual to save the cost of postage. Several weeks later when I was staying with Mary at her home in Hoddesdon, we came back from playing tennis in the municipal park one afternoon to receive a message that a Mr Anthony Brown of MacGibbon & Kee had telephoned, having got the number from my mother in Brockley, and asked if I would call him back, which I did immediately, standing in the cramped hall of 72 Lord Street, where the telephone squatted on the window ledge at the foot of the stairs. So it was in the home of the family that had partly inspired *The Picturegoers* that I received the news every tyro writer dreams of: 'We like your novel, and we want to publish it', or words to that effect. There was only one caveat: Anthony Brown said they thought the book needed some more work, and publication would depend on the delivery of a satisfactory revised text, but meanwhile I would get a contract and an advance. I was happy, indeed ecstatic, to agree to these terms, but warned him that I would not be able to work on the novel until I had finished my MA thesis. To my relief he was unperturbed by this information.

The contract when it came was, by today's standards, simple. The four-page document promised me an advance of £75 in three instalments: £25 on signature, £25 on acceptance of the revised novel and £25 on publication. After allowing for inflation, this still constituted a very small risk for the proprietor of MacGibbon & Kee who signed my contract, Howard Samuel, a left-wing multi-millionaire who had bought the firm with the proceeds of his property business. Needless to say, I did not quibble about the terms. Not long after our telephone conversation I met Anthony Brown, a young, enthusiastic editor, at MacGibbon & Kee's offices in Great Portland Street, and was pleased that he had no radical changes to my novel to propose but left it to me to recognise where it could be improved. He introduced me to Timothy O'Keeffe, whose title was 'Managing Editor' but who did not seem to have yet read *The Picturegoers*. He may have replaced Tom Maschler, who had recently moved to Cape, where he became a celebrated publisher of literary fiction.

Before he left MacGibbon & Kee Maschler had commissioned, edited and published a book under their imprint called *Declaration*, a collection of manifesto essays by Kenneth Tynan, John Osborne, Doris Lessing, John Wain, Lindsay Anderson, Stuart Holroyd and Bill Hopkins, which did much to disseminate the idea I touched on earlier, that an exciting new wave of writing in drama, fiction, film and criticism, loosely associated with the catchphrase Angry Young Men, was gathering momentum in Britain in the 1950s. As Maschler himself later admitted in his autobiography, the success of *Declaration,* which sold 20,000 copies in hardback, was surprising, since the contributors were a heterogeneous bunch, and two of them, Holroyd and Hopkins, had not yet published a book and were chiefly famous for being friends of Colin Wilson. Wilson's *The Outsider,* an ambitious survey of the alienated intellectual in literature and real life, covering major writers and thinkers in Continental Europe as well as Britain and America, was the literary sensation of 1956. Philip Toynbee, the most influential journalistic critic of the day, described it in *The Observer* as 'an exhaustive and luminously intelligent study of a representative theme of our time . . . truly astounding'. The book's fame was boosted by the romantic circumstances of its composition reported in the press: an impoverished twenty-four-year-old with no academic credentials when he came to London, Wilson had researched and written it in the British Museum Reading Room, encouraged by his namesake, the novelist Angus Wilson who was then a senior librarian there, and spent his nights on Hampstead Heath in a sleeping bag. I actually bought *The Outsider* soon after it was published – a rare extravagance – and thought I perceived a certain kinship between the radical rejection of the Enlightenment model of civilisation by Wilson's Outsiders, like Nietzsche and Henri Barbusse, and the antihumanist attitudes of the Catholic writers and thinkers I was interested in, from Newman to Graham Greene, who denied the perfectibility of fallen man. (The title I initially proposed for my MA thesis was in fact 'The Literary Expression of Anti-humanism in Catholic Literature from Newman to the Present Day'.) Thus inspired, I wrote an article on 'The Outsider and the Catholic Novel', which I touted unsuccessfully to a number of literary periodicals, hoping to associate my recondite research topic with a fashionable young author. I was easily impressed by *The Outsider* because I had read hardly any of the works Wilson discussed, and this was probably true of some enthusiastic reviewers. In due course qualified judges began to point out serious flaws and errors in Wilson's book, and the appetite he and his friends showed for personal publicity provoked a change of sentiment in literary circles. When Wilson published his second book, *Religion and the Rebel*, in 1957 there was a backlash of critical opinion and it was rubbished by the very critics who had praised *The Outsider*. Philip Toynbee described it in *The Observer* as 'a deplorable piece of work . . . futile to the point of meaninglessness', and even retrospectively revised his opinion of the earlier book, now described as merely 'interesting and praiseworthy' but 'clumsily written and still more clumsily composed'. I was fascinated by this story and I wrote a piece about Wilson for *New Phineas*, entitled 'Requiem for an Angry Young Man', saying: 'his fantastic reputation was a fabrication of the publicity machine, and the spectacle of the machine devouring its own creation is not an edifying one'. When I became editor of the magazine on its next appearance I invited Wilson to comment, and he wrote an interesting and good-humoured piece, in which he gave some choice examples of the misrepresentation he suffered during the media's feeding frenzy and looked forward with calm confidence to 'a day when readers would come to my books without any knowledge that I had once been labelled as an Angry Young Man'. He continued to write and publish books which received less and less attention as time went on. His friend and associate Stuart Holroyd, who had been a student for one year at UCL, and whom I interviewed in another issue of *New Phineas*, slipped more rapidly into obscurity, while Bill Hopkins never really emerged from it. The fact is that the interests and attitudes of these writers, which included phenomenology, existentialism, mysticism, parapsychology, and political philosophy of a fascist tendency, had nothing in common with the general trend of new writing in Britain at this time, manifested in novels like *Saturday Night and Sunday Morning* and *Lucky Jim*, the poetry of Philip Larkin and other Movement poets, and most of the plays being put on at the Royal Court Theatre: namely, a realistic and/or satirical engagement with contemporary social life. When that disparity became apparent the media simply lost interest in Wilson and his associates. But the new wave was something that *The Picturegoers*, for all its religious preoccupations, could surf on, and that, perhaps, was why MacGibbon & Kee took it.

They were, however, open to other kinds of fiction. I suggested to Park Honan that he should try sending *Eat Rocks, Tame Tigers*, a black-comic dystopian novel set in the future, to Anthony Brown, who responded with enthusiasm and gave him a contract with exactly the same terms as mine, publication being conditional on delivery of a satisfactory revised text. Like me, Park had to postpone this task to complete his thesis because he was in the last year of his GI Bill grant, but he was very pleased and – in spite of the meagre signature fee – hopeful that the book might in time help to relieve his financial debts. The symmetry of these positive developments in our literary efforts cemented the friendship between us.

15

'In the fifties, everyone was waiting to get married, some longer than others,' observes the authorial narrator of *How Far Can You Go?* Nobody in our circle of friends waited as long as Mary and I. Tony Petti married Lorna, a Classics student at UCL who was the star singer of his choir, and their wedding was one of two Mary and I attended on the same Saturday in 1957, Tony's in the morning and that of a relative of mine in the afternoon. In 1958, the year that Martin and Jeswyn got married, Derek Todd met a shy, gentle young woman called Iris with as yet hidden talents as an artist, and after living together discreetly in a flat in Old Street they married too. That summer Mary and I at last got formally engaged, and together we chose a second-hand ring, platinum with a small sapphire set in a circle of diamond chips. Mary was now almost as impatient as I was to bring this inordinately long courtship to a conclusion, having overcome whatever doubts she had once had about marriage or me. She was securely settled in her career, having obtained her PGCE by part-time study, and was enjoying the challenge of teaching English at Eltham Green Comprehensive, a huge new school on the borders of south-east London and Kent, where she demonstrated her quality by turning a notoriously delinquent class known as '4F4' (the very sound of which would make colleagues shudder) into her devoted pupils. She had moved from the flat in Endsleigh Street to a bedsitter in Brockley near the St John's railway station, which was on a direct line to Eltham; and at the end of the working day I would often pop round on the Vespa for cocoa and a cuddle and to talk about future plans. We decided on a Whitsun wedding in 1959. Mr Jacob asked Mary if we could wait another year or two so he could save up enough money to host the wedding, but she firmly refused and we undertook to meet the cost ourselves.

This meant that I had locked myself into a tight timetable. To obtain my MA in the summer of '59, I would have to submit my thesis in April. At that point I had got as far as the 1890s in writing my history of the Catholic novel. When I drew up a list of the novelists I still had to cover I realised there was no question of writing first drafts of these chapters and returning to them later: there simply wouldn't be enough time. I therefore compiled a calendar allotting a precise number of weeks to reading and writing about each author according to their importance. Mrs Wilfred Ward, Montgomery Carmichael and Robert Hugh Benson, for example, would receive less attention than G.K. Chesterton, Hilaire Belloc and Maurice Baring, and those in turn less than Evelyn Waugh and Graham Greene. I kept to this schedule faithfully: each chapter, when it was written in longhand, was typed in finished form and put on the growing pile. I was in a similar situation to Pascal when he wrote to a correspondent, 'I apologise that my letter is so long; I lacked the time to make it shorter', and it was fortunate for me that there was no word-length limit for a London MA thesis at this date. When mine was finished it ran to 760 quarto pages, and at a rough calculation totalled about 180,000 words. Another MA candidate in English Literature submitted a thesis of over 700 pages in the same year, after which the University introduced a limit of less than half that length.

It astounds me now, as I move words, phrases and sentences around on a computer screen, and effortlessly undo, revise, cut, paste, and insert footnotes, before pressing a key that instantly produces pages of pristine typescript, that I typed this monster of a thesis myself on my Oliver portable. I did so to save money, for the cost of having it typed professionally would have made a large hole in my getting-married savings, but it was a formidable task. Four copies of the finished work were needed: one for the University of London, which would be deposited in the Senate House Library, one for UCL and its library, one for myself, and a spare copy for lending to interested friends and sending hopefully to publishers. So four sheets of paper separated by three sheets of carbon had to be inserted into the Oliver's roller and the keys had to be struck with enough force to ensure that the fourth sheet received a legible impression – and at a slow tempo, for I could not type quickly without making mistakes. I gained extra time by taking advantage of a rule that allowed candidates to submit their theses unbound, which made it simpler to make any small corrections which the examiners might require before the degree was awarded, and with enormous relief I delivered the two top copies of my thesis just before the April deadline, each contained in a pair of stout spring-backed looseleaf binders. There

would be a written exam to sit in due course, and an oral examination of the thesis, but for a few weeks I was free to concentrate
on making arrangements for our wedding and finding somewhere
to live afterwards.

I didn't look much further into the future, because it was so
uncertain. In spite of having waited so long, I was getting married
without having a job or a firm prospect of one. I was bent on
becoming a university teacher, a profession which I thought would
be congenial and also give me enough freedom and spare time to
write creatively, but I was well aware of how difficult it was
to enter. The great post-war expansion of British universities did
not begin until the next decade; vacant posts were few and far
between, and the competition for them was keen. I was very
pleased to be shortlisted for an assistant lectureship at King's
College London at about this time, in spite of not yet having the
letters MA after my name; but the interview was disappointingly
perfunctory and gave me little opportunity to shine (one member
of the committee asked me fatuously if I played any sports). I sat
in an anteroom with the other candidates in pensive silence until
the interviews were completed, and after a short interval a registrar
appeared at the door to summon 'Dr Gregor' back to the
committee. A short, stocky man with sparse sandy hair jumped
to his feet with a smile and strode out of the room to accept the
appointment. His face had seemed vaguely familiar, and the name
reminded me that a year before I had heard him give a talk on
Graham Greene to the UC Catholic Society and that he had been
introduced as a research fellow at King's College. I realised that
the job had always been destined for the internal candidate and

that the rest of us were only there to go through the motions of impartiality. But it had been useful experience, and I felt no resentment at the outcome, because the man already had a PhD, and his talk on Graham Greene had been a good one – good enough to provoke a twinge of proprietorial jealousy. I did not guess that Ian Gregor would later become a cherished friend.

My most hopeful prospect of employment in the coming academic year was at UCL, where the English Department had a research assistantship in its gift. Its duties consisted mainly of helping Professor James Sutherland with his scholarly work, but there was also an opportunity to do a little tutoring. The salary was not much more than a postgraduate scholarship, but the job provided a useful bridge between student status and a proper appointment. Tony Petti and Derek Todd had both had it for a time, and it would soon become vacant again. Either Sutherland himself, or another senior member of the Department close to him – I cannot at this distance in time remember who it was – hinted to me that I would stand a good chance of getting it if I were interested, and I put my name forward. It was a purely internal appointment, without the formalities of advertisements and interviews. I thought it would be an ideal position for me during the first year of our marriage, Mary's salary providing the major part of our income while I looked for something more permanent.

Arranging the wedding itself didn't take us too long. We had a limited budget – about £200 I seem to remember – and weddings were simpler affairs in those days than now, when the typical cost is between £16,000 and £20,000 (estimates vary). The nuptial mass was to be celebrated in Hoddesdon, in a chapel belonging to an order called the Canons Regular of the Lateran which served as the Catholic parish church – cramped for that purpose but perfect for a wedding with a guest list of only forty-odd people. A country hotel in the neighbourhood that we fancied for the reception was too far out of town to be convenient, so we hired a room in the Hoddesdon Town Council building and the hotel agreed to provide a finger food buffet, with Pomagne (a superior kind of cider bottled like champagne) to drink the toasts. I had a new suit made to measure by Burtons, of charcoal grey worsted with a faint stripe, and Mary made her own wedding dress, which by tradition I was not allowed to see until the day.

I found us somewhere to live in the small ads of the *Evening Standard*. It was a first-floor unfurnished flat in a street of compact Victorian terraced houses off Battersea Park Road: a living room, bedroom and kitchen, and a bathroom shared with a single male lodger in an attic room. The very pleasant landlady, who lived on the ground floor with her elderly mother, obviously saw us as desirable tenants, but stressed, for future reference, that children would not be acceptable. We assured her that we had no intention of starting a family any time soon. We both assumed that one day we would have children, but we looked forward to enjoying some years together free from such responsibilities. There was of course no question of our using reliable contraception to this end, for its prohibition was absolute for practising Catholics. Our belief that artificial contraception was a mortal sin was as firm as our belief in the divinity of Christ or the doctrine of transubstantiation – indeed firmer, since it was easier to grasp. It was based on what was called Natural Law, which was actually not natural at all, but theological: the principle that the primary, God-given purpose of sexual intercourse (and the reason for confining it to married couples) was procreation, and to frustrate that purpose was to set human will against God's. Our assent to this teaching was helped by the fact that, from the little we knew about contraception, it seemed an ugly intrusion into the act of love, always attended by a kind of sniggering shame even among those who resorted to it. There were no love poems celebrating, or even referring to, the French letter or the Dutch cap. We had heard about the Safe Method, sometimes called the Rhythm Method, abstinence from sex in the period of the wife's menstrual cycle when she was likely to conceive, which was approved by the Church if used responsibly (i.e. not to avoid having any children at all) and seemed a much more attractive alternative. Wasn't the intention just the same as using contraceptives? Yes, but the crucial difference was that every act of intercourse was open to new life. In other words, the method was permissible because it might not work, and, as we would discover, it was much more likely to fail than artificial methods, and was known to disillusioned American Catholics as 'Vatican Roulette'. At the time, however, we blithely placed our faith in it, and went to see a counsellor at the Catholic Marriage Advisory Council who gave us some information on how to chart Mary's monthly cycle.

We were delighted with our new home and set about furnishing it, initially with a couple of armchairs and a sofa that folded out into a bed. I designed a pair of stepped bookshelves to fit into the alcoves each side of the fireplace in the living room, and a neighbour in Millmark Grove who was a carpenter-joiner constructed them. We bought curtains and emulsioned walls. It was the first time we had exercised our own taste in the décor of our habitat, and we enjoyed the process. Mary moved into the flat for a week or two before the wedding.

Saturday the 16th of May was a lovely sunny day, perfect for the occasion. Mary looked dazzlingly beautiful in her wedding dress, a ballerina style that was then fashionable, with a pretty scalloped neckline in a subtly textured silk material that looked white at first sight but had the faintest pink tint to it. And I looked like the cat who had finally got the cream, according to one of Mary's pupils in 4F4 when she showed them the wedding photos. They clubbed together to give us one of our nicest presents: a cut-glass dessert bowl and six matching dishes. At the time of writing this, we still have the bowl, our last surviving wedding gift along with two long-stemmed wine glasses from a set of six given by Dan Moynihan, or Danny as we now called him, like his actor friends. We had kept in touch through the years since he embarked on that career. As he was my oldest male friend, and a Catholic, I asked him to be my best man, but a few weeks before the wedding he had to drop out because the date clashed with a show he was in at the Bristol Old Vic. I was disappointed but I knew enough about the nature of his profession to forgive him, and asked Tony Petti to step into the breach.

The chapel of St Augustine where we were married had bosky grounds which provided an attractive background for photographs after the nuptial mass. They were taken in black and white, because our budget did not run to colour, but one picture was actually enhanced by monochrome. It was the last one the photographer took, and the most informal: Mary and I, smiling and happy, walk arm in arm towards the camera as if stepping confidently into the future, backlit by the noonday sun filtered through an archway of trees. Only if you look very carefully can you see that I have a cigarette between the fingers of my free hand. Martin Jones had a good camera and took a generous number of colour pictures which he kindly gave us on slides in due course, and we were able to recapture the bright polychrome reality of the day by peering at them through a pocket viewfinder bought for the purpose. I don't remember much about the reception, except that people generally seemed to be enjoying themselves and were satisfied with the modest repast we gave them. In my speech I quoted Dr Johnson's observation that 'marriage has many pains but celibacy has no pleasures', saying that I trusted he would be as wrong on the first count as, in Mary's company, I had found him on the second.

We left the party fairly early in the afternoon, for we were going to Dublin for our honeymoon and had a plane to catch from Heathrow. The destination was my idea, but Mary embraced it readily. I had never been there, Mary only very briefly, and it proved a good choice – a city full of historical and cultural interest, but also surrounded by scenic coastal landscape. We enjoyed making our own Joycean pilgrimage before the Irish Tourist Board had commercialised it, visiting sites immortalised in *A Portrait of the Artist* and *Ulysses* such as St Stephen's Green, Sandymount Strand and its Martello tower. We took an extraordinary ride over the hill of Howth (where the young Molly Bloom said *'yes I will Yes'* to Leopold) on the open top deck of a tram, swaying and lurching through gorse and bracken on a track which a few years later was put out of commission as unsafe. We visited the Irish National Gallery and viewed the Book of Kells in the Trinity College Library. The Abbey Theatre, where Yeats had mounted his poetic dramas and Synge had shocked the Dublin audience with *The Playboy of the Western World*, had been destroyed by fire in 1951, but we saw a play at the Queen's Theatre, which was the company's temporary home. As a holiday it was very successful; but of course that wasn't the main point of a honeymoon.

After comparing a few prospectuses and rates I had booked a double room for the week in a small hotel which would probably earn two stars today. The bathroom was not en suite, but the room itself was reasonably comfortable and the staff friendly. I have little doubt that they quickly identified us as a honeymoon couple. After supper in the hotel's dining room, we retired to bed. When two virgins, who have known each other for years but never indulged in heavy petting or had access to explicit sex manuals and videos, have intercourse for the first time, the earth is unlikely to move. There is bound to be some awkwardness and embarrassment and perhaps disappointment. We were no exception; but '*amor vincit omnia*'. We had got the hang of the basic act in the missionary position by the time we returned home and began to get mutual pleasure from it, albeit in a somewhat furtive fashion (in the dark, under the bedclothes, impeded by nightwear). Gradually we became less inhibited and more versatile lovers – but it was very gradual, over many years, progress being slowed by circumstances as well as the scant sexual know-how with which we started married life. This retardation was not without its benign effects. I was only twenty-four and Mary twenty-five. We were marrying for life, till death did us part – or so we believed, and so far it seems that we were right. Given that premise, there is much to be said for an unhurried exploration of the possibilities of erotic love, which may prevent desire from burning itself out early in a marriage and enable the enjoyment of physical intimacy to continue into old age. Nevertheless, in the early years of our married life we could have done without the extra constraints imposed by the Catholic teaching on birth control.[1]

Shortly after our return from Dublin I sat the written examination on the period of my research. Because this stretched from 1840 to the present, I had to choose between the nineteenth- and the twentieth-century papers, and opted for the former. In fact I had had very little time to read any of the major writers of either century while occupied with my enormous thesis on a host of mainly minor ones, and since submitting it I had done no special preparation for the exam, being confident of having enough accumulated knowledge to pass. I didn't even bother to look up papers from previous years. It turned out to be the hardest as well as the last written examination of my life. It lasted the usual

---

1 I was struck recently by the candid account of a modern couple who approached marriage with very different experience and expectations from ours, which vividly illustrates changes in sexual mores over the last fifty years or so. '"I hope we do stay together for ever," I said to my fiancée, Farah. "But, you know, we might not." . . . "I know," Farah said. "What do you think the chance is? Fifty-fifty?" "Maybe," I said. "Seventy-thirty?" Eight months later, in Marylebone register office, we made a 100% promise. I've read the brutal figures, nearly half of all UK marriages end in divorce – and every serious relationship I've had, prior to this one, has failed. We've both had broken hearts . . . Most of all, we're realists. We may be newly married, but we've been together for nine years, cohabiting for eight. It's long enough to have pushed through periods of domestic hostility and to know what happens to all that sex. It's long enough for us to understand that, solemn as our oath might have appeared, "Till death do us part" is the sound not of guarantee, but of hope.' (Will Storr, 'My Chemical Romance', *Guardian Weekend,* 9th February 2013)

three hours, but instead of answering three questions candidates had to answer just one. Scanning the paper, I couldn't see a single topic on which I could write extempore for three hours. Eventually I chose one about the influence of Italy on English writers and began to write an essay about Browning and Clough and the Italian Risorgimento, which I had studied for A-level history and which was an issue in some of the Catholic novels I had read because of its challenge to the Papal States; but I was well aware that it was a rambling and flagrantly padded piece of work. It was four years since I had sat a written examination (excluding the Army Clerk's trade tests) and in that time I had become a habitual cigarette smoker, accustomed to lighting up at moments of compositional stress. This became so powerful a craving during the exam that I asked for an invigilator to accompany me to the men's toilets so that I could have a quick drag in one of the cubicles.

It was a horrible and humbling experience, and I was seriously worried that I might fail the exam and have to resit it before getting my MA, even if the thesis passed with flying colours. My external examiner was Kathleen Tillotson, Professor of English at Bedford College (a small women's college of London University situated in Regent's Park, later merged with Royal Holloway College) and the author of a fine book entitled *Novels of the Eighteen-Forties*. She was a tall, thin, elegant lady, one of the very few female professors of English in the country at that time, married to Geoffrey Tillotson, professor at another London college, Birkbeck, and a specialist in the same period who would soon examine Park Honan's PhD. In the distant past postgraduate candidates 'defended' their theses in public, and on the Continent they still do, often with pomp and ceremony. Later in my career

I acted as one of the judges of a PhD dissertation on the poetry of Philip Larkin at the Catholic University of Leuven in the Netherlands. We sat on a stage in our academic robes and the candidate answered our questions in front of a packed audience that included a large contingent of his family and friends, who applauded his every response like spectators at a tennis match, and cheered at the end when he passed. I believe that at Oxford and Cambridge post-graduate examinations are still open to any member of the University, but very seldom attended by anyone except the candidate and the two examiners. At most other British universities they are private conversations between these three persons, in which the internal examiner, who is also the supervisor, plays a subordinate role. It always seemed to me when I examined postgraduate theses later in my career that these occasions were very tame conclusions to three or more years of dedicated effort, but at the time, like most candidates, I dare say, I was glad to have no observers of my oral. Kathleen Tillotson relieved my anxiety at the outset by telling me that I had passed the written examination, not without a dry hint that it was by a narrow margin. She was complimentary about the thesis, did not complain, as she might have done, about its excessive length, and had no reservations about passing it except to ask that a number of minor errors and typos she had noted should be corrected before it was bound and deposited in the libraries. I shook hands with her and MacDonald Emslie, and went jubilantly home to give Mary the good news.

Unwelcome news soon followed. I received a letter from James Sutherland informing me that someone else had been appointed to the research assistantship: a young woman who may have returned to the Department after an absence, because I hadn't been aware of her existence when I formed the Endsleigh Street discussion group. I recognised her name, but knew nothing else about her. I had not, of course, been promised the job, but nevertheless I felt let down. At about the same time Mary became fairly sure she was pregnant, and a visit to the doctor confirmed it. We wondered if she had miscalculated her monthly cycle, though in fact it was more likely that the emotional upheaval of getting married had disturbed it. This was a double blow to our plans, and it says something for our youthful resilience that we were exhilarated by the prospect of having a child, even though it was sooner than we had wished. I felt I was experiencing real independence, and the responsibility that came with it, for the first time, and relished the challenge. Our greatest regret was that we might have to leave the flat which we had only just begun to make into a home; but I was applying for every university post for which I was eligible and it was more than likely that if I were successful we would have to move from London. I had in fact just applied for one at the University College of Wales in Bangor. In the meantime, we could make love whenever we felt like it, without bothering to consult the calendar.

Mary decided to resign from her job at Eltham Green with effect from the end of the school year, and look for a supply job nearer to Battersea for the autumn term. She found one quickly at a technical college in west London, teaching English and French at a better salary than she was getting from Eltham. I also looked for occasional teaching work, and was hired for a few weeks by the French Lycée in Kensington to teach English literature to a class of eleven- and twelve-year-old boys, who all seemed to be the children of diplomats and glamorous media people, and were incredibly assured and precocious. Their set book at the time was *Mansfield Park,* generally considered to be Jane Austen's least reader-friendly novel, but my pupils had no problems with it. I had in fact never read this book, and quickly did so. It interested me exceedingly, and thanks to that stimulus I published a scholarly article about it later – the first one unconnected with my MA thesis. I was also employed to tutor a young man in a TB sanatorium in A-level English Literature, visiting him once a week after having a BCG injection to protect me from infection. At the same time I started revising the text of *The Picturegoers,* conscious that its acceptance by MacGibbon & Kee had acquired an additional importance and urgency.

I was shortlisted for the post at Bangor, and called for interview in early July. The long vacation had begun and the candidates – there were four of us – easily identified each other as we strolled like tourists around the eerily quiet and empty campus, situated on green hills above the town. Because of Bangor's location in north-west Wales the candidates had to stay overnight as guests of the college prior to the interview and we spent a more-than-usual amount of time in each other's company. This was not an entirely comfortable situation, but it had narrative possibilities that I explored soon afterwards in the script of a play written speculatively for television called *The Interview,* which never found a producer. I was unsuccessful once again at Bangor, but disappointment was mingled with a certain relief for, picturesque though it was, it seemed to me a deeply provincial place where I would feel like an exile if appointed, all the more so since it was in a Welsh-speaking part of the principality. I had not yet received enough rejections to feel like one of the characters in *The Interview*, William Pritchard, who says: '*I tell you, the sweetest words in all the world to me, the words I want to hear more than any others, are: "Mr Pritchard, the committee would like to see you again for a few minutes."*'

I communicated my lack of progress on the job front to Park Honan in Brittany, where he and his family were spending the summer with Jeannette's parents, as was their custom. He commiserated with me in characteristic style, which might have seemed effusive coming from a compatriot, but from him was palpably sincere and comforting, in a three-page single-spaced typed letter that began, 'I don't think you could possibly write a letter to me that would have anything but a cheering, brightening effect. It's wonderful to hear from you – your letter's just come – despite the burden of grim news. Life *is* a bloody insecure business, perhaps a little farcical, too, a bit of a cosmic joke.' Park's PhD thesis, which he had written in a six-month burst of concentrated effort, had been accepted, and he had obtained a teaching job at Connecticut College, a well-regarded liberal arts college for women, which he was due to take up in August, and he offered to fix me up with a job there if I wanted it – 'Froggy and I would be deliriously happy if you did . . . and if you find it interesting at all you should get in touch with me immediately.' He also referred to the recent abrupt departure of Anthony Brown from MacGibbon & Kee, which I had reported to him. 'We're terribly sorry to hear it, of course, because of our loss of a real ally there – your loss and my loss, and the grim shadow this casts over our struggling novels – but also because Brown is an awfully nice guy. They must be raving nuts at Mac & Kee.' Finally he responded to a remark I had made about maybe taking a short holiday in France, and perhaps visiting them. 'How wonderful a surprise visit would be! I hope you meant that seriously . . . nothing would do us more good than to see you both.' He told me the best way to get to St Brévin-les-Pins, and we accepted the invitation gratefully, conscious that it would be our last such opportunity before the baby arrived.

St Brévin-les-Pins is a residential resort on the southern side of the Loire estuary where it broadens out to meet the Atlantic, and almost opposite the port of St Nazaire, to which we travelled by train via Paris. Park met us there with his father-in-law, Monsieur Colin, known in the family as 'Papy'. A genial but largely silent man who looked a little like the elderly Picasso, he drove us in that quintessentially French car, a Citroën Deux Chevaux, to the one-storey house in St Brévin where he and his wife spent a good part of the year in their retirement from schoolteaching. It was situated among many similar houses on a sandy lane not far from the beach, with a patio shaded by a big tree and a garage in which we were accommodated. We did not complain about that: it was a nice clean garage, often used for guests, provided with a springy double bed and other basic pieces of furniture, and it was extremely generous of the Colins to put us up in any fashion. Mme Colin was the dominant presence in the home, with a very firm idea of how things should be done, and Mary, fluent in French and with an au pair's experience of the French bourgeoisie, got on well with her. Park's French was as bad as mine, but he spoke it with less inhibition. For me the week we spent in St Brévin was an education in the French way of life, including such oddities as serving a plate of green beans all on their own as a course in the main meal of the day. The purchasing of the food for this meal in the local shops and market, its preparation and cooking, occupied most of the morning for the womenfolk of the party, supervised by Madame Colin, and the men washed up afterwards. For leisure there was the beach: when the tide was up, you swam, and when it was out you strolled on the huge tract of exposed sand or paddled and caught shrimps in the shallows. In the evenings Park and Jeannette put their children to bed – the twins, Matthew and Natasha, were now just over one year old – and joined us in the garage, where we chatted and played a game I knew as Coffee Pot, though it has other names, in which one player thinks of a famous person of the past or present and the others have to try and guess who it is by asking questions of a formulaic kind. Park was addicted to this game, and would keep us at it for hours until poor Jeannette, who was exhausted from looking after 'Thieu and 'Tasha, all day, fell asleep where she sat.

For the Honans this summer in St Brévin had an elegiac feeling because at the end of it they would be going back to the States. Connecticut College was located in a place called New London, rather poignantly for them, for they had greatly enjoyed their three years in old London. Park knew he would be returning to a much more regimented and competitive academic culture, which did not suit his temperament so well. Jeannette would miss her British friends and the relative proximity of her family. Still, they would have significantly more money to live on than the £58 per month of Park's US government grant, and Jeannette hoped to earn enough by teaching French to allow them to return to Europe every summer. We looked forward to seeing them again, and vowed to keep in touch by mail in the meantime. Park would prove to be, especially over the next few years, the best correspondent – the most regular, most engaging, most encouraging and most eloquent – that I ever had.

Surprisingly, for it was late in the academic year, an assistant lectureship in nineteenth- and twentieth-century literature at Bedford College was advertised shortly after we returned to England, having stayed in Paris for a few days on the way. I applied immediately – and hopefully, thinking that Kathleen Tillotson's favourable opinion of my thesis would give me a real chance of success. I was summoned to an interview and joined the other candidates in a pleasant room overlooking Regent's Park. The ambience was more informal than it had been at King's College or Bangor – there was even coffee provided – and we chatted among ourselves while waiting for the interviews to commence. The last one to arrive was a tall, handsome young woman with curly blonde hair, dressed with casual elegance, and as soon as she walked through the door I guessed that she would get the job. She reinforced my hunch by telling me that she had been attending the Salzburg Seminar and had come straight from Heathrow. The Salzburg Seminar, I gathered from our conversation, was a prestigious interdisciplinary conference on American Studies held in the Austrian city, attended annually by a select group of invited academics of various ages and nationalities, and lavishly funded from the USA. That she had been invited to it although her own research field was nineteenth-century English literature was evidence that she was a high-flyer. She had a B.Litt. from Oxford and was working on a PhD. Her name was Gillian. I can't remember what her second name was, but I knew her later as Gillian Beer, Fellow of Girton College, Cambridge, subsequently King Edward VII Professor of English Literature and Dame of the British Empire. She got the job at Bedford, of course (and met her husband, John Beer, who was on the staff there). That I had predicted it did not prevent me from feeling, when she was summoned back to meet the committee, a little more like William Pritchard in *The Interview*.

There was no further chance of getting a university appointment for the new academic year; but the British Council advertised a post of assistant at their London Overseas Students Centre which seemed to offer interesting and useful experience to someone in my situation, and I applied for it. The Council's mission is chiefly to promote British culture abroad, but in those days it also provided a range of services to students from foreign countries who came to study in the UK. About half of them were postgraduates in a variety of disciplines and the other half were students of English from Europe spending a year in Britain as part of their degree courses, often as colloquial assistants teaching modern languages in our schools. The duties of the assistant at the Council's London Centre were mainly to teach English language classes and to give a weekly lecture on English literature, and the salary was about the same as the starting salary of a university assistant lecturer. I was soon called for an interview with the Director of the Centre at its premises in Brook Street, off Regent Street. He was Richard Auty, who had only recently been appointed to the position. I think he more or less offered the job to me on the spot, but the euphoria of getting it probably compressed the process in memory.

Richard was a delightful man, cultured, clever, witty, and quite without pomposity. He was rapidly climbing the British Council's career ladder, and would end his own in the plum job of Council Representative in Paris. He was, I suppose, then in his early forties, and married to Anne, a French lady somewhat younger, who reminded me of my aunt Lu, warm-hearted and vivacious. The Autys became great friends, and took an almost parental interest in our welfare, the only thing that we couldn't agree on being religion. In the later years of the war Richard had worked in the Army Bureau for Current Affairs, an organisation providing educational programmes for servicemen which was widely credited with encouraging an estimated eighty per cent of them to vote Labour in the general election of 1945, and his and Anne's views were those of the secular left. (So were those of Park and Jeannette but with them, by tacit agreement, we seldom discussed religion.) I remember Richard saying to me as we shared the rather antiquated Brook Street lift one day, 'You know, David, the Catholic Church will have to change its mind about birth control', and my saying firmly but without animus, 'No, it never will. It simply can't.' Our failure with the Safe Method hadn't shaken my faith in the teaching. When Anne discovered that Mary was pregnant she asked if we knew about the Lamaze/Vellay method of natural childbirth, or Childbirth Without Pain as it was known then, which was well established in France but almost unknown in England. This was opportune, because Jeannette Honan had told Mary about *Accouchement Sans Douleur* when we were in Brittany, and urged her to look into it. Anne was an enthusiastic advocate of the method, and lent Mary a book and an LP which explained and illustrated the breathing techniques to control contractions, which she would demonstrate in due course to the sceptical custodians of the St Thomas's Hospital maternity ward.

The first assignment in my new job had nothing to do with teaching English. I was drafted, along with a number of other Council employees, some from Head Office, to take part in a series of short residential courses provided at the beginning of every academic year for foreign students just arrived from countries in Asia and Africa, some accompanied by their wives and children. These courses were designed to introduce the newcomers to aspects of British life which might be challengingly unfamiliar: for instance, how to light a coin-operated gas fire, how to eat a kipper, and how to use a toilet with a flushing mechanism and a seat. There was a lady whose job it was to take certain students aside and tactfully explain that their surnames were homophones of obscene words in English, and that it would be advisable to modify them during their residence here. Those from hot climates were warned about the British one, and I led sorties out of the college in Greenwich where the courses took place to the local Marks & Spencer, where the students bought long johns and other winter underwear. There were also a few excursions to places of cultural and historical interest, and by leading one of them I saw inside the Tower of London myself for the first time.

Not having had any training in teaching English as a foreign language, a discipline which in any case was in its infancy, I found this part of my work disconcertingly difficult at first, but also illuminating. I hadn't been properly attentive to Randolph Quirk's lectures on modern linguistics at UCL, and the old-fashioned Latin-based grammar I had been taught at school was not much use for explaining how modern English actually worked. We learn the rules of the mother tongue as children intuitively and by imitation, but foreign speakers need them to be made explicit. It had never occurred to me, for instance, before I studied the text-book my students were using, that in order to use a verb in a negative sense in English you have to combine it with the verb 'do'. The part of my work that most interested me, however, was the weekly lecture on English literature, which was aimed mostly at the Continental *assistants*. It seemed to be expected that over the next nine months I would survey the history of English litera-ture from *Beowulf* to Virginia Woolf, and beyond. Lacking the confidence to speak from notes, I wrote out the lectures week by week and in the process plugged some of the gaps in my own knowledge. As the lectures were held in the evening, Mary came to hear me, and told me that in trying to cover too much ground I was speaking much too fast for the students to take in the information. I had to admit that as they scribbled their notes they sometimes lifted their heads and looked up at me rather desperately as they flipped over the pages in their notebooks. It was all useful preparation for the university job I still hoped to obtain. Whether she attended the lecture or not, Mary would join me afterwards and we would have a meal in a little restaurant in Carnaby Street which served a very tasty pork goulash.

This was an enjoyable time for us. We were both earning, and making the most of our freedom before the arrival of the baby, which was expected in mid-February. We went often to the Royal Court Theatre, which we had patronised for several years, and which was now only a short bus-ride away across the Thames. It was the chief showcase for the new wave of British dramatists in the late fifties and we saw much of Arnold Wesker's early work there, *Roots*, *The Kitchen* and *Chips with Everything*, and plays by John Arden, Ann Jellicoe, N.F. Simpson and others. Nothing ever quite matched the thrill of seeing the first production of *Look Back in Anger*, but I revived it in a fashion at the Overseas Students Centre, when I put on a rehearsed reading of the first act, playing the part of Jimmy Porter myself, and casting one of the secretaries as Alison. The students found it hilarious, the young men from traditional patriarchal cultures being especially amused by Jimmy's bullying of his wife as she plied the iron on the ironing board. We also went to the Sunday night members' performances at the Court when experimental work was put on, and sometimes fights broke out afterwards between playwrights and critics in the pub next door. One Sunday evening I particularly enjoyed featured Christopher Logue reading his poetry to the accompaniment of a cool jazz group in his inimitable throaty voice, the phrases lingering in the air like perfectly formed smoke rings. I bought the EP recording, called *Red Bird*, and I wish I still had the equipment to play it now as I write this.

In the late summer of 1959 I received my author's copies of a small paperback book, about 25,000 words long, called *Introducing Jazz*. It was published by St Paul Publications, and followed the same formula as *About Catholic Authors*, though it did not appear in the same series, and had a colourful cover design incorporating a photograph of Louis Armstrong. I had proposed the idea to a senior Paulist editor in the spring of 1957 when I was still in the Army and submitted some specimen chapters, as a result of which the book was commissioned in November of that year and delivered in April 1958, so it had taken a long time to appear. The frame story is set in a Catholic youth club that boasts its own jazz band. One evening the pianist injures his hand, and an American priest recently seconded to the parish strolls in, sits down at the piano and astonishes the members by playing a scintillating boogie-woogie. It transpires that he was a professional jazz musician before he found his vocation as a priest. The young people ask him to talk to them about the history of jazz and he obliges over several sessions. It was an act of extraordinary chutzpah for someone who didn't play an instrument, couldn't read music, and possessed only a small collection of records, to write a book about the development of jazz from its origins and in all its varieties: New Orleans, blues, Dixieland, swing, revivalist, bebop, West Coast, cool and fusion. Skimming through this book some fifty years later, I thought the discourse sounded much more like the voice of an English postgraduate student than an ordained American ex-jazz-musician, but I was surprised by how knowledgeable I had managed to make him seem. For example:

'I want you to listen now to *Improvisations,* composed by one of Stan Kenton's brilliant young arrangers, Bill Russo, and featuring altoist Lee Konitz. This recording clearly illustrates Kenton's remarks about the role of the soloist, and shows how the regular beat of orthodox jazz can be disrupted to great effect. It also exemplifies the big band under complete control, the massed effects being used with economy to dramatise the long saxophone solo. The alto sax is the *vox humana* of jazz.'

I know that last aphorism was my own because I gave it to the hero of *The Picturegoers,* but the book as a whole was heavily dependent on secondary sources, especially *Hear Me Talkin To Ya': the story of jazz as told by the men who made it,* by Nat Shapiro and Nat Hentoff, which I acknowledged, and Rex Harris's *Jazz*, which I'm afraid I did not. Perhaps conscious that my bluff might be called by somebody, I hid my authorship behind the initials 'D.J.L.', and in consequence only a few assiduous collectors of my work have discovered it. I wrote the book for the money, such as it was, but I learned a lot in the process. Dad was impressed by the book, and sent a copy to the editor of *Melody Maker*, who had been a patron of the Studio Club, hoping that the paper might commission some articles from me. He received a courteous reply, with a kind word for the book, but a firm statement that the paper was fully supplied with material by its own staff.

It did not take me long to finish revising *The Picturegoers*. I had matured considerably since I submitted the first version, the faults of which seemed very obvious on revisiting it. I was sure that I had improved it, but, following the departure of Anthony Brown, my editor at MacGibbon & Kee was now Timothy O'Keeffe, and I was not at all confident that he would like the novel when I handed over the typescript to him in Great Portland Street. He was a reserved, quietly spoken Irishman who that year brought back into print Flann O'Brien's *At Swim-Two-Birds*, which had been totally eclipsed by the outbreak of war when first published in 1939. It soon became a modern classic and encouraged the melancholic and alcoholic author to begin writing again. Tim O'Keeffe was the friend of several other important Irish writers, but he did not waste time or words in his dealings with me. In all the eight or nine years of our professional relationship, I don't recall that he ever took me out to lunch, and can think of only one occasion when he stood me a drink. That didn't surprise or disappoint me, as I had no experience of author–publisher relations; and I was delighted to get a letter from him two days after delivering my MS to say, 'I would like to tell you that I read THE PICTUREGOERS after you left yesterday and it struck me as a very fine piece of work indeed. Also, I think it stands a very good chance of being noticed and being sold.' Publication was scheduled for the following spring.

Park sent in the revised version of his novel in October but, alas, it was turned down. I empathised with him at this disappointing outcome all the more because of my own better luck, and offered to save him postage by delivering his novel to other London publishers. This I did several times over the months that followed, forging his signature on the covering letters. He reciprocated by touting my MA thesis around American Catholic university presses, after MacGibbon & Kee and a couple of other London publishers had turned it down. These twin efforts often elicited tantalising expressions of interest, but no offers. We cheered each other up by cursing the fickleness and obtuseness of publishers. 'Yes I *do* think your novel should be published, Park,' I wrote to him when his faith in it was dwindling, 'and I am honoured to transport it round the cretinous publishers. I'm just reading John Braine's second, *The Vodi*, and it's lousy.' I had actually begun reading that novel while waiting for our first child to be born in the early hours of 16th February 1960, nine months almost to the day after our wedding.

16

They are sexually innocent to a degree that they will scarcely be able to credit when looking back on their youth in years to come. They know about the mechanics of basic copulation, but none of them could give an accurate account of the processes of fertilization, gestation and birth, and three of the young men do not even know how babies are born, vaguely supposing that they appear by some natural form of Caesarean section, like ripe chestnuts splitting their husks.

So says the authorial narrator of *How Far Can You Go?* about a group of Catholic students aged eighteen to nineteen, gathered together at mass on St Valentine's Day in February 1952. No reader of my own generation has ever questioned the plausibility of this description of their ignorance, so I presume that it would have applied to a much larger sample of this age group in real life at that date. I knew a little more than the three fictional young men when I got married, but I followed a steep learning curve after

Mary became pregnant. I did not accompany her to the antenatal classes – husbands were not invited – but I took a keen interest in the Childbirth Without Pain exercises she did at home and learned how to help her when she went into labour. Our commitment to this innovative procedure was ideological as well as practical, and for Mary it was a precursor of the Women's Liberation movement which began a decade later, but it was viewed with scepticism and suspicion by those members of the British medical profession who had heard of it at all. There was no possibility of my being allowed to be present at the birth, but after some negotiation with the staff at St Thomas's, the large teaching hospital where Mary was booked in, they grudgingly agreed that I could be with her in the early stages of labour and briefly when she was taken into the delivery room. As it was a first baby, we were expecting a fairly long labour and that we would practise the breathing at home for a while before it was time for me to call the ambulance from the telephone box at the corner of the street (we had no phone and neither did our landlady). What actually happened I described in a letter to Park and Jeannette, written two days later, in which I borrowed something of the demonstrative buoyancy of Park's own epistolary style for the occasion. (It is one of the very few private letters of mine that have survived from that period, because Park kept it.)

The big news is I'M A FATHER of – (*pace* Poopie and Tasha) – the most beautiful daughter in the world, name of Julia Mary! You will be delighted to know that the Lamaze/Vellay method worked like a charm. You were the first to put us on to it, and we can't thank you enough. The story is briefly as follows: at about 3 a.m. on February 16th Mary's waters broke, and contractions started coming pretty intensely at about *one a minute*. I said it would be a quick birth, and was I right! Mary got working on the shallow breathing while I got things together and phoned the ambulance. We didn't rush and were admitted to St Thomas's Hospital just after four. After a great deal of persuasion I had got the authorities to agree to my staying with Mary for the first part of the labour, and arrived with books, prepared for several hours of waiting afterwards. To our astonishment and joy she was found to be fully dilated and taken straight into the delivery room. I was allowed to see her for a few minutes there as she began to push out the baby. She looked marvellous. Julia was born at 6 a.m., and I saw Mary soon afterwards. She was cuddling the baby and looked still more marvellous. I saw the baby weighed (6 pounds 14 ounces) and went home in a cheerful daze, restraining myself with difficulty from telling bus conductors and passers-by the news.

The whole thing took only three hours from start to finish, and was accomplished without pain or anaesthetics. Unfortunately the cack-handed student who delivered the baby managed to tear Mary a little with the baby's shoulder (he said 'Sorry'!) and she had to have a few stitches. The whole thing was a wonderful experience for both of us, and next time nobody's going to keep me out of the delivery room. I don't think I have ever admired Mary so much . . . She has shaken the hospital's scepticism about C.W.P. and students are trooping in [to the ward] all day to ask her questions about it.

Like most young couples with a first baby, we were not really prepared for the consequent disruption to the rhythm of our lives, especially of sleep. Getting up in the middle of the midwinter night to feed Julia in a house without central heating was a challenge. At first I felt obliged to keep Mary company as she suckled the child, gazing enviously the while at the voluptuously enhanced breasts her tiny fingers kneaded; later I tended to feign sleep, but when Mary supplemented her breast milk with a bottle I learned to take my turn with that. The flat was not ideal for bringing up a baby. The small kitchen sink, concealed in a cupboard, was the only place to wash things, and a clothes line on a pulley outside the kitchen window the only place to dry them, so we extravagantly subscribed to a dedicated laundry service that collected and delivered every few days, keeping the soiled nappies in a vessel filled with a sterilising liquid called Milton. The incongruous association with the great poet fixed the name in my memory for ever. In due course we acquired the pram in the hall that Cyril Connolly famously called 'the enemy of art', an aphorism I intended to refute, and wheeled it into Battersea Park to give Julia a modicum of the fresh air that folk wisdom prescribed for her health. (American friends used to say that you could always tell British infants by their raw red cheeks and runny noses, caused by prolonged exposure to the elements.) We were indebted to our landlady for her tolerance of the pram and its occupant, but in truth she and her aged mother were enraptured with the baby and it gave a new dimension of interest to their lives. They may have been worried that we might conceive another before long, because the mother, a very old lady who never left the house, took the opportunity when Mary brought Julia to see her one day to offer some advice on birth control. 'You just pull away, dear,' she said, lowering her voice discreetly. 'Pull away at the right moment.' Before we resumed sexual relations we paid another visit to the Catholic Marriage Advisory Council, and were instructed in a new and more reliable way of identifying the safe period of a woman's monthly cycle by recording the rise and fall of her bodily temperature, most efficiently by employing a rectal thermometer. The inconveniences of this method were comically portrayed some years later in my novel *The British Museum is Falling Down*; but it did work – for about a year.

Winter gave way to spring, and spring to summer, and I still had no university job in prospect. In that academic year I applied for assistant lectureships at Keele and Hull without being short-listed for either of them, and was called for interview only once, at Birmingham. It was for a fellowship in the Arts Faculty, tenable for three years, which offered young scholars an opportunity to pursue their own research while doing a limited amount of teaching in the appropriate department. I was hopeful about this opening because the Head of English at Birmingham was T.J.B. Spencer, who had been at UCL when I was an under-graduate, and might remember giving me a straight A for my term paper on the History of Lit Crit. He had also been Mary's tutor in her third year, but it was unlikely that he knew we had married. The Arts Faculty of Birmingham University was due to move to the Edgbaston campus in a year's time, and was still housed in the centre of the city, in a building that had a worn, neglected aspect and smelled faintly of drains and gas inside. The selection committee consisted only of Spencer and the Dean of the Faculty, and the interview was relaxed – too relaxed to bode well, I thought, and I was not surprised when the fellowship was offered to someone else. Afterwards, as I was leaving the building, Spencer said a few private words of commiseration which showed that he remembered me from UCL, and I took the opportunity to mention that my wife was his former tutee, Mary Jacob.

In May a lectureship in the English Department at Birmingham was advertised, and my hopes were ignited again. But I heard nothing after the acknowledgement of my application, and resigned myself to another rejection – in some ways the most disappointing of all. I knew that I could probably stay on at the Overseas Students Centre for another year, but it was a job with no future unless I signed up for a career with the British Council, and I didn't want that. I was seriously thinking of applying to teach in technical colleges, though Park urged me not to, 'until all other possibilities are exhausted'. As usual, his hyperbolic rhetoric cheered me up. 'I simply can't believe that a university with sanity and judgment wouldn't jump to get you now,' he wrote. 'They must be flooded by relatives, bribes, incest and non-compos-mentis Departmental Chairmen pressured by moneyed alumni.' I took every opportunity to remind senior academic contacts of my existence by sending them offprints of articles that I had carved out of my thesis. One day I heard a talk on BBC Radio by George Kane, who had been Mary's tutor in her second year, and had taken an interest in our post-graduation lives as a couple, once inviting us to tea at home with his wife. He was now occupying a chair at Royal Holloway College, and hearing his talk prompted me to send him the offprint of an article on Edmund Randolph, one of the few Victorian Catholic novelists who deserved to be rescued from obscurity, which I had just published in the *Aylesford Review,* a small literary magazine edited by the maverick Carmelite monk Brocard Sewell. Kane thanked me for the offprint, which he claimed had made him want to read Randolph's novel *Mostly Fools,* and continued: 'I am glad that the British Council work is going well, but grieved because you have not yet got the university job which you want. You should be being called to interview. What do you think is going on? Is JRS [James Sutherland] perhaps not writing you a strong enough letter? I shall try to remember to get at him for not having placed you yet.' He went on to give me some excellent advice, which, in a nutshell, was that I should not waste any more time on minor Catholic writers, but get myself a 'mainline project' for a PhD or book, to show that I could be trusted to teach the canonical authors of English literature.

In fact I had already come to this conclusion myself. At that time even Graham Greene and Evelyn Waugh, the stars of my thesis, were not regarded as major writers by either the academic establishment or its opponents – the critical school of F.R. Leavis and his followers. While doing my MA I had become increasingly conscious that what distinguished novelists of genuine originality and literary merit (whether 'major' or 'minor') from the legions of instantly forgettable ones was their feeling for the expressive possibilities of language, and I was vaguely meditating a book on the language of fiction that would deal with classic authors and have a theoretical dimension. Kane's advice encouraged me to pursue the idea. (Curiously, when I mentioned this to Park in a letter, he said he was pondering a similar project, a book about style in a group of twentieth-century novelists including Hemingway and Waugh.) But what most interested me in Kane's letter was the glimpse it afforded into the hidden network of patronage and personal contacts which controlled the academic job market. Sutherland had already passed me over for the post of his research assistant. Could it be true that he was not strongly supporting my applications elsewhere, perhaps because he was referee for other candidates for the same jobs?

Through an extraordinary coincidence fifteen years later I came across some fascinating if ambiguous evidence to support this speculation. In 1975 I was asked by the magazine *New Society* to review a book called *Scaling the Ivory Tower: merit and its limits in academic careers* by Lionel S. Lewis, an American professor of sociology, published by Johns Hopkins University Press. Lewis's basic argument was that appointments and promotions are generally determined not by objective assessments of merit but what he called 'ascribed merit' and 'sponsored mobility' – namely that bright young students who impress their teachers for a number of different reasons, not exclusively academic, are chosen and groomed for the same profession, and started on their career paths by recommendations to senior colleagues in other institutions who got there by the same means, and who share the same values and prejudices. Confidential references for applicants for academic jobs play a crucial part in this process, and one of the most interesting chapters in Lewis's book was one in which he analysed and interpreted selected passages from large samples of such references, with names deleted, obtained apparently with ease from various universities in America, and in one case, with difficulty, from Britain. (Lewis expressed some amusement at the 'solicitude and secrecy' surrounding such documents on this side of the Atlantic.) I was particularly interested in his discussion of the British collection of fifty-seven letters written on behalf of thirty-three candidates for a post in an unnamed department of English, and even more interested when I realised that I was one of them. Two passages revealed this to me. The first was:

> Compare the remarks made about a female scholar who completed a study of a female literary figure with those made about a male who, even if lacking innate intuition, is still obviously qualified: 'a sympathetic and judicious under-standing of her subject, both as a woman and as a writer'; and 'The subject of his thesis was Catholic Fiction . . . and though I did not examine it I understand it was a very good piece of work. ([He], by the way, is a Catholic.)' The issue, then, is not one of sex (or religion) per se, but of trusting an insider to find and recognize the truth.

The truth, in this case, evidently being that the woman was the stronger candidate, though why Lewis inferred that I lacked 'innate intuition' was not clear. Any doubt as to the identity of the male candidate was dispelled by the second passage: 'His post at the British Council is not the usual job, lunching with visiting oriental professors and introducing them to various people, but is mainly concerned with teaching.' Lewis cited this as an example of the adversative 'but' to conceal or minimise a 'deficiency' in the candidate. I am fairly sure the passages quoted were written by Sutherland rather than another of my referees (the reference to not examining my thesis is a clue) and it has to be said that they lack enthusiasm. I had some fun with my discovery in reviewing the book, and some weeks later received a courteous but guarded letter from Professor Lewis conceding that I could have been the subject of the reference quoted (from which all names had been removed) and explaining that 'innate intuition' was intended as a humorous allusion to the idea of 'female intuition'. He apologised for making me feel 'unecessarily uncomfortable'. At that point in time I was sufficiently secure in my academic career to feel nothing but amusement at a coincidence that would have been condemned as incredible in a campus novel.

In June 1960 my spirits were lifted by the arrival of six author's copies of *The Picturegoers,* the publication of which had been postponed from spring to July. Nothing in a novelist's life quite equals the thrill of handling and opening the first mint copy of one's first novel. It had an attractive cover, a steep bank of red cinema seats occupied in places by well-observed portraits of some of the characters. I had not seen it before; if I had, I would have corrected a mistake in the blurb ('noviciate' for 'novice'). It would be some time before I learned to insist on checking everything connected with a new book before it went to press – or had the confidence to do so. Like most hardback novels of that period it was a compact duodecimo, clearly printed on pages that were gathered and bound so that the book opened comfortably in the hands. There was no organised publicity for it – I don't think MacGibbon & Kee possessed a publicity department as such, or if they did I was not aware of it, either then or later. Publishing literary fiction was a simple business in those days: your book was sent out into the world without your participation, and you sat back and waited for the reviews. But at least you could feel confident of *getting* some reviews, which cannot be said of most first novels today. Far fewer titles were published in 1960, and they were usually reviewed in batches of half a dozen, which gave most authors a good chance of being noticed.

In none of my applications for university jobs did I mention that I had written a novel accepted by a reputable publisher, even when its publication was assured. Nowadays that would be a feather in the cap of any candidate for a post in a university English department, but I thought that including it in my CV might be counter-productive, suggesting that I was not a serious, dedicated scholar. In hindsight I'm sure it would have helped rather than hindered my chances of getting a job; but the decision foreshadowed the way I subsequently conducted my twin careers of novelist and academic for many years, giving equal effort to both, but keeping them in separate compartments of my life as far as possible.

The novel was priced at fifteen shillings, equivalent to about £15 today, but £34 in purchasing power. This caused me great anxiety because there were more than five people to whom, for various reasons, I would have liked to give inscribed copies; but now that Mary was no longer earning, and we had the expenses of a baby, our income was stretched to its limit and I could not afford to buy extra copies, even at author's discount, to include them all, without breaking into our modest savings. Mum and Dad, of course, had to have one, because the novel was dedicated to them, partly in acknowledgement of their love and support, but also to signal to the reader that the rather unlikeable parents of the principal male character were not based on them. Aunt Eileen, Uncle John and *Tante* Lu, the Jacob family and Park accounted for four more copies, leaving one for myself. A consequence of this distribution was that I wrote a letter to Malachy Carroll telling him that I had a novel coming out shortly, that I hoped he would read it, and that I would be very interested to know what he thought of it, since I owed so much to his advice and encouragement in the past. I had not had much contact with him for a year or so, and it was even longer since we had met face to face, so it did not surprise me that he did not reply immediately. I assumed he was waiting to read the book. But whether he read it, and what he thought of it if he did, I never discovered, for he did not answer my letter, and eventually I had to draw the conclusion that he was offended because I had not presented him with a copy. At first I shrugged off the rebuff, but the episode caused me increasing *agenbite of inwit*, the Middle English phrase meaning 'remorse of conscience' that Stephen Dedalus applies to his guilt about refusing to kneel and pray with his dying mother, especially after I heard that Malachy had died suddenly in middle life from a heart attack. It seems blindingly obvious now that I should have bought and sent him an inscribed copy, even though he could easily afford to buy it and at the time I could not. I acted from a principle of parsimony which had been bred in me from childhood and, if such a trait can be genetically transmitted, was probably inherited from my father. It took me a long time, and the attainment of a degree of affluence, to overcome it.

The qualms I may have felt on this score in the summer of 1960 were quickly forgotten in a flurry of good news for myself and my friends in July. Park wrote at the beginning of the month to say that his PhD thesis had been accepted by Yale University

Press 'lock, stock and barrel, and they hope to get it out by spring 1961'. It was the first American publisher he had tried, and a very prestigious one. He could hardly believe in his own success, and he was perhaps cautioning himself against hubris when in the same letter he advised me to prepare myself for hostile reviews of *The Picturegoers*: 'you must expect the worst of the worst . . . and then – lo! *some* of them, a couple of them, may just be struck with good sense and a minimum of discernment'. But the reviews were more positive, and in more prominent places, than I had dared to hope. 'An excellent first novel . . . suggests unlimited promise,' said the anonymous *Times*. Kingsley Amis described it as 'sharp and real – an individual first novel' in *The Observer*, and was surprisingly tolerant of its religious content, complaining only of the occasional 'pea-Greene simile'. Elizabeth Jennings, one of the poets in the influential 'Movement' anthology *New Lines*, and herself a Catholic, described the novel as 'an arresting achievement for a twenty-five year old author' in *The Listener*. This generous reception did not make me instantly famous – far from it. The reviews were not unanimously favourable, and the only other interest the book attracted in the media was connected with a well-known supporting actor in British films called David Lodge, who revealed that he was getting a lot of mail from friends and fans congratulating him on writing a novel about a cinema. The producers of the film in which he was currently performing invited me to meet its star, Norman Wisdom, and my namesake on the set at Pinewood, and a photograph was taken of me standing between them, which appeared in an evening newspaper without occasioning a rush on the bookshops. Although the *The Picturegoers* sold reasonably well for a first novel (probably something over

2,000 copies), it was not reprinted by MacGibbon & Kee. I was well satisfied, however, and still more in retrospect, because great acclaim for a first novel is an ambivalent gift of fortune. *The Picturegoers* was published in the same week as Stan Barstow's first novel, *A Kind of Loving*, and sometimes reviewed alongside it. *A Kind of Loving* was a real hit and, helped by a very popular film adaptation, set Barstow up for a long career as a writer, but he never enjoyed the same degree of success with a book afterwards, and that experience, of which there are many other examples, must have been demoralising.

In mid-July, just before these reviews appeared, I received a benign bombshell of a letter from Terence Spencer, which he said (apologising for a cramped page) he had typed himself on University of Birmingham notepaper. In summary it stated that the job for which I had applied was going to 'a rather senior person' who could not take it up immediately, and consequently he could offer me a temporary post for one year as an assistant lecturer at the usual starting salary of £800. He was sorry it could only be for one year, but 'possibly you might find it better to apply for a university post *from* a university post . . . for you would then seem to have experience and qualifications to improve your chances'. This was of course absolutely true, and I didn't hesitate to accept the offer, with Mary's complete agreement. It so happened that Derek Todd, who had also been glumly contemplating a career in the technical college sector, was appointed to a job at Queen's University Belfast at the same time. When I wrote to Park, who knew Derek, to tell him of our good fortune he replied: 'Well, if *this* sort of thing keeps up, none of us will have anything more to complain about & *then* where will we be? What marvellous news!'

In mid-August I received a letter from the Secretary of Birmingham University confirming my appointment as temporary assistant lecturer for one year, beginning on the 1st of October. There were no other formalities. I resigned from the British Council with effect from 23rd September, and I had twelve days' leave owing to me which we used to take an economical holiday. A relative of Dad's owned a small clapboard chalet at the edge of a pebbly beach on the south side of the Thames Estuary, east of Gravesend, and they were willing to rent it to us cheaply for a week or so. I invited Mum to join us, and Dad, though tied up as usual with work, promised to come down for a couple of days. It was a rather desolate spot and the chalet was minimally equipped and furnished; Julia was fractious, probably because she was teething, and Mum's attempts to advise Mary caused some friction. It was not an idyllic holiday, but nothing could dampen a deep internal glow of satisfaction in getting my first academic job and successfully publishing my first novel.

Shortly after the start of this holiday I received a letter from Dad about *The Picturegoers*. Although he was due to join us soon for a couple of days, he obviously found it easier to put his thoughts into written form than to speak to me about the novel, for reasons I could understand. There is nearly always a certain reserve between a creative writer and his or her close family members when the latter read the work of the former, especially if they are not familiar with the literary genre to which that work belongs. What it reveals, or seems to reveal, of the writer's inner life, and perhaps of their outer life too, may be surprising and even shocking. My father, who had read no modern literary fiction later than Evelyn Waugh's stylised comedies of upper-class decadence, was shocked by my realistic take on contemporary life in south-east London, innocuous as it would seem to any reader of literary fiction today.

Dear Dave, I have just finished your book. I will not pretend that it is my type of reading but I have nothing but admiration for the entire production, particularly for your courage in setting out to write as you have which I consider taking something of a chance in your first novel which after all is *the* foundation stone of any future a writer may have in published work. The idea of the book is very good and in my humble opinion, the writing – top class. The way you write cannot fail to impress whatever the subject.

The book I would class as a 'shocker'. That is, it is going to shock a lot of people who are going to tell a lot of other people how shocking it is who will then chase around so that they can themselves be shocked, and that is what you want, or most certainly what the publishers want. The competition amongst the young female assistants round at the Library to get hold of it will undoubtedly set a record. I only hope that our friend the chief Librarian (who has ordered three copies) is not of the Methodist or Salvationist persuasion or I fear it may not get as far as the assistants. I note the few anecdotes from your own life from time to time (or rather experience). The 'open-mindedness' with which you have obviously looked upon life up to now is most noticeable and praiseworthy and it will be universally agreed by one and all that 'there are no flies on this author'. That's all for now, I feel as if I have written a book myself. Love to Mary and Baby, hope to see you, Dad.

I can't remember whether he did join us in the chalet, but if so, I'm sure that we wouldn't have discussed the subject of his letter. That was the pattern of our relationship as far as my writing career was concerned: he followed it with keen interest, especially its practical and financial aspects, and took pride in my successes, but we never discussed my novels in any detail, and I'm far from sure that he read some of the later ones. As for my mother, I don't think we ever exchanged a word about the content of my books, nor did she write to me about them, though I'm sure that she read them, and took pleasure in my growing reputation. I sent them copies of the more favourable reviews I received, and other press cuttings I thought would interest them, and it was on that level that, by mutual tacit agreement, we communicated about my writing.

When he wrote that letter about *The Picturegoers* Dad was no longer leading his own trio at the Studio Club, but had returned to 'gig' work of various kinds. Times were getting harder for traditional dance musicians like himself, with the first stirrings of a new kind of popular music in the form of skiffle and rock and roll. But the violin had come back into favour as an instrument in certain contexts, so Dad took his fiddle out of its dusty case, practised his fingering, and began to get work as someone who could perform a melodic solo as background music for a banquet, and do reels for hunt balls, as well as playing the saxophone and clarinet for ballroom dancing. The story of his life was one of constant versatility in adjusting to changing circumstances, and I admired him for it, in the original Latin sense that means 'wonder at'. In the course of the sixties the development of pop and rock music dominated by amplified guitars, the rise of the discotheque and the waning of ballroom dancing signalled the end of Dad's profession, and he diversified into acting – i.e. performing as a non-speaking 'extra' in films and the rapidly expanding field of television drama. He got himself an Equity card and an agent, made fleeting appearances in many popular sitcoms like *Porridge* and *Dad's Army*, and could be glimpsed getting out of a lift behind Peter Sellers and Goldie Hawn in the feature film *There's a Girl in My Soup*. He enjoyed this work and took a pride in being picked out by a director for a role that required a bit of character-defining 'business'. In the early seventies he would sometimes meet and chat with Danny Moynihan in the studios or on location, because Danny then had a steady job as the prosecutor in a long-running drama series on ITV called *Crime of Passion*, based on French court cases. By the time I began writing television scripts that got produced, beginning with my adaptation of *Nice Work* in 1989, Dad had retired from acting, but his experience enabled him to engage with and comment on my work in this medium more readily than he could with my novels, partly because he had a professional understanding of what was involved, but partly also because drama is a less intimate, more impersonal form than the novel.

While I was at the chalet I set up a rickety table and chair on its wooden porch and worked for a few hours a day on the first draft of *Ginger, You're Barmy,* writing with a fountain pen on a foolscap pad, as was my practice then and for some time after: I would write the whole book to the end in longhand with many cancelled and corrected passages, and then type it up, using that process as an opportunity for further revision. I had made a start on *Ginger* in the spring, aware of the proverbial challenge of 'the second novel', and that it would be as well to have it on the stocks before the first one was published. My National Service was now far enough in the past for me to feel detached from it, and yet recent enough to be recalled in some detail, and I decided to use an 'I' narrator for this novel, to give it a documentary, truth-telling tone. The main formal problem was to construct a story that could stretch over the two-year span of National Service, without getting bogged down in the dull repetitive routine which was its defining characteristic. The most dramatic part of the experience was the rude shock of initiation into military life; after that one's existence was always measured by the slow attenuation of the months, weeks and days before one escaped from it. My solution was to have the narrator, Jonathan Browne, recall his basic training in a series of retrospective episodes, framed by his last week in the Army, during which the banal nature of his employment is evoked. My own mild rebelliousness in basic training, and subsequent success in securing a cushy job at Bovington, I distributed between the two main characters: the impulsive, idealistic Catholic Mike Brady, who carries rebellion into violence, and the prudent, sardonic, agnostic Jonathan, who dissociates himself from his friend's reckless behaviour, but is left with residual self-doubt. That they are both attracted to the same girl, Pauline, gives an extra tension to their relationship, and a twist in the plot brings Mike back to disturb the ritual of release from the Army that Jonathan had been looking forward to. Long after I published the novel I realised that I had borrowed this structure from Graham Greene's *The Quiet American*, his Fowler, Pyle and Phuong corresponding to my Jonathan, Mike and Pauline. The 'e' at the end of

Jonathan's surname may have been inserted by my unconscious in acknowledgement of the debt. Perhaps there is also a pale trace in the relationship between my two main characters of that between Charles Ryder and Sebastian Flyte in Evelyn Waugh's *Brideshead Revisited*, a novel with a first-person narrator and a frame story of military service. As these novels were both key texts in my thesis on the Catholic novel it is not surprising that I had assimilated their narrative strategies subliminally and reproduced them in writing about similar themes in a different milieu. Intertextuality is an inescapable element of writing, whether it is conscious or not. That useful word did not then exist, however. Coined in 1967 by the French academic Julia Kristeva, *intertextualité* belongs to a movement in the theory and practice of literary criticism that would seek to revolutionise the profession which I was about to enter.

17

I advertised in the *Birmingham Post* for a suitable flat and in August I went there on my own to look at the most promising one of those that were offered, taking the steam train from Paddington to Snow Hill station, then the main route between the two cities. In my wallet I carried £100 in cash, having with-drawn virtually our entire savings from the Woolwich Building Society for 'key money'. The rent of the flat was legally controlled and therefore very reasonable, but there was a black market in this kind of property which obliged one to pay a premium to the outgoing tenant, trusting that it would be recoverable in the same way when one left. I knew nothing of Birmingham apart from what I had gleaned from the half-mile walk between the station and the Arts Faculty of the University on my previous visit: a vague impression of old-fashioned office buildings, a soot-stained baroque church (St Philip's) that seemed too small to be the Anglican cathedral of England's second-largest city, and friendly natives whose accent I couldn't understand when I asked them the way to Edmund Street. This time I was escorted from the city centre by an estate agent to an inner suburb called Handsworth. It was already a home for immigrant communities from the Indian subcontinent and the Caribbean, but it was not yet associated in the national media with riots, prostitution, drug dealing and other criminality. The flat was in a block probably built between the wars in a quiet residential street. It was shabby but spacious, with three bedrooms, the smallest of which I could use as a study instead of the corner of our bedroom which served that purpose in Battersea. Looking at the bus map of Birmingham, I calculated that the location was not more than half an hour from the University campus in Edgbaston, which seemed negligible travelling time to a Londoner; so I took the flat, without being able to consult Mary since we had no telephone, and next day, having spent the night in a gruesome commercial hotel, discreetly handed over my key money to the outgoing tenant in the estate agent's office. When I got back to London there was a letter waiting for me, responding to my advertisement, offering us a suitable flat ten minutes' walk from the University, with no key money required, and I deeply regretted having committed to the flat in Handsworth – all the more after we moved there and I caught the expressions of surprise and pity on colleagues' faces when I told them where we were living.

Soon, however, this disappointment was overridden by the exciting novelty of my new job, shared to some extent by my colleagues, since they were moving into a brand-new building that was luxurious compared to the one in Edmund Street. Every member of the academic staff, even a temporary assistant lecturer, had their own office, with fitted bookshelves and cupboards, a desk and filing cabinet, and a table around which students could sit for tutorials and small classes. At the end of the corridor was a Senior Common Room with easy chairs where coffee and tea were served in the morning and afternoon. The Faculty of Arts was the last to move to the Edgbaston site, which had been astutely acquired at the beginning of the century by the first Chancellor of the University, the dynamic local politician Joseph Chamberlain. This part of Edgbaston, lying between the Hagley Road and Bristol Road arteries, is an unusual – perhaps unique – inner suburb of a large industrial city in having no commercial centre and a great deal of green open space, including a golf course, an artificial lake, a nature reserve and two botanical gardens. There are still parts of it where, standing only a mile from the city centre, you can't see a single building for trees. Here, in the late eighteenth and nineteenth centuries, many of the industrialists who generated Birmingham's wealth built fine houses to the west of their fuming factory chimneys, taking advantage of the prevailing wind. The Calthorpe Estate, which owned and managed the land, restricted later residential development and looked favourably on the University's expansion. It was the ideal situation for a civic university, embedded in the city and yet occupying a quasi-pastoral bit of territory in its own right. At the hub of the campus Joseph Chamberlain's initiative is memorialised in a phallic redbrick clock tower known locally as 'Big Joe', modelled on the Torre del Mangia in Siena, but taller – indeed, the tallest free-standing clock tower in the world. From the window of my room I looked out over the central grassed quadrangle, with the clock tower to my left and the massive redbrick Library built in the 1950s to my right, at a striking concrete-and-glass Staff House in the final stages of construction on the far side, designed by Sir Hugh Casson, who had general oversight of the architectural development of the campus. The University had an air of being well established and confident of its future. I knew I would be sorry to leave it after a year, but with the optimism of youth I did not brood on that prospect. Perhaps something would turn up to obviate it.

The ethos of the English Department was conservative and traditional. Several of the academic staff had been there since before the war, and I was the only one under the age of thirty-six. Historically the Department had been dominated by Ernest de Sélincourt, an authority on Wordsworth, who was its head from his appointment in 1909 till his retirement in the 1930s. I once interviewed the Birmingham-born novelist and critic Walter Allen, who had been taught by him, and asked what de Sélincourt was like as a teacher. Allen replied, 'I thought he was a stuffy old bore', and he looked it in the photographic portrait which hung on a wall in the Department. A product of Oxford himself, he ensured that the undergraduate syllabus followed the Oxford pattern. Undergraduates were required to study Old English for at least two years and final examinations in literature stopped at 1900. There was, however, a recently devised first-year lecture course, 'Introduction to the Novel', based on a long, slightly eccentric list of texts which extended into the twentieth century, and Terence Spencer asked me to give lectures on several of them including Henry James's *The Ambassadors* and H.G. Wells's *Tono-Bungay*. Like most young academics at the start of their careers, after two years of specialised postgraduate research I had to work hard filling the gaps in my knowledge to keep ahead of my students, but it was an enjoyable and stimulating workload. Both *Tono-Bungay* and *The Ambassadors* figured prominently in my first book of criticism, *Language of Fiction,* some years later.

In those days there was no instruction of new recruits to the academic profession on how to lecture or teach smaller groups. You just tried to imitate the best of your own former teachers and avoid the faults of the worst. It was not done for the senior staff to monitor the teaching of junior ones, still less that of their peers, so it was possible for someone lacking elementary communication skills to repeat their failures for an entire career without correction. I myself hadn't really taken Mary's comment on my British Council lectures to heart. I continued to write out my lectures in full, and they were usually too densely packed with information to be easily taken in through the ear, certainly in an uninterrupted discourse of fifty minutes. Research has established that the maximum attention span of auditors of such discourse is about twenty minutes, after which it comes and goes in spasms. Much later in my career I began to experiment with the form of a lecture, using visual aids and handouts, and inviting questions to break up the relentless flow of information, but by that time I was getting deaf and had difficulty hearing the questions. Nowadays at Birmingham, and I presume at other universities, newly appointed junior members of staff are required to attend courses provided by the Education Faculty on lecturing technique and other aspects of teaching. This does not necessarily solve the problem – a formulaic PowerPoint presentation that ponderously repeats information summarised on a screen can be deadly boring. Originality, enthusiasm, charisma and wit, which all effective teachers must possess in some measure, cannot be taught.

The liveliest teaching in the Department when I joined it was in medieval literature, led by Derek Brewer and Geoffrey Shepherd, who went out of their way to welcome me. They were in their late thirties and both had served in the armed forces during the war. Derek later moved to Cambridge, where he became Professor of Medieval Literature and Master of Emmanuel College. Geoffrey was eventually given a personal chair at Birmingham, and inspired a special devotion in those he taught. They ran a dialogic seminar together on Friday afternoons for second- and third-year students, and waves of laughter emanating from the packed seminar room attested to its popularity. Another member of staff who quickly became a good friend was Elsie Duncan-Jones, wife of Austin Duncan-Jones, the Head of the Philosophy Department. She had been one of the Cambridge undergraduates who took part in the legendary classes of I.A. Richards from which he drew the material of his seminal book *Practical Criticism* (1929), and at a young age she had published the first monograph on the poetry of Gerard Manley Hopkins. Subsequently she published little, subordinating her career to her husband's, but she was immensely well read in English literature, major and minor, up to the twentieth century. She had a grace and elegance that made it hard to believe she came from a very humble rural background in the West Country. I always associated her with *To the Lighthouse*, for she combined the intelligence and literary acumen of Virginia Woolf with the sensitive concern of Mrs Ramsay for her children, friends and rather aloof philosopher-husband. Elsie must have been a beauty in youth and was comely in middle age. Her warm, sympathetic personality invited confidences, and I was not the first or the last young man to fall under her spell and value her friendship, which we kept up after she retired until her death.

Terence Spencer was something of an enigma to one and all. He had left UCL shortly after Mary and I graduated, to take up the chair of English at Queen's University Belfast, but stayed there only three years before moving to Birmingham. He had ambition, and Birmingham gave him scope to exercise it. He was not only Head of Department, at a time when heads had almost autocratic power ('the Barons' was how he liked to refer to his peers in the Arts Faculty), but also Director of the Shakespeare Institute in Stratford-upon-Avon, founded by his predecessor, Allardyce Nicoll. This postgraduate institute for research into Shakespeare and his contemporaries occupied Mason Croft, the former home of the novelist Marie Corelli, a charming old house in spacious grounds just a few minutes' walk from Shakespeare's birthplace and the Royal Shakespeare Theatre. Though the ambience was appropriate, the Fellows and students were twenty-odd miles away from the intellectual life and library resources of the Edgbaston campus, and Spencer planned to bring the Institute back to Birmingham, while hanging on to Mason Croft as a venue for extramural courses and conferences. When the new Staff House was completed he arranged to move the Institute into Westmere, a Victorian mansion close to the campus which had been the Staff Club. With the bait of an honorary degree, he successfully wooed Eugene Black, President of the World Bank, for a handsome contribution to the cost of this project, and the Institute flourished in its new location, which of course was much more convenient for its director. It became the academic base of the Penguin Shakespeare, of which he was General Editor, with considerable powers of patronage. (Two decades later it moved back to Stratford, under the directorship of Stanley Wells, partly to ward off a threat from the University of Warwick to set up a rival institute there.)

One of the mysteries of Terence Spencer was how, although his range of knowledge was undoubtedly impressive, he achieved his eminence without very much to show in terms of published scholarship. His only book, sifting through a very large swathe of English literature, was *Fair Greece, Sad Relic: literary philhellenism from Shakespeare to Byron* (1954), which he would wryly refer to as 'Fair Greece, Sad Remainder' in acknowledgement of its limited fame; and for the subject of his Inaugural Lecture at Birmingham he chose two authors not normally studied in English departments, though perhaps they should be: Edward Gibbon and Charles Darwin. His later published works, in no great abundance, were editions of texts and periodical articles. But he was far from idle: his energies were consumed in organising and directing the work of others and by a wide range of high-level academic activities at home and abroad. I never saw him without a book or a file in his hand, as if he always read as he ran. His colleagues in the Department respected his learning, but they did not love him, and most did not much like him. He was a tall man, with a large balding head that seemed to bulge with knowledge, and a full-fleshed face that was faintly cratered with pockmarks like the surface of the moon. At close quarters he could make people feel uneasy. He had a habit, which some found intimidating, of calling male colleagues 'Brother' and clamping a heavy hand on their shoulders to keep them stationary while he delivered himself of some opinion or advice. But I doubt if he ever tried that on John

Russell Brown, who was just as tall as Spencer, younger, and the most dashing figure among the staff. He was a Shakespeare specialist, focusing especially on the plays in performance, and took a practical interest in the Drama Society of the Student Guild (i.e. Union), directing some of their productions and inspiring a number of students in the Department, including Terry Hands and Peter James, who went on to have successful careers in the theatre, before he left to be head of a new department in the Faculty, of Drama and Theatre Arts.

I can't remember when I discovered whose place in the English Department I was temporarily filling. It may have been as late as halfway through the spring term of 1961, when Terence Spencer told me this person was not, after all, going to take up his appointment at Birmingham. He was Laurence Lerner, who had been a colleague of Spencer's at Queen's, Belfast, and he had decided to go to the new University of Sussex instead. I didn't know much about him, but I blessed him for his decision when I heard of it, and for long afterwards, because it created a vacancy for which I was eligible. In fact Terence said at once that he wanted to keep me on. He had consulted colleagues, and he did not bother to advertise the post and interview other candidates. Such was the power of an academic Baron. I was soon officially informed that I had been appointed assistant lecturer, on two years' probation from the following October, my present appointment counting as one of the normal three. It is hard to exaggerate the importance of this piece of luck or the intensity of my relief. 'Probation' in those days was a threshold you could only fail to cross if you were seriously incompetent or delinquent – very different from the rigorous competition for tenure in American universities. In effect I had obtained a secure position in the profession of my choice at one of its major institutions, without ever satisfying a normal appointment committee. In fact I would rise to the rank of full professor without ever doing so, since I chose to stay at Birmingham for the rest of my academic career, and on the few occasions when I applied or was invited to apply for chairs in other universities, I was never offered one.

Now that I was an established member of staff I took a keen interest in departmental meetings, which were novel enough not to bore and irritate me as they did my colleagues. Spencer was not a good chairman of these occasions and let people argue without check. Sometimes I suspected that he did so deliberately, knowing that they would eventually cancel out each other's views and allow him to act as he wanted. There was one person whom he could always rely on to provoke others, and that was I.A. Shapiro, familiarly known as 'Ship'. He was one of the oldest members of staff, a graduate of Birmingham, with a goatee which wagged as he enunciated his opinions in slow-paced declarative sentences. He had spread frustration and fury in the academic world well beyond Birmingham. As a very promising young scholar before the war, he had been given an enviable commission to edit the letters of John Donne for Oxford University Press. He took many years over the task, and when it was approaching completion the unique copy of his manuscript with all his notes and references was stolen in a bag taken from his car. He had to start again from the beginning, but progress was slow, if in fact he had made any progress, perhaps being so traumatised by the catastrophe that the project was in mental lockdown. At any rate, he had failed to produce the edition for which Donne specialists and other Renaissance scholars had been waiting impatiently for two decades, and continued to disappoint them, defying all attempts by OUP to cancel his contract and give the task to someone else until the end of his long life in 2004. He was actually a very kind, civilised man at heart, but stubbornly convinced of the rightness of his own opinions on everything.

Department meetings concerned with examinations were of particular interest to me, having previously been on the other side of the wall that separates examiners from examinees. In the spring term the staff assembled to approve the Finals examination papers, and we went through them question by question, emending them if necessary, an opportunity to display learning, pedantry and wit which few could resist, so that several adjournments and new meetings with diminishing attendance were required to complete the process. The climax of the academic year was the week of the Examiners' Meeting in June, when we sat in conclave round a long table piled with marked scripts to decide whether students who had failed first-year examinations should be allowed to resit them, and to determine the class of each finalist's degree in the presence of an external examiner, who adjudicated on marginal or disputed marks. At London the scripts of Finals candidates were identified by a number not a name, and the examiners were selected from several different colleges, so assessment was genuinely impersonal. I was surprised and slightly shocked at first by the intimacy of the process at Birmingham, where every candidate was well known to most of the staff, and tutors would often plead for their tutees, if their marks had been unexpectedly disappointing, by revealing difficult personal circumstances. There was, however, a professional ethic, personified in the external examiner, which ensured that on the whole justice was done. What was surprising, perhaps, was the unexamined consensus on what qualities, or lack of them, in the short essays that literature examinations mostly required, corresponded to the various marks, on a scale from alpha plus (exceedingly rare) to gamma double minus, which cumulatively determined the degree class of a candidate. These qualities certainly couldn't be quantified, and if we had been asked to define them in order of priority I doubt whether there would ever have been unanimity; but generally the Finals results corresponded to most people's estimates of the ability and industry of the students they had taught. There were some lucky, or unlucky, exceptions, and for the latter in those days there was no realistic possibility of appeal.

In the Easter vacation I attended the annual conference of University Teachers of English, which was hosted by a different university each year and in 1961 was held in Cambridge. This was an exciting experience for me, an opportunity to meet and mingle with a broad cross-section of the profession I now belonged to, and to hear some of its stars do their stuff when they gave papers at the plenary sessions, such as Frank Kermode, then Head of English at Manchester, and an American visitor from Yale, W.K. Wimsatt. Wimsatt was a giant of a man, for whom the lectern had to be artificially raised. I had never heard of him, but quickly learned that he was a leading theorist of the American New Criticism, and especially well known for a very influential article written with a colleague, the philosopher Monroe C. Beardsley, called 'The Intentional Fallacy', which I looked up when I got home. Its argument, which struck at the heart of much historical and biographical scholarship, was that the attempt to interpret a literary work by reference to the author's intention is vain because the only intention that is relevant is the one encoded in the language of the work itself. In a way it was a counter-intuitive theory, because nobody writes anything, from a letter to a novel, without an intention to do so, but it is also true that the meaning of such texts always inevitably differs from what the authors might formulate in advance of their composition or might offer by way of explanation afterwards. I found this idea encouraging to my own germinating plan for a study of the language of fiction.

As well as many new acquaintances, I made a new friend at the conference: Bernard Bergonzi, who had recently been appointed at Manchester by Frank Kermode. He sought me out because he had recently read *The Picturegoers*, through an interesting chain of events. His sister-in-law, Bernadine Wall, had achieved some fame the previous year when, a Cambridge undergraduate, she was selected to give evidence at the *Lady Chatterley* trial as a witness to the novel's non-corrupting effect on an intelligent young woman who was also a practising Catholic. She had subsequently written a novel drawing on the life of her cultured Catholic family (her father, Bernard Wall, edited a periodical, *The Twentieth Century*, and her mother, Barbara, was a novelist), which she submitted to MacGibbon & Kee. Though they did not take it, they sent her a copy of *The Picturegoers*, and she passed it to Bernard. He read it with great interest, partly because he immediately recognised the location of the story as the bit of south-east London where he had spent his own Catholic boyhood. We had in fact grown up in neighbouring parishes, he in Lewisham and I in Brockley, unaware of each other's existence. Bernard was older than me by five or six years. His education was interrupted and hampered by illness in childhood, and he went to Wadham College, Oxford, not by the conventional route, but as a mature student via Ruskin College. By the time I met him he had a growing reputation as a contributor of essays and reviews to various journals on modern and contemporary literature, and was a published poet in the Movement vein. At the Cambridge conference he introduced me to Frank Kermode and as a result I found myself sitting with a group late one evening in somebody's room, sipping whisky out of teacups and bathroom mugs, listening to Frank discoursing in his relaxed, drily amusing style. Unfortunately I cannot recall anything he said on that occasion except his enjoyment of the drive down from Manchester in his Mini, then a new and trendy vehicle; but in time he would become an inspiration to me as a critic and a personal friend.[1] Bernard became a closer friend, especially after he moved to the new University of Warwick in the late sixties. Bernadine, whom I met a few times at Bernard's home, wrote several novels in two groups with a lengthy gap between them. *Unexpected Lessons in Love,* published in 2013, the year of her death, treated the experience of bowel cancer both wittily and movingly, and was posthumously shortlisted for the Orange Prize.

I cannot recall anything of particular interest Mary did in that academic year 1960–61, and neither, I'm afraid, can she. I was having all the fun. The University Wives' Club provided some agreeable social

---

1 See my essay, 'Frank Remembered – by a Kermodian', in *Lives in Writing* (2014).

gatherings for those with young children, but living in Handsworth and dependent on buses for transport, she was not able easily to develop the friendships she made, and she spent most of her days looking after Julia and the flat, with shopping excursions to the Soho Road, where the ladies loitering on street corners in all weathers excited even Julia's infant curiosity. Now that my future at Birmingham was secure, I was impatient to move from Handsworth to somewhere near the University when our lease on the flat expired, and we started to look for a small house with a garden. We were hampered by our lack of savings for a deposit and the building societies' insistence on a prudent ratio of income to mortgage, but eventually we found a very small two-bedroomed semi-detached house in Selly Oak which we could afford, with a long narrow garden that backed on to a drained reservoir – hence its address, Reservoir Road. Its great attraction to me was that it was within comfortable walking distance of the University, which could also be reached by bus from the end of the road. We viewed the house on a sunny day when the garden looked quite inviting, and suppressed our doubts about its mean proportions and cheap-looking build. When I inspected the bathroom I observed a turd floating in the toilet bowl, which I should have taken as a warning that the house was crap.

The houses in Reservoir Road were examples of the worst kind of jerry-built inter-war semis. I was told by long-term residents in the street that they cost only £250 when new, and that the first few had to be knocked down when half built because the contractors had omitted to provide them with external doorways. This story was plausible because the front door to every house was, unusually, at the side. It opened on to an area, too small to merit the term 'hall', between the two ground-floor rooms, and the staircase went straight up in front of you as you entered, passing under the beams of the first floor. When we moved in it proved impossible to get our double bed up the staircase, and it had to be taken away, sawn in half and converted into a hinged bed, while we slept on the mattress in the meantime: not an auspicious start to our residence. We also found that the previous owners had stripped every removable object, including curtain rails, light bulbs and most of the rose bushes, from the property when they departed. It soon became apparent that the man of the house had been a DIY enthusiast whose attempts to improve it had generally made it worse. The rear ground-floor room was designed as a kitchen–dining room, but had been partitioned to make two rooms inconveniently small for their respective purposes. Like the vast majority of British houses at that time, it had no central heating, was poorly insulated and had single-glazed windows which frosted up inside on cold winter nights. The front room doubled as our lounge and my study, with a desk in one corner, so in that respect we had taken a step backwards in domestic amenities.

Several weeks had passed since I sent *Ginger* to Timothy O'Keeffe without any response from him, and I was beginning to get anxious. In September, just before handing back the keys to the vacated flat and recovering my key money, I paid one last visit to check if there was any mail there, and indeed there was a letter from Tim O'Keeffe. He apologised for the delay, explaining that the firm had been in upheaval following the disappearance of its owner, Howard Samuel, who was observed walking into the sea on holiday one day and never seen again – a mystery that remained unsolved. Tim was 'glad to say' that they would publish the novel with an advance of £125, of which £75 would be paid on signature and the balance on publication. It was a less-than-generous offer considering the modest success of *The Picturegoers*, the paperback rights of which had been bought by Pan Books, but I was too relieved to argue. He said that Simon King, the new head of the firm, would read the book and might have some editorial suggestions for improvement. I have no memory of King's comments, but they may have prompted me to add another narrative frame to the novel before publication, in which Jonathan, whom some readers found an unsympathetic narrator, introduces the story of his National Service, describes the sequel, and conveys an awareness of his self-centredness and his efforts to become a more generous person. It seems to me now, however, that the real weakness of the book is the characterisation of Mike Brady, whose motivation is never entirely convincing.

Not long after we moved to the Reservoir Road house its limitations became more obvious when Mary proved to be pregnant again. The house would soon feel even smaller, and Mary's hopes of returning to teaching one day were further postponed. Still, we reflected, we didn't want Julia to be an only child, two years was a good interval between siblings, and perhaps it was as well to get the early parenting over and done with. So we were not too cast down by another failure of the so-called Safe Method. Mary was now less isolated from other university wives than she had been at Handsworth, and began to form friendships with neighbours. I was happily employed in the Department, especially with teaching a new optional course on modern literature for final-year students that Terence Spencer had planned to give to Laurence Lerner. I was also seeking new ways to make extra money by writing. I had submitted a few articles in the past to *The Tablet*, the most cultured of Catholic weekly publications, which were turned down by the literary editor, Maryvonne Butcher, a formidable lady of forthright views. However, she had been impressed by *The Picturegoers*, and invited me to review books for the journal, which I was very pleased to do. Later, through Bernard Bergonzi's recommendation, I began reviewing fiction regularly for *The Spectator*, which paid more and sent me a dozen new novels from which to choose five or six. Any I didn't wish to keep I could sell to a dealer in London for half the cover price. One of those I kept was John McGahern's debut, *The Barracks*, which I was greatly impressed by and compared to Joyce's *Dubliners*. McGahern wrote to thank me for the review, and in a later letter said he had tried to buy *The Picturegoers* but discovered it was banned in Ireland, and had to wait till he came to England to obtain a copy. Whether it was the novel's treatment of sex or of Catholicism that offended the notoriously philistine Irish censorship board, I do not know – perhaps both.

An element in Terence Spencer's expansionist plans for the Department was to appoint a specialist in American literature who could teach a course in that subject and also contribute to the English Literature syllabus. He obtained approval and funding from the appropriate quarter, and the post was advertised. Perhaps regarding me as in some sense his protégé, he occasionally took me into his confidence, and one day he drew me into his office to show me an application for the new post from a man called Malcolm Bradbury. When I had scanned it, he said, 'I don't think we need interview anyone else, do you?' and I agreed without hesitation. Bradbury was a little more than two years older than me, and the idea of having a colleague in my own age group was attractive, especially one with a CV as intriguing as his. A product of West Bridgford Grammar School, Nottingham, he had a First-class BA from University College Leicester at the time when its students took the London External degree examinations, and an MA from Queen Mary College London, so our education had followed very similar paths. After that, however, they diverged: he had spent two separate years in American universities on a fellow-ship and as an instructor, had begun a PhD on American literary expatriates at Manchester University, and was currently a tutor in the Department of Extra-Mural Studies at Hull. He had an inter-estingly varied list of publications to his name, including a good deal of journalism and a novel, *Eating People is Wrong*, published in 1959, which I knew of, but had not read. Of course I read it, and of course Malcolm read *The Picturegoers*, before he arrived with his wife Elizabeth in Birmingham in January 1962.

Being a comic-satirical campus novel set at a provincial redbrick university, *Eating People is Wrong* (a title taken from a well-known comic song of the time, 'The Reluctant Cannibal' by Michael Flanders and Donald Swann) was inevitably bracketed by reviewers with *Lucky Jim*, and it does have features in common with Amis's book, notably some farcical set pieces; but, as I realised much later, it owed more to the example of early American campus novels, especially Mary McCarthy's *The Groves of Academe* and Randall Jarrell's *Pictures from an Institution*, in which the comedy is more intellectual and morally complex. An epigraph from Epictetus defining the vocation of a philosopher sets the tone. Unusually in a first novel by a young writer, the central character is in early middle age. Professor Henry Treece embodies a theme on which Malcolm played several variations in his career: the plight of the liberal humanist who discovers he is an impotent spectator of, and sometimes involuntary collaborator in, the illiberal machinations of others in the society to which he belongs. Succumbing to the charms of a pretty postgraduate, Treece drives a gifted but unstable student into madness, and is punished by being hospitalised at the end of the novel, a black-comic episode which drew on Malcolm's own experience. As a young man he was diagnosed with a serious heart condition, thought he was going to die, and wrote the first draft of *Eating People* in the shadow of that fear; but happily he made a full recovery after undergoing one of the first successful hole-in-the-heart operations performed in England. His first novel was more mature and poised than mine, and I was impressed by its sparkling wit and range of intellectual reference. Malcolm probably found the religious themes in my novel more difficult to relate to, for his outlook was essentially secular, but he relished my parodic representation of popular culture, and his subsequent encouragement of the comic strain that was present but subdued in my first two novels is my greatest debt to him.

We quickly became friends, as did Mary and Elizabeth. I have described our relationship at some length in another book, and I cannot convey its nature more economically than by quoting a few passages from that account.

Close friendships between writers have a special character, especially when they are formed fairly early in their careers, when both parties are developing their work, showing it to each other, discussing it, perhaps collaborating on it . . .

Inevitably there is an element of competitiveness in such a relationship, which can cause some tension later, but at this early stage it is a constructive rivalry, as between two athletes specialising in the same events who train together. For three academic years . . . I enjoyed that kind of relationship with Malcolm continuously. We saw each other nearly every day at the University in term time, had offices on the same corridor, took coffee together in the Senior Common Room and shared lunch in Staff House. There was always much to talk about: new books, new writing projects, departmental politics . . . Several post-war British novelists began their careers with a 'day-job' teaching in a university, but most of them gave it up as soon as they felt able to do so. Malcolm and I were unusual in being equally committed and ambitious in our academic and creative careers. This was partly because the life of a freelance writer simply seemed too risky, especially for a married man with a family (Mary and I had two children by 1962 and the Bradburys had their first the following year) but it was also because we were genuinely interested in the academic study of literature, and wanted to make our mark on it. So we set ourselves up for a very busy life, combining teaching, writing and reviewing scholarly books and articles, with writing novels, short stories, and in due course, scripts for stage, radio and TV, as well as doing a good deal of journalism, including regular reviewing . . . We would not have been able to maintain this tempo of work if we had not married on the pre-Women's Lib assumption that the husband was the breadwinner whose work had priority and the woman the housewife and mother whose career was suspended during the early years of childbearing.[2]

Malcolm's versatility, his ability to shift from one genre and one stylistic register to another, contributing regularly, for instance, to both *Punch* and the *Critical Quarterly*, inspired imitation. Perceiving that useful supplementary income could be obtained from the lighter kind of writing, I placed a few humorous pieces in *Punch* and *The Tablet* myself.

1962 was an eventful year in many ways, personally, professionally and publicly. There was a spell of extremely cold weather over Christmas and the New Year, and when we returned to Reservoir Road from a visit to Mum and Dad we had some difficulty in opening the outside door because it was frozen to the door frame. Being a novice house-owner, I had omitted to turn off the mains water supply before our departure, and the storage tank in the loft and the pipes in the house had frozen and burst. Their contents had thawed and leaked and frozen again. Water had cascaded down the stairs to form an icy lake of congealed mail and late Christmas cards on the doormat, and had poured down the walls in the dining room behind the wallpaper and frozen, forming blisters which crackled when you pressed them. From the toilet bowl I removed a perfectly formed ice sculpture in the shape of an oversized meerschaum pipe.

We were rescued by a small family building firm recommended by neighbours – cheerful and helpful folk very appropriately called Godbyhere – and they carried out the necessary repairs and

---

2 'Malcolm Bradbury: Writer and Friend', *Lives in Writing* (2014)

redecoration promptly. I was not insured against this kind of mishap, and the cost nearly wiped me out financially. There came a day when I had only £40 in my bank account. I went to see Terence Spencer and told him I needed a pay rise. He was sympathetic and said he would see what he could do. I did get a small rise, and better still I was told in March that I would be promoted to lecturer from 1st October. At about the same time the editor in charge of literary fiction at Pan Books wrote to say that they planned to publish the paperback edition of *The Picturegoers* in October, when another advance would be payable, and he casually mentioned that he had read *Ginger* in typescript and agreed to publish it. That was the first I had heard of this welcome news. When I enquired of my current editor at MacGibbon & Kee, Martin Green, he wrote apologetically, 'Our agreement with Pan books was signed on 21 September last year . . . I assumed you were told.' I was too diffident to complain, but I accepted Malcolm's advice that I should get an agent. He introduced me to his own, Graham Watson, a director of Curtis Brown, one of the leading London agencies, who took me on. Graham could not, of course, do anything about the terms for *Ginger, You're Barmy*, but looked forward to representing me with my next novel.

Ever since we arrived in Birmingham, Park Honan had been writing his long, racy letters, complaining of the suffocating atmosphere of life in a small town and small women's college – citing, for example, his colleagues' disapproval when he organised a not-for-credit reading group for students on the work of James Joyce which proved very popular. He was determined to move from Connecticut College and in January '62 wrote to say that he had obtained a post at Brown, one of the prestigious Ivy League universities, which would begin in the fall. He had also applied for a Guggenheim Fellowship to do post-doctoral research in England, though with little hope of getting it so early in his career. In March he informed me that he had just ordered forty-three copies of *The Picturegoers* for the Connecticut College bookstore, explaining that sophomore students were required to read one good contemporary novel in the May reading week, and he had made mine the set text. He invited me to submit some questions for the exam they would have to sit, and promised to send me the better papers for my comment. I presumed that as he was leaving the college he didn't care what his colleagues thought of his unusual choice, and gratefully thanked him for the boost to my sales. In early April he announced that to his surprise and delight he had been awarded a 'Guggie' and, as Brown was willing to postpone the commencement of his appointment, the Honans would be coming to Europe in June for a whole year. A second letter dated the same day congratulated us on news just received – the birth of our second child, Stephen, whom he promptly nicknamed 'Dedalus'.

Stephen was born at home with the assistance of a midwife by Mary's wish, so that she could practise natural childbirth without interference from hospital staff and with my co-operation. Unfortunately he arrived suddenly, four weeks earlier than expected, in the Easter vacation, while I was away from home with Malcolm, attending two conferences held successively in Hull and London. At the latter I was called out of the first morning's session to receive a telephoned message that I was a father again. I hastened home immediately, relieved that mother and child were well, and pleased that the baby was a boy, but deeply disappointed that I had missed the birth. Apparently the labour had been even quicker than on the previous occasion and there was no way I could have been summoned home in time. Fortunately Mary's mother had come to stay with her while I was away, so she had had a helper in addition to the excellent midwife. Mrs Jacob declared that she had never seen a baby born before, because the doctors who delivered her own had always instructed her to close her eyes, and it had been an amazing revelation to her. Stephen was almost a premature baby, and certainly a small one, but sound and healthy.

When Stephen was baptised his godmother was Mary's youngest sister, Margaret, who was a student in the English Department, now in her second year. At the time she had applied I administered the interviewing of candidates for admission, which put me in a moral dilemma: should I reveal to my colleagues that Margaret was my sister-in-law or not? I decided I should not, but allocated her to Elsie Duncan-Jones, who I thought would be a sympathetic interviewer. Fortunately Elsie recommended acceptance. She reproached me later for not telling her of the connection, but it was bound to come out, and I was happy that I could not be accused of nepotism, nor Margaret of benefiting from it. We saw a good deal of her in term time, and also of her boyfriend, Ioan Williams, who was reading English at St Catherine's College, Oxford. He was of Welsh parentage but brought up in Hertfordshire near Hoddesdon, and they had met on the day of our wedding, when Margaret went to a dance in the town that evening wearing her bridesmaid's dress. Ioan had the build of a Welsh miner and the face, Elsie told Margaret when she met him, of an angel. He was as chastely and possessively in love with Margaret as I had been with Mary at the same age, and also as academically competitive. When he visited Margaret at weekends he picked my brains for his tutorial essays, and argued with a pertinacity that I sometimes found exhausting. I was not surprised when in due course he was awarded a First, after paying to dictate his copious but illegible Finals papers to a typist under invigilation – a facility we did not offer candidates at Birmingham.

At the beginning of August '62 the death of Marilyn Monroe from barbiturate poisoning dominated the media on a scale not equalled until the death of Princess Diana decades later. Like most men of my generation, I had always found her an extraordinarily attractive and fascinating figure on the screen, beautiful, seductive and yet somehow innocent, who magnetised one's attention even in the ropiest film. The pathos of her suicide – the fact that a woman who was idolised, envied, and in fantasy desired by millions should be so unhappy and lacking in self-esteem that she took her own life – prompted me to write a poem, a form of literary expression I very seldom tried after adolescence, called 'Epitaph for a Film Star'.

> Passing the hoarding where she was displayed,
> From which destructive nails had peeled
> Long ragged strips of irregular depth,
> (Breast and buttock in the gutter fade)
> One glimpsed beneath the wounds she smiled above,
> Fragments of other images, appeals:
> A baby's limb, a page half-turned,
> *Ban the – Save the – Dancing – Love.*
>
> Now eyes and speculation stick
> Where nails have scraped through to the stark brick.

I sent it speculatively to Ron Bryden, literary editor of *The Spectator*, and to my surprise he liked it enough to publish it, in the issue of 19th October. 'It's a marvellous image for her and all of them,' he wrote. About twenty years later I was invited by Richard Adams, the author of the bestselling children's book *Watership Down*, to contribute to an anthology he was editing of poems by well-known writers who were not recognised poets. It was called *Occasional Poets*, published by Viking in 1986, and included work by nearly fifty authors, including Alan Ayckbourn, Beryl Bainbridge, C.S. Lewis, William Golding, Doris Lessing – and Malcolm. I suspected that Adams had dreamed up the idea in order to get his own poetry into print prominently but unpretentiously, and no doubt the rest of us were pleased to collaborate for the same reason. I submitted four poems, written at long intervals, including the one on the death of Monroe. Reviewing the book rather disdainfully in *The Observer*, Blake Morrison, himself an established poet, commented that 'the shadow of Philip Larkin's "Sunny Prestatyn" falls heavily over David Lodge's "Epitaph for a Film Star".' It was true that Larkin used the image of a defaced poster depicting a beautiful young woman rather similarly in his poem, but a little research revealed that in fact 'Sunny Prestatyn' had been published after mine, in the *London Magazine* in January 1963. I had the satisfaction of pointing this out in a letter to *The Observer* the following weekend, concluding, 'I do not, of course, suggest that the shadow fell the other way.' Blake subsequently sent me an apologetic note.

At the beginning of the new academic year the Birmingham English Department acquired a second professor, Richard Hoggart. The appointment had been made some time before, but his arrival had been postponed at his request because he felt he had obligations to the University of Leicester, to which he had moved only a few years earlier from Hull, where he occupied the position in the Extra-Mural Department that Malcolm took over. (Small world.) He had been head-hunted by Birmingham and needed some persuasion to leave Leicester, where he was very happy as a senior lecturer. Eventually he accepted the appointment on condition that he could set up a postgraduate institute in a new subject area called Cultural Studies, which would combine the methods of literary criticism and sociology and apply them to the whole range of contemporary cultural production in different media and milieux.

It was a shrewd appointment by Birmingham. It was the beginning of the sixties, in a cultural as well as chronological sense, when old disciplinary boundaries would collapse and the mass media would become vehicles of cultural innovation. Richard was a rising intellectual star popular with progressive staff and students in universities, especially those who, like himself, came from the lower end of the British class system, and *The Uses of Literacy* was never out of print. He had been one of the most effective witnesses for the defence in the *Lady Chatterley* trial of 1960 which, more than any other single event, freed writers to describe sexual behaviour explicitly, and an influential member of the Pilkington Committee which met in the same year to consider the future of broadcasting, and successfully defended the BBC's charter for public service broadcasting against the commercial interests of independent television. Richard himself was not a radical in politics, methodology or morals. In many ways his values were old-fashioned, those of the self-respecting working class he had celebrated in his book, and his critical method was intuitive and suspicious of theory. But the Centre for Contemporary Cultural Studies which he set up became a powerhouse of innovative research, engendering similar graduate programmes and eventually undergraduate degrees in cultural studies at other universities. Much of that development occurred in the 1970s and '80s, under the stewardship of Stuart Hall, after Richard had left Birmingham. But he was the 'onlie begetter' of the Centre, which had an influence and reputation out of all proportion to its modest size and resources, until for various reasons it ceased to exist in the less sympathetic academic climate of the next century.

In the autumn of 1962 all that was hidden in the mists of the future. What was immediately clear was that Richard was an exceptionally nice man, honest, decent and caring in all spheres of his life, and prodigiously industrious. Although his priority was to establish the Centre on a firm foundation (with financial help from Allen Lane, owner of Penguin Books), and he was drawn into much faculty and university committee work, he made sure that he tutored some undergraduates from the first year upwards, to keep in touch with English as a living, developing discipline. He was small in stature, and confessed poignantly in his auto-biography that the only thing he regretted in his life was that he hadn't been a few inches taller; but he made up for the lack of an imposing physical presence by his energy, sincerity and a verbal fluency which, like his prose, was not that of the cultural mandarin class but salted with humour, homely analogies and slightly old-fashioned colloquialisms. Most people immediately felt at ease with him, as they did not with Terence Spencer, and it soon became evident that the two professors did not get on with each other. It was another enigma posed by Spencer: he must have strongly supported the effort to lure Richard to Birmingham – indeed it is likely that he instigated it – but why? The two men had nothing in common, personally or intellectually, and this must have been evident to Spencer as soon as they met. If he imagined that Richard would be content to defer to him out of gratitude for the appointment, he made a grave mistake. In the incompatibility of the two men lay the seeds of trouble in departmental politics during the increasingly turbulent Sixties.

One of the main issues discussed at the *Lady Chatterley* trial in which Richard had figured was the legitimacy of Lawrence's frequent use of the words 'fuck' and 'cunt', the argument of the defence being that the novelist was seeking to redeem them from vulgar usage in an honest celebration of sexual love. But the effect of the verdict was also to permit the printing of these words as mere expletives, in order to give colloquial dialogue in fiction authenticity. This was a matter very relevant to *Ginger, You're Barmy*, which was mostly written before the trial. I had decided to follow Norman Mailer's example in *The Naked and the Dead*, rendering the soldier's favourite expletive as 'fugg' and the vulgar term for vagina by a 'c' followed by a dash, which was curiously elongated by MacGibbon & Kee's printer so that it looked more like an eight-letter than a four-letter word. I did not venture to change my text in the light of the trial, but even so I felt it necessary to preface the book with a warning to readers who might be offended. By 1970, when a second paperback edition of the novel was issued by a different publisher, Panther, this note looked exceedingly quaint. I deleted it, and took the opportunity to have the four-letter words printed in full. It was a strange experience to sit down with a copy of my own novel and, like some conscientious vandaliser of library books, inscribe obscene expletives in the margin of nearly every page for the printer. When I read the new paperback I found that the explicitness was distracting, because it didn't match the general reticence of the novel's style, and when it was reissued again, in 1982, by Secker & Warburg, the original version was used with the expletives bowdlerised, as seemed appropriate in what was by then a period piece.

Ginger, You're Barmy was due to be published early in November. In late October the Cuban Missile Crisis came to a head. Having discovered that Russia was building missile sites on Cuba, the USA blockaded the island, which the Soviet Premier Khrushchev described in an open letter to President Kennedy on the 24th of October as an act of aggression threatening to cause a nuclear war. 'Just my luck to be publishing a novel as the third world war breaks out,' I said to Malcolm and Elizabeth when they invited us round to their flat for a meal. The flippancy concealed a genuine anxiety – the whole world held its breath in those few days – but I was not as terrified as many people were at the time. I always thought that nuclear catastrophe would more likely happen by accident than by a deliberate decision to engage in mutually assured destruction. (At this time of writing, given the alarming political situation in the Middle East, I am not so sure.) Happily the Soviets backed down, and the Cuban crisis passed into history a few weeks before my novel was published.

Its reception was, as the trade says, 'mixed', which means for the author disappointing. Only the anonymous *TLS* reviewer offered unqualified praise. Most saw some merit in the book but complained of the flatness of the prose and the unsympathetic character of the narrator. Christopher Ricks in the *New Statesman* rightly questioned the characterisation of Mike Brady, but having done National Service himself 'found the total recall agreeably unnerving'. Older ex-soldiers were inclined to share Anthony Burgess's reaction: 'David Lodge speaks the truth about this sad limbo of a cold-war army, but it's not a new truth, nor is it newly illuminated . . . Get some in lad: your number's not dry.' But he was kind enough to add, 'Now that he's purged these two nasty wasteful years, he'll write, I prophesy, something to make us really sit up.' All in all, I felt I had scraped through the test of the second novel, and began to make notes for a third, based on and around my holiday in Germany in 1951.

18

The winter of 1963 was even colder than the previous year's. There was heavy snow, and then a period of exceptionally low temperatures which lasted through January and February. It was so cold in Birmingham that the water froze not only in the internal plumbing of houses but also in the mains pipes deep in the earth under the roads, and many homes were without water for several weeks. Warned by our experience of the previous year we managed to keep our rabbit hutch warm and dry, its small size becoming an asset in the arctic weather. I was astonished when the Vice-Chancellor of the University, Sir Robert Aitken, whose tall, distinguished figure matched his elevated position, called at our house one day during the great freeze. Standing on the trodden snow in our side way, with his chauffeured limousine waiting in the street, and to my relief declining to come inside, he invited us to a dinner party at his official residence a few days hence. It was short notice and we had no telephone, but it seemed an extraordinary visitation. As I thanked him I remembered that he had seemed rather taken with

Mary recently at some university function and decided he must have desired her presence at his dining table strongly enough to call in person. I did not suspect him of any more predatory motive. We enjoyed the dinner and the drinks before and after, served with some ceremony by a team of servants in the spacious and well-heated house on Edgbaston Park Road, but I felt embarrassed that the VC had been put to such trouble to invite us. Soon afterwards I decided we could afford a telephone and applied for one. It is almost incredible to me now that I had managed for so long without it, professionally as well as privately.

I also decided it was time to take driving lessons and get a car. In purchasing the car I made the same mistake as in buying the house, but with less justification. My career was going well, I was earning increasing income as a writer, and I could have afforded to get into debt without worrying, but Dad's example or genetic input guided my choice once again. I should have bought a new Mini on what was then called 'hire purchase'; instead I looked for a cheap second-hand car. I took what I believed was reliable advice from a neighbour, Michael, whose little boy was a playmate of our Julia. His father had been in the motor trade and Michael seemed to know a lot about cars himself, so I asked him to accompany me to inspect a Ford Popular several years old that was advertised in the *Birmingham Mail* for £100. We had a test drive in it, and Michael peered under the bonnet and pronounced it a bargain, so I bought it. It was in fact a clapped-out vehicle that was able to complete a gentle drive of a few miles around residential streets, but broke down when asked to do anything more strenuous. That summer we made a journey to visit friends in Cardiff, a distance of about 90 miles, which took us eleven hours, entailing calls at four different garages for repairs on the way, one of them requiring the removal of the entire engine to replace the clutch. In due course I had to replace the engine too. In fact it seemed to me that in the eighteen months I owned that car I replaced almost every moving part. It performed well by the end, but had cost me several times what it was worth.

The car blighted what was in other respects a time of interesting new developments and new contacts. I made the acquaintance of Brian Wicker, an English Literature tutor in the Birmingham extramural department who was a Catholic convert of left-wing political views, especially on the issue of nuclear weapons, and through him I got to know Ian Gregor, who had got the job at King's College London for which I was interviewed in 1959. He had since moved to the University of Edinburgh, and sometimes visited the Wicker family. They both belonged to a network of Catholics in university English departments, extensive enough to support a conference which met annually at the Dominican Priory and retreat house at Spode, in Staffordshire, to discuss connections between religion and literature. I attended the conference in 1963, as did Ian and Bernard Bergonzi, and fairly regularly for some years after. The bar opened punctually at lunchtime and in the evening, manned by a friar in the white Dominican habit, a novel experience. Participants included some interesting postgraduates and research fellows from Cambridge, known as the *Slant* group after the magazine they edited, which articulated a Marxist interpretation of authentic Christian faith, identifying the Kingdom of Heaven with Revolution on earth. Its leading lights were Terry Eagleton and Adrian Cunningham, though I missed the former's attendance at Spode, and met him much later elsewhere.

The English Department was engaged in the long-postponed but inevitable process of revising its syllabus. No issue is more important to the academic staff of any department, or more contentious, since the syllabus defines the subject to which they have dedicated their professional lives, and the status of each one's special field within it. Twentieth-century English literature and American literature had recently been added to the curriculum, and Malcolm and I, supported by Richard, thought there should also be more teaching on critical theory and methodology. It was not practicable to squeeze all this new subject matter into the existing degree structure. After many exhausting departmental meetings it was decided that there would be a new first-year syllabus introducing all students to the whole range of English studies, and then in the two years leading to their finals they would elect to join one of three groups, A, B and C, who would pursue some 'core' courses in common but choose options in medieval, Renaissance and modern literature respectively. As might have been predicted, the largest group of students opted for C group, which caused some concern to teachers belonging to the other groups, including Spencer, who was the figurehead of B group, though he preferred to use the faintly derisory term 'platoon', as if to distance himself from the exercise. He had had a good war, serving on the General Staff in Egypt and rising to the rank of lieutenant colonel, sailing on the Nile in off-duty hours with Brigadier Enoch Powell.

The students were a bright and interesting set of young people – and so they should have been, because the competition for admission was intense. We had about 400 applications for 40 places in the Single Honours course and interviewed all who seemed eligible, making them first write a commentary on a short literary text for an hour, so that both oral and written evidence of their potential could be assessed. It was a time-consuming exercise but worthwhile, for we would have to teach them for three years. Most of the successful candidates were the first members of their families to go to university, like the majority of us teachers, and it was fascinating to see how quickly they changed and developed intellectually and in other ways in the new environment.

A student I had tutored in my first year in the Department who had particularly impressed me was Jim Duckett, a lad from Coventry, to whose essays I frequently gave marks in the 'A' range. He also revealed talents as a writer and performer in occasional student entertainments, the exercise of which probably prevented him from getting a First. But he did get a good enough 2.1 to begin postgraduate research. In the summer term of 1963, he wrote, produced and performed in a revue consisting of satirical sketches and songs, which he put on in the Faculty of Arts. Malcolm and I watched some rehearsals, and Malcolm was sufficiently impressed to invite John Harrison, the recently appointed Artistic Director of the Birmingham Rep, to come and see the show, which he enjoyed as much as we did. It was funny and intelligent and slickly presented. Malcolm had got to know John years before in Nottingham when he was in charge of the Playhouse there, and John had suggested Malcolm should now try writing a play for the Rep. Instead, Malcolm proposed that he, Jim Duckett and I should write a revue together, and to my astonishment John commissioned it. At this time satirical revue was very much in vogue, helped by the huge success of *Beyond the Fringe* on stage and *That Was the Week That Was* on television, but John was taking a considerable risk, since none of us had any professional experience of writing for the theatre.

Revue is an essentially collaborative genre and Malcolm was an enthusiastic collaborator throughout his life. He claimed that he and a young American friend at Indiana University used to write short stories together sitting on opposite sides of a table, typing energetically until one of them said 'Blocked!' upon which they would change places and continue the other's work – an anecdote which itself has the makings of a revue sketch. He, Jim and I quickly began to write sketches and song lyrics to show John, and he was sufficiently satisfied to schedule our show for a four-week run at the Rep in November, while demanding more material to choose from. It was a genuinely collaborative process: each of us would write drafts of sketches and songs at home and bring them to joint sessions in Malcolm's office in the University, where we tried them out and rejected or reworked them, Malcolm typing the revised scripts as Jim and I prowled around him. There was much hilarity at these sessions, and I'm not sure that writing was ever such unadulterated fun for me again. From writing humorous pieces for *Punch* and *The Tablet* I had acquired the habit of spotting aspects of contemporary life ripe for parody or satire, and I did not find it difficult to develop these ideas in the form of drama, and even song lyrics. I had a record I played to Julia and Stephen of traditional songs sung by young children, including 'The Derby Ram' with the refrain '*It's a lie, it's a lie, it's a lie, lie, lie*', and we composed verses in which spokesmen for the various political parties made statements which received that rejoinder, ending with a topical reference to the Profumo Affair. We had a Brechtian pantomime, and an 'All Purpose Sentimental Song' and a 'Sunday Newspaper Service' ('"*Thrice was I beaten, twice was I thrown out of pubs, and once I was sent to prison. All because I would not reveal my sources.*" Words, my dear readers, taken from Acts of the Reporters, page 5, column 3'). We had a Festival of Folk Song and Dance which began with Bavarians in lederhosen singing demonstratively: '*With a yodel yodel elly, yodel elly, yodel elly elly Eye Ay! Oh, we slap our bottoms 'cause we like it and it's warm on a cold day!*' and ended with a troupe of Morris dancers singing: '*They say that life is just a dream, With a heigh-ho, heigh-ho nitty ditty day-do, soho, yoyo, derry down dum.*' It was silly but hilarious, and John shrewdly chose it to end the first half of the show. The curtain rose after the interval on the exhausted dancers still staggering round in a circle, grinding out their song.

The Old Rep, as it is now known, situated close to New Street station in the city centre, is a theatre with a long and distinguished history, founded in 1913 by Sir Barry Jackson who was its artistic director for most of his life. Many of the most famous actors on the British stage performed there – Laurence Olivier, Edith Evans and Ralph Richardson before the war, for instance, and Albert Finney, Ian Richardson and Derek Jacobi after it. John Harrison, speaking at an event to celebrate the Rep's centenary in 2013, explained that they loved playing there because their voices could reach every person in the audience without strain. He knew, having worked there himself as an actor in the 1940s. He called it a Stradivarius among theatres. It has about 400 seats in a steep rectangular rake, not much wider than the proscenium, a deeply unfashionable shape today, but one which ensures that every member of the audience can see and hear perfectly. In 1963 there were plans afoot to build a much bigger theatre deemed more appropriate to England's Second City, and in consequence the fabric and amenities of the old Rep had been neglected. It has since been handsomely renovated and one can appreciate what a gem it is; but shabby though it was then, we couldn't have had a better venue for our first attempt at writing for the professional stage.

There were no stars in the company of seven that performed *Between These Four Walls,* as our revue was called, though Linda Gardner, John Harrison's wife, was an enchanting and versatile actress, and Ralph Nossek would have a long and successful career as a character actor. There was, however, a star just about to be born: twenty-three-year-old Julie Christie. Her aspirations were focused on film but she had joined the Rep for a season to get acting experience, at £16 a week. While our show was in rehearsal she was given leave to attend the Venice Film Festival, where the film of *Billy Liar,* in which she was one of Tom Courtney's three girlfriends, was premiered. It won instant acclaim and Julie's performance was especially praised, launching her on a brilliant career in movies. She showed no sign of having her head turned by this success during the production of *Between These Four Walls,* which was just as well because she really wasn't very good as a stage actress, though she tried hard and humbly accepted advice – even from Jim Duckett. I have a memory of the postgraduate student coaching the future film star in the delivery of a song during a break in rehearsals, Julie nodding gratefully.

Between These Four Walls opened on the 19th of November. J.C. Trewin reviewed it next day in the *Birmingham Post* kindly and at length, under the headline, 'The University Wits of Station Street', praising its 'sustained good temper, gaiety and zest'. Other reviews in the local press were generally favourable, and box office bookings were encouraging, but soon our luck ran out. At first I went every night to the show, fascinated by the experience of hearing my own lines spoken and observing whether they worked or not for the audience, something a novelist can never do. There was a sketch in the first half about a job interview, and the candidate showed his insouciance by entering with a transistor radio playing pop music in his hand. One evening it was suddenly interrupted by a news flash that President Kennedy had been assassinated. The audience laughed uneasily at what seemed to be a joke in poor taste. In the interval they discovered that it had been a real broadcast and a genuine announcement, and the house was very subdued in the second half. Nobody felt like going to the theatre for some time after that event, certainly not to a light-hearted revue, and our audience figures slumped, recovering somewhat in the latter part of the run. A West End management manifested interest in transferring the show, but this too petered out. We had to be content with about £40 each in royalties, and a creative experience which was in fact priceless.

Meanwhile, I had been pursuing possible ways of spending a year in America, an aspiration of many young academics in those days. American universities were wealthy, numerous and expanding, and the best had staff ('faculty', in American usage) who were leaders in their fields, including literary criticism. American novelists like Salinger, Bellow, Mailer, Malamud and Updike seemed more ambitious and innovative than their British contemporaries.

For a young English writer and critic America was 'where it's at', to use one of the many phrases we borrowed from its colloquial speech to enliven our native idiom. My experience of American expatriate life in West Germany, my friendship with Park and Malcolm's anecdotes of the two separate years he had spent there all strengthened my desire to see the country for myself.

There were two ways of doing this: to take a job as a visiting teacher at a university, or to get a grant or fellowship for study and research in the USA, taking unpaid leave of absence from Birmingham in either case. I was tempted by the first alternative because American salaries were more generous than the British equivalents and would enable me and my family to live comfortably, while still making a profit on the trip. Richard Hoggart had enjoyed a spell at Rochester University and elicited an attractive offer to me through his contacts there. But I had also applied for a Harkness Commonwealth Fellowship, which funded one or two years' study and travel in the USA for young professionals in various fields, and I reached the final stage of the highly competitive selection process. I had first heard about this fellowship from Tony Petti, who had been a Fellow in 1959–60, and strongly recommended it. It was a counterpart to the Rhodes Scholarships which brought so many bright young Americans to Oxford, cementing the 'special relationship' between the two countries, but the Harkness was much more comprehensive, flexible and imaginative in its operation. Fellows could attach themselves to an institution of their choice, but did not register for degree courses. They proposed their own programme of work – mine was to acquire, *in situ,* a basic knowledge of American literature, of which I knew very little prior to the twentieth century. The fellowship was not worth as much as a visiting teacher's salary, but it covered the transatlantic fares of spouses and children. Fellows were required to travel for three months in America, visiting at least three different major regions of the country, and a hire car was provided for this purpose. All you had to do to earn this largesse was to write a long essay about your experience at the end of it. When I wrote to Park in March 1964 saying I was wondering whether to take the fellowship if it was offered rather than the better-paid job at Rochester, he replied bluntly, 'I'd turn down as much as $10,000 for three courses there, if I could get $6000 (plus fares) for doing nothing.' Of course he meant by the latter phrase the freedom to do whatever one wanted to do, and of course he was absolutely right. When I looked back later on what was probably the most liberating and productive twelve months of my life, I trembled at the thought that I had once hesitated about seizing the opportunity. It was my last chance to do so because I was just under the age limit for applicants.

I accepted the fellowship when it was offered in April, but not without qualms at the prospect of travelling to and around America with children aged four and two. To make things as easy as possible for the family I proposed to spend a semester at Brown University studying American literature, so that we would have the advantage of the Honans' friendly presence there before setting off on our travels. The Brown English Department was strong in American literature, so the location made academic sense, and the Harkness people were very pleased with my choice because most Fellows wanted to be attached to more prestigious universities like Harvard, Yale and Berkeley, where they all had much the same experience. The Honans for their part were delighted at the prospect of having us as neighbours in Providence for five months. We had seen disappointingly little of each other during Park's Guggenheim year in London, simply because we couldn't accommodate each other's families for overnight visits. He and Jeannette exerted themselves generously to take the stress out of our American adventure, finding us an apartment near the Brown campus at a very reasonable rent, and giving invaluable advice on what to pack, and what not to. ('Only a madman would bring a dinner-suit or tuxedo to America,' Park assured me in answer to a question of mine.) They even offered to drive to New York and meet us off the *Queen Mary*, on which we were to cross the Atlantic in August, but we did not put them to that trouble. I was glad that earlier in the year I had been able to do Park a small favour, when I declined an invitation by the *Encyclopaedia Britannica* to write a long article on Style with a recommendation that they try Park, who accepted it gratefully. His Guggenheim project had not really taken shape, but this gave him the stimulus to put all his notes and thoughts into a coherent but condensed form, and its appearance in this highly esteemed publication would look good on his CV.

In the months before our departure I strove to finish my own book on the language of fiction, then called 'The Novelist's Medium', so that I would not have to take all my notes and drafts with me to the States, and could start my fellowship year with a clean sheet. I had by this time completed the first section, about a third of the book, which was theoretical, though illustrated with close analyses of a number of extracts from classic and modern fiction; and I had written most of the second part, which consisted of essays on individual novels with particular attention to their verbal texture.

The premise of the theoretical section was: 'that if we are right to regard the art of poetry as an art of language, then so is the art of the novel; and that the critic of the novel has no special dispensation from that close and sensitive engagement with language we naturally expect from the critic of poetry'. It seemed to me that the neglect of this principle was especially evident in the work of F.R. Leavis and his disciples, who constituted the most influential school of literary criticism in Britain and the Commonwealth in the mid-twentieth century. Leavis's book *The Great Tradition* (1948) asserted that the novelists who belonged to it were characterised by 'a vital capacity for experience, a kind of reverent openness before life, and a marked moral intensity' – ethical rather than aesthetic values, which he seemed to think could be demonstrated by plonking long quotations on the page, without any analytical effort to trace the effectiveness of these passages to the diction and syntax employed by the writers. He proclaimed an austerely restricted canon of indisputably great novelists consisting of Jane Austen, George Eliot, Henry James and Joseph Conrad (later to be supplemented by D.H. Lawrence and later still by a revaluated Dickens), but even some of the chosen few failed to satisfy him at times. *The Ambassadors,* he complained, 'produces an effect of "disproportionate doing" – of a technique the subtleties of which are not sufficiently controlled by a feeling for value and significance in living'. I defended James's late style by a detailed analysis of his rendering of the superb climactic scene of *The Ambassadors*, when the hero belatedly realises he has been deceived by those he thought were his friends.

Other critics, notably the American Mark Schorer, had applied to prose fiction the close reading tools, honed on poetry and poetic drama, of the New Criticism, but they tended to favour modernist fiction, which was most amenable to this approach. I defended H.G. Wells, whose prose in *Tono-Bungay* had been criticised by Schorer to throw into relief the beauty and subtlety of Joyce's in *A Portrait of the Artist as a Young Man,* by arguing that Wells had quite different aims and priorities in what was generically a 'Condition of England' novel. Its core strengths are its powerful descriptions of the social systems encoded in the physical fabric of London and in the cultivated, enclosed English countryside, and its registration of the accelerating rate of change that was overwhelming both in the early twentieth century. It seemed to me then, and I have not changed my opinion since, that a theory of the novel, or general poetics of prose fiction, ought to encompass the whole spectrum of modes and subgenres, and not just those favoured by an individual critic or school of criticism.

Where I was mistaken at that point in time was in thinking this could be achieved by attention to verbal style alone. As I wrote in the afterword to a new edition of the book published in 1984:

> I accept that narrative is itself a language, a code of signification (or bundle of codes, like a multi-core cable) that functions independently of specific verbal formulations. Some of the meanings attributable to a narrative will remain constant when it is translated from one language to another and from one medium to another; and some of the crucial decisions and choices by which a narrative is produced are in a sense prior to, or performed at a deeper level than, the

articulation of the surface structure of the text, and may be
analysed without reference to it.

I might have formulated these axioms earlier by introspection, reflecting on my own practice as a novelist, but instead I derived them from the Continental European tradition of structuralist criticism, which began with the Russian Formalists of the 1920s, was developed in France in the 1970s and '80s, and had an increasing influence on Anglo-American literary criticism from that time onwards. Fortunately my ignorance of this work at the time of writing did not fundamentally affect the validity of the commentaries on individual texts in my book, or the interest of the theoretical questions it raised. In spite of the flaws in its argument, *Language of Fiction* is still in print.

The Catholic Church had been going through a period of very interesting change since Mary and I married. In 1958 Pope Pius XII, whose pontificate began in 1939, died, and John XXIII was elected in his place. The new pope, smiling and portly, was a very different character from his austere and tight-lipped predecessor. Since John was seventy-six he was at first labelled a 'caretaker pope', but he soon disproved this assumption by calling for a Second Vatican Council – a gathering of cardinals, bishops and theologians from all over the world – to review the Church's teaching, liturgy and mission in the modern world; this opened in Rome in October 1962. The First Vatican Council (1868–70), convoked by Pius IX, had declared the Infallibility of the Pope, under strictly defined conditions, to be an Article of Faith, and inaugurated a period of authoritarian top-down government of the worldwide Church by the Vatican. John XXIII declared that it was time to open the windows and let in some fresh air, and although his pontificate was short, and he died in 1963 while the Council was still in progress, he initiated an upheaval in Catholic life comparable to, and as important as, the political and cultural revolutions of the 1960s – with which indeed it was often intertwined.

Not all Catholics, whether clerical or lay, were pleased with this development, which has divided the faithful ever since, but as young, progressive Catholics Mary and I welcomed the new order and most of the innovations it produced. We approved of mass celebrated in the vernacular language of each country instead of Latin, and the more meaningful participation of the laity in the liturgy this made possible; we welcomed the relaxation of rules about fasting and abstinence, and the option (for a few years, until the Vatican managed to withdraw it) of substituting a collective liturgy of reconciliation for private confession. We were delighted with the new spirit of ecumenism, the respect for other Christian denominations and other faiths that the Council's deliberations encouraged, and the removal of invidious expressions like 'the perfidious Jews' from the Easter liturgy. But the crucial moral issue on which married Catholics hoped for change was birth control. There was an expectation, encouraged by some bold moral theologians, that the Council would consider whether the traditional natural law arguments against contraception still commanded assent. In fact neither Pope John XXIII nor his successor, Pope Paul VI, who reconvened the Council after John's death, had any intention of letting the Council debate this sensitive topic, and instead Paul set up a commission of suitably qualified clergy and laity to advise him on the matter. As is well known, he declined to accept its overwhelming majority opinion in favour of change and reiterated the traditional teaching in his encyclical, *Humanae Vitae*, in 1969. But in the early summer of 1964, as we prepared to leave for America, there seemed reason to hope that a more liberal statement might emerge from the deliberations of the Council.

I finished typing the manuscript of 'The Novelist's Medium', and sent it off to Colin Franklin, a senior editor at Routledge & Kegan Paul, who had discovered what I was working on and expressed keen interest in it. I had intended to take to America the preparatory notes and first draft pages of the novel inspired by my German holiday in 1951, and to go on with it there; but instead I was seized with the idea of a novel about the moral dilemma of married Catholics over birth control. As far as I was aware, the subject had never been treated in any detail in a novel, and I knew all about it, in theory and practice. From the beginning I thought of it as a comic novel. Although the Church's teaching has undoubtedly had tragic consequences for countless lives, in sexual deprivation, marital stress and damage to women's health, I thought that a serious treatment of such experience would be unlikely to engage non-Catholic readers, who would grow impatient with characters subjecting themselves to such unnecessary misery on what would seem irrational grounds; nor would I much enjoy writing about them. The subject had to be presented as a manifestation of the eternal comedy of human sexuality, the gap between the fantasy of unalloyed erotic bliss which we desire and the reality of married love, which is always vulnerable to unerotic contingency. But I doubt whether I would have reached this conclusion so promptly, or acted on it with such gusto, if I hadn't been stimulated by Malcolm to develop the strain of humour in my writing, and had the experience of writing comedy for performance in our revue. I felt eager to start. The weather was fine one bank holiday weekend. There was a shed in our garden at Reservoir Road with a kind of porch under which I set up a table and chair, and began to write the first chapter.

I invented a character called Adam Appleby, a Catholic postgraduate student at London University who has three unplanned young children, and wakes up one morning troubled by the awareness that another may be on the way because his wife Barbara's period is three days overdue. He mentally composes a short article on 'Catholicism, Roman' for a future Martian encyclopaedia.

As far as the Western Hemisphere is concerned, it appears to have been characterised by a complex system of sexual taboos and rituals. Intercourse between married partners was restricted to certain limited periods determined by the calendar and the body temperature of the female. Martian archaeologists have learned to identify the domiciles of Roman Catholics by the presence of large numbers of complicated graphs, small booklets full of figures and quantities of broken thermometers . . . Some scholars have argued that it was merely a method of limiting offspring . . . but as Roman Catholics produced more children on average than any other section of the community, this seems untenable.

Imitating the style of encyclopaedia articles gave me the idea for another thread in the novel – which I thought it needed, because Catholic hang-ups about birth control couldn't sustain it alone. Adam is working daily in the round Reading Room of the British Museum on a stylistic thesis about modern fiction and, stressed by anxiety over Barbara's possible fourth pregnancy, he has episodes of delirium in which commonplace events are present to his consciousness in parody or pastiche of the novelists he is studying. I thought I would call my novel 'The British Museum Had Lost Its Charm', a line from a George and Ira Gershwin song definitively recorded by Ella Fitzgerald:

> *A foggy day, in London town*
> *Had me low, had me down.*
> *I viewed the morning with alarm,*
> *The British Museum had lost its charm.*

And that in turn determined the time span of the novel's action: it would be a single day, a foggy day in London. I packed the draft of the first chapter and notes for its continuation in my luggage, labelled for the *Queen Mary*, cabin class.

19

In the mid-1960s most people we knew who travelled to and from America went by sea because of the high cost of air fares, but it was typical of the generosity of the Harkness Foundation that they paid for Fellows to cross the Atlantic in cabin rather than tourist class. Mum accompanied us to Southampton by train and was allowed to spend some hours on board the *Queen Mary* before it sailed. According to a letter from Dad, she couldn't stop talking to all her acquaintance for weeks about the size and luxurious appointments of the ship. We enjoyed the voyage, learning the quaint ways of shipboard life, which seemed to belong to a pre-war culture and class system, and managed to keep the children occupied and reasonably happy for four or five days. It was certainly the ideal way to arrive in America for the first time, watching the skyscrapers of Manhattan rise into view and sliding past the Statue of Liberty, with smaller ships and boats in the harbour hooting a welcome, before docking. The Director of the Fellowship programme, Lance Hammond, and some colleagues were there to greet us and some other new Fellows who had been on the voyage. They transferred the group to a hotel and gave us dinner that night, and a quick tour of Manhattan the next day, after which we took the train to Providence, and a tumultuous reunion with the Honans. How glad I was that we had these good friends to receive us and help us settle in.

Rhode Island is not an island, but is the smallest state in the Union, with a history that goes back to colonial days. By the mid-twentieth century its capital, Providence, was an economically depressed industrial city which sometimes reminded me of Birmingham on a smaller scale, the charming university campus and the tree-lined residential streets around it encircled by tracts of decaying property, disused factories and dull canals. The Honans had found us an apartment Park described in a letter as 'just a few blocks from the campus' and I had visualised the blocks as tall apartment blocks, whereas in fact our flat on Brook Street was on the first floor of a two-storey clapboard house, next door to a friendly Armenian shoe-mender's shop. Our landlords were Italian immigrants who had converted, decorated and furnished the place in a cheerfully unpretentious fashion and we felt immediately comfortable there. There were three bedrooms, the smallest of which I could use for a study. On the floor below lived a group of postgraduates, one of whom, a physicist called Stuart, became a friend. He gave me a paperback copy of Thomas Kuhn's *The Structure of Scientific Revolutions* in an effort to leaven my lamentable apathy towards science, but I'm afraid I did no more than glance at it: the aversion-teaching of this subject at St Joseph's Academy still exerted its influence.

The Brown campus was only a short walk away. It is one of the oldest universities in America, and the original buildings are pleasing to behold, plainer and more dignified than the overdone neo-Gothic of some other historic American universities, while the tree-shaded spaces between them provided a useful place to take the children for an airing in the warm weather, since we had no garden in Brook Street. According to Park, Brown was at this time fairly low down in the Ivy League as regards academic distinction, and tended to attract students from affluent families who were mainly interested in having a good time, though it has since grown in stature and currently has a world ranking of 52. My status there was ambiguous. I was registered as 'an occasional postgraduate student', although in qualifications and experience I was equivalent to a young assistant professor, except that I did not have a PhD. We mixed socially with faculty, helped by our association with the Honans, and everyone we met was very friendly and hospitable. At the parties we attended we were startled at first by the casual use of expletives in conversation, especially the f-word never heard in similar gatherings at home, and Mary was so offended by one person in this respect that she reproached him to his face, much to his surprise. Another difference from Birmingham I noted was the passion with which people discussed politics, local and national, for I had no idea how most of my English colleagues voted.

The Harkness Foundation paid postgraduate fees to Brown so that I could take courses if I wanted to, but I planned to work mainly on my own – and not exclusively at acquiring knowledge of American literature. For that purpose I had brought with me a compendious just-published anthology edited by Geoffrey Moore, from which I got the basic historical outline and plenty of suggestions for further reading. I did, however, join a graduate course on modern American fiction taught by a colleague of Park's, with whom he shared an office, Mark Spilka: a gentle, intelligent, somewhat depressive Jew, very quietly spoken – the absolute antithesis of the booming, boisterous, extrovert Yankee, so that it was surprising they were friends (and indeed the friendship came under severe strain later). Mark was very interested in Freudian psychoanalysis and had written, or would go on to write, esteemed books about Virginia Woolf, Ernest Hemingway and D.H. Lawrence from that perspective. At the time we met he identified strongly with the eponymous hero of Saul Bellow's *Herzog*, which had been recently published to great acclaim, and insisted that I read it. I did so with qualified admiration. To my mind Bellow was always straining a little too hard to impress us with his hero by saturating his consciousness with showy rhetoric and intellectual referencing. But this stylistic obtrusiveness, I discovered, as I extended my reading, was a typical feature of American literature from the nineteenth century onwards, because the ambitious American writer felt he had to invent a literary language that was distinctively different from the inherited British one. Hawthorne, Melville, Whitman – they all put words and phrases together that were never seen in company on the same page in canonical English literature. Mark Twain's use of American vernacular was another, different way of resisting the stylistic decorum of the old world – one which, according to Hemingway, shaped the subsequent development of American literature.

A prime example of the American writer's urge to 'make it new' (in Ezra Pound's celebrated words) was the work of John (Jack) Hawkes, who taught creative writing at Brown, and was highly esteemed by aficionados of avant-garde fiction. He was quoted as declaring: 'I began to write fiction on the assumption that the true enemies of the novel were plot, character, setting and theme, and having once abandoned these familiar ways of thinking about fiction, totality of vision or structure was really all that remained.' Park was an admirer and personal friend of Jack Hawkes and had hoped to introduce us, but unfortunately he and his family left Providence for San Francisco on a year's sabbatical leave just before we arrived. In another respect it was fortunate, because he wanted to sublet his rented apartment in SF in the summer of '65 at just the time we would be in need of one, for our plan was to drive to California in easy stages in the spring and make San Francisco our last place of residence before returning home. The sublet was agreed by correspondence between Jack and me, during which time I read two of his verbally exciting, narratively baffling novels, *The Lime Twig* (set in an unrecognisable version of England) and *Second Skin*, while he read my conventionally realistic *The Picturegoers*, and we exchanged polite compliments about each other's work. Not surprisingly, he was experiencing difficulty getting his books published in England.

My own luck was exactly the reverse. Early in September I was astonished and delighted to receive a phone call from a man called Tom McCormack, an editor at Doubleday in New York, saying they wanted to publish *Ginger, You're Barmy*. I had had no inkling of this possibility. I wasn't aware that the novel had been submitted to any American publishers, and it was a most unlikely book to appeal to them. I suppose Tom McCormack must have told me how it came to him when he invited me down to New York for lunch at the Ritz, but if so I have forgotten. It was certainly not from MacGibbon & Kee. Tim O'Keeffe communicated the news of Doubleday's offer with his congratulations in a letter which was sent by surface mail and therefore arrived weeks after the deal was done. I wrote a little humorous piece about the difference between the way British and American publishers treated their authors, which was published in the American *Saturday Review* and entertained Tom McCormack hugely. I liked him a lot, and was very sorry when he told me in October that he was leaving Doubleday – whether he jumped or was pushed I don't know, but his cheerful tone suggested the former – and handed me over to another editor. Meanwhile I was getting on well with the British Museum novel, and negotiations for the publication of 'The Novelist's Medium' jointly by Routledge and Columbia University Press in New York were proceeding promisingly.

Life was not entirely trouble-free. I had to have a tooth extracted, the first since childhood, because I couldn't stand the pain of the root canal treatment that was required to save it (so much for the vaunted American dentistry – or perhaps I was unlucky with the recommended dentist). Then Mary was stung in the foot by a wasp on the Brown campus on her way to the launderette with the children, and went into a state of cataleptic shock from which she might have died if the launderette's attendant hadn't noticed and called me in time to get her to a doctor, who administered the necessary shot of adrenalin. Otherwise we basked in good fortune. Lance Hammond came to Providence to check up on my progress, and told me that because we had two children the Foundation had decided to give us a hire car for nine months instead of the usual three. I went down to New York to collect the car, a brand new Chevrolet Bel Air, which I drove out into the honking, heaving mid-town Manhattan rush hour, struggling with the unfamiliar steering column gear-shift and peering nervously over the dashboard at the vast expanse of bonnet, which I steered down one of the infinitely long avenues for block after block, not daring to turn left or right, until I found a place where I could safely park. I spent the night in the tiny apartment of Charles Tomlinson, a charming and dazzlingly handsome theatre designer from North Carolina whom Mary and I had met years before as student hosts at a London University summer school for American students, and had kept in touch with ever since. Next day I took the turnpike to Providence, a drive of several hours' duration. Oh, the quiet power of the engine, the smooth, bump-absorbing ride, the soothing sound of the radio, as the miles slipped effortlessly by. What a magical change from the Ford Popular!

As Mary had not learned to drive in England, she did so in Providence, where it was in fact easier to pass the test, for the driving school instructors and the examiners seemed to be on intimate terms with each other. Her own instructor guaranteed that she would pass the test at the first attempt, and he was right. When she had difficulty reversing round a corner in her test, the examiner put his hand helpfully on the wheel to guide her. The instructor also ran a funeral parlour and, amazed to learn that she had no knowledge of such a facility in England, insisted on talking about its merits all the time she was driving with him. Mary was soon a safe, confident driver, however, and coped well with the nearest thing we had to an accident in our American year – when a rear tyre blew out at about 60 mph on a highway in Nevada, and she controlled the resulting skid to bring the car to a safe halt on the central reservation. While we were still in our seats, recovering from the shock, a highway patrol car drew up behind us, the Stetsoned policeman approached and, not noticing the flat tyre, sternly warned us that we were illegally parked – but he soon helped us to get on our way.

Having the Chevvy immediately enhanced the quality of our lives. We could shop at big supermarkets, and make expeditions to places of interest, like New Bedford on the south Massachusetts coast, with its famous whaling museum. And we ventured further north to Boston and environs, staying for a weekend with Bernard and Gabriel Bergonzi, who were living there with their two children while he was a visiting teacher at Brandeis University, and also met the large, hospitable family of Bernard McCabe, brother of the Dominican theologian Herbert McCabe, the inspiring mentor of Terry Eagleton and the *Slant* group back in England. We were introduced to the McCabes through Martin Green (not to be confused with my editor at MacGibbon & Kee), whom we had met in Birmingham on a couple of occasions as a guest of the Bradburys when he was in England visiting his parents, and who taught at Tufts University with Bernard. I now belonged to a network of British academics temporarily or permanently employed in America who kept in touch and helped each other in various ways.

Martin Green was a particularly interesting member of this group, a remarkable man of whom we would see a good deal in the years to come. Some eight years older than me, he came from a poor family in rural Shropshire, no member of which had had a secondary education until he won scholarships to grammar school and Cambridge, where he read English. He was a victim of what

I called earlier the 'First-degree culture' of English academia, and its one-chance-only final examinations. If ever there was a true intellectual, who deserved to be paid to think, write and teach in a university, it was Martin. But he got a poor first degree. I'm not sure whether it was a Lower Second or a Third, or what the cause was – whether it was overwork or anxiety or recklessly opinion-ated exam scripts – but this result effectively barred him from postgraduate study and an academic career in Britain. After various forms of employment in England, France and Turkey, he got a PhD at the University of Michigan, which qualified him for an academic career. He caused something of a stir in 1961 with a book in the Angry Young Man mode called *A Mirror for Anglo-Saxons,* about culture and society in England and America and his personal search for identity between these two nations, in which he put forward as his ideal Englishman an unlikely combin-ation of qualities possessed discretely by D.H. Lawrence, F.R. Leavis, George Orwell and Kingsley Amis. While writing that book he had read C.P. Snow's celebrated attack on the anti-scientific bias of British education and the governing class it produced, *The Two Cultures and the Scientific Revolution* (1959), and was persuaded by it to spend much of the next four years studying science at MIT and Cambridge in order to make his own contribution to the debate, *Science and the Shabby Curate of Poetry,* published in 1964. By the time we met him he had resumed teaching at Tufts, and was writing mainly about American literature in a provoca-tively independent way. The senior professor in the field at Brown, Howard Waggoner, told me that Martin's recent book on Hawthorne, 'though wrong', was the most important thing written about the author that year. He could be a rather formidable person in company: serious, sardonic and disinclined to engage in small talk. He had a sense of humour, but his laughter seemed more like a physical effort than a euphoric release of tension.

As a young man Martin had been converted to Catholicism, which explained why he was intimate with the McCabe family. He had previously seemed to us to have a settled bachelor persona, but at the McCabes' he was evidently an item with a handsome young woman called Carol, who taught at a local Catholic college. I recall discussing with her on that occasion the current speculation that there might be a change in the Church's teaching on birth control, and she said that she knew several Catholic couples who had decided to make their own conscientious decision on the matter while continuing to go to mass and communion. This was the first time I had heard of such a course of action, and I didn't quite know what to make of it. It is hard to convey to those who have not experienced the kind of Catholic education Mary and I had received how all-embracing and all-controlling was the faith which it instilled. This was more marked in northern European countries, where Catholicism had assimilated something of the spiritual scrupulosity of Protestantism, than in the southern Latin ones, where the laity had a more relaxed attitude to contradictions between principles and behaviour. To us the Church was like a club: it had a rule book which covered all the possible contingencies of life, and if you kept them, or received absolution for breaking them, you were assured of eternal life and God's help in the trials of this one. It seemed obvious that you couldn't ignore the rules which you found inconvenient without forfeiting membership, and for this reason many Catholics had 'lapsed' over the issue of birth control. Of all the mortal sins, contraception was one of the most deliberate and habitual by its very nature, and incompatible with 'a firm purpose of amendment' in the sacrament of Penance; therefore couples who took the conscientious personal decision route would have to either make confessions that were invalid and possibly sacrilegious according to the rule book, or stop going to confession altogether – which was what vast numbers of Catholics did in due course. Mary and I were not yet ready to take that step.

I was getting towards the end of my novel about Adam Appleby. I had put this character through a series of farcical and alarming experiences in the course of a foggy November day, and I had decided early on in the compositional process to relieve his anxiety that Barbara might be pregnant again before the single day of the action came to an end (it was, after all, a comic novel). But I was preoccupied with the problem of how to combine that resolution with the thread of literary parody and pastiche in the novel, which had become more and more prominent as it developed. Paragraph-length passages echoing D.H. Lawrence and Joseph Conrad, for instance, had been followed by whole episodes in the style of Ernest Hemingway and Henry James. It was essential that the last chapter should raise this game to its highest level. But how? The rationale for Adam's propensity to reveries or delusions coloured by the style of various novelists was that he is writing a thesis on 'The Long Sentence in Modern Fiction'. It occurred to me belatedly that the longest sentences in all modern fiction must be in that greatest of all circadian novels (i.e. those with a one-day action), James Joyces's *Ulysses*. Molly Bloom's twenty-five-thousand-word stream-of-consciousness monologue which concludes it contains only two full stops, one in the middle and one at the end. Problem solved! I could switch the novel's point of view from Adam to Barbara in the final chapter, and have her half asleep in bed when he comes home late (like Bloom to Molly), relieved that her period has started in the course of the day, musing drowsily on the problems and paradoxes of sex, marriage and human fertility. When I remembered that Molly also starts her period halfway through that episode of *Ulysses*, I realised that there is such a thing as writer's luck. But did I dare take this liberty with the writer I revered above all others? I couldn't resist, because I saw that this shift of perspective to the wife's viewpoint was exactly what the novel needed thematically, to provide a balanced view of its central topic:

> . . . well perhaps the church will change and a good thing too there'll be much less misery in the world but it's silly to think that everything in the garden will be lovely it won't it never is I think I always knew that before we were married perhaps every woman does how could we put up with menstruation, pregnancy and everything otherwise not like men he has this illusion that it's only the birth control business that stops him from getting sex perfectly under control . . .

And in place of Molly's affirmative keyword, 'Yes', with which *Ulysses* ends, I gave Barbara the more tentative 'perhaps', recalling Adam's forecast of their marriage when they were courting:

> . . . he said it'll be wonderful you'll see perhaps it will I said perhaps it will be wonderful perhaps even though it won't be like you think perhaps that won't matter perhaps.

The air temperature dropped and the first snow came. Old Providence looked pretty under its deep white covering, and we enjoyed trudging through it as the sun shone from a clear blue sky. We drove to Toronto to spend Christmas with Mary's sister Eileen and her family. She had married John, a technical draughtsman, in the same year as Mary and I got married, and they had two boys about the same age as Julia and Stephen. We had planned to have a look at the Niagara Falls on our way, but the weather turned unseasonably mild just before we set off, and they were swathed in fog, so we could only listen to the roar of the water as we stood at the rail of the viewing platform. Eileen and John entertained us kindly in their suburban apartment, and Christmas Day was enhanced by the excitement of four children opening their presents. On Boxing Day we went to an open-air ice skating rink in the centre of the city so that Eileen's elder boy could try out his new skates, but the surface was wet with melting ice so that if you fell over you got soaked. Back in Providence, the cold high-pressure weather returned, and we skated a few times on a frozen river wearing borrowed and second-hand skates – one of the most exhilarating experiences I have ever had. Going round and round a rink never seemed worth doing afterwards.

The Columbia University Press publishing committee had finally decided that 'The Novelist's Medium' was worthy of publication under their imprint, but only on condition that I changed the title. By 'medium' I meant 'language' of course, but perhaps they thought it might be interpreted as a reference to spiritualism. I offered a number of alternatives including *The Language of Fiction*, which they accepted – only to quibble again a month or so later. They thought it implied a more comprehensive study of the subject than the book actually attempted, and proposed that I should drop the definite article. To clinch the deal and speed the process of publication, I agreed, as did Routledge for the same reasons, but I regretted it later. 'Language of Fiction' on its own is an unnatural locution, and consequently the book is often cited inaccurately as *The Language of Fiction*. MacGibbon & Kee were delighted with 'The British Museum Had Lost Its Charm' when they received it in February from Graham Watson, but I would have trouble with that title too in due course, and meanwhile Graham was frustrated by a clause in my contract for *Ginger, You're Barmy*, which he described as 'a villainous document', not only giving them the option to publish my next novel, but retaining subsidiary rights in it too. These rights he managed to prise from them eventually. I was just happy to have secured the publication of the two books before we set off on our trek to California.

In February I received disturbing news from Malcolm, with whom I had been corresponding at intervals by airmail. The new University of East Anglia had head-hunted him for an appointment there, with the prospect of early promotion to senior lecturer and the opportunity to design an American Studies programme from scratch. New universities were springing up all over the country, often on the outskirts of pleasant cathedral towns like Norwich, and there were plenty of such enticing job opportunities. In the same month I was approached by Ian Gregor about my possible interest in one at the University of Kent at Canterbury, to which he had just moved from Edinburgh, and which was about to open its doors, but I was not tempted, much as I liked Ian. Malcolm obviously *was* tempted, but said, 'I'm in a state of great indecision: one thing it makes me realise is how attached I am to Birmingham and how if I went I'd miss you.' I was dismayed at the prospect, and wrote him a long letter laying out all the reasons I could think of why he should stay at Birmingham. In March, just before we left Providence, I heard that he had accepted the job at UEA. He told me later that he agonised over the decision and when he *had* to make it he went out with two letters in his pocket, one saying Yes and the other saying No. At the pillar box he decided to post the No letter, but someone at UEA phoned him next day and said, 'You don't really mean it, do you?' and he agreed that he didn't. Malcolm hated to say no to any invitation, as many people in academia and the media learned to their advantage, though not always to his. I wrote back, 'Oh Malcolm, how could you do it? How could you turn your back on Brum? We're really desolated.' I felt that if I had not been in America at the vital moment I might have persuaded him to stay in Birmingham, but as time went on it became increasingly clear that such a separation was inevitable and essential if we were to develop our careers as novelists independently. Even so, as two academics who wrote satirical campus novels we were confused often enough in the minds of many people, and were frequently congratulated on writing each other's books, a compliment difficult to receive gracefully.

At the end of March 1965 it was time to leave Providence, to pack our belongings in the capacious boot, or rather 'trunk', of the Chevrolet, bid farewell to the Honans and thank them for all their many kindnesses. The last of these was a list of the names and addresses of friends living in California which Jeannette compiled;

she had written to them, and assured us that they would be very glad to meet us and even put us up. She and Park were sorry to see us go, partly because we were a link with their happy years in London. Neither of them, for different reasons, really loved the American way of life, which for Mary and me, liberated as we were from the chores and frustrations of our existence in England, had all kinds of novel attractions. When I came to write my essay on our year in America for the Harkness Foundation I called it 'The Bowling Alley and the Sun', a phrase taken from a poem by the seventeenth-century American poet Edward Taylor which celebrates God's creation of the universe by asking a series of rhetorical questions, e.g. *'Who Spread its Canopy? Or Curtains spun? / Who in this Bowling Alley bowld the Sun?'* I explained:

The Bowling Alley, the modern bowling alley, that curious place of popular resort and recreation, where half the fun of the simple and repetitive game lies in watching the machinery reset the pins and return the balls – this stands for everything in American life that is designed to tickle and appease our appetites as consumers, everything that seems to make the ordinary humdrum business of life require less effort and yield more pleasure than it does in England: motels and super-markets, big cars and big refrigerators, central heating and ice cubes, bathroom showers, urban expressways, heated open-air swimming pools. And the sun stands for itself (for one sees so much more of it in America), but also for all the natural wonders of that vast and infinitely various country . . . America is a country peculiarly rich in euphoria, and one becomes more conscious of this the further one drives west . . .

378

Since 1965 England has acquired bowling alleys and most of the other amenities I celebrated in that passage, and we take them for granted now, while America, after decades of wars, assassinations, terrorist violence and economic crisis, has become a less euphoric place, but that was how it felt to me at the time. America provided the perfect 'Abroad' experience for me. It was fascinatingly different from home in topography, history, architecture, politics, manners and many other respects, especially the ways people used the English language in speech and writing. But because their language *was* a variety of English, I quickly acquired its different vocabulary and idioms and was able to understand and interact with the natives as I never could in any European country.

We took about two months to drive to California, a journey of a scale we would never have contemplated in Europe with two young children, but which was feasible in America because of the ubiquity of comfortable motels and restaurants used to catering for families. From Providence we went first to Philadelphia and Washington, where we did some sightseeing, and then drove south into Virginia, visiting Thomas Jefferson's house, Monticello, where the American genius for making domestic life easier was manifested early in Jefferson's interior design ideas. Here we stayed for a few days at the University of Virginia in Charlottesville, where we coincided by arrangement with a visit by Jack Hawkes, who was giving a reading there. We enjoyed his company, but it was the only time we ever met. Before his reading there was a reception at which black waiters served drinks wearing white gloves, an index that we were now in the South. We did not venture further in that direction because it was the time of Civil Rights demonstrations, which were violently resisted by local white communities, and we had been advised that to take a car with New York number plates into the Deep South was to invite trouble. Consequently we turned north into Kentucky and crossed the great plains through Indiana, Illinois and Missouri until we paused at Hannibal, Mark Twain's boyhood home on the Mississippi. Then we made for the snow-capped Rocky Mountains, which rose up slowly and majestically on the western horizon, and specifically for the University of Colorado at Boulder, where Malcolm's introduction had secured me an invitation to the Conference on World Affairs, an annual event which he had attended and enthused about. Still going strong, it consists of a week of panel discussions on every possible subject by a hundred or so guest speakers from all over the world, attended by large enthusiastic audiences. I was asked to speak on, among other things, 'Camp', a term lately appropriated by Susan Sontag in a celebrated essay to describe a wide range of cultural attitudes and practices. I felt I should explain that in Britain it applied more narrowly to a stylised kind of speech and behaviour especially associated with homosexuality (the term 'gay' was not yet in general currency), and amused the audience with a letter home describing the Boulder campus and conference from a visitor who was a cross between Oscar Wilde and Kenneth Williams.

There was a party every night that week, and at one of them Mary and I met a nuclear physicist from the National Laboratory at Los Alamos, in New Mexico, where the atom bomb was designed, who invited us to visit him there after the conference. By this time I had lost my native caution and reserve and said yes to any offer of a new experience. It was a long drive through an arid empty landscape until we reached the oasis of the Laboratory and the large settlement that had grown up around it to house and service its population of scientists, technicians and their families. There was an air of anticlimax about the place, as if the inhabitants were aware it had passed its peak of fame and achievement, and my most vivid memory is of the disaffected teenage daughter of our host, who described it as being at night 'like a graveyard with lights'. From this desert citadel of science we made a literary pilgrimage to the D.H. Lawrence ranch near Taos, which the writer's wealthy admirer Mabel Dodge Sterne gave to him and his wife Frieda. Here he wrote *The Plumed Serpent* and here Frieda eventually brought his ashes after his death in the South of France. It is owned and maintained by the University of New Mexico, but was unattended and looked rather neglected when we made our visit, though the little whitewashed memorial building was open, and I signed the visitors' book, noting the names of several writers I knew above mine. It occurred to me that I was making the twentieth-century equivalent of the Grand Tour of Europe.

On the other side of the Rockies was Arizona, with its natural wonders – the Painted Desert, the giant Meteorite Crater and the Grand Canyon. What can one say about the Grand Canyon? This vast cleft in the earth is beyond sublime – the Romantic poets who were moved to eloquence by the Lake District or the Alps would have been rendered speechless by it, it is so monumentally indifferent to the human beings who creep along its edges and peer nervously down at the ribbon of the Colorado River a mile below. From beyond sublime we went to beyond ridiculous in Nevada – to the surreal architecture of Las Vegas. We stayed two days, lounging round the motel pool by day, seeing extravagant floor shows in the evenings which the casinos put on at modest prices to lure customers, and left the town having gambled just once, with a 50-cent piece on a fruit machine, perhaps a record.

From there we went to Palm Springs, the Californian desert resort favoured by Hollywood celebrities and wealthy retirees, where we had a reunion with my aunt Eileen. After living for some years in San Francisco, and then in Vancouver, she had sought a warmer, drier climate, and Palm Springs certainly had that. One day I left a small transistor radio on the dashboard of the car in the sun, and when I came back the plastic casing had softened and curled so that it resembled something painted by Salvador Dalí. Eileen had found a job with a PR firm, her beautiful manners and perfect diction serving her well in this sphere. She was delighted to see us, and to meet the children for the first time, and we stayed for several days in the comfortable motel suite she had found for us, with the luxury of a kitchen and two bedrooms. We had a lot to talk about and catch up on. Eileen seemed pleased with her situation, but before long she would be on the move again: she went on holiday to Hawaii and was enchanted by the place, feeling that she had at last found the perfect climate – tropical sunshine cooled by the trade winds – and an ocean you could comfortably swim in all year round. She moved there, soon found a job in Waikiki, an apartment ten minutes' walk from the beach, and was very happy until the impact of mass tourism made the location less idyllic.

Then we were off again, across the Joshua Tree desert to the Californian coast – to La Jolla, near San Diego in the extreme south, and then north to Los Angeles, where we visited Disneyland for the children's sake, and for my sake Forest Lawn, the huge cemetery-cum-theme-park satirised by Evelyn Waugh in *The Loved*

One. In both locations we were hospitably entertained and escorted by friends of Jeannette's. The generosity of the people we met in this way never ceased to amaze me and caused occasional twinges of guilt, but they showed no signs of feeling exploited.

A two-day drive from Los Angeles up the scenic coastal Route 101 took us to our home for the summer in San Francisco. The apartment was shabby, as Jack Hawkes had warned us, but it was spacious, with a room on the ground floor which I could use as a study, and the situation was superb, high up on one of the city's many hills, above the Marina, where we sometimes went on Sundays to watch the yacht racing, and joined in a kite-flying competition on Independence Day. From the crest of the hill you could see the whole bay spread out between the Golden Gate and Bay bridges. The former took us to the green hills of Marin County, to the arty-crafty little port of Sausalito and the Pacific rollers breaking on Stinson Beach; the latter to Berkeley, and the vast University of California campus, which turned out to have a campanile almost identical to Birmingham's, but built of white stone instead of red brick. Brian Cox, senior lecturer at Hull and co-editor of the *Critical Quarterly*, in which I had published some articles, was a visiting professor in the English Department and introduced me to its current chairman, Mark Schorer, whose essays on style in the modern novel had fed into *Language of Fiction*. We were invited to parties given by Schorer and his wife, a charming and hospitable couple, in a house perched on a hill so steep it had a chairlift to the front door; and Brian invited us to dinner to meet a rising young star in the English Department called Stanley Fish, and his wife Adrienne.

Stanley had written a well-received book on the sixteenth-century English poet John Skelton, and was now working on one about Milton. He and Adrienne had both grown up in Providence, which provided us with an immediate conversational topic, and had Jewish family backgrounds. One of the things that had struck me about American universities was the very high proportion of Jews among the faculty compared to England, but Stanley stood out from the crowd. Faculty who specialised in English literature, especially older English literature, tended to be Anglophile, took every opportunity to study or do research in England, cultivated English manners and even dressed like Englishmen, in tweed jackets with leather elbow patches. Stanley had never been to England or anywhere else in Europe, and appeared to have no wish to do so. He was typically American in all his tastes, enjoying movies, popular music, television, cars, shopping, baseball, and basketball – which, though short and slight in stature, he liked to play as well as watch. He was very ambitious and made no attempt to disguise it, and in argument spoke wittily and pungently in perfectly formed sentences. He was not loved by all his colleagues, but I found his openness engaging and stimulating, and the contrast between his character and his academic specialism fascinated me. Adrienne was less assertive, but had a sly sense of humour, some-times turned on her spouse. We quickly became friends of this lively couple.

On my quite frequent trips across the double-decker Bay Bridge to Berkeley I observed with interest the nascent Free Speech movement organised by the students to resist attempts by the authorities to suppress political speeches, demonstrations and publications on campus. Initially focused on domestic civil rights, the FSM increasingly attacked the 'military-industrial complex' and its influence on US foreign policy, especially in Vietnam. I attended one of the first 'teach-ins' – occasions when students invited sympathetic celebrity speakers to address them in an open-air amphitheatre on campus – and heard Norman Mailer doing his oratorical stuff to a large and enthusiastic audience. I sensed that something of more than ephemeral import was happening at Berkeley, and wrote a report about this event for *The Tablet*.

After our long holiday on the road, I was keen to do some writing in the three months we were to spend in San Francisco. I had discovered that Columbia University Press published a series of pamphlets, about 15,000 words in length, on individual authors of the twentieth century. They were called Columbia Essays on Modern Writers, and I offered to write one on Graham Greene. In contrast to the Press's previous leisurely pace, they accepted promptly and asked if I could deliver it by September, so I bought or borrowed Greene's novels, re-read them, and set to work. I was distracted for a while by a crisis over my British Museum novel, which was going through the editorial process at MacGibbon & Kee, scheduled for autumn publication. Tim O'Keeffe wrote, rather late in the day, to ask if I had obtained permission to use the line, 'The British Museum had lost its charm', for the title. Inexperienced in these matters, I had not done so. I applied to the Gershwin Publishing Corporation for permission, which was refused. I pleaded and offered to pay anything within reason, but they were adamant, claiming that they might want to use the line themselves as a title. I learned later that the publishers of popular song lyrics are, of all their kind, the most jealously protective of copyright. Tim O'Keeffe asked me for an alternative title, and I suggested a line from *Paradise Lost*, 'Adam from the cold sudden damp re-covering', which they didn't like. I sent them a long list of other titles, of which my own preference was for 'Wombsday', which they rejected. The last on the list was 'The British Museum is Falling Down', and that was what we agreed on. There was a false fire alarm in the Reading Room in the novel which gave some warrant for this title, and there is a theory of some relevance that the nursery rhyme which inspired it was originally an apology to 'my fair lady' for erectile dysfunction, but I mourned the loss of my original choice. The best I could do to repair the loss was to use the first four lines of the song as an epigraph to the first chapter (every chapter of the novel had an epigraph refer-ring to the British Museum), for which MacGibbon & Kee managed to get permission.

At the beginning of July, Doubleday's representative in San Francisco took us out to lunch to celebrate the publication of their edition of *Ginger, You're Barmy*, and organised some publicity. I was interviewed on local TV and donned headphones for a radio phone-in programme (a form of broadcasting as yet unknown in England) to answer questions about the British Army from people in the Bay Area who had nothing better to do. There was one rave review, in a Chicago paper, but the rest were mostly unenthusiastic. I was not surprised – the surprise was that Doubleday had bought a book which had not been very successful in England in the first place. I was not surprised either when later they turned down *The British Museum is Falling Down*. My new editor there, James Ross, loved it and described himself as 'disturbed, distressed and depressed' by the decision, which might have been different if *Ginger* hadn't been a flop.

Meanwhile we made the most of the pleasures of San Francisco, about which I rhapsodised in my Harkness essay:

the sense of living on the very crest of civilization, serene and poised as a surf-rider, that graced the simplest experience: riding the steep, roller coaster hills, browsing in the City Lights Bookshop, seeing a ship slide past the end of a city street, having tea in the Japanese Tea Gardens, watching the white fog creep in through the Golden Gate like a living thing, wondering idly, what shall we do this evening, shall we go down to North Beach and see Lenny Bruce at the Hungry i, or hear Charlie Byrd play his guitar, or have a Mexican meal, or call up some friends and invite them over?

Then, suddenly, it was time to go home, first traversing those thousands of American miles. We chose a more direct and northerly route than our outward journey, aiming to cover it in about three weeks, with breaks of a few days at the Yosemite and Yellowstone National Parks, and in Chicago. The Chevrolet was not air-conditioned – only luxury cars were in those days – and to avoid the summer heat of the day we developed a routine of going to bed early, getting up at three or four in the morning, and driving for five or six hours with the children in sleeping bags on the back seat, extended by an ingenious arrangement of luggage, and then looking for a nice motel with a pool.

. . . it was pleasant driving quickly along empty roads with the children asleep in the back, talking quietly and sipping black coffee picked up from an all-night café, the dawn spread across the sky as we drove straight into the rising sun. We saw many tremendous dawns, angry red and yellow over Nevada, sad pastel shades over South Dakota. We climbed the 10,000 foot Powder River Pass over the Bighorn Mountains, Montana, in the dark; but when we got to the plateau at the top it was dawn, and as we began to descend it was like being in an airplane, we were looking down on the cloud cover, and startled deer looked at us from the side of the road.

Sometimes Stephen would wake up and ask, 'Where are we going?' to which I would reply, 'To a motel,' upon which, apparently satisfied, he would fall asleep again. Poor Stephen! He was much too young to get anything out of our year in America, while Julia, though old enough to enjoy many things at the time, has little or no memory of them. Sometimes I feel a little guilty in retrospect on this account, but no regret. There are moments in life when you have to be a little selfish to make the most of it, and accepting the Harkness Fellowship was one.

20

It takes a bit of getting used to, England. You have to re-acquire the taste for it: for the change that sprains your wrist as the bus conductor pours it into your hand. For five different shops to buy five different kinds of food. For politeness when it is least needed ('*Please* tear off,' it says on the tab inside the matchbox). For the National Health Service (I've been limping about on a verruca for months, determined to wait for free treatment. 'Most people do it themselves,' said my doctor. 'Just take a razor-blade . . .') For pedestrians who prance out at oncoming cars like bull-fighters, arching their backs as you brush past them. For houses all identical on the outside, all with different electrical sockets on the inside. Tiny, tiny houses, like cosily furnished hen-coops. And in one such hen-coop I lie on my bed, my nose streaming, my throat itching, my eyes watering – with, in short, the common English cold. Back.

Thus I concluded an article for *The Tablet* about the experience of returning to England in 1965, and it expresses pretty well how our *annus mirabilis* in America had defamiliarised my native land, afflicting me with withdrawal symptoms and depression. The chief source of discontent was our wretched house, which we had let in our absence to a young lecturer in the Philosophy Department, Margaret Boden, who went on to have a notable career in the field of cognitive science at the University of Sussex. She had looked after it well, but it seemed more than ever inadequate to our needs. I don't know why it took us until the following summer to find something satisfactory – probably my innate financial caution again, and anxiety not to make a mistake for a third time. I did, however, draw on the funds I had accumulated to buy a brand-new car, to avoid breakdowns. It was an Anglia Estate, the smallest of its type in the Ford range to which I remained inexplicably loyal.

Though I was depressed, the children were positively glad to be home, and Mary was grateful to have them off her hands for a few hours a day. Julia started at our parish primary school, and Stephen was placed at an excellent nursery school much favoured by University parents. Mary began to think about returning to teaching part-time next year. My own low spirits were partly due to the fact that Malcolm had left not only Birmingham but also England, for a whole year. He had postponed his move to Norwich in order to take up an American fellowship similar to the Harkness, and had planned a programme much like mine, spending time at three very different universities – Harvard, Indiana and the University of California at Davis. He sailed to America with Elizabeth and their infant son Matthew just before we returned, so that we weren't able to meet for even a few days to discuss Malcolm's second novel, *Stepping Westward*, which had just been published by Secker & Warburg, and another revue that John Harrison had commissioned from the same team as before, plus David Turner, for production at the Rep in November.

Stepping Westward, written, like most of Malcolm's novels, over many years at intervals between other projects, followed the droll fortunes and misfortunes of a diffident provincial English novelist who journeys to a Midwestern university in a town called Party and fails to understand the plots in which he becomes involved. Notable for its dense, witty and exact observation of English and American manners and speech, it was well received, but might have made more impact if he hadn't taken so long to write it, because there had been three recently published novels about the adventures of Englishmen in America, two of them set on university campuses, by Kingsley Amis, Julian Mitchell and Thomas Hinde. The new revue was something Malcolm had told me about when I was on my travels and felt that I could hardly contribute usefully to it, but I did send a few sketches from San Francisco and wrote some more when I got home. At least one of these must have been performed, because I had a contract for my participation, but I have a strangely blank memory of the show, no recall of rehearsals or performances, and I cannot now even find a copy of the script. The revue was called *Slap in the Middle*, a reference to Birmingham's geographical position, and had a much more local focus than its predecessor, which probably didn't inspire me. Jim Duckett, who had abandoned postgraduate research for a career in the theatre, was involved as John's assistant director, writer and performer. As far as I remember, the revue was not as successful with audiences as *Between These Four Walls*, and perhaps for this reason I quickly forgot it.

It was some compensation for Malcolm's absence that he had been replaced in the Department by Martin Green. Knowing that Martin wanted to return to England, I had recommended him to Richard Hoggart, who fixed the appointment – I don't remember how. We were lucky to get someone who was, like Malcolm, equally well qualified in English and American literature. After a while he returned to the States to marry Carol, the young woman I had met in Boston, and brought her back to Birmingham, where she soon found employment as a teacher. Other interesting appointments had been made while I was away. There were two young men with Cambridge Firsts who couldn't have been more different: Michael Green, tall, handsome, left-wing, interested in modern literature and cultural studies, and Tom Shippey, tall, muscular, right-wing, interested in Anglo-Saxon, Tolkien and science fiction. Michael had become a close friend of the Bradburys while we were away, and would soon become one to us. Richard Hoggart's postgraduate Centre was now established, with Stuart Hall as his deputy director, and they had a programme of open seminars every week which brought a stream of notable outside speakers to the Department and were invariably packed with auditors. Stuart, a Jamaican who had come to England for his higher education and stayed, was a very shrewd appointment by Richard, for he had a grasp of political and sociological theory that complemented Richard's very personal and intuitive style of cultural commentary. He was also a man of great personal charm. Richard and his wife Mary and two younger children (the eldest,

Simon, having left home and started his journalistic career) had now moved to Birmingham, and occupied a large Victorian house in Edgbaston almost opposite Terence Spencer's even larger pile, which they could afford to buy and modernise because it had a limited lease left to run, and where they did a lot of entertaining. Richard, who had written his first book on W.H. Auden, nominated the poet, born and brought up in Birmingham, for an honorary degree, and entertained him as a house guest for the occasion – one of several interesting events we had missed by being in America.

Another significant appointment that year was John Sinclair, to a new Chair of English Language. The story behind this was told to me as follows. There had been growing awareness at various levels in the Faculty of Arts that it lacked expertise in modern linguistics: the systematic study of language both as *langue* (language as a phenomenon and its grammatical structures) and *parole* (language in use, oral and written), to use the terms of Ferdinand de Saussure, generally regarded as the father of modern linguistics. It is a subject distinct from historical philology, which traces the evolution of languages and the etymology of words. The much-discussed 'linguistic turn' in philosophy was beginning to show up in other disciplines in the humanities, and it was felt that the Faculty needed a Department of Linguistics. The trouble was that it already had one, occupied by a single member of staff, Professor Alan Ross, and his secretary. Ross was chiefly known as the author of an article published in an obscure Finnish journal in 1954, coining the terms 'U' and 'Non-U' to categorise different words with the same referent used by upper-class and middle-class English speakers, like 'napkin' and 'serviette' or 'WC' and 'toilet'

– the 'Non-U' terms being more genteel and euphemistic than the 'U' equivalents, which were also used by working-class speakers. This observation was pounced on with glee by Nancy Mitford, who developed it in an article of her own in *Encounter,* and instigated a wider debate about language and class in Britain. 'U' and 'Non-U' entered the language, and Alan Ross became famous. After joining the Birmingham English Department in 1948 as a lecturer he had been rapidly promoted to the rank of professor. He was responsible for the teaching of Old English, but students complained that his classes were incomprehensible, and he aggravated his colleagues in several other ways, to the extent that in 1951 they conspired to get him out of their hair by creating a Department of Linguistics just for him. There his only teaching duty was to give an annual series of lectures on general linguistics, open to all students in the Faculty, which by the fourth week of each academic year he would cancel because the audience had rapidly dwindled to zero. He was then free to pursue his own research and travel the world visiting countries whose languages he claimed to speak, though no natives could ever understand him. It was impossible to remove him, or to persuade any reputable linguist to work under him; so modern linguistics was smuggled into the Faculty by recruiting John Sinclair from the Department of Linguistics at Edinburgh University and calling him Professor of English Language.

Some eyebrows were raised by this appointment, because John was only thirty-three and had few publications to his name. In fact he never published a great deal, but he rewarded the faith placed in him. His forte was organising and supervising the efforts of others in the field of discourse analysis and corpus linguistics,

394

using computerised data to analyse and define the way language is used in reality, not as in the model sentences of traditional textbooks. Perhaps his most important single achievement was CoBuild, the database which underpinned the invaluable *Collins COBUILD English Dictionary*. Although it is intended especially for people for whom English is a second language, I quite often consult it – for instance when uncertain about which preposition follows a particular noun or verb in contemporary English usage. CoBuild attracted the largest amount of research funding in the history of the University up to that time, which was one in the eye of scientists who looked down superciliously on the activities of the Faculty of Arts. John's work, and that of his staff and students and visitors, stimulated my own writing, both critical and creative, in various ways over the years, and he and his wife Myfanwy became personal friends. They were famous for their New Year's Eve parties, at which John would wear his kilt with all the trimmings.

The British Museum is Falling Down was due to be published early in October, at the height of the autumn publishing season, which was some indication of the hopes MacGibbon & Kee had invested in it. Waiting for the reviews of a new book, and then reading them as they appear, is always an anxious time for writers. Even those who claim they never read their reviews know that these will have a significant effect on the sales of their books and on their own reputation, and it is almost impossible to remain entirely ignorant of the reception of a new work unless you leave the country for a while (as at least one novelist of my acquaintance often does). I have never pretended to be indifferent to reviews, which, in spite of all the back-scratching and backbiting, the envy and self-promotion, that contaminate many of them, collectively give an author the first reliable indication of whether his new book is a hit or a miss or something in between. In Britain book reviews appear very soon after the publication date, and sometimes before, in spite of publishers' pleas to the contrary, so you know pretty quickly how you have fared. Imagine my feelings, therefore, as I scanned the newspapers and weeklies for ten days after *The British Museum* was published without finding a single review. When I phoned Tim O'Keeffe he was as puzzled and disappointed as I was. He thought that the large number of novels by big-name authors published at the same time had crowded out mine, and said that if the dearth of reviews continued they would have to consider sending out another set of copies, perhaps early next year. He didn't propose to take any other action. Publishers are understandably reluctant to appear to be pressuring literary editors to review their books, and authors even more so, but it seemed to me that a polite hint, in the guise of an enquiry as to whether the review copies had been received, would not be out of order. When another week passed without reviews, my patience snapped. I phoned the *Birmingham Post,* for which I reviewed books myself, and asked the literary editor's assistant if they had received my novel. The answer was no. I phoned a national newspaper and a weekly magazine with the same question and received the same answer. I phoned Tim O'Keeffe with this information and he said he would look into it at once. He soon reported that apparently not a single review copy had reached its destination, and that they would send out another batch immediately with a covering letter of explanation.

The mystery of the missing review copies was never solved. The menial who took them in their jiffy bags to the post office swore he had mailed them, but the GPO could find no trace of them. Park commented in a letter, 'Mac & Kee ought to be put to torture', and if I had been more assertive I would certainly have demanded a more thorough investigation; but at the time I was too relieved that my novel had not, after all, been contemptuously binned by all the literary editors in the British Isles, and too concerned about its fate in the delayed reviews, to expend more time and energy on discovering the truth of the matter. The reviews came out in November and were generally favourable, but they might have been better if it hadn't been for a misjudgement of Tim O'Keeffe's. I had suggested that the blurb on the jacket should draw attention to the literary parody thread in the novel, but his opinion was that this might put off some potential readers and it would be better to let reviewers discover it for themselves. Consequently very few reviewers noticed the full extent of the parodies and some never mentioned them at all, while complaining of the unevenness of tone and style in the novel. When it was published in America in 1967 I made sure that the parodies were mentioned in the jacket description and they were recognised and enjoyed. It was widely and on the whole very favourably reviewed there, helped by a puff from Graham Greene.

When my Columbia pamphlet on Greene was published in 1966 I sent it to him with the British edition of the novel. He replied:

Thank you so much for sending me your pamphlet on my books which I have read with interest, although I never much enjoy reading about myself. Your own book *The British*

Museum is Falling Down is another matter and I am enjoying it enormously. It's very funny, but very important at the present time. I wish you would send a copy of it to Cardinal Heenan saying that it was at my suggestion!

It took quite a long time to find an American publisher for the novel because it was obvious that Doubleday had passed on their option. When Holt, Rinehart & Winston eventually accepted it my editor asked if there were any well-known writers who might be approached to give a supporting quote. I wrote to Greene to ask if he would be willing to have his letter used in this way, and he not only agreed but tweaked the wording for the purpose. When I confessed that I had not sent the novel to Cardinal Heenan (for reasons partly of timidity, partly of economy) Greene said he would send his own copy. I presumed that he must have had a private conversation or correspondence with Heenan on this issue, but I do not know whether the prelate responded to the gift. From then onwards I sent Greene a copy of each of my novels as they appeared, which he always acknowledged, but I troubled him only once more with a request to quote his remarks, for the American edition of *How Far Can You Go?* – to which he again acceded. He was often generous to other writers in this way.

The British Museum is Falling Down, dedicated 'To Derek Todd, in affectionate memory of B.M. days; and to Malcolm Bradbury, whose fault it mostly is that I have tried to write a comic novel', was the most successful of my novels to date, without being a palpable hit. Pan passed on the paperback rights, but they were picked up by a new imprint, Panther. (The paperback revolution was gathering pace.) A young film producer called Peter Katz, who didn't seem to have yet produced any films, optioned the film rights for a very modest sum, and commissioned me to write an outline treatment. Malcolm wrote from America in April, 'if they are looking for writers to collaborate with you, don't forget your old mate'. In the same letter he responded to some other news – that Mary was pregnant again: 'the most cogent advice I can give you on the baby question is, don't give the hero of your next novel 4 children'. He was invoking one of the epigraphs at the front of *The British Museum is Falling Down*: 'Life imitates art – Oscar Wilde'. Another was: 'I would be a Papist if I could, but an obstinate rationality prevents me – Dr Johnson'.

This third unplanned pregnancy should have convinced us of the obstinate irrationality of the Church's teaching on birth control, but we made no decision on the matter. There was, after all, no reason to do so until the baby was born, and we were preoccupied with the immediate practical consequences – the greater urgency of finding a bigger house, and also the blow to Mary's hopes of returning to teaching. She had been interviewed by the Head of a new Catholic comprehensive school, due to open in the autumn, who was ready to appoint her to a part-time post, and she now had to write withdrawing her application. But at least, and at last, in the late spring we found a suitable house, advertised on the noticeboard of the University's Staff House. It belonged to David Eversley, a social historian who was moving to the new University of Sussex, where he would soon occupy a chair in Population and Regional Studies. It was a large, three-storeyed semi-detached house, built in the early 1900s, in Norman Road, Northfield. The only major drawback was that the location was a couple of miles further away from the University than Reservoir Road, and that Julia would have to move to a new school after only a year. In other respects it was pretty much ideal. It had five bedrooms, one of which, the master bedroom on the first floor at the front of the house with windows on two sides, we earmarked for a play-room, while we took a cosier room at the back for our bedroom. A great attraction for me was the study which Eversley had created for himself by partitioning the dining room into two. It was too small to pace up and down in, but it was snug and fitted with 150 feet of bookshelves which extended into an alcove with a store cupboard. There was a decent-sized sitting room, a rather elegant staircase with a gallery landing, and a cellar. Due to its situation on a bend in the road there was no back garden but one at the side of the house, with a climbing frame and a Wendy house and a big enough lawn for our needs. The house had central heating with old-fashioned but effective radiators. We waited impatiently to move in.

Our last visitors of note in Reservoir Road were the Fishes. Stanley had sabbatical leave and Adrienne had persuaded him that they ought to see something of Europe. They had flown to Milan to buy an Alfa Romeo sports car from the factory, which Stanley had driven to London, where I met them in the spring. He was raving about the new Beatles album *Revolver*, and played 'Eleanor Rigby' to me in the apartment they had rented. For the first time I registered the true importance and originality of these musicians. The Alfa Romeo was too long to fit into the minimal drive of our house when Stanley and Adrienne visited us, so it had to be parked in the street, to the wonderment of the neighbours. We gave the Fishes our bedroom and slept on the put-u-up sofa in the sitting room/study, and if they were appalled at the pinched dimensions and limited amenities of our habitat, they did not show it, and seemed to enjoy their visit. Adrienne wrote an effusive thank-you note later, and Stanley a characteristically professional one, about *Language of Fiction*, a copy of which I must have given him, being flush with complimentary copies from Columbia as well as Routledge:

> You will remember how surprised I was to realise after you left San Francisco that you were a critic like me and not merely a novelist. But I think the truth of the matter never quite got home to me until I began reading your book. It's great. Beautifully written, clearly argued, and you may quote me for a blurb . . . I find it as rigorous as my old dogmatic heart could desire. Naturally I have some quarrels. Chiefly I disagree with your acceptance of Cameron's statement about the paraphrasability of locutions in ordinary discourse. Verbal communication is always a happening and each one happens only once and cannot be reproduced. More about this when we meet. When are we going to meet?

There was no opportunity before they returned to California, and more than two years passed before I saw Stanley again – which I regretted because my mind seemed to work twice as fast as usual in his company.

When *Language of Fiction* was published in England in the spring it got a number of reviews in the daily and weekly press, something that would be astonishing for a book of academic criticism today, for two reasons: firstly, because there weren't so many such books issued in those days, the huge expansion of higher education, and the pressure on its teachers to publish their research, being still in the future; and secondly, because younger academic critics today tend to write in a style saturated in the jargon of post-structuralist literary theory which is impenetrable to the general reader, so literary editors largely ignore their efforts. *Language of Fiction*, as previously mentioned, was comparatively innocent of Continental European literary theory, and presented no such challenge for reviewers, who found it stimulating even if they didn't always agree with it. The reviews in academic journals that followed later were also mostly favourable, Tony Tanner going so far as to describe the book in *Modern Language Review* as 'something of a minor milestone in English criticism'. Sales were good enough for Routledge to order a reprint later in the year.

So I was feeling pretty pleased with myself in the summer of 1966. My two new books were successfully launched, and film interest in the novel took a promising new turn when Peter Katz went into partnership with Mel Frank, the Hollywood producer of *A Funny Thing Happened on the Way to the Forum* and other successful movies, to develop a film of *The British Museum is Falling Down*. Malcolm and Elizabeth returned from America with their son in late July and we were able to put them up comfortably on their way to their cottage in Yorkshire, and to give a party for all their Birmingham friends that doubled as a house-warming. What an unaccustomed pleasure it was to entertain in a spacious home! The icing on the cake was that England won the World Cup while the Bradburys were staying with us. We didn't have a television, but Stuart Hall, who of course did have one, was going away that weekend and kindly gave me the keys to his flat, where Malcolm and I watched England beat West Germany 4–2 in extra time (the fourth goal was particularly satisfying since there was some doubt about the legitimacy of the third), so we shared in the general jubilation at this famous victory.

Mary and I had never had a television, at first because we couldn't afford it, and later because, like many educated parents, we thought it might retard the mental development of our infant children, while I feared that it would be a distraction from my work. However, we had noted that Julia took every opportunity to go down the road to watch children's programmes in her playmate's home. Now that we had a big house I decided that I would get a TV and put it in a room all by itself on the top floor, where the children could watch programmes of their choice for a prescribed amount of time – as could adults if they were motivated enough to climb two flights of stairs. Meanwhile we converted the huge master bedroom into a splendid playroom, and it did our hearts good to watch Julia and Stephen taking possession of its expanse of fitted carpet, scattered with toys and play equipment. There would be ample room for another child there – and, I felt, in the life that was opening out so promisingly before us.

21

We had decided to call the new child Christopher if it was a boy, simply because we both liked the name. He was born in the early hours of Friday 14th of October, at home in our bedroom, which had a wash-hand basin in one corner, a convenience appreciated by the midwife when she arrived. We were well prepared. I helped to get the bed ready with plenty of protective newspaper covering the mattress, and timed the contractions. Mary was practised in natural childbirth by now and in complete control, which impressed me – and the midwife – no end. She never seemed to be in pain, but was like a trained athlete in a strenuous event, concentrating, pacing herself and saving her strength for the final push. At last I saw a child of mine born, and like everyone who has had that experience I was astonished and awed as he slithered into the world and, after the midwife snipped and sealed the umbilical cord, took a breath and began to cry. She washed him, swaddled him, and gave him to Mary to hold. When the other two children woke they were allowed into the room to see him;

then I gave them their breakfast and took them off to their respect-ive schools. A busy but happy weekend followed, phoning family and friends with the good news, and on Monday morning I went into the University to teach my classes. It was before the days of paternity leave.

I came home early in the afternoon and went straight upstairs to Mary and the baby. She was sitting up in bed, with Christopher asleep in a cot beside her. As soon as she saw me come smiling into the room she began to cry. I sat down on the edge of the bed and put my arm round her shoulders. 'What's the matter?' I said, already filled with dread. 'It's the baby,' she said. 'The doctor came. He says the baby is a mongol.' 'What does that mean?' I said. I had heard the word, and it had an unpleasant resonance, but I didn't know what condition it referred to. Apparently the midwife had noticed something was wrong with the baby, but hadn't told us. Instead, quite correctly, she had alerted our GP, and he had called earlier that day and told Mary that our child was a mongol, and would grow up mentally and physically handi-capped. Suddenly I had a flashback: a crocodile of shambling children and youths led by an adult coming towards me on a pavement, all grinning and dribbling and twitching, and one of them clumsily banging into me as they passed. It was an image I associated with the word 'mongol'. I looked at Christopher: he seemed perfect. 'How can they tell?' I said. 'There are signs,' she said. 'The lines on the hands are different from normal. And they usually have slanted eyes, that's why they're called mongols.' 'He doesn't have slanted eyes!' I said. 'No,' she said, 'but he has the lines on the hands.' 'What causes it?' I asked. 'It happens at the moment of conception, apparently,' she said. 'Nobody knows why. Dr Evans had a cousin who was one.' We had registered with Dr Evans only recently and did not know him well, though he and his family were neighbours and would become friends. Like all doctors in this situation he had a difficult decision to make: whether to tell the parents immediately, or wait until they begin to have misgivings themselves about the baby. Alan Evans decided it was better to tell the truth quickly and avoid a cruel disillusionment later, and I think he was right, but he should have waited until we were both present. By talking about his cousin he was trying to domesticate the event, to convey that it was part of life, something that could happen to anyone, but it seemed that his relative was severely handicapped and the picture he conjured up had upset Mary.

Later we would learn to call Christopher's condition Down's syndrome, after the Victorian doctor who identified it. Down was a clever and humane man, who ran his own home for the mentally handicapped on progressive principles for many years, but unfortunately he shared the racial prejudices of his time and place. In a medical paper called 'Observations on the Ethnic Classification of Idiots', he named this particular condition 'mongolism' because of the slightly Asiatic features of those born with it, thus encouraging their stigmatisation as alien and ugly. The word 'mongol' is no longer acceptable usage – one of the few linguistic effects of 'political correctness' which I wholeheartedly approve of – but it was current for much of Christopher's childhood. We would also learn what Dr Down had no means of knowing, since it was not discovered till 1959, that his syndrome is caused by an extra copy (three instead of two) of the twenty-first chromosome out of the twenty-three involved in cell division in the embryo, a blip in the biological processing that produces a human being which causes a number of physical and mental abnormalities as the foetus develops. Nobody knows why it occurs. Mothers over thirty-five are more likely to have Down's babies, and there is a variant of the condition that may have a hereditary element, but neither of these factors applied to Mary. In Christopher's case it was a completely random genetic abnormality, unpredictable and unpreventable. Neither Mary nor I had any previous knowledge of it.

In fact it had never occurred to me that anything at all could be wrong or go wrong with the child in Mary's womb. She had produced two healthy and intelligent children, and I confidently awaited a third. I knew nothing about congenital disorders or the possible causes of brain damage at birth. Such a state of blissful ignorance could hardly occur today because of several developments since then: advances in medical knowledge and practice, the large amount of information about mental and physical disability disseminated through the media, and more enlightened social policy towards those afflicted. Up to the time of Christopher's birth, having a mentally handicapped child, especially among the middle and upper classes, was regarded as a tragedy best kept private, and often swathed in secrecy and shame. In fact he was born just as attitudes to such children were about to become more positive, but that was not evident in the information we received from people who should have known better, including a health visitor and a friend who was the wife of an eminent child psychologist. We were told that Christopher would never learn to read or write, that he had a very limited life expectancy (estimates varied from twenty to forty), and were advised to place him as soon as possible in a mental subnormality hospital. All wrong assertions and bad advice – but we weren't to know that, and were very distressed. Those who tried to comfort and encourage us said that mongol children were usually affectionate and lovable, which turned out to be true of Christopher, but at the time it was hard to imagine how that could compensate for all the other aspects of his condition.

For me it was a profound shock. I had supposed I was on an escalator bearing me and my family to higher and higher levels of fulfilment, pleasure and happiness, and suddenly it had stopped, irreparably. The vague visions I had entertained of the future did not include looking after a mentally handicapped child. The first days and weeks after the event were very hard to bear for Mary and me: having to keep up a cheerful front for the sake of Julia and Stephen, who were delighted with their baby brother, having to break the news to parents, friends and colleagues, and having to live with being the object of so much concern, sympathy and pity in response. I went to work on the day after we learned the truth about Christopher, and my first tutorial group came in looking solemn and subdued. Someone – I guessed it was Michael Green, who I had spoken to by phone – had told them, with the best of intentions, of our misfortune. Ironically the subject of the tutorial was *Tristram Shandy*, with its Rabelaisian humour about conception and childbirth, and the discussion was constrained. A few days later the disaster at the Welsh mining village of Aberfan occurred, when a waterlogged colliery tip suddenly collapsed and engulfed the school in an avalanche of slurry, killing 116 children and 28 adults. The horror and pity that gripped the whole nation for many days somehow merged with our own private sorrow and added to my gloom.

In those early days it crossed my mind, as I suppose it does with many people in such a situation, that it would be a blessing if the child died peacefully and painlessly, but there was no prospect of that. He was in essential respects a healthy baby, and although he had difficulty taking sustenance from the breast or bottle, he began to put on weight when Mary started feeding him with a spoon. Dr Evans had put us in touch with a paediatrician who offered to arrange a visit to a Birmingham subnormality hospital. Mary was reluctant but I thought we should at least see what it had to offer, so we went by appointment. When the staff discovered we had not already made up our minds to place Christopher there they refused to show us round the wards, which was enough for both of us to decide firmly against this option. From then onwards we were united in a determination to give Christopher as normal a life as was possible without a detrimental effect on his brother and sister, or on our own relationship. Inevitably the main burden of this project fell on Mary, especially in Christopher's early years, but it was greatly assisted by the fact that he was our youngest child, always stimulated by interaction with his older siblings and never disheartened by being overtaken by one younger than himself.

In one respect Christopher caused a positive improvement in our marriage. Not long after he was born Mary decided to go on the pill, without any prompting from me but with my unhesitating agreement. Suddenly it seemed a very simple decision. Random though the extra copy of chromosome 21 was, mothers who gave birth to a Down's baby were more likely to have another, and the effort of bringing up one was going to be demanding enough. We made a simple pragmatic decision, but it was enormously significant: we took responsibility for our own lives, instead of being governed by a code invented by theologians which looked increasingly irrational and had no demonstrable basis in the teachings of Jesus Christ. I'm sure we would have made this decision eventually anyway, but Christopher gave us the impetus to act without further delay, to the great enhancement of our intimate life. This is not to say that my peace of mind was unaffected by his advent. Henceforward I became more prone to anxiety when confronted with unexpected events and difficult decisions. The first such challenge came quite soon.

In the spring of 1967 I received a letter from my former colleague, Derek Brewer, now a fellow at Emmanuel College, Cambridge, to tell me that there was a vacant lectureship in the Faculty of English and that several people there hoped I would apply for it. It was followed up shortly afterwards by John Holloway, a member of the Appointments Committee, pressing me to do so. The vacancy was created by the resignation of Denis Donoghue, a highly esteemed Irish critic who had been in the post for little more than a year, and having decided that he did not wish to bring his large family to live in Cambridge was returning to University College Dublin. The date for applications had officially passed so there was some urgency about the matter if I was interested. Derek kindly offered to put us up for a weekend if we would like to consider the possibility *in situ*. This approach from what was generally regarded as the top English department in the country couldn't have come at a more inopportune time, but I could not be indifferent to it. The appointment would bring with it a fellowship, possibly at King's, where Donoghue had been, with its perks and privileges, eight-week terms, and more money than I was getting at Birmingham, not to mention the beauty of the city's ancient core, and the fact that it was in easy reach of Norwich and the Bradburys. So in early February we got someone to look after Julia and Stephen, and took Christopher with us in his carrycot to stay with the Brewers. John Holloway gave us lunch in his rooms at Queens' College, and I met L.C. Knights, who had recently been appointed to the King Edward VII Chair of English at Cambridge. Since he had been a pupil of F.R. Leavis, who had been denied the title of Professor by his enemies, Leavisites disapproved of Knights's acceptance of this position, and I heard a story that, shortly after he arrived in Cambridge, Leavis's wife Queenie crept up behind him in the University Library and hissed '*Traitor!*' in his ear. In our brief conversation Knights mentioned that he and others involved in the lectureship appointment had been particularly impressed by the way I took on Leavis in *Language of Fiction*. The notorious factionalism of Cambridge English was one reason to be chary of moving there. Another was that we would have to sell the house we had just acquired and look for another in a place where property prices were twice Birmingham's, and disturb Julia and Stephen's schooling once again. But when I wrote to Holloway to say that I had decided not to apply, I emphasised another reason:

> I suppose the decisive factor was a feeling that to be a Cambridge don would not be a good thing for a novelist to be, at least for me personally, at my present stage of devel-opment (if, as I hope, development is what it is).

I knew that Cambridge English was a very competitive, critical, self-obsessed community, and that, in spite of the short terms, I would have to work hard to hold my own there, endangering the balance I had tried to maintain between my creative and academic writing. For all these reasons I decided against applying, with Mary's relieved agreement. It was a thoroughly sound decision, and in the long term seemed more and more so. But soon after communicating it I began to have doubts and regrets. Had I turned down a golden opportunity that most of my peers would have seized with alacrity? Of course I could not be certain that I would have got the job if I had applied for it, but that somehow made no difference to my state of mind, and before long I had argued myself into a state of depression. In retrospect it seems obvious that I was transferring feelings associated with Christopher's condition, a random event over which I had had no control, on to one for which I was responsible and could have managed differently. I must have confided in my father, for I have found in my files a long and very moving letter of counsel, which concluded by saying he had mentioned my regrets about Cambridge to a man he was playing golf with.

> He said, 'Oh not to worry. It will come again.' Okay, so he doesn't know, and it might not come again, but then it *might* come again and who's to say on this earth what is going to happen in the future and perhaps everything is going to be for the best and all the fretting was needless.

Wise words, and I wish I had taken them to heart. Dad thought I was overworking my brain, and wanted me to get more physical exercise ('I would like to hear of you going for a good walk every day now without your pipe'), but my own programme for recovery was to start working on the novel that was already entitled *Out of the Shelter* in my head, since that was the prime reason why I had decided not to apply for the job at Cambridge.

I had study leave coming up in the summer term which offered a good opportunity. I felt I needed to refresh my memory of Heidelberg, and asked the British Council in London if they could arrange some lectures or seminars for me at Heidelberg University. That proved impossible but they did organise a short lecture tour to speak at the universities of Frankfurt, Marburg and Mainz, and I added on a visit at my own expense to Heidelberg, where a young lecturer in the English Department kindly kept me company. The trip was interesting and useful, and I was in a good mood as I waited for a train at the beginning of my homeward journey. There was a newspaper booth on the platform, where I bought a copy of the previous Sunday's *Observer*. Inside it was a full-page article about Cambridge by Michael Frayn, who had been an undergraduate there. He described its charms with lyrical nostalgia and declared that he could not imagine a more blissful place in which to spend one's life. My good spirits evaporated instantly.

I was looking forward to a holiday with the Honans and the Bradburys, whom I had put in touch with each other during Malcolm's fellowship year. He and Elizabeth had enjoyed a visit to Park and Jeannette in Providence, and Park had inspired a plan for all of us to get together in St Brévin in the summer of '67. We and the Bradburys arranged to share a rented bungalow very near the Colins' place for two weeks in July, and planned to drive there together in our respective cars. Before then, however, something happened which I still find distressing to recall: I had a serious

413

car accident with the whole family, and my mother, who was staying with us, on board. There was just room for them in the Anglia estate: Mary beside me in the passenger seat, Mum in the back with Julia and Stephen, and Christopher in his carrycot on the flat floor behind the back seat. It was a Sunday in June, and we were going to visit Mary's sister Margaret and Ioan, who had been married for about three years. Ioan was now a lecturer in the English Department at the University of Warwick and they had bought a new house in Wellesbourne, near Stratford.

There were several factors that contributed to the accident. On our way we ran into a thunderstorm and rain so heavy that I stopped the car in a lay-by and waited for it to pass over. I suffered badly from hay fever in those days, and the deluge, so far from clearing the air, forced the pollen down and I suffered a paroxysm of sneezing. I swallowed a Piriton tablet, which was the medication Dr Evans had recently prescribed. Its tendency to cause drowsiness is better known now than it was to me then, and it's possible that it slowed down my reactions when we proceeded shortly afterwards. Just past the church at Wootton Wawen I approached a bend with steep grass banks on each side. The rain had poured down the banks, bringing a good deal of mud with it and forming a slick surface on the road. I was doing about 30 mph, and eased my foot on the accelerator to slow the car down, but this had no effect, even when I lifted my foot completely, so I touched the brake pedal. The wheels locked and the car skidded into the left-hand bank, bounced off it, turned over and ended up lying across the middle of the road on its side, the driver's side. I felt utter surprise, helplessness and dismay as the world went topsy-turvy. Mary said she felt anger and resentment, sure that we were going to die – and if another vehicle had come fast round the bend towards us we might have done. Fortunately no other vehicle was involved, though one soon appeared and its flabbergasted occupants opened the doors of ours and helped us climb out. We were all strapped in except for Christopher, who was protected by his carrycot, and my mother, who must have been held in place by the other two children. She had a bruised rib later, but astonishingly none of the rest of us had any injury. People from a neighbouring cottage came out and kindly invited us in to have a cup of tea and use their telephone, while some strong men from the other cars that had by now come to a halt managed to lift the Anglia on to its four wheels and pushed it to the side of the road. I phoned Margaret and Ioan to tell them what had happened, and ordered a taxi to take the family back to Norman Road. Stephen, who had lost a sandal in the crash, said that if we could find it he would prefer to walk, but was dissuaded. The Anglia was badly scratched and dented on the driver's side, but seemed to be otherwise in working order, so I drove it cautiously home.

The main cause of the accident was that the car did not slow down when I took my foot off the accelerator. There was a reason for this: the car had been serviced the day before at a local garage, and the mechanic had obviously set the carburettor incorrectly. I had been compensating for this by using the brake, which in slippery conditions caused the skid. What I should have done was to call in the AA to verify the malfunction, and then sue the garage, but I was too shocked by our narrow escape from a dreadful tragedy to take any such action – and too remorseful, for I blamed myself for not noticing the high revs of the engine when idling. But this carelessness in turn was traceable to stress and anxiety associated with Christopher. It was not coincidental that later Mary had an uncharacteristic and potentially serious accident with a second car I had bought for her. But I could not bear to think of the guilt I would have felt if I had survived a crash in which any of my family had been killed or seriously injured. We had had an escape of a kind that is colloquially described as 'miraculous', and devout Catholics like my mother-in-law would have ascribed it to the special intervention of God, and thanked Him effusively for it. But I did not. It would imply that God had declined to bestow the same favour on all the people who were killed or seriously injured in car crashes that day, many – perhaps most – of them no less deserving than us. I no longer believed in such a God. I knew we had survived by luck. I felt the emotion of gratitude, but there was no recipient. I was chastened, I was relieved, and I set myself to make the most of our luck – first of all, by going ahead with the planned holiday. I had the car checked out for safety but postponed the bodyshop work it needed and drove it in its battered state to St Brévin.

Park's letters about Christopher over the past year had been typically positive and encouraging, but he was as restless and dissatisfied with his own situation as ever. He had abandoned his project of a book about style in the novel, and had gone back to Browning, agreeing to complete a biography left unfinished at his death by a distinguished Browning scholar, William Irvine, whom Park knew well. It involved a huge amount of research work to check and improve Irvine's manuscript as well as writing completely new chapters, and corresponding with the scholar's wife, who took a keen interest in the project, all of which delayed the publication of the book for several years. He was also in constant dispute with Mark Spilka over the editorial management of a new journal based at Brown called *NOVEL* in which they were both involved. I had taken part in some preliminary discussions about the project when I was there and my name appeared on its list of editorial advisers, but I never understood what the dispute was about. It was, however, one of the factors that made Park hanker after an academic post in England, as he often mentioned in his letters. He was aware that he was much better off in America as regards salary, teaching load and funding for research, but as he had explained in a letter of 2nd May, 'my reason for wanting to go to England is that I seem to be able to think and write there much more freely than I can here . . . I can't and won't teach American lit but I'll make myself into a specialist in anything ENGLISH overnight, so please for God's sake keep your eye out for me at Birmingham.' I promised to do so.

We had a happy reunion with the Honans and Bradburys in St Brévin, and the holiday passed in a pleasantly relaxing way. One day Malcolm and I made an excursion along the Loire in his Rover 2000, pausing to visit a number of chateaux; but most days we occupied ourselves swimming and lounging on the beach, amusing the children, shopping for food (a chore at home, but it acquired a pleasing novelty abroad) and later enjoying an aperitif at a café and a meal which we took turns to cook. Not for the first time I regretted my poor French, especially after Mary complained to the tourist office about some bad milk we had been sold which the shopkeeper refused to exchange. That afternoon I was in the village on my own and a gendarme who evidently recognised me said something which I could not understand. A small, interested crowd gathered round us, and someone interpreted for me: 'He says tell your wife to meet him here at four o'clock this afternoon.' It was of course to resolve the milk issue (in our favour) but some of the spectators sniggered as if I was revealed as a complaisant cuckold. It made a good story to amuse the others that evening.

Not long after we returned home from this holiday we received a letter from the local health authority asking if we would be willing to take part in an experiment that a child psychologist, Mr Rex Brinkworth, was conducting into improving the learning abilities of mongol children. We replied promptly in the affirmative and were soon visited by a slightly built, soft-spoken man with a moustache and an unpretentious manner that nevertheless inspired immediate confidence. He explained that in collaboration with a doctor in Northern Ireland he had developed a programme for maximising the potential of mongol children by stimulating them in infancy. It was based on the little-known fact that the human brain continues to develop after birth, so it was possible in this period to teach them to respond to their environment in ways that normal children learn unaided. This made immediate sense – it revealed in a flash the folly and inhumanity of consigning such infants to a hospital where they would get a minimum of stimulation and thus confirm the pessimistic prognosis assigned to them – and we waited eagerly to learn more. The snag was that Mr Brinkworth had already assembled a group of children on whom to test his latest programme, and was looking for some to form a control group who would not take part but would be tested periodically for purposes of comparison. Naturally we said we wanted Christopher to be part of the experiment, not the control group, and after some discussion Rex agreed to help and advise us outside the experiment. He examined and played with Christopher, and encouraged us by praising his responsiveness, remarking that we must have intuitively applied the principles of his own system in several ways, so we had not lost too much time by being ignorant of it. Before he departed that day he gave us a copy of the schedule of exercises and activities he had designed, and he left us feeling immeasurably more hopeful about Christopher's future. Here at last was a knowledgeable person telling us how to do something positive for him instead of merely accepting him. He turned out to be a very rewarding child to bring up, with a distinctive personality that charmed most people who met him – confident, affectionate, and for a Down's remarkably articulate – even witty. Inevitably most of the necessary effort was made by Mary, especially in the early years, but he bonded strongly with me and I shared the satisfaction we felt later, when he learned not only to read and write, but also to use public transport, to make speeches at family celebrations, to beat me routinely at pool, to carve beautiful wooden bowls on a carpenter's lathe, and to paint pictures that people would buy. His life was not to be without problems and anxieties, for him and for us, but it has been mostly a happy and (given his limitations) a fulfilled one. For that we owe a lot to meeting Rex Brinkworth at the right moment.

Rex had been motivated to develop his ideas about improving Down's children by having one himself, his daughter Françoise. The short book he wrote with his collaborator Dr Joseph Collins, first published in 1969, and subsequently revised and reissued many times as *Improving Babies with Down's Syndrome*, has been of enormous help to many parents. He founded the Down's Babies Association in Birmingham, which subsequently became a nation-wide charity known as the Down Syndrome Association, based in London, and he was awarded an MBE, the least public recognition he deserved for his contribution to society. He died in 1998.

22

While we were enjoying our traditional seaside holiday in a small unfashionable French resort, a hundred thousand young people converged on San Francisco to create a 'Summer of Love', and the singer/songwriter Scott McKenzie urged everyone planning to visit the city to wear flowers in their hair, in a pop song which has been called the unofficial anthem of the 1960s counterculture movement'. The Sixties as a cultural phenomenon did not of course begin in 1960, and it would be hard to say when exactly it did begin, but by 1967 it was in full spate. This revolution, or rebellion, against the established order of things in Western society was led by the young, though inspired by certain older sages and heroes; and it had two aspects, the sexual and the political. As a monogamous married Catholic of liberal principles, suspicious of ideological extremes and over the age of thirty, when according to a popular slogan of the day you should never be trusted by those younger, I was not likely to get personally involved, but I observed what was going on with a novelist's interest.

At first it was the sexual revolution that was most striking, especially in universities. The strict code of sexual behaviour that had long been enforced in colleges and university halls of residence, and had resulted in many young men being 'sent down' for having women in their rooms, or being in women's rooms, after the permitted hours, collapsed under pressure from the increasing permissiveness of society at large, which was driven by the lifting of taboos on the representation and discussion of sexuality in the arts and media, and facilitated by the availability of the contraceptive pill. In the third volume of his memoirs, *An Imagined Life* (1992), Richard Hoggart describes two incidents, one historic, one in his own experience, which exemplified the change. He learned that in 1962 the barber who worked in a small shop on the Birmingham campus was asked to leave because he had been selling condoms to customers. Five years later, when Richard was standing at the reception desk of the University's Health Centre:

> I noticed a box of what looked like packeted pills on the right-hand side, placed in much the way supermarkets put sweets near their tills to tempt impulse buyers . . . Were those packets of The Pill, which I'd heard of but never seen? Yes, said the nurse-receptionist. Are they available to anyone? Not quite; they have to be having a serious relationship. How do you discover it's serious? We take their word for it.

Although Richard welcomed the greater openness about sexual relationships, he was aware that there were losses as well as gains in this new freedom. I believe it is now generally accepted that it was mainly young women not young men who paid a price for it, emotionally and physically, but it was hard for them to swim against the tide of the time. As a tutor one saw some of them grow up and change with astonishing rapidity, from shy innocent schoolgirls to young women conscious and confident of their sexual allure, dressing and behaving accordingly. Across the Faculty and the University there were stories and rumours of relationships between staff and students, and staff and staff, leading in due course to the break-up of some marriages, though the Birmingham English Department was less licentious (or liberated, according to your point of view) than some others, to judge from what we heard about UEA from the Bradburys.

Relations between staff and students also became more relaxed in less controversial ways. Most staff stopped wearing gowns to lecture and began to address students by their first names in tutorials and seminars. I did so myself, though I stopped short of inviting them to call *me* by my first name, as some younger colleagues did. In the English Department we initiated an annual Reading Party for first-year students in the Reading Week halfway through the autumn term, which was highly successful as a bonding experience. It was held at Spode Priory and lasted several days, consisting of talks, tasks and small-group discussions on a theme. Some members of staff went for one or two days, and some for the duration, the latter returning home completely knackered. The Priory's somewhat austere dormitories discouraged sexual activity, but people stayed up late talking, and the event ended with a party, skits and a disco in the galleried theological library, its desks and chairs moved back against the walls by permission of the tolerant Prior. Although the new-style dancing entailed no physical contact, or even partners necessarily, its body language was sexual in a primitive, promiscuous kind of way. It had by now displaced ballroom dancing in youth culture, and older folk had to join in or look like fogies. I enjoyed opportunities to join in. It became customary to have a departmental party after the Finals examiners' meeting at the end of the academic year, held by permission of Terence Spencer at the Shakespeare Institute in Westmere. The postgraduate students set up a bar and a buffet, to which staff contributed dishes, in the spacious hall, and the largest teaching room was cleared for a disco. Some of the bolder finalists would also come to this event by unofficial invitation, get drunk and covertly smoke cannabis. I remember seeing the supine bodies of several of them stretched out on the carpet of a darkened room on my way home from one of these occasions, which Spencer himself spent closeted in his comfortably furnished, wood-panelled office with selected young admirers, mostly female, thus both exploiting and distancing himself from a cultural revolution which was alien to him.

The nascent Free Speech movement at Berkeley whose demonstrations and teach-ins I had witnessed in the summer of 1965 had grown more militant as the Vietnam War escalated, and spread to other American campuses. But that wasn't in the forefront of my mind in the autumn of 1967 when I decided to accept an invitation from Berkeley, prompted by Stanley Fish, to be a visiting associate professor there from January to June 1969. I hoped to recover the sense of well-being I associated with our Harkness year, and finally throw off the depression that had followed the Cambridge episode. Mary was willing, and we thought in more than a year's time Julia and Stephen would be old enough to get something valuable and memorable out of the experience. Accordingly I applied for six months' unpaid leave of absence from Birmingham to teach the first two 'quarters' of 1969 at Berkeley, where the academic year was divided into four equal segments. I had recently acquired the normal American qualification for this position by submitting *Language of Fiction* for a Birmingham 'official degree', a very convenient procedure available to academic staff of some years' standing, whereby you could submit published work in lieu of a thesis. This was read by an external assessor who awarded the level of degree it merited, in my case deemed to be a PhD.

Meanwhile Park's letters expressed an increasingly urgent desire to move to England. Towards the end of 1967 Martin Green, who had spent so much of his life shuttling restlessly between England and America, announced that he had decided to return to Tufts and would leave us at the end of the academic year. That would create a vacancy for someone to teach American literature at Birmingham. After sounding out Richard Hoggart, who had met Park on one of his flying visits to the States and had formed a favourable impression of him, I asked Park if he would be interested in an appointment that was partly dedicated to American lit. Revising his earlier attitude, he said yes, if it was not more than a third of his teaching load, and stated the very reasonable minimum salary he would require. The matter was under discussion into the New Year, and became quite exciting when Warwick entered the fray and offered Park an equivalent post, subject to an interview for which they would pay the return air fare. Birmingham couldn't, or wouldn't, afford that, but Richard persuaded the higher levels of the university administration that his personal acquaintance with Park was sufficient to support the latter's impressive CV, and he was appointed in March, with effect from September. I believe the post was advertised, but I do not recall that anyone was interviewed. Park and Jeannette were delighted, though well aware of the problems the family would face in making the transition, and Jeannette came to England ahead of him with the children, to arrange their schooling and settle into a university-owned flat that was fortunately available while they looked for a house. Park stayed behind to clear their Providence home and arrange the shipping of their possessions to England. He sent his books to be stored in the Department, in 117 parcels.

I'm conscious that many of the appointments I have mentioned in this narrative, including my own, were determined by the personal influence of individuals in the appointing department, without strict observance of the normal procedures, which may seem scandalous by today's standards. The fact is, however, that the 'normal procedures' of that time were defective, as I would discover later when I served on appointment committees. The process usually consisted simply of a small committee taking references from the most promising of those who applied, sampling the publications they might have produced, making a shortlist and interviewing the candidates for thirty to forty minutes each. The references were often unreliable and sometimes deceitful, and the interviews too brief to really test the candidates. It was almost impossible to gauge how effective they might be as teachers. Yet on that evidence we appointed people who, given the perfunctory nature of 'probation' which obtained in those days, might be colleagues for life. It is not surprising that we made some unfortunate appointments over the years, and I was involved in one or two of them. Nowadays, following the American practice, short-listed candidates usually visit the appointing department well ahead of the final interview, meet people in various constituencies within the Department who feed back their views to the committee, and may be invited to give a lecture or seminar paper. That is obviously a better and fairer system, though time-consuming and not infallible. I don't think any of the 'irregular' appointments I have mentioned turned out badly.

In the spring of 1968 there were demonstrations in many countries by young protestors, mainly but not exclusively against the Vietnam War. In March a large crowd surrounding the US Embassy in London's Grosvenor Square clashed with police and people were hurt. There were similar events in West Germany, and in April an assassination attempt on Rudi Dutschke, the leader of the student movement, triggered more protests and violent responses which I watched on the TV news with particular interest and concern, because I was due to go to West Germany shortly on another British Council lecture tour. I did go, without encountering any trouble, speaking at universities in Aachen, Cologne, West Berlin and Freiburg, and deviating from my itinerary to refresh my memory of Baden-Baden for *Out of the Shelter*. West Berlin by this time was a lively, confident, increasingly hedonistic city that had recovered from the war, but someone at the British Council took me through Checkpoint Charlie one day and showed me a completely different place. It reminded me a little of London at the end of the war, but more of the London George Orwell described in *Nineteen Eighty-Four*, with drab, badly maintained buildings, vacant bomb sites, no colourful advertisements, no goods worth buying in the shops, goose-stepping soldiers guarding official buildings, and a cowed, sullen-looking population, some of whom stared hostilely at us when we entered a bleak café to buy the black tea that seemed to be the only available drink.

The baton of student protest passed from West Germany to France with '*les événements*' of May in Paris, when students occupied their university buildings, erected barricades and marched alongside militant workers to such effect that de Gaulle's government was seriously threatened. The revolution did not happen, but the revolutionary impulse crossed the Channel. In the first term of the new academic year there were organised student demonstrations and occupations at several British universities, notably the London School of Economics, where the gates of the institution were knocked down with symbolic effect, and the University of Essex, where something like siege conditions existed for a time. The Birmingham manifestation of the Zeitgeist was a comparatively mild and short-lived affair. The Guild demanded student participation in university government by representation on committees and subcommittees at various levels of administration from departments to Senate. This was brusquely rejected by the new Vice-Chancellor, Robert Hunter, who had just taken over from the retiring Sir Robert Aitken, and lacked his predecessor's executive finesse. On 27th November several hundred students occupied the VC's office and other offices in the Aston Webb Building, allegedly breaking into filing cabinets, then spilled into the Great Hall, where they heard speeches and eventually held a disco before settling down for the night on the floor. The occupation continued for some days, adroitly led by a temporary assistant lecturer in the Sociology Department, Dick Atkinson, who had experience of radical action at LSE. After some concessions and promises of further discussion of the issues had been offered by the administration, on the advice of liberal professors like Richard Hoggart, the occupation was called off at a mass meeting of students held outside the Library on 5th December. Campus life returned to something like normality, though many older professors, including Terence Spencer, were profoundly shocked by what had happened, realising that their power and authority would never again be quite the same.

Meanwhile the publication of Pope Paul VI's encyclical *Humanae Vitae* at the end of July, reaffirming the traditional teaching on birth control, had precipitated something like a Catholic equivalent to the secular revolt of youth in America and Europe. Leaks from the Vatican had previously indicated that the commission set up by John XXIII to investigate the issue, and enlarged by his successor with qualified laymen and -women, had given the Pope a report recommending, by a very large majority, a change in the rules in the light of modern knowledge. There was widespread disappointment and disillusionment among the laity, which would lead eventually to many of them leaving the Church, and an increasing number of priests leaving the priesthood. As the authorial narrator of *How Far Can You Go?* comments:

Of course, if the Pope had come down on the other side of the argument, there would no doubt have been an equally loud chorus of protest and complaint from the millions of Catholics who had loyally followed the traditional teaching at the cost of having many more children and much less sex than they would have liked, and were now too old, or too worn-out by parenthood, to benefit from a change in the rules – not to mention the priests who had sternly kept them toeing the line by threats of eternal punishment if they didn't. The Pope, in short, was in a no-win situation.

But he had got himself into it. More leaks revealed that the argument of the small minority on the commission, all clerics, which had prevailed with Paul, was simply that the Church could not admit to having been wrong about this important moral issue without losing its authority. But the commission had been set up on the basis that there might be new reasons for change, and this was an old reason for no change, which made the whole exercise seem futile. *Humanae Vitae* triggered a crisis in the Church which has still not been resolved. Since it was agreed, even by supporters of the Pope, that he was not speaking *ex cathedra* (i.e. infallibly) there was still some room for conscientious dissent, and Mary and I were not in the least deterred from continuing with the decision we had made. I signed an 'Appeal to the Pope and Bishops of the Catholic Church', which was organised from the Catholic University of Louvain and signed by some 100 academics from ten countries, pointing out the flaws in the arguments of the encyclical and calling for a more flexible pastoral response to the issue.

The crisis was widely discussed in the media, and invested *The British Museum is Falling Down* with a certain topicality. Panther decided to reissue their paperback edition and I wrote a brief authorial note for it, saying that if I were writing the novel in 1968 I would not leave the two principal characters with their dilemma unresolved, and that: 'there is of course only one possible resolution that would be consistent with the realities of their situation, with reason, with modern Christian thought, and with the demands of a comic literary structure'. My editor at Holt, Rinehart & Winston, Joe Cunneen, who had been disappointed by the lack of interest in the paperback rights of the novel in the USA, wrote to me jubilantly to say he had sold them to a small New York publisher called Lancer. They wanted to rename the novel *Vatican Roulette,* and had already printed the cover with that title in their haste to get the book out, and he had agreed, 'since I was not in a mood to stop them from cashing in on an immediate sale'. I objected strongly to this cavalier treatment for several reasons, and Joe was contrite, but there was nothing to be done. My mood was not improved when I saw the actual book, a cheap-looking object which didn't even earn me much in royalties. I didn't like the new Panther edition either, which had a sensational cover depicting a woman taking a pill while dangling a rosary with crucifix over her open mouth. I felt my novel was being vulgarised and misrepresented.

I finished *Out of the Shelter* in time to deliver two copies of the bulky typescript to Graham Watson in late December before we departed for California, travelling this time by air. Martin and Carol Green had invited us to break our journey in Boston and stay with them at Christmas, and it seemed a better idea than taking three young children on a twelve-hour economy flight over the pole, so we accepted gratefully. The Greens made us welcome, but the journey proved taxing. The BA flight to Boston from Heathrow was delayed for some hours for technical reasons, and the packed United DC8 that took us to San Francisco seemed to have something wrong with the quality of the air in the cabin, for we all felt increasingly ill as the flight went on, Mary particularly. That we all had colds didn't help. We were scarcely able to walk off the plane and through the airport on arrival.

Stanley and Adrienne had kindly found us accommodation to rent in an area a few miles from Berkeley called El Cerrito. It was a three-bedroom house built into the hillside, with a large and habitable semi-basement, big picture windows overlooking the Bay, a garden at the rear and a pond with a waterfall which you could turn on and off by pressing a button in the kitchen. It belonged to a retired couple called Weede (pronounced Weedy) who had gone to Europe for six months. El Cerrito was in fact popular with middle-income retirees, and therefore parsimonious in voting money for the local junior school where we enrolled Julia and Stephen, so its curriculum and facilities were fairly limited. But it did its best for our children, who were comfortably ahead of their age group in ability and were contented there. Julia did a successful science project growing a sweet potato, which may have inspired her eventual decision to become a biologist. Mary found a play-school for young children with various kinds of disability that was mainly staffed by their mothers and found it rewarding to participate with Chris. A helpful couple lived across the street from us, with children about the same age as ours who soon became regular visitors, fascinated by our different accents and manners. El Cerrito was a rather dull little suburb, but it was friendly and safe, and a better place for us than volatile Berkeley. We needed a car, and for a few hundred dollars I bought a second-hand Ford Falcon with an alarming number of miles on the clock and shock absorbers that barely absorbed, which nevertheless served us for the duration of our stay without breakdowns or accidents.

Berkeley is one of several campuses in the federal University of California, which is governed by a board of Regents. The Governor of the State is a Regent *ex officio,* and at this time he was a right-wing Republican and ex-Hollywood film star soon to be President of the whole country, Ronald Reagan. My arrival at Berkeley co-incided with an organised strike by students belonging to ethnic minorities who were demanding the establishment of a Black Studies Department or Third World College. Governor Reagan predictably rejected these demands and authorised the use of some force by the police against demonstrators. The usual battleground for such confrontations was the Sather Gate entrance to the campus leading to Sproul Plaza, where the Free Speech movement was born, and the steps of Sproul Hall, where many a revolutionary speech was made. One day police broke up student pickets there and chased them through the campus, and I could hear the yelling and popping of tear gas grenades from my office in the English Department. The strike was called off before the end of the quarter, when the University put forward plans for a new Department of Ethnic Studies, but it had disturbed the educational functioning of the institution. One had the feeling that many students had become addicted to the excitement and drama of protest and would soon be looking for another issue.

I was teaching two courses, mainly with my novelist's rather than my critic's hat on, by my own choice, as a change from Birmingham where I kept my novel-writing in a private compart-ment separate from my academic work. One course was a work-shop in novel-writing for a small group of senior students, which met once a week for two hours or more and stretched over two quarters; and the other was a larger class of sophomores which combined creative writing exercises with critical analysis of model texts, meeting three times a week for ninety minutes. I knew how to run that one, but the creative writing course was more of a challenge. Most of the dozen students had a novel in progress which they had worked on for some time previously in other courses. I didn't think any of them were likely to become published writers, though that was their aspiration. They were easily upset by criticism of a technical kind, and preferred to talk about their lives and their feelings, so it always threatened to turn into a kind of encounter group. The keenest member was a black student (as he called himself in the latest approved terminology, though he was a very pale brown) who had taken refuge in my office when police were rampaging through the campus, but he was not conspicuously talented. Decades later when he was in England, he looked me up and kindly invited me to lunch at Claridge's, where he was staying; he had become a wealthy lawyer specialising in medical litigation, but still hankered after writing a bestseller.

In addition to these classes I kept office hours when students could see me individually about their work. Courses were assessed by the teacher at the end of the quarter, and counted for credit towards the student's final degree. This modular course system resulted in a rather patchy education in the student's 'major' subject, but it struck me as a much more efficient way of managing large numbers of students and courses than the British system, and eventually we would adopt something very like it. From the teacher's point of view, it allowed time to cover a few subjects in some detail, instead of dealing hurriedly and superficially with many different ones in the course of a single week in one-hour tutorials, seminars and lectures. But the biggest difference, and the most surprising to me, was that the teacher's performance was assessed by the students at the end of each course – twice: once on official forms which were distributed and collected by the teacher and passed to the relevant Dean's office, and once in a guide compiled and published by the student body, which pulled no punches and had a large readership. This was something even the most extreme student activists at home had not thought of demanding, though student assessment of teaching is now common practice in the UK.

Stanley showed me the ropes, answered my questions, and introduced me to his friends and colleagues – not identical categories, though Leonard Michaels, who taught creative writing and Romantic literature, belonged to both. Lenny was a Jewish New Yorker, about my age, who specialised in short stories which were funny, shocking, arresting and written in a style all his own – urgent, fragmented, unpredictable and honed to a sharp edge. His first collection, called *Going Places,* was about to be published. This is how one of the stories, 'A Green Thought', starts:

> I yelled; she ran in; I pointed. 'Why is it green?' She clapped her mouth; I shrieked, 'Why is it green?' She answered . . . I shrieked, 'Vatchinol infection!' She whispered . . . 'Green medicine!' I wouldn't let her mitigate; shoved her aside. 'No mitigations!' She picked up a wash cloth. I wouldn't let her wash it. 'No washing it!' I lunged into my clothes, laughed ironically, slammed out . . . subway steps, downtown express, eighty miles an hour. Hot, cold, nauseated. Nevertheless, nevertheless, nevertheless.

It was writing absolutely antithetical to mine, especially to the novel I had just finished, but I responded to its energy, mainlined into the reader's brain. I discovered several other American novelists during those six months whose work surprised and stimulated me – Donald Barthelme, Richard Brautigan, Robert Coover, among others. It was a great period for innovative fiction writing in America, but in Lenny's case the impact was increased by his personality. Perhaps it was because we belonged to such different literary cultures that we became friends so quickly, because he viewed the American one as a snakepit full of jealous rivals and malevolent reviewers, and sometimes he was right. He had a lean, angular frame, a long mobile Jewish face that creased and uncreased as he laughed and lamented, and a mop of curly black hair. His wife Priscilla was his opposite in every way: pale, blonde, willowy, quietly spoken. Mary and I liked Priscilla, but there were tensions between her and Lenny, who had been married before and would be married again – twice. He fell in love very easily. We saw a good deal of this couple.

Soon after we settled in El Cerrito I began to get bad news about *Out of the Shelter*. In mid-January Joe Cunneen explained in a long letter why Holt, Rinehart & Winston were rejecting it: basically it wasn't interesting enough. The central character 'is a nice guy, we wish him well, but he is not Stephen Dedalus'. Shortly afterwards Graham wrote to say that after speaking to Tim O'Keeffe he thought MacGibbon & Kee would also pass on the novel, and confessed that he had been holding back his own negative opinion: 'it just doesn't seem to me to work on any count . . . This is a "grey book" whereas I think the *British Museum* proves that your fictional forte lies in humour.' I was devastated by these reactions, which I described in reply to Graham as 'a major crisis in my writing career'. Tim O'Keeffe confirmed Graham's prediction by writing a rather stilted letter mixing regret with disappointment and concluding, 'it seems to me that it might be time for a change of publisher'. Not long afterwards I heard that he had left MacGibbon & Kee involuntarily and with some bitterness; within a year or two the firm was swallowed up by Granada's publishing company and the imprint expired. Meanwhile Graham undertook to seek another publisher for *Out of the Shelter*, though without inspiring much confidence in me, and I glumly left the book's future in his hands. Weeks went by and I heard nothing.

Soon there was more bad news of a different kind. Mary got a cable from her brother Brian to tell her that her father was seriously ill and not likely to live much longer. This presented her with a painfully difficult decision: whether to fly home. It would mean taking Christopher with her, because I couldn't manage all three children on my own and do my teaching. The memory of the ghastly flight from Boston was still vivid to her and, as I discovered, all flights from San Francisco to London at that time went via Los Angeles, extending the journey by a couple of hours and entailing a second landing and take-off, which she always found the most stressful part of flying. While we were deliberating, a second telegram arrived to say that Frank Jacob had died. Mary could not face the ordeal of the journey to England and back to attend his funeral. It was some consolation that her father, in hospital and aware of his condition, had written to say she was to stay with her family in America. But inevitably she felt upset and self-reproachful, knowing that her mother and siblings were gathered in Hoddesdon and conscious that some of our American friends, to whom long-haul flights were routine, would not understand her reluctance to join them. Perhaps for the first and last time in her life, she suffered depression (she is discontented at times, and angry, but not depressed) and with typical decisiveness, she sought help.

A condition of my appointment at Berkeley was that I and the family had health insurance covered by contributions split between myself and the University. This entitled us to treatment at a Kaiser clinic that included psychiatry, and Mary was lucky to find a psychiatrist who took a counselling, not a pharmaceutical, approach to her problem. He seems in retrospect to have used something like what we later came to know as cognitive behavioural therapy, challenging her negative views of herself and prompting her to take a more proactive attitude to her situation. The result was a renegotiation of our marriage, though I did not immediately see it as such. I promised to support her, when we returned to England, in pursuing a fulfilling career by paying for whatever assistance with Christopher she needed, and to take a bigger share in domestic chores (mainly by learning to cook). Mary did not wish to return to ordinary teaching, but to train as a school counsellor. She had done some voluntary work in Birmingham on behalf of the organisation Mencap, visiting parents who had just had a baby with a mental handicap to give them practical advice and encouragement, and had found it rewarding. She wanted to pursue this kind of interpersonal work in an educational context, and she had heard of a course in Birmingham which led to a qualification in school counselling. With this aim in view for our return to England, her spirits improved quickly.

So did my own spirits when I received a Western Union telegram from Graham Watson: 'OUT OF THE SHELTER MACMILLANS WRITING DIRECT MAKING EDITORIAL SUGGESTIONS STOP WILL UNDERTAKE PUBLICATION GIVEN YOUR ACCEPTANCE SUCH SUGGESTIONS STOP WILL NEGOTIATE CONTRACT SUBSEQUENTLY.' What relief! At last a publisher who wanted the novel. I had always expected to do more work on it, and looked forward to doing so in collaboration with an editor. Shortly afterwards I got a letter from Kevin Crossley-Holland, a young editor at Macmillan who was also at the beginning of a productive career as poet, novelist and translator. He said he and his colleagues thought the novel was 'a sharply observed and endearing study of how a protected small boy grows and develops . . . but is really far, far too long'. He concluded by saying that if I could see my way to cutting the novel 'by as much as a third' Macmillan would be pleased to publish it. A third was an awful lot of words. I didn't see how I could cut that much and not end up with a very different and much slighter work. Perhaps I could manage a quarter. I offered to cut it by a quarter, and Macmillan accepted this compromise.

With this anxiety resolved, I was able to enjoy more fully the pleasures of being back in the Bay Area. The weather helped: our first couple of months had been cool and rainy, but then the sun came out, and stayed out. Christopher learned to walk in our garden, to his great delight, and was happy to be floated in an inflatable jacket in El Cerrito's open-air swimming pool. My mother and her brother John took our presence in California as an encouragement to make a trip to Hawaii to visit Eileen, breaking their journey to stay with us for a few days. It was the first time that Mum had travelled by air and it was a testing initiation, but she stood up to it very well, and looked as if she was enjoying herself in the few snaps we have of the visit. They stayed with Eileen in Waikiki for a couple of weeks and (I gathered) the three of them talked their heads off and laughed and cried and quarrelled as they always did when they got together. I was quite sure Mum wouldn't have made such an epic journey if we hadn't provided a staging post, and I was glad to have given her the incentive to see something of the big wide world beyond England and Belgium.

My taste in music began to change with the times. Mary and I went one evening to an open-air arena in Berkeley for what was advertised as a jazz concert. The first half featured Dizzy Gillespie and his band, the second half the gifted singer/songwriter/ composer of eclectic jazz-based music, Nina Simone, followed by the Northern California State Youth Choir, who were currently high in the pop charts with a funky gospel arrangement of the eighteenth-century hymn 'Oh Happy Day'. Dizzy Gillespie, one of the giants of early modern jazz, second in fame only to Charlie Parker, was the support act! Nothing could have told me more clearly that vocal music, drawing on and combining various sources – folk song, blues, gospel, country and western, rock and roll, Latin American, Caribbean – was displacing instrumental jazz in Sixties culture. The cool music of the decade was that of Bob Dylan and Simon and Garfunkel, Joan Baez and Joni Mitchell, and the ever-surprising Beatles. I bought albums by some of these and similar artists to play on the Weedes' record player.

Stanley and Adrienne led us to see the movie of the moment, *Bullitt*, a police thriller located in and around San Francisco, with a famous and much-imitated car chase filmed on the very streets, hills and freeways that we had driven on ourselves. Another film that derived a special impact from being viewed in that place, at that time, was the British director Lindsay Anderson's *If . . . .*, in which a group of public-school boys rebel against the sadistic and repressive ethos of their school by massacring a crowd of teachers, pupils and parents with machine guns from the school's neo-Gothic battlements. At this savage climax the youthful Berkeley audience rose to its feet and cheered. The Living Theatre came to Berkeley and we queued up to see this venerable experimental troupe, who had been presenting anarchic avant-garde drama influenced by Antonin Artaud's Theatre of Cruelty for decades, but had found an enthusiastic new audience in the Age of Aquarius with an ensemble piece called *Paradise Now*. As you went into the theatre you were accosted by actors who uttered bitter complaints like 'I am not allowed to smoke marijuana . . .' or 'I am not allowed to take my clothes off . . .' and during the show they were apt to jump from the stage and walk through the auditorium, stepping on the backs of the seats between the ducking members of the audience, some of whom invaded the stage to participate in the Dionysian climax of the performance.

People who *were* allowed to take their clothes off were the go-go dancers in the bars on Columbus Avenue in the North Beach district of San Francisco. It so happened that our residence in the Bay Area coincided with a licensed replacement of topless performers with totally nude ones, provoking some controversy in the local press. Lenny and I sampled – purely for the purpose of cultural research, of course – one of the small 'Topless and Bottomless' bars which had proliferated to exploit this development, before going on to a rock concert at Fillmore West. The ambience was quite unlike a sleazy strip club: the patrons included women with their dates, and there was no stripping. The girls, who looked like nice young women working their way through college, danced to recorded disco music in turn, solo and quite naked, in a pool of coloured light on a tiny stage, and in a decorous style that was more akin to exercise than eroticism. There were, I gathered, raunchier venues, but we didn't look for them.

It was not long before bared female breasts acquired a different significance – as a motif in the iconography of political protest in Berkeley. The new *casus belli* was a park, the 'People's Park', as it was called by those who created it on a vacant lot a few blocks from the campus, which was owned by the University and intended for use as a playing field, but had been left undeveloped for two years and was something of an eyesore. On 20th April about 200 students and hippies, or 'street people' as they were known locally, occupied the land and began to lay down grass and plant flowers. The concept of the park appealed to several different sections of the community: students, hippies, environmentalists, left-wing radicals and ordinary families. They all worked together voluntarily on the Park and frequented it. The Regents put pressure on the moderate but weak-willed Chancellor of Berkeley, Roger Heyns, to suppress this project, and on 30th April the University's Public Relations office announced that work would begin on the playing field in July, pointing out 'the disutility of any additional labour' on the site. The Park people carried on regardless. On 13th May Chancellor Heyns commented: 'Most people are worried about a confrontation, although some people are afraid there might not be one . . . [They] have the perfect issue: the people versus the heartless University, creativity versus bureaucracy.' Having shrewdly defined the trap, he proceeded to walk into it. At dawn on 15th May, police surrounded the Park, evicted all, and arrested some, of those who had spent the night there and stood guard while the San Jose Steel Company rapidly erected a chain-link fence around it. At noon there was a rally in Sproul Plaza and the crowd marched off to demonstrate at the Park, where they were met by a large body of police. Stones were thrown and the police retaliated with clubs, tear gas and, for the first time, shotguns loaded with birdshot and in some cases buckshot. A colleague and I heard the distant hubbub, climbed to a balcony of the Union building and watched as the police rolled the crowd back along Telegraph Avenue and chased them through the campus.

Over the next few weeks violent confrontations between demonstrators and police on and around the campus escalated. One apparently innocent person was killed, another blinded, and many injured, by police firing shotguns. Ronald Reagan declared a state of emergency and called out the National Guard. An army helicopter sprayed tear gas over the campus: it drifted into offices, into the Cowell hospital, and into the Strawberry Canyon Recreation Center where faculty wives and children were swimming. Five hundred people were arrested on the street one morning for defying the ban on public gatherings and made to lie face down on the asphalt of the County Prison compound for two hours. The conflict had its lighter aspects. The National Guard (somewhat like the British Territorial Army) was largely composed of young men who had joined it to avoid being sent to Vietnam, and many were sympathetic to the demonstrators. The young women protestors embarrassed them by stripping off their tops, opposing bare breasts to the soldiers' weaponry and putting flowers in the barrels of their rifles, a photo opportunity that student and underground newspapers found irresistible. But the methods of law enforcement used by the authorities provoked shock and horror in the community and radicalised many people previously detached from the struggle, including academic staff. An 'ad hoc' assembly of 250 faculty passed a series of motions censuring the authorities and declaring their inability to continue teaching while the campus was occupied by police and military. I joined a large number of them holding a vigil of protest on the steps of Sproul Plaza. Though I shared their views, I felt more like a war correspondent reporting in a foreign country and collected documentary souvenirs of the unfolding story – newspaper cuttings, photographs, flyers, manifestos, and personal experiences that were written up and circulated in the University. I knew I would use this bit of history in a novel one day, though not exactly how.

The climax of this sequence of events was as dramatic as any novelist could invent. A compromise solution to the main issue was proposed: that the Park should be taken over by Berkeley City Council. Its nine elected members were divided on the matter, and a meeting was scheduled for the evening of 5th June, when they would hear opinions from citizens. Meanwhile the Park supporters planned a huge rally and march through the streets to be held on Memorial Day, 6th June. As many as 50,000 supporters from all over the country were expected to attend, and local people viewed the prospect with foreboding. The first issue discussed at the Council meeting was whether the march should be permitted to take place the next day. The proceedings were covered live on local television, and I was enthralled and moved as I watched, for it was a demonstration of American democracy at its best. The Berkeley Police Chief was confronted by the organiser of the march and accused of bad faith over permits. Sensationally, the charge was supported by one of the City Council's officials, and the permit was granted. The proposal that the Council should take over the Park was passed by a single vote, one member having changed his mind on the issue, and the meeting broke up amid liberal rejoicing. The great march next day passed off peacefully in a carnival atmosphere. The Park, I believe, is still in place.

That was really the climax of our six months' stay, but there was time for a restful week's holiday at beautiful Stinson Beach, in a rented house which we shared with Lenny and Priscilla and their boys. It was situated on a narrow spit of land with the beach on one side and on the other a lagoon, which unlike the ocean was calm and warm enough to swim in. Then it was time to return home. This time we flew over the pole, in a Pan Am Boeing 707. I booked our journey for the 4th of July, Independence Day, guessing that the flight would have fewer passengers than usual. Indeed the plane was almost empty: we each stretched out across several seats, slept peacefully for hours, and were waited on solicitously by the underemployed cabin crew. It was the most comfortable long-haul economy flight I ever experienced.

23

We had let our house for a very modest rent to my colleague
Michael Green and Tim Moore, a young lecturer in the Philosophy
Department, confident that they would look after it well, as they
did. By arrangement, Michael was at the house to welcome us
back and hand over the keys. He insisted on taking me that very
day for a spin in his Hillman Imp to see the new roadworks that
had just been completed in Birmingham: twin tunnels under the
city leading to a multi-lane freeway (as Americans would call it)
which joined the M6 motorway at an intersection already dubbed
'Spaghetti Junction' because of the complexity of its curves and
connections; this enabled drivers to travel from just outside the
city centre to the M6 without encountering a single traffic light.
It was an impressive feat of civil engineering, but part of a development plan which throttled the central area with the concrete
collar of a ring road, forcing pedestrians down into dismal and
soon squalid underpasses. The plan also encouraged the indis-
criminate destruction of older property and the erection of a

great many cheap and nasty commercial buildings which weathered badly. This New Brutalist makeover of the city centre came under increasing criticism, and has since been undone and replaced by more user-friendly and architecturally eclectic developments; but my first reaction to Michael's exhilarating guided tour was that it had transformed Birmingham into something like an American city, and blown away the dull grey provincial ambience which had permeated it like a fog when we first came there, and hung around until now.

Michael, who was always the first member of the Department to latch on to new cultural and intellectual trends, had got hold of an American edition of Kate Millett's *Sexual Politics,* shortly to be published in Britain, and asked if we had read it. We hadn't even heard of it. It seemed that Birmingham was somewhat ahead of Berkeley in this respect. The first manifestation of what was then called Women's Liberation and is now termed second-wave feminism (the first wave being that of the New Woman and the suffragettes earlier in the century) was a demonstration against the Miss America Pageant in Atlantic City in the fall of 1968, but it was a very inconspicuous element in the Californian counterculture of 1969, which was steeped in unacknowledged male chauvinism, to use a term put into currency by Kate Millett. One of the counterculture's venerated heroes was Henry Miller, and another was D.H. Lawrence, *Tropic of Cancer* and *Lady Chatterley's Lover* being regarded as prophetic books heralding the age of sexual liberation. Millett pilloried both authors as reactionaries for their patriarchal and phallocentric treatment of relationships between the sexes, an indictment that became entirely plausible once traditional assumptions about gender were questioned. It would be hard to exaggerate the effect of this book and of Germaine Greer's broader polemic, *The Female Eunuch*, published in 1970, on literary and cultural studies. One consequence was the steep decline in status of D.H. Lawrence in Eng.Lit. syllabuses, and therefore of the influence of Leavis and his followers who had invested heavily in his reputation. Another was the emergence of a distinctively feminist criticism, which set out to revise the literary canon by reinterpreting and rediscovering women writers of the past. For some time the proportion of women studying English at university had been steadily increasing and they were now in the majority. Feminist criticism gave their studies a new motivation and a new excitement. As a formalist myself I was wary of critics who, as Northrop Frye put it (I paraphrase from memory), judged literature according to criteria derived from something that interested them more. But as a social phenomenon I welcomed the movement, not least because the women it touched seemed to become much more interesting in consequence.

In Birmingham a lively Women's Lib group had already formed, composed mainly but not exclusively of women associated in some way with higher education, including wives of academics, such as Mary, who had subordinated their careers to those of their husbands. She joined it soon after we got back, and it provided exactly the encouragement she needed to act on the counsel of her Californian psychiatrist, though she criticised some of the more extreme views expressed by the sisterhood, and their neglect of practical issues in pursuit of the ideal. She went off one weekend with Christopher to a big national gathering of women's groups from all over the country, while I looked after Julia and Stephen at home. The conference was held in a holiday camp, out of season.

The room set aside by the management as a crèche had no toilet facilities and Mary was obliged to lend desperate mothers with infants the special portable loo (a potty in the form of a small toilet) which she had trained Christopher to use. Holding this object by way of illustration, she made a short speech to the 500 delegates suggesting that the episode was a concrete example of women being treated as second-class citizens.

Soon we both became involved in the Catholic Renewal Movement, an association of laity agitating for radical reform in the Church which had something in common with Women's Lib, for there was no institution so comprehensively patriarchal as the Roman Catholic Church. The CRM had a fairly short life under its original name, and mutated into a similar organisation called Catholics for a Changing Church. If you google 'Catholic Renewal Movement' all the results refer to the Charismatic Renewal which developed a little later in the Catholic Church and was akin to Protestant Pentecostalism. Our movement arose out of the controversy that followed the publication of *Humanae Vitae*. A number of bishops censured or suspended priests who voiced their dissent from the encyclical, and two groups of laity were formed to support them, one based in Surrey, and the other in Birmingham. These soon merged and established a national network of Catholics concerned not only with the birth control issue but also that the reforming impetus of Vatican II should be maintained and extended to all aspects of Catholic life – including the role of women. In due course Mary and a friend, Barbara McLoughlin, published a forceful article in the *Catholic Herald* (then a much more liberal paper than it is today) making a case for the ordination of women, and deploring the way in which the figure of the

449

Virgin Mary in Catholic tradition had been used to legitimise the subordinate position of women in the life of the Church.

The initial stimulus that created the Birmingham group of the CRM, however, was to support Father John Challenor, a priest at the Birmingham Oratory founded by Newman, who was in dispute with his fellow Oratorians and the archdiocese over *Humanae Vitae*, and our first positive action was to tackle that issue. We collected a good deal of anecdotal evidence in the form of letters, some of them heartbreaking, of the stress and suffering the traditional teaching had caused to individual couples, and resolved to prepare a leaflet addressed to troubled Catholics, setting out the grounds for conscientious dissent from *HV,* which would be made available in clinics of the Family Planning Association, who were keen to co-operate. I took on the task of writing it, and after a few emendations it was approved by the group, printed and distributed. It was about 1,000 words long, not counting a number of supporting quotations from respected sources, including the statement David Frost had skilfully wrung from Cardinal Heenan in a much-publicised TV interview, that 'Nothing in this Encyclical interferes with the primacy of conscience – that a person's ultimate decision depends on himself'. (It would have been unrealistic to regret that he did not add 'or herself'.) The FPA distributed nearly 100,000 copies of the leaflet before the Catholic hierarchy put pressure on them to desist. I doubt if anything I wrote before or after it did as much good. After the censorship of our leaflet we requested a meeting with the Archbishop of Birmingham, George Dwyer, a cousin of the novelist Anthony Burgess, though he did not boast of the connection. He listened to us courteously, and recognised our good intentions, saying, 'I will not quench the smoking flax' – alluding to a passage in Isaiah about the servant of God, rendered in the modern Jerusalem Bible as: 'He does not break the crushed reed, nor quench the wavering flame.' But the archbishop could not of course agree with the argument of the leaflet. When one of our number told him of the evidence we had collected of marital stress caused by the ban on efficient contraception, he replied that our faith sometimes required heroic sacrifice from us. A note in the summary John Challenor made of the meeting mentions that I interjected, 'But in this case, is it worth it?'

What preoccupied me professionally following our spell in California was the progress of *Out of the Shelter* to publication, which turned out to be inordinately slow. Cutting the original typescript by a quarter was much more time-consuming than it would be today on a computer, but I finished the task not long after returning home. Kevin Crossley-Holland had moved on from Macmillan, and I was assigned an editor called James Wright. I had a couple of meetings with him and a young female colleague, as a result of which I made some further 'fine-combing' cuts to the text, for they were still concerned about its length. While this was in hand James wrote to me to say that Macmillan had begun to use computerised typesetting, then a brand-new technology, 'with considerable success', and they wanted to produce my book by this method. The advantage, he said, was that it was both cheaper and quicker than conventional typesetting. The only drawback was that I would not be able to correct proofs, because these would be in a form that only a computer expert could understand. 'He will, of course, take the utmost care: his reputation depends upon it.' Eager to please and to speed the process, I suppressed my misgivings and agreed. Publication was scheduled for early in June 1970. I cannot improve on a brief account of the sequel which I wrote in an introduction to the new edition of the novel published by Secker & Warburg in 1985:

In April the publication date was postponed till August. In May it was postponed again till 10 September. In August it was postponed again till 24 September. By this time I had seen an advance copy of the book and was appalled. The text was riddled with misprints . . . many of them grotesquely obvious (like *u* for *you*). A pun had been removed, and a joke transformed into a meaningless banality by the correction of a deliberate misspelling, in spite of the fact that I had written in the margin of my MS '*Joke! Do not correct spelling.*' The lines of type were bumpy, the spaces between words grossly uneven, and there were strange gaps within words, notably between the *o* and the *th* of my central character's name, Timothy, which occurred two or three hundred times. Those lonely words at the beginning of a line that printers call 'widows' abounded, as did awkward hyphenations at line endings. In short it was the most hideous piece of printing I had ever set eyes on, and there was absolutely nothing I could do about it.

James Wright was sympathetic and apologetic when I complained, but he concealed the true scale of the incompetence to which my novel had been subjected. Many years later I chanced to meet, at a dinner party given by a Birmingham colleague, a man who had worked in the production department of Macmillan at the time. He told me that the text that had so appalled me was actually a second attempt, and that the first printout was so garbled that they had to destroy the tape and start all over again, which explained the repeated delays and postponements.

The only good thing to be said for the finished book was that it had a striking cover, featuring a naked female, half-Rhinemaiden, half-floozie, wearing a Nazi armband and the Stars and Stripes as a cape, flying through the air above the figure of Timothy and a montage of the story's chief locations. The novel was eventually published on 1st October and it soon became obvious that it was a flop. There were very few reviews, and only two really good ones, one of them written anonymously by my friend Bernard Bergonzi for the *TLS*, which was sincerely felt but not disinterested. The horrible printing cannot be blamed for this disappointing response, though it obviously didn't help; neither did the book's delayed appearance at the very peak of the autumn publishing season, when several novels by well-known authors were dominating the literary pages. The main reason, I believe, was that it was simply not a novel for the 1970s. Change and revolution, excess and experiment were in the air, and there was not much interest in a realistic, nostalgic evocation of growing up in wartime and post-war England. When Secker & Warburg proposed to reissue the novel I decided to revise the text once more, since it would have to be re-set anyway, restoring some of the cuts while making some new ones and other minor adjustments. In that form it was well received and has been in print ever since. But in 1970 I was deeply dejected by its failure. There was no prospect of a paperback edition or an American sale. Macmillan printed 3,000 copies of their edition but bound only 2,000, and when these were sold or otherwise disposed of they pulped the remaining sheets, as I discovered some time later. 'God seems to have sent the publishing profession to save you from self-love,' an Irish friend, Nuala O'Faolain (then a producer of videos for the Open University, later to achieve considerable fame as a writer), commented in a letter when I told her of the novel's final fate. Ironically, it became in consequence a rare book and the most valuable of my first editions, copies with the jacket in good condition being currently offered by dealers at prices over £1,000.

The poor reception of a novel in which I had invested so much time and effort plunged me into a depression, from which I recovered in an unexpected and rewarding way: by giving up smoking. This had been a contentious issue in the family for some time, for it was by now incontrovertibly established that smoking caused lung cancer. In California Julia and Stephen had been disturbed by short public service films on television in which smokers in the last stages of this disease earnestly enjoined others to quit, followed by a caption giving the date on which they had died. The children pestered me to give up the habit, and Mary, who had never smoked, took the same view, refusing any longer to buy for me the latakia-laced pipe tobacco I favoured (Three Nuns Empire Blend) when she went shopping. I had switched to the pipe because it was supposed to be healthier than cigarettes since one did not inhale, but I only had to look at the disgusting goo that collected in the bowl, or the smoke-stained ceiling of my study, to see that it could not be good for me. I wanted to give up, but I doubted whether I could do without something that had become an indispensable aid to reflection and concentration in

454

the writing process, and an essential prop for small-group teaching (what else could so simply cover a moment's pause for thought as the act of lighting or relighting a pipe?). In fact I seldom had a pipe out of my mouth for long, apart from at mealtimes and in the hours of sleep. In the late autumn of that year I succumbed to a bad bout of flu, and for ten days or so I really had no desire to smoke. It occurred to me that this was an opportunity to try and overcome the addiction, and I made it a project in my convalescent state. Several days went by without my succumbing to the lure of the pipe, though there was a half-full tin of tobacco in my desk drawer. I recovered from the flu, and began to count in weeks instead of days, distracting myself from temptation by looking forward to meals and drinks, which acquired a forgotten intensity of flavour as my palette recovered its sensitivity. I realised that this was a life-enhancing, life-extending project I could actually accomplish, and by Christmas I was certain I had done it. I never smoked again.

That achievement did much to restore my self-esteem, but the best way to recover from the failure of a novel is of course to start a new one that won't be vulnerable to the same criticisms. I knew it would need to have some of the comic invention and stylistic exuberance that had made *The British Museum is Falling Down* my most popular work of fiction to date, and I had brought back a rich haul of material from my six months at Berkeley, but for some time I was uncertain how to use it. Given the number of novels about British academics on American campuses published in recent years, including Malcolm's *Stepping Westward*, it was essential to find some new variation on this theme. Mulling over the problem, it occurred to me that no one had written a novel about a visiting American teacher at a British university – a less common phenomenon, usually part of an exchange scheme between two institutions. That thought immediately presented the solution to my problem: a novel about *two* academics, one British, one American, exchanging jobs for six months, a narrative that would cut back and forth between the locations, based loosely on Birmingham and Berkeley – call them 'Rummidge' in the English Midlands, and 'Plotinus' on the Bay of Esseph in the State of Euphoria – with opportunities for comic-satiric observation of the contrasting environments and manners of each university. Dramatise these differences by setting the story at a time when both institutions are rocked by a wave of student protest. Make the two main characters epitomise the competitive professionalism and humane amateurism of the two academic cultures: the Brit someone whose finest hour had been his brilliant First in Finals and whose failure to publish has retarded his subsequent career, the American a prolific author of theory-driven critical interpretations of the novels of Jane Austen designed to silence all rival scholars in the field. Call them Philip Swallow and Morris Zapp. Let these two professors (the humble British lecturer would acquire the title of 'Associate Professor' in America) change as a result of exposure to the opposite of what they were used to. Make them both forty years of age, a time when a man takes stock of his life and may be tempted to change direction; one of them in a marriage that is going stale and the other in a marriage on the brink of breaking up. Could they in the course of the story exchange wives as well as jobs? Why not? Comedy licenses such symmetries and coincidences. I imagined them passing each other in the air on their way to change places, and began to write the opening paragraph. '*High, high above the North Pole, on the first day of 1969, two professors of English Literature approached each other at a combined velocity of 1200 miles per hour . . .*' A comic novel whose plot entailed double adultery between the four main characters meant of course that they could not be Catholics, burdened with theological guilt, and that was a kind of liberation for me. I thought I would enjoy writing this novel, and I did.

The character of Philip Swallow contains some traits of mine, as that of Morris Zapp owes something to my acquaintance with Stanley Fish, but they are essentially representative *types*. Zapp has been identified by academic readers with several other American professors, some of whom I never met, and Philip differs in several respects from me, not least in his professional barrenness in the matter of publications. One year in this period I noticed that there were more entries under my name in the University's annual Research Report than those mustered by the entire French Department. I was still pursuing a twin-track career, as novelist and academic critic, equally committed to both activities and making connections between them. In 1971 I published a collection of essays written over the previous few years entitled *The Novelist at the Crossroads,* including 'Choice and Chance in Literary Composition: a self-analysis', in which I anatomised the development of a short story of my own from inception to published text. I gambled that readers would find the exercise interesting rather than narcissistic, and wrote several similar pieces in later years.

The title essay of the 1971 collection was indebted to *The Nature of Narrative* by the American critics Robert Scholes and Robert

Kellogg, and engaged with Scholes's more recent and more polemical book *The Fabulators*. He argued that the synthesis of realism and romance from which the classic European novel evolved was now irreparably shattered, and in consequence literary novelists were turning increasingly to various combinations of fantasy, allegory and myth, which he called 'fabulation'. It seemed to me, however, that there was no single mode of writing which was dominating the literary fiction of our time, as did the panoramic social novel in the nineteenth century or the modernist novel of subjective consciousness earlier in the twentieth century; instead there was a wide range of contrasting and coexisting practices from which the writer could choose as he or she stood at a metaphorical crossroads. Ahead lay the path of realism which was still followed by many respected novelists and their faithful readers, but which was increasingly disparaged by avant-garde critics and writers because, as one of them said, 'reality isn't realistic any more'. Doubts about the validity of traditional realism might encourage a writer to take one of the two alternative paths that led away from it in opposite directions: fabulation, exemplified by novels like John Barth's *Giles Goat-Boy* and Günter Grass's *The Tin Drum*, or the fact-based non-fiction novel, like Truman Capote's *In Cold Blood* and Norman Mailer's third-person memoir, *Armies of the Night*. Alternatively, I argued, the novelist hesitating over which direction to follow might build that hesitation into the novel itself, which then became what I called the 'problematic novel' (because I had not yet picked up the newly coined and more appropriate term 'metafiction') – the novel partly about its own processes, for example John Fowles's *The French Lieutenant's Woman* or Doris Lessing's *The Golden Notebook*. This kind of reflexivity in works of fiction was not totally new, of course – you find it as far back as *Don Quixote* and *Tristram Shandy* – but it acquired a new importance in the late twentieth century when, as Elizabeth Hardwick wrote in the *New York Review of Books* while I was writing my essay, 'many novels show a degree of panic about the form. Where to start and where to end, how much must be believed and how much a joke, a puzzle . . . the mood of the writer is to admit manipulation and design, to exploit the very act of authorship in the midst of the imagined scene.'

When asked how I would characterise my own work in this scheme I usually answered: 'basically realistic but with elements of metafiction'. Of late I have been drawn to fact-based narrative in two biographical novels about writers, Henry James and H.G. Wells, but I never wrote another novel like *Out of the Shelter*, which seeks to give its fictional story an unbroken illusion of reality by adopting a single point of view and a uniform style. *Changing Places* contains a lot of realistic detail based on personal experience and observation, but each chapter is written in a different mode: intrusive authorial narration; narration focalised through the consciousness of the two main characters, at first in synchronised alternation and later in two sequential blocks; narration in the form of letters between the main characters and their wives; narrative inferable from extracts from newspapers, flyers, official bulletins, etc. read by the characters; and finally narrative in the form of a film script. I did this partly to offset the symmetry of the plot, which might otherwise have seemed somewhat mechanical and predictable. But, like the passages of parody and pastiche in *The British Museum is Falling Down*, these shifts in narrative method also have the metafictional effect of foregrounding the artificiality of all narration, the irreducible gap between the world and the book which the realistic novel seeks to disguise by its stylistic decorum. I am often asked how I manage to combine writing novels with the practice of analytical literary criticism, implying that the latter must inhibit creativity. On the contrary, I have found that it makes me more aware of the expressive potential of various techniques and helps me to solve problems I encounter in composition, while being a novelist undoubtedly helps me as a critic to analyse other novels by other writers. The compatibility of the very different professional personae of the novelist and the academic was another question, more difficult to answer.

The English Department was in a volatile state at this period. In 1970 Richard Hoggart obtained three years' leave of absence to take up the post of Assistant Director General at UNESCO's headquarters in Paris. It was an opportunity to participate in the formation of cultural policy on a global scale which he couldn't resist, and also a welcome respite from his increasingly difficult relationship with Terence Spencer, whose habit of blocking or postponing by devious means any decision on departmental matters which he saw as threatening his own status caused Richard intense frustration. Simon Hoggart, chatting to me at a literary party more than forty years later, still remembered how his father would come home from the University beside himself with anger after some fruitless argument with Spencer. Disturbed by the new assertiveness of students since the events of 1968, and evidently feeling that the Department he had built up was developing in ways he could no longer control, Spencer began to adopt an attitude of prophetic despair. A 'teach-in' was arranged in the spring term of 1969, when I was away in Berkeley, at which a panel of the four professors – Terence, Richard, John Sinclair and Geoffrey Shepherd – were to confront the Department's entire student body, and, evidently alarmed by this prospect, Spencer summoned an evening meeting of senior staff at Westmere, of which Park sent me a vivid account:

Scene: Terence's hushed, book-lined office, wine bottles out, nine or ten staffers staring hard at the floor, Terence – with folded hands – gazing benevolently at the ceiling: 'And so, in short, I am a total failure . . . all of the plans, all of the work over the past ten years has now been shown to be misguided. Utterly futile. It is clear that the Department is no longer respected by anyone at the University – by the students, by the Administration – the only hope now being, perhaps, for us to break into smaller groups and . . . simply survive . . . [*one had the impression that the Nazis had just landed, and we were all to take to the hills*] All that I have done has been to make things a little less catastrophic . . . For example, I felt it was important to have a novelist on the staff. David has been successful . . . He has been protected, and we must continue to protect him . . . So a few things, almost by accident, we have done well . . . But I want to tell you *all* that your arrangements, the way you run this Department, are absolutely *wrong* . . .'

Apparently it emerged from the subsequent discussion that Spencer wanted seminars abolished, tutorials limited to two students and, bizarrely, a compulsory course for all undergraduates on literature

since 1950, though he must have been well aware that these suggestions would never win wide support from his colleagues. Whether
he was aware when he appointed me that I was about to publish
a novel I doubted, but I was touched that he considered me
deserving of protection. He had given me a vital start in my
academic career, and I would always be grateful to him for that.
But like everyone else I found it increasingly difficult to have a
normal conversation with him.

In the early seventies Terence absented himself from Department meetings and left us to conduct them as a kind of collective.
There was general agreement that the syllabus was unsatisfactory,
and that we were all teaching too many hours on a diversity of
subjects in the effort to make it work, but no consensus on what
should be done, and Richard's absence compounded the lack of
direction. It was partly for this reason that in 1972 I applied for
chairs at two other universities, one by invitation and the other
on my own initiative. The first was at Edinburgh. I was flattered
by the interest of this large and prestigious Department, since I
had only recently been promoted to senior lecturer at Birmingham.
Never having been to Edinburgh, or indeed Scotland, I was
doubtful whether I would want to move myself and family so far
north, but thought I had nothing to lose by finding out what its
attractions might be. The interviewing panel was formidably large.
It included Frank Kermode, the external assessor, who gave me a
genial smile when I sat down, but questioned me shrewdly when
I professed an interest in Continental structuralist criticism,
exposing some gaps in my knowledge. I forfeited the approval of
Alastair Fowler, the Regius Professor of English Literature at
Edinburgh, by refusing to agree that our job was to teach students

to read literature correctly, since I did not accept that interpretation was ever final, and I left the interviewing room under no illusions that I would be offered the job, but not disappointed. I had taken a walk round Edinburgh that morning and decided that, beautiful and impressive as it was, it felt almost like a foreign city, a place where I would never feel at home. The other candidate whom I met on that occasion was Norman Sherry, then at the new University of Lancaster, soon to become the authorised biographer of Graham Greene, and he was of the same mind. After some time had elapsed I was informed that a considerably older man than either of us had been appointed: Wallace Robson, for most of his career an Oxford don, and currently a professor at the University of Sussex. This created a vacancy for a professorial appointment in Modern Literature at Sussex, which was duly advertised, and I decided to apply for it.

In retrospect I cannot really understand why I thought moving there would be worth all the upheaval; but Sussex was the most fashionable of the new universities, having quickly built up a reputation for cutting-edge research and innovative courses, and was attracting many bright students who would previously have gone to Oxbridge. It was also in a location that appealed to me, near London and by the sea (from which Birmingham was as far as one could be in England). Mary was not keen, but would not stand in my way. I wrote in June to ask Richard to be one of my referees, and in his reply he spoke positively of Sussex, whose VC, Asa Briggs, was a friend, and thought I would fit in happily there. He also told me that the Director General of UNESCO had asked him to stay on after 1973 for another two years, when the DG's own term of office would expire, and hinted that he was likely to agree, even though he would have to resign his chair at Birmingham, as he could not expect the University to extend his leave of absence. I was not surprised when his resignation was confirmed soon afterwards. The Hoggarts had kindly invited Mary and me to spend a week with them in Paris, and I had sensed how absorbing and exciting he found the job, for all the frustrations he encountered in UNESCO's Byzantine bureaucracy and political infighting. In particular he and Mary valued the opportunities to fly all over the world visiting sites of cultural importance with expert guides. But whether he realised it or not, he was making a decisive career choice of administration over teaching and research. The Centre for Contemporary Cultural Studies was attracting bright young graduate students from all over the country and had moved out of the English Department into spacious accommodation in the Muirhead Tower. (This was a new building next to the Arts Faculty with an intriguing type of lift called a paternoster, a continuously moving belt of open compartments which passengers had to step nimbly in and out of, and which I promptly incorporated in my novel-in-progress.) Under the direction of Stuart Hall the Centre had become a thriving hothouse of radical 'isms' – Marxism, feminism, structuralism and various combinations and revisionist versions of these conceptual systems. Richard probably intuited that he would never feel comfortable in this babble of theoretical discourses and that he should allow the institution he had founded to evolve without him.

His resignation, however, created a professorial vacancy at Birmingham for which I would be eligible, and I pondered whether to apply when it was advertised. It would be awkward to seek promotion over older colleagues who might apply; on the other

464

hand, I wouldn't relish having any of them promoted over me. I gathered that there was a plan afoot to have the four professors in the Department acting as chairmen in rotation while each remained head of their autonomous graduate programmes, but it was being stymied by Terence's determination to hold on to his office and status in the English Department, as well as at Westmere. Whatever happened, it looked as if Richard's replacement would have to battle with Spencer as he had, and I didn't feel equal to that. In this context the chair at Sussex, not attached to any specific administrative responsibility, became more enticing. Julia and Stephen were strongly opposed, however, and Mary doubtful, so when the invitation to an interview during the school summer holidays came I took the family down to Brighton on the day so that they could get a sense of its attractions.

I left them sitting on the beach while I went off for my interview. The University is situated on undulating open country where the Sussex Downs slope towards the sea between Brighton and Lewes. I walked up through the campus, which had grown considerably since I attended a conference there in 1966. The development of the site had been overseen and partly designed by Sir Basil Spence, and the architecture, though elegant in a restrained modernist way, seemed to me almost eerily pristine and harmonised, as if it had all sprouted magically from the green turf at the same moment. Since it was the long vac, the campus was largely deserted – so probably was Birmingham's that day, but it was embedded in a city whose hum was always faintly audible, whereas this one was exposed to the silent sky and the Downs. Although the day was sunny, the Sussex campus made a slightly chilly impression on me. So did the interview, when with some difficulty

I found the appointed room in the largely empty building where it took place. I don't recall who conducted it, but I think there were only three of them, and I didn't see signs of any other candidates. In fact I can't remember much at all about the occasion, but I left with a sense that they had been looking for reasons to eliminate me rather than to appoint me. When I got back to the family sitting on the pebbled beach Julia exclaimed, 'Father!' (She had adopted this old-fashioned and slightly ironic style of address as a way of putting me in my place.) 'For heaven's sake don't make us live here, it's *horrible!*' Stephen echoed her protest. They hadn't taken to brash, commercialised, slightly grubby Brighton and its holiday crowds, perhaps because their last two summer holidays had been spent in Connemara and the Swiss Alps. I assured them that I didn't expect to be offered the job, and would decline it if I were. Mary was as pleased as the children, for she was due to begin a postgraduate diploma course in Counselling and Health Education the following year at Birmingham Polytechnic, and we went home a contentedly united family.

I didn't hear until May 1973 that Sussex had appointed someone else to their chair, but by then I had long ceased to give it a thought. I had just been made Reader at Birmingham, a title given to staff for achievement in research and publications, which carried a negligible rise in salary but implied a degree of what Spencer had called 'protection' from humdrum duties. That position suited me very well, and I decided I would not apply for the vacant chair when it was advertised. (Eventually the University tired of the English Department's internal wranglings, rejected the idea of a rotating chairman and in 1975 appointed James Boulton, an outside candidate from Nottingham University, as Professor of English Literature and Head of the School of English, which proved to be an excellent decision.) I had nearly finished my new novel, provisionally entitled 'Exchange', and had started work on an ambitious critical book which I referred to privately as 'Son of *Language of Fiction*', but would eventually publish in 1978 as *The Modes of Modern Writing: Metaphor, Metonymy, and the Typology of Modern Literature*. It drew on a good deal of reading in Continental European literary theory, especially the work of the great Russian linguist Roman Jakobson, but I will not attempt to summarise its content here.

I sent the novel to Graham Watson in June. Mary had read it, of course, as had Park and Malcolm, and Lenny Michaels had checked a draft for the idiomatic accuracy of the American speech when he visited us in December '72, in the course of a sabbatical in Europe. They had all liked it, but I waited in some suspense to hear Graham's verdict. In my first years at Birmingham it was possible to make and receive outside calls on one's desk telephone via the switchboard (I remember receiving one from a man asking me to settle a bet by declaring whether or not I was the same person as Malcolm Bradbury) but later this facility was withdrawn, and you had to make them and take them in the departmental office. When I was summoned there one day to take a call from Graham Watson, who had just read 'Exchange' and was bubbling over with enthusiasm for it, I had to mute my reciprocal delight and conceal as far as possible the subject of discussion from the ears of the secretaries, especially as his main concern was that it might contain some libellous portraits of my colleagues. He was sure Macmillan would exercise their option on the novel, and very hopeful that it would find an American publisher. I wrote a follow-up letter to set his mind at rest on the libel issue, and said I would insist on Macmillan's printing the book by conventional methods to avoid another 'computerised catastrophe', adding blithely, 'presumably there would be no problem about getting it out in spring '74.'

Towards the end of July Graham wrote to say that Macmillan had passed. 'They like the novel enormously but have reservations about being able to sell it in view of their results with *Out of the Shelter* . . . I have not the slightest doubt that we shall find a publisher elsewhere and we have in the meantime sent it to John Guest at Allen Lane since he is an admirer of your books.' I was not sorry to be free of Macmillan, but puzzled by Graham's first choice of an alternative. This hardback imprint, named after the founder of Penguin Books, now belonged to the recently merged Longman Penguin Group, though that was not clear to me at the time. I did not associate it with literary fiction, but I trusted Graham's judgement. After an interval John Guest invited Graham and me to tea at his bijou dwelling in Chelsea or there-abouts. He was a man of about sixty with a striking resemblance to Angus Wilson, in more ways than one. After a polite explora-tory conversation Guest came to the point: although he liked the novel in many respects he would not publish it unless I agreed to rewrite the more stylistically deviant chapters – the letters, the extracts from printed sources, and the film script at the end – as straight narrative: in short, to turn it into a conven-tional novel. I declined emphatically even to consider doing so, giving my reasons, and the meeting quickly terminated. Graham understood my decision, but I had the impression that his faith in the book was a little shaken. I suggested that we should try Jonathan Cape, currently the trend-setting publisher of literary fiction, and he agreed.

Cape, however, rejected the novel, without giving any particular reason. I was by now feeling quite demoralised, and Graham did not cheer me up by suggesting that if we had another rejection it might be wise to put the novel in a drawer for a while. I wrote to Malcolm, lamenting my failure to find a publisher, and he suggested that I should try Secker & Warburg, who published his own novels. Since the recent retirement of Fredric Warburg, this firm had been headed by Tom Rosenthal who, he said, was a very dynamic and supportive publisher of new fiction. This was a typically generous suggestion. Malcolm was writing *The History Man* at this time, and not many novelists would invite another writer working on similar subject matter, even if he was a friend, to join their own publisher's list. In fact Graham may have abstained from making the same suggestion for that very reason. When I told him it came from Malcolm he said it was an excellent idea and acted on it at once. Towards the end of the year I heard that Tom Rosenthal would publish the novel if I cut it by 15,000 words. I did not quibble, but accepted gratefully, and had a letter from Tom early in January 1974, after the contract had been signed, welcoming me to the Secker list. He described reading the novel on a train journey, 'causing prodigious discomfort to my travelling companions who were very put out by the spectacle of a perfectly ordinarily dressed man with a briefcase giggling helplessly as he turned over the pages of your typescript'. When I finally met Tom I wondered a little about his idea of ordinary dress, for he favoured boldly striped shirts and bright red braces, but for various reasons it was a long time before I had that pleasure.

Meanwhile I worked on reducing the length of the text with an editor, John Blackwell, and it was a happy collaboration. I discovered that he was already a fan of my novels when 'Exchange' arrived at Secker's, and recommended it warmly to Tom Rosenthal. There was no doubt that the novel was improved by being cut, but John often defended passages I proposed for deletion and in the end the text was reduced by about 12,000 words, perhaps fewer. He was an in-house desk editor of a kind that hardly exists any more – not the 'creative' type who likes to be involved in the composition of a book, but one who worked on a completed manuscript, tuning and refining it by patient questioning and tactful suggestion, removing wrinkles and blemishes, and ensuring that nothing would interfere with the communication of meaning between writer and reader. He was also an inspired blurb-writer, an indefatigable source of exquisitely polished and highly amusing letters of the kind that light up an author's day, and an exceptionally nice man. It was always a pleasure to climb the stairs, in the tall narrow building in Soho that housed Secker & Warburg, to his eyrie on the top floor, crammed with books and manuscripts in a state of organised chaos, and scented with the smoke of Gauloises, to chat over a glass or two of white wine from the bottle he had cooling in a small fridge. He edited all my novels until he died in 1997 at the age of only sixty, greatly missed by his authors, a notable list that included Malcolm.

In Britain 1974 was a year marked by two miners' strikes, an energy crisis and three-day working, which slowed down all forms of production and caused a logjam in publishing schedules. In August, while correcting the proofs of *Changing Places: a tale of two campuses* (as I had decided to call it), I wrote to Lenny Michaels who, now that Park was a colleague in Birmingham, was my chief transatlantic correspondent:

> It seems that the novel won't be out until January next year, more than four years after I started it. I thought then that I would take two forty-year-old heroes as a challenge, and try to write about early middle age before experiencing it; now I shall be exactly forty when the novel appears, my birthday being January 28th . . . I have dedicated it, by the way, to 'Lenny and Priscilla, Stanley and Adrienne, and many other friends on the West Coast', which I trust won't actually lose me any friends.

As publication drew near, however, I began to fear that I might forfeit the friendship of my colleagues at Birmingham. I had taken the precaution of inserting a prefatory note emphasising the fictional nature of the narrative:

> Although some of the locations and public events portrayed in this novel bear a certain resemblance to actual locations and events, the characters, considered either as individuals or as members of institutions, are entirely imaginary. Rummidge and Euphoria are places on the map of a comic world which resembles the one we are standing on without corresponding exactly to it, and which is peopled by figments of the imagination.

Such disclaimers are so common as to carry little weight, but I had taken care not to portray any recognisable person in my characters, with the exception of Stanley, who I was sure would love the fictional version of himself (as indeed he did, putting 'Morris Zapp' on his door at Duke University years later). My satire was directed at two contrasting academic cultures, not at individuals, and I did not fear any libel suits. Also it would be obvious to my colleagues that the fictional Rummidge English Department was much smaller and much less distinguished than the one they belonged to. But, it belatedly occurred to me, they might reflect that most readers of the novel would not know that, and, given the resemblances between Rummidge and Birmingham as cities, would suppose that the novel was an accurate reflection of reality. In which case my colleagues and friends might be very displeased.

That thought, coming on top of the anxiety that builds up in every author as the publication of a book approaches, was enough to throw me into a state of panic, and for several weeks I was in a state of extreme apprehension, which caused me many sleepless nights. I knew intuitively that there was one thing which could save me from shame and embarrassment when the novel appeared: it must be a literary success. Like all comic novels, *Changing Places* was an extended joke, and I was inviting my colleagues to relax and enjoy it. If it didn't amuse them, and if it wasn't seen to be amusing a lot of other people, it would seem tasteless and offensive. Everything therefore depended on the reviews, and as I had no pre-publication interviews with journalists, I had no idea how it would be received. As the fateful time drew nearer John Blackwell fed me with hopeful messages which I clutched at gratefully: 'our sales reps are distinctly keen – and our production department are extremely enthusiastic: if there is a precedent for that, I have missed it'. In the week before publication day, finally fixed for Monday 10th February, he reported that there had been an unusual number of requests from newspapers, including *The Observer* and the *Sunday Times*, for photographic portraits of me, indicating that at least the novel wouldn't be ignored.

There is a very good scene in Frederic Raphael's TV drama serial *The Glittering Prizes*, broadcast by the BBC in the following year to great acclaim, in which the character who is a novelist is shown coming downstairs early one morning in dressing gown and slippers and sitting on the bottom steps for some time, staring fixedly at the front door of the house, until suddenly several newspapers are thrust through the letter flap and fall on to the doormat. The novelist quickly picks them up and sits down again on the stairs to read his reviews. I had decided some time ago that I didn't want to experience this moment of truth at home, in my familiar domestic environment, then go off afterwards with the children to mass at our parish church and spend the rest of Sunday in the usual routine way. I wanted to be away somewhere pleasant, where I was not known and not under observation. I booked myself and Mary into a hotel in Bath recommended in the *Good Hotel Guide* for the night of Saturday 8th February. We left the children at home in somebody's care, drove to Bath, had a pleasant stroll around the town, enjoyed a delicious dinner, and made the most of a warm, luxurious bedroom. I slept well for the first time in many days. When we woke, Mary went to the door to collect the two Sunday papers we had ordered the night before. 'See if there are any reviews,' I said, 'and tell me what they're like.' She sat down, leafed through the pages, found a review in each and read them. I watched her from the bed: her expression gave nothing away. At last she finished reading and handed the newspapers to me, saying with a smile, 'They're very good.' I scanned the reviews quickly, then read them again more slowly. They were both raves. Jill Neville in the *Sunday Times* said, 'Not since *Lucky Jim* has such a funny book about academic life come my way.' From that quote alone, I knew I had written a successful book, and anxiety instantly left me, like a spell magically removed.

The reviews that were published in the following days and weeks reinforced the verdict of the first two, and I have never had such a unanimously favourable press for a novel since. It also received a fortuitous boost on television: Asa Briggs, who was moonlighting as a co-presenter of the BBC's *Book Show*, started reading a copy of *Changing Places* he found at his bedside in the Hoggarts' Paris apartment when he was staying with them, carried it off to finish it, and recommended it on the programme. Graham Watson wrote to congratulate me on the 'ecstatic reviews' which he was forwarding to Curtis Brown's co-agency in New York, confident that they would stimulate keen interest from American publishers. Dick Odgers, who handled film and TV at Curtis Brown, was soon in negotiations with two producers about the film rights. To my delight the paperback rights were sold for a substantial sum to Penguin, an imprint I had always longed to be published under. Going through my files recently I found numerous forgotten letters of congratulation from friends and strangers, including one from Fredric Warburg ('the Schweppeslike tingle of your wit is rare and delicious') and another from Frank

Kermode, who said, 'I thought the novel a real beauty and am grateful for it.' But the most moving discovery was a short letter from Dad, when he was halfway through the novel: 'it's great. Just how I would have liked to write if I had been a writer.' As for my colleagues, it was some time before most of them got round to reading it, but Elsie Duncan-Jones was quick off the mark. Her positive reaction was a great relief to me and proved indicative of the general tenor of responses within the University. Very occasionally I sensed the disapproval of some individuals, but it was expressed through reserve, not explicit comment. As I had hoped, most of my colleagues enjoyed the book for what it was, a work of comic fiction.

The only downer in this euphoric period was that my long-promised celebratory lunch with Tom Rosenthal had to be postponed yet again, and for a very unfortunate reason. It was his custom to cycle to work from his home in Primrose Hill, and as he did so in the morning of the appointed day he was knocked over by a careless van driver, and injured badly enough to be taken to hospital. John Blackwell and I had a subdued lunch for two. Tom recovered and soon returned to work, but he suffered from back pain for the rest of his life in consequence of the accident. Later in the year he rang me to say that the *Yorkshire Post*, who awarded an annual prize for fiction, had told him they had reduced the field to two contenders, *Changing Places* and Malcolm's *The History Man*, which had been published that autumn. This was the first occasion when our close association took a slightly awkward competitive turn – an accidental result of the miners' strikes, because I'm sure Tom's original plan had been to publish my book in 1974. It was a very small prize in monetary terms

– £150 – but it would be a first for either of us. We made light of the situation on the phone, Malcolm quipping that the winner would get to sleep with Barbara Taylor Bradford, the bestselling, impeccably respectable Yorkshire novelist, but one of us was going to be disappointed, and in the event it was Malcolm. I suspected Tom would have wished him to win because of their longer association, but he was in Leeds to greet Mary and me warmly when we went up for the Literary Lunch at which the prize was presented – on this occasion by Lord Longford, already well known for his campaigning against pornography. The person who met him off the train at Leeds told me later that he had read my novel for the first time on his journey and had been greatly shocked by it. Apparently he was particularly upset by the scene in which Philip Swallow discusses his concern about the size of his penis with Morris Zapp's wife Désirée, with whom he is having an affair. Lord Longford made his disapproval fairly clear in his speech presenting the award, and I almost had to prise the cheque from his fingers when I stepped up to receive it. Never mind: it was the first such feather in my cap, and I spent the money on a dish-washer, which could be described as buying more time for writing. Later I was surprised and delighted to be told that I had won the Hawthornden Prize, also of small monetary value but much more prestigious, having been won by several distinguished writers in its quite long history. Happily Malcolm won the Royal Society of Literature's Heinemann Award for *The History Man*, but neither of us was shortlisted for the Booker Prize, though the judges that year rather snootily decided that only two novels were deserving of the honour instead of the usual six. The exclusion of *The History Man* was the more surprising, since it was a more serious, less playful novel than *Changing Places*, and in most people's opinion, including my own, Malcolm's masterpiece.

Changing Places was undoubtedly my 'breakthrough' book, and raised my profile significantly in the literary world. But it was not a really big, life-changing success, like *Lucky Jim,* or *Room at the Top.* The hardback appeared on no bestseller lists – I would guess it sold about 3,000 copies in its first year or two – and Penguin waited three years to bring out their edition, with a first printing of 15,000 which indicated a low expectation of sales. It sold out in two weeks, was rapidly reprinted, and has remained in print ever since, refreshed from time to time with new jacket designs. But to my surprise and disappointment it proved impossible to find an American publisher. Some seventeen of them turned it down, and the comment of a senior editor at Knopf was representative: 'this is a very funny and lively example of a genre of English novel that is pure hell to do anything with here'. In his defence it must be said that *Lucky Jim* sold only 2,000 copies when it was first published in America. But when Penguin USA were persuaded to issue *Changing Places* in 1978 as a paperback original, with little or no promotion, it quickly found a readership, especially on university campuses, became essential reading for all American academic visitors to Britain, and again has been in print ever since. A Spanish translation was published in 1978 and a Czech one in 1980 but it was a long time before the book was available in some twenty other languages. The film rights were finally sold to the producer Otto Plaschkes, who had made a successful movie called *Georgy Girl* but proved unable to make one of *Changing Places,* although he tried hard for many years with an excellent script by Peter Nichols. Unfortunately it was customary in those days to sell film rights in perpetuity, thus preventing other interested producers from having a try.

That *Changing Places* acquired its reputation and increased its readership gradually, over decades, was in fact all to the good for my development as a writer. Producing a huge bestseller can be a burden for literary novelists, creating expectations that they will continue to produce the same kind of work – expectations which they may not wish or be able to fulfil. The reception of *Changing Places* restored my self-confidence as a writer of fiction, but it did not inhibit me from writing other kinds of novels subsequently. My next one would contain some comedy, and even farce, but in a darker and more ironic vein than its predecessor, as it followed the fluctuating fortunes and attitudes of more than a dozen Catholic men and women, from their youth in the early 1950s to the late '70s, coping stressfully with courtship and marriage, faith and doubt, in an era of sexual revolution and an increasingly conflicted, pluralistic Catholic Church. The aim was to represent in less than 250 pages, by a kind of fast-forwarding narrative method, the great changes that had taken place during that period in Catholic belief and practice, including my own. In the process of researching and writing *How Far Can You Go?* my faith had been demythologised, and I had to recognise that I no longer believed literally in the affirmations of the Creed which I recited at mass every Sunday, though they did not lose all meaning and value for me. But that is a subject, among others, for another book.

ACKNOWLEDGEMENTS

I am grateful to Park Honan for permission to quote numerous passages from his unpublished letters to me, and for checking the accuracy of my references to him and his family. Sadly he died, at the age of 86, as I was checking the proofs of this book. I am also grateful to Curtis Brown on behalf of the Estate of Malcolm Bradbury, another deceased friend, for permission to quote extracts from his unpublished letters to me. Kath Chater gave me expert assistance in tracing my ancestry. Patricia Allen, Jean Pearson, and two ladies whom I first knew by their maiden names as Mary Wood and Jenefer Smith helped me to recover facts about my parents and grandparents, and to revive my own childhood memories, by their reminiscences and generous gifts of photographs. Carol Green, Jeswyn Jones, Daniel Moynihan, John Sutherland and Derek Todd kindly supplied information which I requested. Dominic Bradbury, Paul Hoggart and Corinna Honan responded very helpfully to my appeal for photographs of their parents as they were half a century ago.

I am grateful to my agent Jonny Geller for his encouragement and advice on this project from its inception, to my editor Geoff Mulligan for numerous suggestions for improving the text, and to Liz Foley, Publishing Director at Harvill Secker, for her enthusiastic support of the book and management of its progress to publication. My wife Mary is always the first reader of my books, but her contribution to this one was especially valuable, as a source of facts during its composition as well as for her comments when it was completed.

D.L.

INDEX